编委会

普通高等学校"十四五"规划旅游管理类精品教材

总主编

马　勇　　教育部高等学校旅游管理类专业教学指导委员会副主任
　　　　　中国旅游协会教育分会副会长
　　　　　中组部国家"万人计划"教学名师
　　　　　湖北大学旅游发展研究院院长，教授、博士生导师

编　委（排名不分先后）

田　里　　教育部高等学校旅游管理类专业教学指导委员会主任
　　　　　云南大学工商管理与旅游管理学院原院长，教授、博士生导师
高　峻　　教育部高等学校旅游管理类专业教学指导委员会副主任
　　　　　上海师范大学环境与地理学院院长，教授、博士生导师
韩玉灵　　全国旅游职业教育教学指导委员会秘书长
　　　　　北京第二外国语学院旅游管理学院教授
罗兹柏　　中国旅游未来研究会副会长，重庆旅游发展研究中心主任，教授
郑耀星　　中国旅游协会理事，福建师范大学旅游学院教授、博士生导师
董观志　　暨南大学旅游规划设计研究院副院长，教授、博士生导师
薛兵旺　　武汉商学院旅游与酒店管理学院院长，教授
姜　红　　上海商学院酒店管理学院院长，教授
薛兵旺　　武汉商学院旅游与酒店管理学院院长，教授
舒伯阳　　中南财经政法大学工商管理学院教授、博士生导师
朱运海　　湖北文理学院资源环境与旅游学院副院长
罗伊玲　　昆明学院旅游管理专业副教授
杨振之　　四川大学中国休闲与旅游研究中心主任，四川大学旅游学院教授、博士生导师
黄安民　　华侨大学城市建设与经济发展研究院常务副院长，教授
张胜男　　首都师范大学资源环境与旅游学院教授
魏　卫　　华南理工大学经济与贸易学院教授、博士生导师
毕斗斗　　华南理工大学经济与贸易学院副教授
史万震　　常熟理工学院商学院营销与旅游系副教授
黄光文　　南昌大学旅游学院副教授
窦志萍　　昆明学院旅游学院教授，《旅游研究》杂志主编
李　玺　　澳门城市大学国际旅游与管理学院院长，教授、博士生导师
王春雷　　上海对外经贸大学会展与旅游学院院长，教授
朱　伟　　天津农学院人文学院副教授
邓爱民　　中南财经政法大学旅游发展研究院院长，教授、博士生导师
程丛喜　　武汉轻工大学旅游管理系主任，教授
周　霄　　武汉轻工大学旅游研究中心主任，副教授
黄其新　　江汉大学商学院副院长，副教授
何　彪　　海南大学旅游学院副院长，副教授

普通高等学校"十四五"规划旅游管理类精品教材

Introduction of China's Major Tourist Source and Destination Countries (Bilingual Edition)

中国主要旅游客源国与目的地国概况

主 编 ◎ 张金霞 王 越
副主编 ◎ 刘 琼

华中科技大学出版社
http://www.hustp.com
中国·武汉

图书在版编目(CIP)数据

中国主要旅游客源国与目的地国概况:双语版:汉、英/张金霞,王越主编. —武汉:华中科技大学出版社,2021.8(2023.1重印)
ISBN 978-7-5680-7342-4

Ⅰ.①中… Ⅱ.①张… ②王… Ⅲ.①旅游客源-国际市场-概况-中国-高等学校-教材-汉、英 ②景点-概况-世界-高等学校-教材-汉、英 Ⅳ.①F592.6 ②K91

中国版本图书馆 CIP 数据核字(2021)第 170158 号

中国主要旅游客源国与目的地国概况(双语版)　　　　　张金霞　王　越　主编
Zhongguo Zhuyao Lüyou Keyuanguo yu Mudidiguo Gaikuang(Shuangyu Ban)

策划编辑：李　欢
责任编辑：陈　然
封面设计：廖亚萍
责任校对：李　琴
责任监印：周治超

出版发行：华中科技大学出版社(中国·武汉)　　电话：(027)81321913
　　　　　武汉市东湖新技术开发区华工科技园　　邮编：430223
录　　排：华中科技大学惠友文印中心
印　　刷：武汉市籍缘印刷厂
开　　本：787mm×1092mm　1/16
印　　张：16.75　插页：2
字　　数：450 千字
版　　次：2023 年 1 月第 1 版第 2 次印刷
定　　价：59.80 元

本书若有印装质量问题,请向出版社营销中心调换
全国免费服务热线：400-6679-118　竭诚为您服务
版权所有　侵权必究

内容提要

本教材是根据"十四五"规划，为适应我国旅游业发展的需要，满足教育部教育教学改革要求和教材建设目标编写的。本书共 7 章：国际旅游业总论、亚洲旅游区、欧洲旅游区、北美洲旅游区、南美洲旅游区、非洲旅游区和大洋洲旅游区。本书系统地阐述了 23 个主要客源国和目的地国的国土疆域、自然风貌、人口民族、发展简史、政治经济、旅游市场和旅游资源等基本概况。介绍每个国家时，第一部分以中文为主，第二部分以英文为主，有利于提高读者的英文阅读水平。本书既可作为高等院校旅游管理类专业的教材，也可作为旅游工作者，特别是出入境旅游者的参考书。

Synopsis

This textbook is written by adapting to China's tourism industry development in the 14th Five-Year-Plan, meeting the education and teaching reform demands and the textbook construction goals from the Ministry of Education. This textbook consists of seven chapters: General Introduction of International Tourism, the Asia Tourism Region, the Europe Tourism Region, the North America Tourism Region, the South America Tourism Region, the Africa Tourism Region and the Oceania Tourism Region. This textbook systematically describes the territory, natural features, population, nationality, brief history of development, politics, economy, tourism market, tourism resources and other basic situations of the 23 major tourist source and destination countries. In each country, the first part is written in Chinese while the second part is mainly in English, which is conducive in developing the reader's English reading skill. This textbook can be used not only as a teaching material for tourism management majors in colleges and universities, but also as a reference textbook for tourism workers. It is especially useful for inbound and outbound tourists.

总序

伴随着我国社会和经济步入新发展阶段，我国的旅游业也进入转型升级与结构调整的重要时期。旅游业将在推动形成以国内经济大循环为主体、国内国际双循环相互促进的新发展格局中发挥出独特的作用。旅游业的大发展在客观上对我国高等旅游教育和人才培养提出了更高的要求，同时也希望高等旅游教育和人才培养能在促进我国旅游业高质量发展中发挥更大更好的作用。

《中国教育现代化 2035》明确提出：推动高等教育内涵式发展，形成高水平人才培养体系。以"双一流"建设和"双万计划"的启动为标志，中国高等旅游教育发展进入新阶段。

这些新局面有力推动着我国高等旅游教育在"十四五"期间迈入发展新阶段，未来旅游业发展对各类中高级旅游人才的需求将十分旺盛。因此，出版一套把握时代新趋势、面向未来的高品质和高水准规划教材成为我国高等旅游教育和人才培养的迫切需要。

基于此，在教育部高等学校旅游管理类专业教学指导委员会的大力支持和指导下，教育部直属的全国重点大学出版社——华中科技大学出版社——汇聚了一大批国内高水平旅游院校的国家教学名师、资深教授及中青年旅游学科带头人，在成功编撰出版"普通高等院校旅游管理专业类'十三五'规划教材"的基础上，再次联合编撰出版"普通高等学校'十四五'规划旅游管理类精品教材"。本套教材从选题策划到成稿出版，从编写团队到出版团队，从主题选择到内容编排，均做出积极的创新和突破，具有以下特点：

一、基于新国标率先出版并不断沉淀和改版

教育部 2018 年颁布《普通高等学校本科专业类教学质量国家标准》后，华中科技大学出版社特邀教育部高等学校旅游管理类专业教学指导委员会副主任、国家"万人计划"教学名师马勇教授担任总主编，同时邀请了全国近百所开设旅游管理类本科专业的高校知名教授、博导、学科带头人和一线骨干专业教师，以及旅游行业专家、海外专业师资联合编撰了"普通高等院校旅游管理专业类'十三五'规划教材"。该套教材紧扣新国标要点，融合数字科技新技术，配套立体化教学资源，于新国标颁布后在全国率先出版,被全国数百所高等学校选用后获得良好反响。编委会在出版后积极收集院校的一线教学反馈,紧扣行业新变化,吸纳新知识点,不断地对教材内容及配套教育资源进行更新升级。"普通高等学校'十四五'规划旅游管理类精品教材"正是在此基础上沉淀和提升编撰而成的。《旅游接待业(第二版)》《旅游消费者行为(第二版)》《旅游目的地管理(第二版)》等核心课程优质规划教材陆续推出,以期为全国高等院校旅游专业创建国家级一流本科专业和国家级一流"金课"助力。

二、对标国家级一流本科课程,进行高水平建设

本套教材积极研判"双万计划"对旅游管理类专业课程的建设要求,对标国家级一流本科课程的高水平建设,进行内容优化与编撰,以期促进广大旅游院校的教学高质量建设与特色化发展。其中《旅游规划与开发》《酒店管理概论》《酒店督导管理》等教材已成为教育部授予的首批国家级一流本科"金课"配套教材。《节事活动策划与管理》等教材获得国家级和省级教学类奖项。

三、全面配套教学资源,打造立体化互动教材

华中科技大学出版社为本套教材建设了内容全面的线上教材课程资源服务平台;在横向资源配套上,提供全系列教学计划书、教学课件、习题库、案例库、参考答案、教学视频等配套教学资源;在纵向资源开发上,构建了覆盖课程开发、习题管理、学生评论、班级管理等集开发、使用、管理、评价于一体的教学生态链,打造出线上线下、课堂课外的新形态立体化互动教材。

在旅游教育发展的新时代,主编出版一套高质量规划教材是一项重要的教学出版工程,更是一份重要的责任。本套教材在组织策划及编写出版过程中,得到了全国广大院校旅游管理类专家教授、企业精英,以及华中科技大学出版社的大力支持,在此一并致谢!衷心希望本套教材能够为全国高等院校的旅游学界、业界和对旅游知识充满渴望的社会大众带来真正的精神和知识营养,为我国旅游教育教材建设贡献力量。也希望并诚挚邀请更多高等院校旅游管理专业的学者加入我们的编者和读者队伍,为我们共同的事业——我国高等旅游教育高质量发展——而奋斗!

总主编

2021 年 7 月

前言

　　旅游业作为世界最大以及发展最快的产业之一，对促进世界经济增长的作用日益显著。近年来，中国旅游业也取得了显著成就，竞争力不断增强，旅游大国的地位和作用受到各国重视。纵观世界及中国旅游发展形势，中国旅游业正处于大有可为的战略机遇期。

　　2019年，中国人均GDP已经突破1万美元，旅游消费的需求呈现爆发式增长。其中，出境旅游业增长最快。早在2014年，我国出境旅游人数已突破1亿人次，2019年达到1.5亿人次，超过了入境旅游人次，旅游消费居世界首位。在这种趋势下，如何正确引导和规范出入境旅游发展是我国旅游业面临的重要课题。

　　基于以上原因，江汉大学旅游管理与酒店管理系和外语学院的相关老师通力合作，共同对本教材进行了规划与编写。为了提升教学水平，适应旅游业发展需要，本教材采用中英文双语编写，力图在适应教育部教育教学改革要求的背景下，在教材结构、内容等方面有所创新。围绕发展中国出入境旅游这一主题，本教材致力于体现教学改革的最新理念，有效结合理论与实际，希望能给学生提供更多、更新、更系统、更有指导性的基本理论和知识，使学生更好地了解世界主要旅游客源国和目的地国的基本情况。

　　本教材的主要特色：

　　一是采用中英文双语编写，既符合我国国际旅游业发展的需要，也符合教育部双语教材建设的要求和教学过程的实际需要，读者在开阔视野、丰富专业知识的同时，也有利于提高英文阅读水平。

　　二是编写模式独特，图文并茂。本书除总论部分外，主要分为亚洲旅游区、欧洲旅游区、北美洲旅游区、南美洲旅游区、非洲旅游区、大洋洲旅游区六大旅游区进行介绍，同时增加了旅游区的示意图，可读性强，实用性广。

　　三是资料更详实，数据更新，内容更丰富。本书采用最新资料，紧跟中国旅游业发展实际，全面介绍各大洲主要国家的国土疆域、自然风貌、人口民族、发展历史、政治经济、旅游市场和旅游资源等基本概况。

四是每章均给出了与本章内容契合的思考题，既注重了知识性，又突出了实际的运用。

五是本教材把一些相关知识以二维码的形式呈现，既丰富了教材内容，又不占用篇幅，同时便于学生学习。

本教材编写的具体分工如下：张金霞编写全书的中文部分，王越老师和刘琼老师主要编写全书的英文部分。全书由张金霞负责编写提纲并统稿定稿。

本教材在编写过程中，得到了华中科技大学出版社编辑陈然的鼎力支持和李欢社长的热情帮助，在此致以衷心的感谢。

由于编者的认识水平和能力有限，本教材中可能仍存在许多不足之处，诚恳欢迎广大读者批评指正。

编　者

Preface

Tourism is one of the world's largest and fastest growing industries. It plays an increasingly important role in the process of world economic development. The Chinese tourism industry has also made remarkable achievements in recent years. Its competitiveness has been strengthened, and its status and role of a big tourism country have been valued by all other countries. Throughout history and the world, China's tourism industry is in important period of strategic opportunity for development.

China's GDP per capita has exceeded $10000 in 2019, the demand of tourism consumption has shown explosive growth. Among them, outbound tourism grew the fastest. As early as 2014, the number of outbound tourists in China has exceeded 100 million, and it reached 150 million in 2019, exceeding the number of inbound tourists. China's tourism consumption ranked the first in the world. In this case, how to correctly guide and standardize the development of the inbound and outbound tourism is an important issue for China's tourism industry.

Based on the above reasons, teachers from the Department of Tourism and Hotel Management and the Department of Foreign Languages of Jianghan University worked together to plan and compile this textbook. In order to improve the teaching level and adapt to the needs of tourism development, this textbook is written in both Chinese and English, trying to make innovations in the structure and content of the textbook under the background of meeting the education and teaching reform requirements from the Ministry of Education. Around the theme of developing China's inbound and outbound tourism, this textbook is committed to present the latest ideas of teaching reform. Through the effective combination of theory and practice, we hope to provide students with richer, newer, more systematic and more instructive basic theories and knowledge, so that they can have a better understanding of the basic situation of the world's major tourist source and destination countries.

The main features of this textbook are as follows:

First, bilingual writing in Chinese and English. This method not only meets the needs of China's international tourism development, but also meets the requirements of the construction of bilingual textbooks by the Ministry of Education and the actual needs of the teaching process. Readers can not only broaden their horizons and enrich their professional knowledge, but also improve their English reading ability.

Secondly, the writing mode is unique and illustrated. In addition to the general part, the textbook is mainly divided into Asia Tourism Region, Europe Tourism Region, North America Tourism Region, South America Tourism Region, Africa Tourism Region and Oceania Tourism Region for introduction. It also increases the schematic diagram of the tourist Region, which embodies the characteristics of strong readability and wide practicability.

Thirdly, the information is more detailed, the data is more novel and the content is more abundant. Textbook adopts the latest information, closely following the actual development of China's tourism industry, and comprehensively introduces the territory, natural features, population, nationality, brief history of development, politics, economy, tourism market, tourism resources and other basic situations of major countries on all continents.

Fourthly, each chapter gives thinking questions corresponding to the content of this chapter, which not only pays attention to the knowledge, but also highlights the practical application.

Finally, the textbook presents some related knowledge in the form of QR code, which not only enriches the content of the textbook, but also saves space for students' further learning.

The division of writing is as follow: the Chinese part is compiled by Zhang Jinxia, the English part is compiled by Wang Yue and Liu Qiong, and the outline planning and final compilation is responsible by Zhang Jinxia.

Here we sincerely thank Ms. Chen Ran and Ms. Li Huan of Huazhong University of Science and Technology Press for their full support and warm help during the compilation process.

This textbook may not fully cover comprehensive knowledge from the perspective of the writer's cognition. We sincerely welcome readers to criticize and feed back.

目录
CONTENTS

CHAPTER 1　General Introduction of International Tourism（国际旅游业总论）　……　1

Section 1　International Tourism（国际旅游业）　…………………………………　2
Section 2　Chinese International Tourism Market（中国国际旅游市场）　…………　16

CHAPTER 2　The Asia Tourism Region（亚洲旅游区）　……………………………　37

Section 1　General Situation of Asia（亚洲概况）　…………………………………　38
Section 2　Japan（日本）　……………………………………………………………　43
Section 3　South Korea（韩国）　……………………………………………………　51
Section 4　Thailand（泰国）　…………………………………………………………　58
Section 5　The Philippines（菲律宾）　………………………………………………　65
Section 6　Singapore（新加坡）　……………………………………………………　72
Section 7　Malaysia（马来西亚）　……………………………………………………　80
Section 8　India（印度）　………………………………………………………………　86

CHAPTER 3　The Europe Tourism Region（欧洲旅游区）　…………………………　94

Section 1　General Situation of Europe（欧洲概况）　………………………………　95
Section 2　Britain（英国）　……………………………………………………………　100
Section 3　France（法国）　……………………………………………………………　108
Section 4　Germany（德国）　…………………………………………………………　116
Section 5　Italy（意大利）　……………………………………………………………　123
Section 6　Spain（西班牙）　…………………………………………………………　131
Section 7　Russia（俄罗斯）　…………………………………………………………　139
Section 8　Switzerland（瑞士）　………………………………………………………　148
Section 9　Greece（希腊）　……………………………………………………………　158

CHAPTER 4　The North America Tourism Region(北美洲旅游区) ……………… 168

Section 1　General Situation of North American(北美洲概况) …………… 169
Section 2　The United States(美国) …………………………………………… 171
Section 3　Canada(加拿大) …………………………………………………… 186

CHAPTER 5　The South America Tourism Region(南美洲旅游区) ……………… 197

Section 1　General Situation of South America(南美洲概况) ……………… 198
Section 2　Brazil(巴西) ………………………………………………………… 202
Section 3　Argentina(阿根廷) ………………………………………………… 207

CHAPTER 6　The Africa Tourism Region(非洲旅游区) ………………………… 216

Section 1　General Situation of Africa(非洲概况) …………………………… 217
Section 2　Egypt(埃及) ………………………………………………………… 221
Section 3　Morocco(摩洛哥) ………………………………………………… 227

CHAPTER 7　The Oceania Tourism Region(大洋洲旅游区) …………………… 235

Section 1　General Situation of Oceania(大洋洲概况) ……………………… 236
Section 2　Australia(澳大利亚) ……………………………………………… 238
Section 3　New Zealand(新西兰) …………………………………………… 246

Reference(参考文献) ……………………………………………………………… 256

CHAPTER 1

General Introduction of International Tourism
（国际旅游业总论）

◇ **LEARNING OBJECTIVES**(学习目标)

1. Master the basic pattern of the development of international tourism and its basic characteristics(掌握国际旅游业发展的基本格局及其基本特征)。

2. Familiar with the basic trend of the development of international tourism(熟悉国际旅游发展的基本趋势)。

3. Master the current situation of China's international tourism characteristics(掌握中国国际旅游的现状特点)。

4. Familiar with the development prospects of China's international tourism market(熟悉中国国际旅游市场的发展前景)。

◇ **LEARNING CONTENTS**(学习内容)

1. The basic pattern of international tourism development; basic characteristics of international tourism development; basic trend of international tourism development(国际旅游发展的基本格局;国际旅游发展的基本特征;国际旅游发展的基本趋势)。

2. The current situation of China's inbound and outbound tourism; development prospects of Chinese inbound tourism market(中国入境和出境旅游现状;中国入境旅游市场发展前景)。

◇ **PROBLEM ORIENTATION**(问题导向)

Is the world tourism market still dominated by Europe and America today?(今天世界旅游市场仍然由欧美主导吗?)

Section 1　International Tourism(国际旅游业)

一　国际旅游业发展的基本格局
(Basic Pattern of International Tourism Development)

1. 发展历程(Development History)

随着世界经济的发展和人们生活水平的提高,旅游已经成为人们休闲的主要方式之一,旅游业已成为世界上最大的产业。旅游业的发展不仅给许多国家提供了大量的就业机会,还给它们带来丰厚的外汇收入。因此,旅游业引起各国政府的高度重视。许多国家的政府通过颁布旅游组织法或旅游基本法、直接投资或减税、设立旅游发展基金、制定休假制度、实行"低门槛"入境和"低门槛"收费政策等,以保证和支持本国旅游业的健康发展。

With the development of the world economy and the improvement of people's living standards, tourism has become one of the main choices of people's leisure, and tourism has become the largest industry in the world. The development of tourism not only provides a lot of employment opportunities for many countries, but also brings them huge foreign exchange receipts. Therefore, the tourism has increasingly attracted the attention of governments around the world. In order to ensure and support the healthy development of domestic tourism, many governments have promulgated the tourism organization laws or the basic tourism laws, made direct investment or tax reduction, set up tourism development funds, formulated vacation systems, and implemented "low threshold" entry and "low threshold" charging policies.

世界旅游组织(以下简称 UNWTO)的数据显示,国际跨境旅游者的数量从 1990 年的 4.34 亿人次增加到 2018 年的 14 亿人次。国际旅游业年发展速度虽然有升有降,各地区增长速度有快有慢,但是总体上一直呈增长趋势(见表 1-1)。

表 1-1　世界各旅游区接待国际游者数量　　　　单位:百万人次

旅游区	年份								
	1990	2010	2012	2013	2014	2015	2016	2017	2018
欧洲旅游区	261.1	484.8	534.4	563.4	588.4	605.1	619.5	673.3	710.0
亚太旅游区	92.8	150.6	233.5	248.1	263.0	284.1	306.0	324.0	347.7
美洲旅游区	55.8	204.9	162.7	167.9	180.6	193.8	200.7	210.8	215.7
非洲旅游区	14.7	49.9	52.9	55.8	56.0	53.6	57.7	62.7	67.1
中东旅游区	9.6	58.2	51.7	51.6	50.3	58.1	55.6	57.7	60.5
全世界	434	948	1035	1087	1138	1195	1239	1329	1401

资料来源:UNWTO, Data as collected by international tourism highlights,1991-2019 Edition。

但是世界旅游业在总体增长的趋势下,也经历了一系列的危机时期,例如 1991 年的海湾战争、1997 年的亚洲金融危机、2001 年的"9·11"恐怖袭击、2003 年的非典型肺炎(简称 SARS)、2004 年和 2005 年的禽流感危机、印度尼西亚巴厘岛、突尼斯和蒙巴萨的爆炸事件、阿富汗战争、印度洋海啸、南亚大地震、2008 年以来席卷全球的金融危机、甲型 H1N1 流感的蔓延等,使世界旅游业更加具有不确定性,且出现区域性的负值增长。UNWTO 公布的统计数据显示,2012 年以来,全球入境旅游年增长率一直保持增长态势,欧洲地区、亚太地区、美洲地区一直保持正增长,而非洲个别年份呈现负增长,中东地区由于局势不稳定,入境旅游年增长率也不稳定,有些年份呈现正增长,有些年份呈现负增长(见表 1-2)。

With the overall growth in the world's tourism industry, tourism sector has also experienced a series of crisis, such as the Gulf War in 1991, the Asian financial crisis in 1997, and the terrorist attacks of September 11, 2001, which made tourism more unpredictable and even appeared a regional negative growth.

表 1-2　2012—2018 年世界入境旅游年增长率　　　　　　　　单位:%

旅游区	年份						
	2012	2013	2014	2015	2016	2017	2018
世界	4.1	4.7	4.7	4.6	3.8	7.0	5.4
欧洲地区	3.7	5.0	3.9	4.7	2.4	8.6	5.5
亚太地区	6.9	6.8	5.3	5.6	7.1	5.7	7.3
美洲地区	4.4	3.5	7.4	5.9	3.6	4.7	2.3
非洲地区	5.2	4.8	2.2	−3.3	7.8	8.5	7.0
中东地区	−5.6	−3.4	4.4	1.7	−4.4	4.1	4.7

资料来源:UNWTO, Data as collected by international tourism highlights,2013-2019 Edition。

世界旅游城市联合会(以下简称 WTCF)与中国社会科学院旅游研究中心共同发布的《世界旅游经济趋势报告(2020)》显示,2019 年,全球旅游总人次(包括国内旅游人次和入境旅游人次)为 123.1 亿人次,较上年增长 4.6%;全球旅游总收入(包括国内旅游收入和入境旅游收入)波动趋势放缓,为 5.8 万亿美元,相当于全球 GDP 的 6.7%。总之,世界旅游业的发展是曲折的,但从大趋势来看是上升的。

2020 年是特别的一年,席卷全球的新冠肺炎疫情对世界经济造成重创,而其中受害最大的产业莫过于旅游业。据 UNWTO 统计,2020 年全球的旅游人次减少 4.5 亿,相比 2019 年减少 60%~80%,国际旅游收入也减少了 9 100 亿美元,全球旅游行业损失 1 亿到 1.2 亿个直接就业机会。

In short, the development of world's tourism is a turns and twists, but the prospect is on the rise as a whole. The year 2020 has been different. The world's economy has been hit hard by the COVID-19 pandemic. The tourism industry is among the first to bear the brunt.

2. 国际旅游业发展的基本格局(Basic Pattern of International Tourism Development)

现代国际旅游市场在不断向纵深发展,世界五大区域的旅游业呈现发展不平衡的态势,进入 21 世纪,五大区域旅游差异化更加明显,已呈现欧洲、亚太和美洲三足鼎立的格局。

The modern world's international tourism market is constantly developing in depth. The tourism development of the five major regions in the world has shown an unbalanced trend. In the 21st century, the five major regions have become more differentiated in tourism, and they have shown a tripartite tourism pattern in Europe, Asia-Pacific and the America.

1)欧洲旅游市场(European Tourism Market)

无论从国际旅游接待人数,还是从国际旅游收入来衡量,欧洲旅游业在国际旅游业中一直处于领先地位。欧洲是国际旅游的中心地区,也是世界上国际旅游业最发达的地区。

随着欧盟成员国的增加和"大欧洲"态势的发展,欧洲的国际旅游人数总体都有增加,自2017年以来,欧洲依然是世界最受欢迎的国际旅游目的地,各区域均出现喜人的增速。2017年欧洲共接待了6.73亿入境游客,同比增长8.6%。2018年共接待了7.10亿入境游客,同比增长5.5%,但欧洲内部发展不平衡,2018年南欧及地中海地区的旅游业增长最快,这与该区域拥有众多成熟旅游目的地息息相关,中东欧其次,西欧第三。(见表1-3)。

表1-3　2017—2018年欧洲地区国际入境旅游人数及增长率对比

区　域	年　份		增长率/(%)
	2017/百万人次	2018/百万人次	
欧洲地区	673.3	710.0	5.5
北欧	78.4	78.9	0.6
西欧	192.7	200.4	4.0
中东欧	134.6	141.4	5.1
南欧及地中海	267.5	289.4	8.2

资料来源:UNWTO, Data as collected by international tourism highlights, 2018-2019 Edition。

Measured by both the number and the revenue of international tourists, European tourism industry has always taken a leading position in international tourism. Europe is the central region for international tourists and also the most developed region in the world. However, there is a growing disparity in European countries.

2)美洲旅游市场(American Tourism Market)

美洲国际旅游业开始较早,在20世纪80年代发展尤为迅速。目前美洲国际旅游业发展水平仅次于欧洲地区和亚洲地区。其中美国是美洲、也是世界头号旅游大国。虽然之前美洲旅游受到世界经济衰退、"9·11"事件和反恐战争等因素的影响,其旅游业发展速度减缓,但2010年后,美洲地区的旅游业摆脱了低迷状态,国际入境旅游人数快速增长。2017年美洲入境游客增长较快,增长率为4.7%,而2018年入境游客增长放缓,增长率为2.3%,其中加勒比地区和中美洲地区甚至出现负增长(见表1-4)。究其原因,以美国为例,美国外交和贸易政策不得人心,其中美国不断制造中美贸易摩擦,使中国赴美游客人数由过去十年的年平均增速23%,下降到2018年零增长。

表 1-4　2017—2018 年美洲地区国际入境旅游人数及增长率对比

区　域	年　份		增长率/(%)
	2017/百万人次	2018/百万人次	
美洲地区	210.8	215.7	2.3
北美洲	137.1	142.2	3.7
加勒比地区	26.0	25.7	−1.2
中美洲	11.1	10.8	−2.7
南美洲	36.6	37.0	1.1

资料来源：UNWTO, Data as collected by international tourism highlights, 2018-2019 Edition。

International tourism in America started early and grew rapidly in the 1980s. At present, the development of international tourism of America is inferior to that of Europe and Asia, but the United States is the No. 1 tourism country in America and in the world.

3) 亚洲及太平洋地区旅游市场（The Asia and Pacific Tourism Market）

随着世界经济贸易的重心向亚太地区转移，加上亚太地区各国政府的重视，亚太地区旅游业发展迅猛，亚太地区在国际旅游业中的地位越来越重要，已跃居世界第二位。2003 年，亚太地区由于受到伊拉克战争和 SARS 的影响，接待国际旅游人数出现下降，2004 年以后，亚太地区各国加大了对旅游业的投入，其国际旅游业迅速恢复和振兴。但是，受 2008 年以来全球金融危机等因素的影响，亚太地区入境过夜游客数量增长放缓，2009 年除东南亚外，其他区域出现负增长。2010 年以后亚太地区，尤其是东南亚和南亚地区的旅游业实现了快速增长。2017 年，亚太地区国际游客为 3.24 亿，同比增长 5.7%，2018 年为 3.48 亿，同比增长 7.3%，在世界五大区域中增长最快（见表 1-5）。

表 1-5　2017—2018 年亚太地区国际入境旅游人数及增长率对比

区　域	年　份		增长率/(%)
	2017/百万人次	2018/百万人次	
亚太地区	324.0	347.7	7.3
东北亚	159.5	169.2	6.1
东南亚	120.5	128.2	6.4
大洋洲	16.6	17.0	2.4
南亚	27.5	32.8	19.3

资料来源：UNWTO, Data as collected by international tourism highlights, 2018-2019 Edition。

With the transfer of the world's economic and trade focus to Asia-Pacific, plus the attention of the governments of the region, the international tourism has developed rapidly. Asia-Pacific region has become increasingly important in international tourism and has taken the second place in the world.

4)非洲旅游市场(African Tourism Market)

非洲的现代国际旅游业兴起于20世纪60年代。70年代后,非洲各国采取了一系列行之有效的措施,其国际旅游业取得了长足的发展。世界政治经济形势的变化,加上该地区内民族纷争、政局不稳定、自然灾害频繁、传染病流行、社会经济及文化不发达等因素的影响,阻碍了本地区国际旅游业的发展,使非洲的旅游业呈现南强北弱的局面。总体来看,目前赴非的国际游客数量正呈快速增长之势。据世界旅游组织统计,2014年,赴非洲旅游的国际游客达到了近5 600万人。2015年受恐怖袭击的影响,赴非洲旅游的国际游客人次下降3%,其中北非国家下降了8%,但非洲国际游客仍达到了5 300万人。2017年非洲地区入境游客人数为6 230万,2018年为6 710万,同比增长了7.0%,其中北非增长高于南非。

Africa's modern international tourism emerged in the 1960s. After the 1970s, the international tourism of African countries has made great progress and achieved obvious economic effects. However, various internal and external factors have hindered the development of international tourism in this region, and formed a strong south and weak north.

5)中东旅游市场(The Middle East Tourism Market)

中东是世界国际旅游业发展最不稳定的地区,但2002年其国际旅游业出现了猛烈反弹。2003年后,中东接待入境旅游人数持续保持增长态势,2008年增长率为18.2%,但2011年以来,受全球经济衰退的影响,加上政治的动荡,该地区国际旅游业出现了连续三年的负增长,直到2014年才由负转正,增长率为4.4%。2015年相比2014年增长3%,达到5 400万人次。2016年圣战分子先后对突尼斯、埃及、土耳其游客集中地发动恐怖袭击后,中东的外国游客减少了2.4%。2017年后中东地区局势趋于稳定,入境游客人数有所增加,2017年为5 770万,2018年为6 050万,同比增长了4.90%。

The Middle East has been the most unstable region in the development of world's international tourism, but rebounded sharply in 2002.

二 国际旅游的基本特点
（Basic Characteristics of International Tourism）

旅游业是脆弱行业,易受金融危机、传染性疾病、山洪海啸、飞机失事、政治动乱等一系列突发事件的影响,世界范围内的入境过夜游客数量变化表现出以下特点:

Tourism is a fragile industry, which is vulnerable to a series of emergencies such as financial crisis, infectious diseases, mountain torrents and tsunamis, plane crashes and political turmoil, etc. Throughout the world, international tourism presents the following characteristics.

1. 世界各旅游区发展不平衡,亚太地区发展迅猛(The development of tourism regions in the world is unbalanced, and the Asia-Pacific region is developing rapidly)

1)五大区域旅游差异化更加明显

从表1-1中的数据可以看到,2018年欧洲旅游区共接待国际游客7.1亿人次,远远高于其他地区,非洲接待了6 710万人次,中东地区仅接待了6 050万人次,二者都不足欧洲的10%,因此国际旅游业发展极不平衡,但这种格局也是动态的,2019年继续维持这一格局。

从全球旅游总收入区域分布来看,亚太地区、欧洲地区和美洲地区呈现三足鼎立局面,2018年三大地区旅游市场份额分别为32.9%、30.7%和31.4%。三大地区旅游总收入合计占比超过95%,非洲地区和中东地区份额合计不超过5%。但从旅游人数和旅游收入对比来看,亚太地区以66.4%的旅游人数创造了32.9%的旅游收入,而美洲地区和欧洲地区分别以15.1%和15.7%的旅游人数创造了31.4%和30.7%的旅游收入,说明亚太地区游客的人均旅游消费水平整体较低,亚太地区人均旅游消费为219.07美元,远远低于欧洲地区人均旅游消费897.65美元和美洲地区人均旅游消费884.35美元。

From the regional distribution of global tourism revenue, Asia-Pacific region, Europe region and America region form a tripod complexion, with the total tourism revenue of the three regions accounting for more than 95%, while the total share of Africa region and the Middle East region is less than 5%. The per capita consumption of tourists in Asia-Pacific region is far lower than that in Europe and America region.

2)全球旅游经济高度集中于T20国家

WTCF将旅游总收入排名前20位的国家和地区称之为T20。总体来看,全球旅游经济80%集中于T20国家。

2012年以来,美国、中国、德国、日本、英国一直占据旅游总收入前五名。前三名稳定不变,第四、第五名交替轮换。T20国家旅游总人次和旅游总收入占全球的比例分别高于88%和78%。T20是当之无愧的旅游大国集团(见表1-6)。

WTCF calls the top 20 countries and regions as T20. Overall, 80% volume of the global tourism economy is centered in T20 countries.

表1-6　2012—2019年旅游总收入排名全球前20的国家(T20)

排名	年份							
	2012	2013	2014	2015	2016	2017	2018	2019
1	美国	美国	美国	美国	美国	美国	美国	美国
2	中国	中国	中国	中国	中国	中国	中国	中国
3	德国	德国	德国	德国	德国	德国	德国	德国
4	日本	英国	英国	英国	英国	日本	日本	日本

续表

排名	年份							
	2012	2013	2014	2015	2016	2017	2018	2019
5	英国	日本	日本	日本	日本	英国	英国	英国
6	法国	法国	法国	印度	印度	印度	印度	印度
7	意大利	意大利	意大利	法国	法国	法国	法国	法国
8	印度	印度	印度	意大利	意大利	意大利	意大利	意大利
9	墨西哥	墨西哥	墨西哥	墨西哥	墨西哥	墨西哥	墨西哥	墨西哥
10	巴西	西班牙	巴西	西班牙	西班牙	西班牙	西班牙	西班牙
11	西班牙	巴西	西班牙	澳大利亚	澳大利亚	澳大利亚	澳大利亚	澳大利亚
12	澳大利亚	澳大利亚	澳大利亚	巴西	巴西	巴西	巴西	巴西
13	加拿大	加拿大	加拿大	加拿大	加拿大	加拿大	加拿大	加拿大
14	俄罗斯	俄罗斯	俄罗斯	韩国	韩国	泰国	泰国	泰国
15	土耳其	土耳其	韩国	土耳其	泰国	韩国	韩国	韩国
16	韩国	韩国	土耳其	泰国	土耳其	土耳其	土耳其	菲律宾
17	泰国	泰国	奥地利	俄罗斯	菲律宾	菲律宾	菲律宾	土耳其
18	瑞士	瑞士	瑞士	瑞士	俄罗斯	瑞士	俄罗斯	俄罗斯
19	阿根廷	瑞典	瑞典	奥地利	瑞士	俄罗斯	瑞士	瑞士
20	瑞典	阿根廷	马来西亚	菲律宾	奥地利	奥地利	奥地利	奥地利

资料来源：中国社会科学院旅游研究中心和世界旅游城市联合会联合发布的报告，2020年。

3）新兴经济体在全球旅游业中的地位更加凸显

2019年，新兴经济体接待入境旅游人次占全球接待入境旅游人次的46.2%，2019年，新兴经济体入境旅游收入占全球旅游总收入的39.3%。

2019年新兴经济体旅游总收入增速为2.0%，高出发达经济体1.4个百分点，旅游总收入相当于GDP的7.0%，高出发达经济体0.5个百分点。也就是说，旅游业对新兴经济体的社会经济发展更加重要，新兴经济体拉动社会经济发展的作用更强。

Tourism is more important to the social and economic development of emerging economies, which will further impel the economic and social development.

4）城市仍是入境旅游者的主要目的地

WTCF的《世界旅游城市发展报告》显示，所选择的100个样本城市中79个国际城市接待了入境旅游总人次的1/3以上，贡献了入境旅游总收入的1/5以上。这些城市主要来自亚太、美洲和欧洲这三个地区，可见，城市格局与旅游经济发展的总体格局高度一致。2018年WTCF发布的排行榜中，世界旅游城市发展综合排行前十名分别为伦敦、巴黎、纽约、东京、北京、首尔、悉尼、迪拜、中国香港、罗马。

In the charts released by WTCF in 2018, the top ten tourism cities in the world are London, Paris, New York, Tokyo, Beijing, Seoul, Sydney, Dubai, Hong Kong (China) and Rome. They are mainly from Asia-Pacific, America and Europe.

2. 全球旅游增长趋缓，但世界旅游经济总量仍很大（The global tourism growth has slowed down, but the world tourism economy is still large）

纵观世界旅游经济，其总量一直在增加，2016年以来，国际旅游人数和国际旅游收入一直呈增长态势，但增长趋缓。

2019年全球入境旅游人次增速同比下降0.5个百分点。2019年全球入境旅游达到13.71亿人次，比上年增长3.4%，增速比2018年下降0.5个百分点。表1-7展示的是2016年以来全球入境旅游收入的增速。

表1-7　2016—2019年全球入境旅游收入增速

年　份	入境旅游收入增速/(%)
2016	1.0
2017	11.5
2018	2.5
2019	1.1

资料来源：根据中国社会科学院旅游研究中心和WTCF联合发布的报告整理，2020年。

究其原因是多方面的：互联网的普及，旅游目的地（国）预定系统日趋完善；国际航运的发展，让洲际间的旅行时间大大缩短；各国出入境手续趋向简化；国际旅游供给水平已经达到了一个新的高度，各国、各地区旅游接待能力提高。总之，世界旅游业的经济总量不断增加，在世界经济中的地位不断提升，旅游业已经成为国际服务贸易的支柱产业。

同样，近年来全球旅游总收入保持增长势头，旅游业对全球GDP的贡献率超过6.0%（见表1-8），带来的工作机会占全球总就业量的10%。

Since 2016, the number of international tourists and international tourism revenue have been increasing, but the growth has slowed down. In short, the total economic volume of the world tourism continues to increase, and its status in the world economy continues to rise. Tourism has become a pillar industry of the international service trade.

表1-8　2016—2019年全球旅游收入及占全球GDP的比例

年　份	旅游总收入/十亿美元	占全球GDP/(%)
2016	5.17	7.0
2017	5.30	6.7
2018	5.34	6.1

续表

年　份	旅游总收入/十亿美元	占全球 GDP/(%)
2019	5.80	6.7

资料来源：根据中国社会科学院旅游研究中心和 WTCF 联合发布的报告整理，2020 年。

三　国际旅游业发展的基本趋势
（Basic Trend of International Tourism Development）

国际旅游业从形成到发展，现在进入了稳定发展时期，21世纪将是国际旅游业发展的第二个黄金时代。国际旅游业成为世界上最大的产业，旅游者将达到空前的规模，来自各个国家、各个阶层的旅游者将把他们的足迹印在世界的每一个角落。尽管各个国家的政治、经济情况以及旅游业的发展模式不同，但就整个国际旅游业而言，将出现下列发展趋势。

International tourism has entered a period of stable development from its formation to development. The 21st century will be the second golden age of the development of international tourism. International tourism has become the largest industry in the world. Tourists will reach an unprecedented scale. Tourists from all countries and all social classes will leave their footprints in every corner of the world. Although the political and economic situation of each country and the development mode of tourism industry are different, the following development trends will appear in terms of the whole international tourism.

1. 旅游业继续保持世界上最大产业的地位（Tourism continues to maintain its position as the largest industry in the world）

旅游业作为世界上最大的新兴产业，每年国际旅游业的交易额已超过 3 000 亿美元。旅游业已取代石油工业、汽车工业，成为世界上最大的创汇产业。早在 1992 年，世界旅游业理事会（以下简称 WTTC）根据总收入、就业、增值、投资及纳税等几个方面的分析，证明旅游业作为世界上最大产业的态势正在形成。因此，WTTC 指出，旅游业是促进经济发展的主要动力，旅游业已成为世界上最大的就业部门，共产生 1.27 亿个工作岗位，约占世界劳动力总数的 6.7%；旅游业是创造高附加值的产业，其增值额已达到 14 490 亿美元；旅游是各国财政中主要的纳税产业之一，全世界的旅游企业及从业人员的纳税总额高达 3 030 亿美元。旅游业对世界经济的贡献，不仅是它产生的产值和提供的就业岗位，它同时还带动其他产业的发展，带来一系列的经济效益。

2019 年旅游产业继续保持世界第一大产业的地位。WTCF 与中国社会科学院旅游研究中心共同发布的《世界旅游经济趋势报告（2020）》显示，2019 年，全球旅游总人次（包括国内旅游人次和入境旅游人次）为 123.1 亿人次，较上年增长 4.6%；全球旅游总收入

(包括国内旅游收入和入境旅游收入)为5.8万亿美元,相当于全球GDP的6.7%,这一比例较上年下降0.1%;全球入境旅游收入与国内旅游收入波动趋势放缓,有望实现"五连增"。

Tourism, as the world's largest emerging industry, has replaced oil industry and automobile industry to become the world's largest foreign exchange earning industry. WTTC points out that tourism is a major driving force for economic development and has become the largest employment sector in the world.

2. 国际旅游区域的重心向东转移的速度加快(The center of international tourism region is shifted to the East, and the speed is accelerating)

欧洲和北美是现代国际旅游业的两大传统市场。在20世纪80年代以前,它们几乎垄断了国际旅游市场,接待人数和收入都占世界总数的90%左右。20世纪80年代后,亚洲、非洲、拉丁美洲和大洋洲等地区一批新兴旅游市场的崛起,使国际旅游业在世界各个地区的市场份额出现了新的分配组合。到了21世纪,亚太地区在国际旅游市场中的份额进一步扩大,欧洲和北美地区在国际旅游市场上的份额进一步缩小,旅游重心由传统市场向新兴市场转移的速度将会加快。随着发展中国家和地区经济的持续增长和繁荣,这些国家和地区的居民去邻国度假必定会增加,区域性国际旅游将得到极大发展。特别是随着全球经济重心的相应东移,亚太地区逐渐成为国际旅游业的热点区域。

例如,近年来邮轮行业发展引人瞩目,根据国际邮轮协会(CLIA)的统计,全球邮轮市场游客量从2004年的1 314人次增长到2017年的2 580人次,复合增长率达到4.9%。其中,世界邮轮旅游重心东移特征明显,2010—2016年亚太地区的占比由原来的1.2%增长到9.2%,亚洲正成为邮轮业新的增长极,而在亚洲市场上,中国游客占比最高,达到47.4%。

近年来,随着国际旅游业重心东移,中国经验、中国市场和中国作用在世界旅游产业格局中的地位更加突显。国际社会普遍认为,把脉世界旅游业大势必须关注中国旅游走向。

中国政府持续拓宽国际合作渠道,拓展国际发展空间,参与国际规则制定,推动中国标准走出去,建立完善"丝绸之路旅游部长会议""二十国集团旅游部长会议""中国-东盟(10+1)旅游部长会议""APEC旅游部长会议""中日韩旅游部长会议""中俄蒙三国旅游部长会议""中国-中东欧国家旅游合作高级别会议""中俄人文合作委员会旅游分委会""中英旅游部长级会议""中美旅游高层对话会"等会议机制,与俄罗斯、美国、印度、中东欧、东盟、欧盟等国家互办"旅游年",倡议主办首届世界旅游发展大会,承办联合国世界旅游组织全体大会活动,彰显了中国对于世界旅游发展方向的主导与引领作用,中国已逐渐由参与者转变为主导者,由跟跑者转变为领跑者。特别是由中国发起的世界旅游联盟的正式成立,为中国向世界贡献旅游新理念、新倡议、新思路提供了全新路径。

Europe and North America are the two traditional markets for modern international tourism. In 21st century, the share of Asia-Pacific region in the international tourism market will further expand, while the share of Europe and North America will shrink, and the transfer of the tourism focus from the traditional market to the emerging market will be accelerated. Especially with the eastward shift of the global economic center, Asia-Pacific region has gradually become the "hot" region of international tourism.

3. 国际旅游客源市场趋向分散化(The international tourist source market tends to be decentralized)

长期以来,国际旅游的主要客源市场在地区结构上一直以西欧和北美为主。这两个地区作为现代国际旅游的发源地,其出国旅游人数几乎占国际旅游总人数的75%左右。但是20世纪90年代以来,随着国际旅游区域的重心向东转移,国际旅游客源市场在地区分布上畸形集中的局面也受到了冲击,世界经济的迅速分化和重新改组,初步形成了北美、西欧、日本、以俄罗斯为主的独联体、东欧和第三世界等六大经济力量相抗衡的态势,直接影响了各地区国际旅游客源,特别是亚太地区的迅速崛起,导致了客源市场分布格局由集中渐渐走向分散。

到21世纪初,亚洲、非洲和拉丁美洲的一些新兴工业国脱颖而出,其国民人均收入的增加,可能逐渐取代传统的旅游客源国,而成为国际旅游的主体市场。世界旅游经济格局已经从多年前的"三个中心"(美国、日本、西欧)逐步转化成"七国集团(G7)+金砖五国(BRICS)"。2018—2019年旅游收入世界排名前十位的国家中,G7国家有美国、德国、英国、日本、意大利和法国,金砖国家有中国、印度,其余是墨西哥、澳大利亚。

表1-9是2019年国际旅游支出世界排名前十位的国家。

表1-9 2019年国际旅游支出世界排名前十位国家

排　　名	国　　家	国际旅游支出/十亿美元	较前年增长/(%)
1	中国	277	5.0
2	美国	144	7.0
3	德国	94	1.0
4	英国	76	3.0
5	法国	48	11.0
6	澳大利亚	37	10.0
7	俄罗斯	35	11.0
8	加拿大	33	4.0
9	韩国	32	1.0
10	意大利	30	4.0

资料来源:中国社会科学院旅游研究中心和WTCF联合发布的报告,2020年。

For a long time, Western Europe and North America have been the main tourist source markets of international tourism in terms of regional structure. By the early 21st century, with the increase of per capita national income, some emerging industrial countries in Asia, Africa and Latin America may gradually replace the traditional tourist source countries and become the main market of international tourism.

4. 国际旅游消费需求向多元化方向发展(International tourism consumer demand is developing in a diversified direction)

国际上传统的旅游方式分为四种，即娱乐型、观光型、疗养型和商务型，大多数旅游活动更多的是各种方式兼而有之。一个国家或地区的旅游方式是由其资源条件、地理位置、市场条件等多方面因素决定的，不同的旅游方式也有不同的产品、价格、市场对策等，同时旅游者也有不同的消费要求和消费特点。随着旅游方式向个性化、多样化、自由化、文化化方向发展，观光旅游、度假旅游和商务旅游等已不能满足旅游者的需求，各种内容丰富、新颖独特的旅游方式和旅游项目应运而生。目前，国际旅游消费需求的基本态势是：从人们出游的组织方式来看，在追求个性化的浪潮下，散客旅游特别是家庭旅游成为全球流行趋势；从旅游动机和目的来看，生态旅游、文化旅游、奖励旅游、探险旅游、科考旅游、潜海旅游以及其他淡季旅游、美食旅游、体验式旅行、环保式旅行等各种形式的主题旅游，构成了人们外出旅游的主旋律。

With the development of tourism mode towards individualization, diversification, liberalization and culturalization, sightseeing, vacation tour and business trips can no longer meet the needs of tourists. Various novel and unique tourism modes and individualized travel products emerge endlessly.

5. 中远程旅游逐渐兴旺(Medium and long-distance tourism is booming)

旅游距离的远近受限于时间和经济等因素的影响，在20世纪上半叶，人们大都只能借助火车和汽车进行旅游活动。当时飞机速度既慢且票价昂贵，还很不安全。因此，那个时代的人一般只能作短程旅游。中远程旅游，特别是横渡大洋的国际旅游的兴起，是二战后航空运输大发展的直接结果。目前，飞机的飞行速度越来越快，续航技术日新月异，世界正变得越来越小，距离在旅游限制因素中的作用逐渐减弱，人们外出旅游将乘坐更快捷的飞机和高速火车。到2010年，新一代的超音速飞机，从伦敦飞到东京，航程9 585千米，只需3小时；短途旅行可坐时速550 km/h的超导火车，速度比现在的高速火车快近一倍。加之闲暇时间增多，今后将有更多的人加入远程旅游的行列。另据国际航空协会估计，世界航空运输中，长途航运将成为主要手段，距离在2 400千米以上的长途客运量可能从目前占航空客运量的6%剧增至40%。2018年7月24日据英国《每日邮报》报道，一家超音速飞机的制造商表示，未来一支包含2 000架超音速飞机的机队将遍布全球各地的城市连接起来，其中从伦敦运到纽约只需3.5个小时，所用时间是目前的一半。因此，随着更加快捷、安全、舒适、经济的新型航空客机投入运营,全球性大规模的远程旅游将成为可能。

With the development of science and technology, the world is becoming smaller, and traveling is not restricted by the distance any longer. People may take faster planes and high-speed trains when traveling. With more new airliners starting operation, traveling will be faster, safer, more comfortable and more economical, and global large-scale long-distance tours will be possible.

6. 国际旅游对旅游安全更为重视(International tourism pays more attention to tourism safety)

安全性和可靠性是所有旅游企业应该考虑的首要问题,保证游客的安全是国际旅游的前提。如果旅游目的地存在安全隐患,应该采取有力的防范措施,提供准确信息,并对不安全地区进行隔离和明示。

世界局势的缓和,使世界避免爆发全球性的毁灭战争成为可能,但世界上局部战争和冲突时有发生。民族冲突、宗教冲突、国际恐怖主义,随时对国际旅游业的发展形成局部威胁。在具备闲暇时间和支付能力的条件下,唯一能使旅游者放弃旅游计划的因素就是对安全的顾虑。旅游者考虑的安全因素主要有:局部战争和冲突、恐怖主义活动、旅游目的地政局不稳定、传染性疾病流行、恶性交通事故的发生、社会治安状况恶化等。旅游者只有对各方面的安全因素确定无疑后才会启程。因此,各旅游接待国或地区都将越来越重视安全因素对旅游市场营销的影响,力求从每一个环节把好安全关。针对一些不可预测的不安全因素为游客预先代办保险,一方面可以减轻游客的后顾之忧,另一方面一旦事故发生,可以将其对市场的冲击力减小到最低程度。

Safety and reliability are the primary issues that all tourism enterprises should consider. How to ensure the safety of tourists is the most important factor in international tourism. Every tourism reception country or region will pay more and more attention to the impact of security factors on tourism marketing and strive to ensure the security in every aspect.

7. 支付方式将改变国际旅游者的旅行生活(Payment method will change the travel life of international tourists)

全球电子商务市场中,电子钱包已打破信用卡的主导地位,成为最常用的支付方式,信用卡和借记卡成为第二和第三大支付手段。据英国支付处理商 WorldPay 的统计,2018年,电子钱包支付占总支付方式的36%,信用卡占23%,借记卡占2%,银行转账占11%,直接借记占8%,货到付款占5%,预付卡占2%,其他方式占3%,而到2020年,电子钱包快速拉大优势,占总支付方式的47%,信用卡占17%,借记卡占17%,银行转账占11%,直接借记占6%,货到付款占3%,预付卡占1%,其他方式占1%。从全球来看,移动支付冷热不均,亚太地区的电子支付发展迅速,其中中国的移动支付发展引人瞩目,居全球第一。支付方式的转变是科技发展的结果,也必将为国际旅游者的旅行带来更多便利。

In the global e-commerce market, electronic wallets have broken the dominance of credit cards and become the most common payment method, with credit cards and debit cards becoming the second and third. The change of payment environment will certainly bring more convenience to international tourists.

Section 2　Chinese International Tourism Market（中国国际旅游市场）

中国历史悠久,文化灿烂,山川秀丽,民族众多,旅游资源丰富多彩而独具特色,改革开放以来,经过40余年持续、快速、健康的发展,中国已实现了由旅游资源大国向旅游经济大国的历史性跨越。

中国入境旅游现状（Current Situation of China's Inbound Tourism）

1. 历史回顾(Historical Review)

从建国初期到党的十一届三中全会的20多年间,由于受国际政治经济环境及国内因素的影响,中国国际旅游业的发展非常缓慢,在有些年份甚至停滞不前;旅游接待工作属于外事活动接待和统战工作的一部分,即始终是"政治接待型"的模式,国际旅游入境人数和国际旅游收入都很少,旅游业对国家的经济贡献微不足道,与世界上许多国家通过发展旅游业而促进经济社会协调发展的现实形成了强烈的反差。

In the early 20 years from the founding of the People's Republic of China to the Third Plenary Session of the Eleventh Central Committee of the Communist Party of China, due to the influence of international political and economic environment and domestic factors, the development of China's international tourism was very slow, and even stagnated in some years. The tourism reception was a part of the reception of foreign affairs and the united front work, that is, it has always been a "political reception" mode. With a small number of international tourists and international tourism income, the contribution of tourism to the country's economy is negligible, which is in sharp contrast to the reality that many countries in the world promote coordinated economic and social development through the development of tourism.

党的十一届三中全会以后,在党中央、国务院的正确领导下,中国旅游业有了长足发展,在世界旅游业中的地位不断提高(见表1-10和表1-11)。

表 1-10 历年来海外游客来中国内地旅游入境人数和年增长率

年份	入境人数/万人次	增长率/(%)	年份	入境人数/万人次	增长率/(%)	年份	入境人数/万人次	增长率/(%)
1978	180.92	—	1992	3 811.49	14.29	2006	12 494.21	3.90
1979	420.39	132.36	1993	4 152.69	8.95	2007	13 187.33	5.55
1980	570.25	35.65	1994	4 368.45	5.20	2008	13 002.74	−1.40
1981	776.71	36.20	1995	4 638.65	6.19	2009	12 647.59	−2.70
1982	792.43	2.02	1996	5 112.75	10.22	2010	13 376.20	5.76
1983	947.70	19.59	1997	5 758.79	12.64	2011	13 531.82	1.16
1984	1 285.22	35.61	1998	6 347.84	10.23	2012	13 240.53	−2.20
1985	1 783.31	38.76	1999	7 279.56	14.68	2013	12 907.78	−2.51
1986	2 281.95	27.96	2000	8 344.39	14.63	2014	12 849.83	−0.45
1987	2 690.23	17.89	2001	8 901.29	6.67	2015	13 382.00	4.10
1988	3 169.48	17.81	2002	9 752.83	9.57	2016	13 844.00	3.50
1989	2 450.14	−22.70	2003	9 166.21	−6.01	2017	13 949.00	0.80
1990	2 746.18	12.08	2004	10 800.00	17.82	2018	14 120.00	1.20
1991	3 334.98	21.44	2005	12 029.23	11.38	2019	14 530.00	2.90

资料来源:根据文化和旅游部的统计资料整理。

表 1-11 历年来中国接待过夜旅游者人数和国际旅游收入在世界旅游市场中的排名

年份	接待过夜旅游者人数/万人次	排名	国际旅游收入/亿美元	排名
1990	1 048.40	11	22.20	25
1995	2 003.40	8	87.30	10
1998	2 507.30	6	126.00	7
1999	2 704.70	5	141.00	7
2000	3 122.90	5	162.20	7
2001	3 316.70	5	178.00	5
2002	3 680.30	5	203.90	5
2003	3 297.10	5	174.10	7

续表

年份	接待过夜旅游者人数/万人次	排名	国际旅游收入/亿美元	排名
2004	4 176.10	4	257.40	7
2005	4 680.90	4	293.00	6
2006	4 991.30	4	339.50	5
2007	5 472.00	4	419.00	5
2008	5 304.90	4	408.00	5
2009	5 087.50	4	396.75	5
2010	5 566.45	3	458.14	4
2011	5 657.00	3	484.27	4
2012	5 772.49	3	500.28	4
2013	5 568.59	4	516.64	4
2014	5 562.20	4	1 053.80	2
2015	5 688.60	4	1 136.50	4
2016	5 927.00	4	1 200.00	4
2017	6 074.00	4	1 234.17	12
2018	6 290.00	4	1 271.03	10
2019	6 573.00	—	1 313.00	—

资料来源：文化和旅游部的统计资料及 UNWTO International Tourism Highlights, 2014-2019 Edition。

1978 年，来华旅游入境人数只有 180.92 万人次，其中外国人 23.0 万人次，华侨、港澳台同胞回乡探亲旅游人数 157.9 万人次，旅游外汇收入只有 2.63 亿美元，但创造了新中国成立以来的最高纪录，超过以往 20 多年的旅游接待人数的总和。

1979 年，在中国饭店基本没有增加的情况下，旅游接待人数增长 132.36%，旅游外汇收入增长 70.7%，其中来自西方国家的游客迅速增长，美国旅游者首次达 6.8 万人次，仅次于日本的来华旅游者。

1983 年至 1985 年，来华旅游人数又开始保持两位数的高速增长。1984 年，海外旅游者来华人数首次突破"千万"大关。旅游外汇收入增长速度达 10% 以上。1989 年，中国国际旅游业受到严重的影响，当年来华旅游人数比 1988 年减少了 22.7%，旅游外汇收入第一次出现负增长，为 -17.2%。此后，中国国际旅游业迅速走出困境，1990 年旅游外汇收入和有组织接待外国旅游人数基本恢复到历史最好水平，这表明中国国际旅游业已具备一定规模，比以前更加成熟了。

20 世纪 90 年代以来,中国旅游业持续发展,在国民经济中所占的比重日益提高,取得多方面的经济效益、社会效益和生态效益,旅游产业定位日趋明确,国际旅游业保持稳定增长,其间国际国内政治经济形势对中国国际旅游业产生了重要影响。1996 年,旅游外汇收入第一次突破 100 亿美元大关。1997 年 7 月 1 日,香港回归祖国,香港同胞回内地进行旅游商贸活动的人数进一步增长。1997 年下半年,东南亚爆发金融危机,包括日本、韩国、泰国等许多国家均受到打击。这些国家是中国国际旅游的主要客源国,因此亚洲市场来华游客人数减少较多。1999 年 12 月 20 日,澳门回归祖国,为中国旅游市场的进一步发展提供了更为有利的条件。澳门与内地的感情更加贴近,更多的人到祖国内地观光游览。1999 年澳门来内地旅游人数为 878.37 万人次,同比增长 23.24%。

2001 年的"9·11"事件,对世界旅游业无疑产生了深刻影响,它不仅给美国的旅游业带来致命的打击,也给世界各地的旅游业笼罩上了一层阴影。2003 年由于 SARS 的影响,中国入境旅游市场受到了严重冲击。

2004 年以来,中国旅游业增长迅猛,入境旅游已成为中国最大的国际服务贸易领域,中国已从旅游资源大国发展成为世界旅游大国。

2008 年至 2014 年,我国旅游业连续遭受金融危机、各种突发事件和不利因素的影响,经受了前所未有的考验,入境旅游市场出现下滑,但是中国接待过夜旅游者人数和国际旅游收入仍然处于世界旅游市场前列。

2015 年至 2019 年,中国入境旅游人数从 1.338 亿人次增加到 1.453 亿人次,国际旅游收入从 1 136.5 亿美元增加到 1 313.0 亿美元。

From 1978 to 2019, the number of Chinese inbound tourists and the international tourism incomes in these 41 years have witnessed the brilliant achievements of China's inbound tourism development. It also indicates that China has grown from a tourism resource country to a big tourism country in the world.

(1)从区域看,中国海外客源市场主体为亚洲市场,其次为欧洲和北美市场,大洋洲和非洲市场比例较低,但近年来也有增长的势头。具体来看,2019 年,亚洲占 75.9%,欧洲占 13.2%,美洲占 7.7%,大洋洲占 1.9%,非洲占 1.4%。

(2)从国籍看,20 世纪 80 年代以前,客源国主要是日本、苏联及东欧国家。20 世纪 80 年代以后,随着中国改革开放的不断深入,中国海外客源市场打破了过去狭窄的地域分布格局,中国客源国数量剧增,遍布世界各大洲,其中日本、美国、俄罗斯、英国、法国、德国、菲律宾、泰国、马来西亚、新加坡成为中国十大稳定的客源市场。进入 21 世纪后,世界政治经济局势进一步发生变化,中国客源市场又发生了较大变化。2019 年列入中国前 20 位的客源国家为:缅甸、越南、韩国、俄罗斯、日本、美国、蒙古、马来西亚、菲律宾、新加坡、印度、泰国、加拿大、澳大利亚、印度尼西亚、德国、英国、朝鲜、法国、意大利(其中缅甸、越南、蒙古、印度、朝鲜含边民旅华人数)。

(3)从旅游目的看,外国旅游者来华旅游的主要目的是观光休闲、参加会议及从事商务活动。2019 年来华旅游者中,观光休闲占 35.0%,会议商务占 13.0%,探亲访友占 3.0%,服务员工占 14.7%,其他占 34.3%。

(4)从性别看,男性旅游者仍是中国旅游客源市场的主体。2019年来华的外国旅游者中,男性占58.7%,女性占41.3%。

(5)从年龄上看,中青年仍是中国海外旅游客源市场的主力军。2019年来华旅游的外国旅游者中近80%集中在25—64岁,其中14岁及以下人数占3.8%,15—24岁占13.9%,25—44岁占49.3%,45—64岁占28.1%,65岁及以上占4.9%。

(6)从入境方式看,变化很大,过去以乘飞机为主,现今徒步为首选,乘汽车和飞机为次要方式。2019年来华的外国旅游者中,入境旅游人数按照入境方式分,船舶占2.9%,飞机占17.4%,火车占2.6%,汽车占21.2%,徒步占55.8%。

(7)从职业看,入境游客的成分比较复杂,分布比较广泛,其中商人偏多,这也正说明前来从事商贸活动较多,是中国经济快速发展的反映。

(8)从入境旅游月份来看,游客较多集中在8—11月,是旅游旺季,特别是10月份形成旅游高峰;而1、2、12月较少,是旅游淡季。

此外,中国旅游研究院发布的《中国入境旅游发展报告2019》显示,来华旅游的外国游客以受教育水平及收入水平较高的中青年群体为主,他们多以自由行的方式来华旅游,在华停留时间为4—15天,参观景点为3—9个。此外,外国游客的重访率较高,有42%的外国游客表示未来一年将再次来华旅游。

The above analyzes China's inbound tourism from the region, nationality, traveling purpose, gender, age, entry mode, occupation, month of inbound tourism and other factors.

2. 客源市场分析(Analysis of the Tourist Market)

经过改革开放40余年的发展,中国逐步形成了具有自身特色、符合旅游业持续发展需要的海外客源市场组合,2018—2019年中国海外客源市场的基本情况见表1-12、表1-13和图1-1。

表1-12　2018—2019年中国海外客源市场的基本情况

地　区	2018年入境外国游客人数占总数比重/(%)	2019年入境外国游客人数占总数比重/(%)
亚洲	76.3	75.9
欧洲	12.5	13.2
美洲	7.9	7.7
大洋洲	1.9	1.9
非洲	1.4	1.4
合计	100.0	100.0

资料来源:中国旅游研究院发布的《中国入境旅游发展报告(2019)》。

表1-12表明,亚洲市场是中国最主要的入境客源市场。2019年,占外国人入境市场的75.9%左右。其次是欧洲和美洲市场,占比分别稳定在13.2%和7.7%。

表 1-13　2016—2019 年中国主要客源国

排　　名	2016	2017	2018	2019
1	韩国	缅甸	缅甸	缅甸
2	越南	越南	越南	越南
3	日本	韩国	韩国	韩国
4	缅甸	日本	日本	俄罗斯
5	美国	俄罗斯	美国	日本
6	俄罗斯	美国	俄罗斯	美国
7	蒙古	蒙古	蒙古	蒙古
8	马来西亚	马来西亚	马来西亚	马来西亚
9	菲律宾	菲律宾	菲律宾	菲律宾
10	新加坡	新加坡	新加坡	新加坡

资料来源:文化和旅游部 2016—2019 年的统计资料。

2019 年度旅行社入境旅游接待人次排名前十位的客源地国家或地区有中国香港、澳门、台湾地区以及韩国、美国、马来西亚、日本、新加坡、俄罗斯、泰国(见图 1-1)。

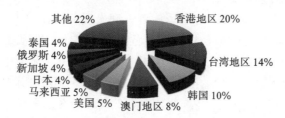

图 1-1　2019 年度入境旅游接待人次排名前十位的客源地国家或地区

资料来源:根据文化和旅游部的统计资料。

表 1-13 和图 1-1 表明,我国主要客源国中,除美国和俄罗斯外,其余均为亚洲国家和地区。

Asian market is the largest source of visitors to China, among which Hong Kong, Macao and Taiwan are still the basic inbound tourist source markets. Next come Europe and North America.

1)持续增长且基数大的亚洲客源地

亚洲是中国最主要的入境客源市场,表 1-13 中近四年的数据显示,虽然位居前十的部分客源国位次有所变动,但这十个客源国家整体保持不变。其中,日本因为其与中国隔海相望的地理位置、悠久的历史渊源和经济文化交流传统,一直是中国最重要的客源国之一。但 2018 年,日本赴华旅游 269 万人次,同比增长仅 0.3%,增长乏力,这一增速远低于同期外国游客赴华旅游市场整体的平均水平(4.7%)。20 世纪 90 年代后,由于中韩两国邦交正常化,韩国来华旅游很快进入快速发展阶段,2018 年,韩国赴华旅游 419 万人次,已经从萨德事件的负面影响中走出来,同比增速高达8.5%,未来旅华旅游增速或将下降。东南亚5国作为中国的近邻,也一直是中国传统稳定的客源国,特别是20世纪90年代以来,随着其经济的发展,旅华市场进入快速发展时期。自2017年缅甸成为中国第一位的客源国,而且近三年一直保持不变。越南出境旅游蓬勃发展,旅华市场保持快速增长,2018年,越南赴华旅游758.8万人次,同比增长16%,是中国第二大入境旅游客源市场。新加坡出境旅游稳步增长,旅华市场继续回升,2018年,新加坡赴华旅游98万人次,同比增长3.9%。泰国出境旅游快速增长,旅华市场同步跟进,2018年,泰国赴华旅游83万人次,同比增长达7.2%,远高于同期外国赴华旅游市场的整体增速(4.7%),2019年泰国赴华旅游也保持较快增长。南亚国家中印度出境旅游市场高速增长,旅华市场增长较快,2018年,印度赴华旅游86万人次,同比增长5.1%。

Asia is the most important inbound tourist source market for China, among which Japan, South Korea and 5 countries of Southeast Asia have always been China's traditional and stable tourist source countries.

2)发展平稳的欧洲客源地

欧洲是中国仅次于亚洲的重要客源市场。作为东亚地区的重要旅游目的地,中国在欧洲游客的远程旅游中扮演着重要角色。20世纪90年代中期以来,欧洲各国来华旅游人数不断增加,1997年香港回归,欧洲游客出现高速增长。此后,一直平稳增长,但是1998年受亚洲金融危机的影响,欧洲游客来华旅游一度出现负增长,2003年SARS和2004年的禽流感,2008年以来汶川大地震、国际金融危机和甲型H1N1流感的影响等,使欧洲游客来华旅游受到一定影响,比例有所下降。但2010年之后欧洲来华人数持续增长,2012年更是达到了591万人次的高峰,之后又有所回落,2014年欧洲来华旅游人数为548.41万人次,占当年来华旅游者的20.8%,而其他年份欧洲游客也平稳增长,其旅游人数占来华旅游者的比例始终保持在20%以上,其中英国、德国、法国、俄罗斯等是主要客源国。其中,俄罗斯出境旅游增长较快,是中国第四大入境旅游国。2018年,俄罗斯赴华旅游242万人次,同比增长2.5%。2019年俄罗斯居民首站到访中国的游客108万人次,同比增长19%。

Europe is China's second most important source market after Asia. As an important tourist destination in East Asia, China plays an important role in the long-distance travel of European tourists, among which Britain, Germany, France and Russia are the main source countries to China.

3)持续平稳增长的美洲客源地

美洲,尤其是北美客源国是中国第三个重要的客源市场,美国和加拿大是中国在美洲的两个主要客源国,20世纪90年代中期以来,它们占据了美洲市场份额的90%左右,来华旅游呈现平稳增长。人数由1990年的28.08万人次增加到2014年的310.65万人次,占当年中国国际入境游客总数的11.78%,特别是美国一直是中国十大稳定的客源国之一,2018年,美国赴华旅游249万人次,同比增长达7.4%,再次超过俄罗斯,成为中国第五大客源市场,且一直是中国第一大远程客源市场,但中美贸易战对2019年全年赴华旅游产生一定的负面影响。加拿大出境旅游出现下滑,但旅华市场稳步增长,2018年,加拿大赴华旅游85万人次,同比增长5.5%,是中国第二大远程客源市场。根据加拿大统计局公布的数据,2018年首站到访中国的加拿大游客共58万人次,其中,超过一半的游客以探亲访友为来华目的。2019年1—8月,加拿大首站来华游客53万人次,同比增长5.4%。

America, especially North America, is the third important source market to China. The United States and Canada are China's two main source countries in America, especially the United States has always been one of the top ten stable source countries to China.

4)发展中的大洋洲与非洲客源地

对于中国海外客源市场而言,大洋洲与非洲国家属于发展中的客源市场,人数还比较少,2019年,中国入境旅游人数为1.453亿,大洋洲占1.9%,非洲只占1.4%。澳大利亚是大洋洲最重要的中国海外客源国,2019年澳大利亚是中国第十四位的客源国。澳大利亚统计局的数据显示,澳大利亚居民出境旅游1 106万人次,同比增长5%,其中赴华75万人次,同比增长2.5%,首站赴华旅游59万人次,同比增长达9.7%,中国是其第五大出境旅游目的地。2019年1—8月,澳大利亚出境旅游757万人次,同比增长2.3%,同期,澳大利亚居民首站赴华旅游41万人次,增速3.9%。

此外,中东地区,特别是"海湾六国"阿联酋、阿曼、巴林、卡塔尔、科威特和沙特阿拉伯居民收入高,出游比例高,2014年出境旅游人次已达5 000万,2030预计超过8 000万,但是这些国家来华旅游人次却是屈指可数。今后随着"一带一路"建设的推进,中国与海湾国家双向合作进一步加强,能源合作及其他领域相互投资的带动效应将更加明显,我们应乘势而为,加大对海湾国家民众的宣传,未来该地区有可能成为中国重要的入境游客源市场之一。

For China's overseas source market, Oceania and African countries are developing source markets with a relatively small number of tourists. With the development of "the Belt and Road initiative", the two-way cooperation market between China and the Gulf countries will be further strengthened, and the region is likely to become one of the important inbound tourism source markets.

3. 客源国特征分析(Analysis of the Characteristics of Tourist Source Countries)

总体而言,中国海外旅游客源国主要有以下四个方面的特征。

1)客源地分布广泛,少数重要客源国居主导地位

中国海外客源国广泛分布于亚洲、欧洲、美洲、大洋洲、非洲各地,客源地组成上具有地域多样性。但从客源国所占来华旅游市场的份额来看,少数重要的客源国提供了大部分客源,居主导地位。具体表现为亚洲居多,欧洲与美洲次之。主要客源国客源输出量累计占外国客源总数的70%左右,其中前五大客源国占50%以上,且近年来这一比例仍不断上升,反映出主要客源国的作用越来越明显。

这种少数重要客源国居主导地位的格局,在一定时期内还会有所强化,并维持相当一段时间。同时,重要客源国在地域上分布广泛,又为中国防范区域性的危机或其他偶发事件提供了条件,从而有利于中国旅游业健康平稳地发展。

China's overseas tourist source countries are widely distributed in Asia, Europe, America, Oceania and Africa, with the regional diversity in the composition of the source countries. However, judging from the share of tourist source countries in the tourist market to China, a few important tourist source countries provide most of the source and occupy a dominant position. Specifically, most of them are in Asia, followed by Europe and America.

2)各大洲分布不均,亚洲客源市场扮演重要角色

近几年,在中国入境旅游客源市场上,亚洲国家始终扮演重要角色,2019年比重达75.9%,呈快速上升趋势,而欧洲、美洲、大洋洲、非洲的比重依次下降。其中,邻国市场如日本、韩国、俄罗斯、蒙古、东南亚各国均为主要客源国。

中国地处东亚,发展亚洲客源市场具有先天优势。一方面距离近,在旅游交通费用在旅游花费中占有较大比重的前提下,这种优势往往被强化;另一方面有相近的文化传统以及频繁的经济往来,国与国之间往来限制放宽、手续简化。此外,日本、韩国及东南亚各国人口密集,在其经济快速发展的背景下,已成为世界上重要的客源产出国。特别是对于这些国家的大多数初访者来说,中国是一个较为理想的旅游目的地。因此,拓展亚洲客源市场,尤其是深层次拓展邻近国家客源市场,对中国入境旅游业的发展来说,是一件事关全局、意义深远的事情。

In recent years, Asian countries have always played an important role in China's inbound tourist source market, while Europe, America, Oceania and Africa have declined in turn. At the same time, neighboring markets such as Japan, South Korea, Russia, Mongolia, Southeast Asian countries are the main source nations.

3)客源国构成与世界主要客源产出国基本相对应

从世界旅游市场的大背景上看,世界主要客源市场依次为欧洲、亚太地区、美洲、中东及南亚地区、非洲。从主要客源国看,主要为德国、日本、美国、英国、法国、荷兰、加拿大、俄罗斯、意大利等。而对中国海外旅游市场而言,德国、日本、美国、英国、法国、加拿大、俄罗斯等国家已是主要的客源地,荷兰、意大利来华旅游也发展得相当迅速。但由于这些客源国都是远程市场,其来华旅游受到一定限制,因而日本、韩国、蒙古、新加坡、泰国等近程客源市场仍将是中国的主要客源地。显然,这种客源市场格局是符合世界旅游市场发展规律的,它将在相当长的时间内支持中国国际旅游业的持续发展。

For China's overseas tourism market, Germany, Japan, the United States, Britain, France, Canada, Russia and other countries have been the main source of visitors, while Japan, South Korea, Mongolia, Singapore, Thailand and other short-distance source markets will still be the main source of tourists to China. Obviously, this kind of tourist source market pattern is in line with the development of the world tourism market.

4）潜在客源地发展前景乐观

受经济发展水平、距离和国民旅游习惯等多种因素的影响，南亚、中东地区、南美、非洲国家来华旅游的人数很少，但它们是中国潜在的客源国，这些地区近年来出国旅游市场发展较快，其迅速发展的势头已引起业内人士的关注。

例如，中国近邻印度是一个极具潜力的客源市场，主要原因在于：①过去20年里印度来华旅游相较于其他主要客源市场表现抢眼，增长速度最快；②印度出境旅游市场增长迅猛，印度近几年来较高的经济增长速度，加上印度13亿的人口基数，未来其出境旅游增长潜力非常可观；③相对于其他亚洲国家，印度来华旅游人数占其出境市场的比重较低，具有较大的提升空间。20世纪80年代末，印度来华旅游人数为1万人次，1995年达5.5万人次，1999年达8.43万人次。2000年达12.09万人次，2015年，印度来华人数达73万人，进入中国前20位客源国之列。近些年来，来到中国旅游的印度游客每年达到100万人次，是中国去印度游客的五倍。

Affected by economic development, distance and national traveling habits and other factors, the number of tourists to Chins from South Asia, the Middle East, South America and Africa is very few, but they are China's potential tourist source nations. In recent years, the overseas tourism market in these regions has developed rapidly and drawn the attention of the industry.

中国出境旅游现状
（Current Situation of Outbound Tourism in China）

近年来，我国旅游业迅速走向全球，我国与联合国世界旅游组织、世界旅游业理事会、亚太旅游协会等保持着密切联系。中国经济的持续增长、人均可支配收入的增加、交通的提升、签证环境的改善等因素使中国出境旅游处于最美好的时代。

2018年，我国的出境旅游市场规模达到1.49亿人次，相比2017年同比增长14.7%。我国出境游客境外消费超过1 300亿美元，增速超过13%。2019年，我国的出境旅游市场规模达到1.55亿人次，2019年中国出境旅游消费依然位居世界第一，达2 770亿美元。不仅中国出境旅游规模在不断增大，中国游客对出游目的地的满意度也在不断提升。2018年，主要出境旅游目的地接待中国游客市场份额排名前15位的国家和地区分别是：中国香港、中国澳门、泰国、日本、越南、韩国、美国、中国台湾、新加坡、马来西亚、柬埔寨、俄罗斯、印度尼西亚、澳大利亚、菲律宾。

In recent years, China's tourism has rapidly become global. China has kept in close touch with the United Nations World Tourism Organization, the World Tourism Council and the Asia Pacific Tourism Association. With the continuous growth of China's economy, the increase of per capita disposable income, the improvement of transportation, the improvement of visa environment and other factors, China's outbound tourism is in the best era.

In 2018, the scale of outbound tourism market in China grew to 149 million tourists, a year-on-year increase of 14.7% compared with that in 2017. The overseas consumption of outbound tourists in China exceeds $130 billion, with a growth rate of more than 13%. In 2019, the scale of China's outbound tourism market grew to 155 million tourists. In 2019, the consumption of outbound tourism of Chinese tourists is still the first in the world, reaching $277 billion. Not only is the scale of outbound tourism in China increasing, but also the satisfaction of Chinese tourists to the destinations is also increasing. In 2018, the top 15 market shares of the major outbound tourist destinations to receive Chinese tourists are: Hong Kong (China), Macao (China), Thailand, Japan, Vietnam, Korea, the United States, Taiwan (China), Singapore, Malaysia, Cambodia, Russia, Indonesia, Australia and the Philippines.

1. 历史回顾(Historical Review)

20世纪80年代中期,中国才开始出现出境旅游,出境旅游真正大发展是在20世纪90年代。刺激中国国内旅游需求最为重要的因素之一是居民可支配收入的增加,另外还有闲暇时间的增多以及生活和消费方式的转变。出境旅游的发展对扩大中国的国际影响、增长国人见识、融入国际大环境等方面具有积极作用。

In the mid-1980s, outbound tourism began to appear in China, and the real development began in the 1990s.

1)试探性发展阶段(1984—1989年)

1984年以前,中国出境旅游基本上是以外事活动为主,几乎谈不上真正意义的出境旅游,年出境人数一般都在200万人次以下。1983年11月广东作为试点开放本省居民港澳探亲游,1984年,国务院批准了侨办、港澳事务办、公安部联合上报的《关于拟组织归侨、侨眷和港澳台眷属赴港澳地区探亲旅行团的请示》,规定统一由中国旅行社总社委托各地中国旅行社承办归侨、侨眷和港澳台眷属赴港澳地区探亲旅行团在内地的全部组织工作,香港地区、澳门地区的中国旅行社负责当地的接待事务,内地公民港澳游扩大到全国。1987年11月,国家旅游局(今文化和旅游部)和对外经济贸易部(今商务部)批准了丹东市对朝鲜新义州市的"一日游"。这个文件标志着中国边境旅游的开始。

在此试探性发展阶段,中国出境旅游人数增长非常缓慢,到1989年出境旅游人数仅达到300万人次。

Before 1984, China's outbound tourism was mainly foreign activities, hardly any real outbound tourism, and the annual number of outbound tourists was generally less than 2 million. In this exploratory stage of development, the number of Chinese outbound tourists grew very slowly and only reached about 3 million in 1989.

2)初步发展阶段(1990—1996年)

1990年10月,国家旅游局(今文化和旅游部)经外交、公安、侨办等部门及国务院批准,出台了《关于组织中国公民赴东南亚三国旅游的暂行管理办法》,它标志着中国出境旅游的真正发展。规定在由海外亲友付费、担保的情况下,允许中国公民赴新加坡、马来西亚、泰国探亲旅游。继开放"新马泰"后,1992年中国公民的旅游目的地国又增加了菲律宾。

在此阶段,中国出境旅游人数从初期的每年300万人次左右迅速上升到1996年的500万人次,但是由于各种原因,因私出境旅游者仍然只有200万人次,年增长速度非常缓慢。

In October 1990, the state issued the Interim Administrative Measures for Organizing Chinese Citizens to Travel to Three Southeast Asian Countries, which marked the real development of China's outbound tourism. At this stage, the number of Chinese outbound tourists increased rapidly, but the growth rate of outbound tourists for personal purposes was slow.

3)规范发展阶段(1997—2000年)

1997年,由国家旅游局(今文化和旅游部)与公安部共同制定并经国务院批准了《中国公民自费出国旅游管理暂行办法》,同期还公布了中国公民自费出国旅游的目的地国家,明确了"出国(境)旅游"的概念,也标志着中国公民出境旅游进入一个崭新的规范发展阶段。出境旅游目的地资格的获得采取了ADS(Approved Destination Status,被批准的旅游目的地国家)协议谈判的方式,到2000年年底,中国正式开放的ADS国家和地区达到14个。

在此阶段,中国公民年出境人数从1997年的532万人次增长到2000年的1 047万人次,几乎增长了一倍,年均增长率达到25.31%;其中,因私出境旅游开始迅速发展,从1997年的244万人次,增长到2000年的563万人次,增长了1.3倍,年均增长达到32%。中国出境旅游的强劲增长势头受到国际旅游业界的关注。

In 1997, the state issued the Interim Administrative Measures for Chinese Citizens' Traveling Abroad Private, marking that Chinese citizens' outbound tourism has entered a completely new stage of normalization development. At this stage, the strong growth of China's outbound tourism attracted the attention of the international tourism industry.

4)快速发展阶段(2001年至今)

2001年12月11日,中国正式成为世贸组织成员国,旅游业发展面临新的机遇和挑战。遵循WTO规则和中国的入世承诺,中国出境旅游管理也相应作出了重大调整。2002年7月1日正式实施《中国公民出国旅游管理办法》。该办法的出台使得中国出境旅游管理逐渐走上了规范化的轨道。

从2002年开始,中国明显加快了出境旅游目的地(ADS)的开放步伐,每年开放国家均在五个以上。2019年中国游客选择出境游已到达全球158个国家,已经有73个目的地对中国游客实行免签、落地签,或者互免普通护照签证(见表1-14),也就是说对于全球的两百多个国家,中国游客可以无障碍地到达大部分国家。

表 1-14　持普通护照中国公民前往有关国家和地区入境便利待遇一览表

入境便利待遇	国　　家
互免普通护照签证	国家(15 个) 阿联酋、巴巴多斯、巴哈马、波黑、厄瓜多尔、斐济、格林纳达、毛里求斯、圣马力诺共和国、塞舌尔、塞尔维亚、汤加、白俄罗斯、卡塔尔、亚美尼亚
单方面允许 中国公民免签入境	国家或地区(18 个) 亚洲(4 个)：印度尼西亚、乌兹别克斯坦、韩国（济州岛等地）、阿曼 欧洲(1 个)：阿尔巴尼亚 非洲(3 个)：摩洛哥、法属留尼汪、突尼斯 美洲(7 个)：安提瓜和巴布达、海地、南乔治亚和南桑威奇群岛（英国海外领地）、圣基茨和尼维斯、特克斯和凯科斯群岛（英国海外领地）、牙买加、多米尼克 大洋洲(3 个)：美属北马里亚纳群岛（塞班岛等）、萨摩亚、法属波利尼西亚
单方面允许 中国公民办理落地签证	国家和地区名单(40 个) 亚洲(19 个)：阿塞拜疆、巴林、东帝汶、印度尼西亚、老挝、黎巴嫩、马尔代夫、缅甸、尼泊尔、斯里兰卡、泰国、土库曼斯坦、文莱、伊朗、约旦、越南、柬埔寨、孟加拉国、马来西亚（注：印度尼西亚同时实行免签和落地签政策） 非洲(15 个)：埃及、多哥、佛得角、加蓬、科摩罗、科特迪瓦、卢旺达、马达加斯加、马拉维、毛里塔尼亚、圣多美和普林西比、坦桑尼亚、乌干达、贝宁、津巴布韦 美洲(2 个)：圭亚那、圣赫勒拿（英国海外领地） 大洋洲(4 个)：帕劳、图瓦卢、瓦努阿图、巴布亚新几内亚

在此阶段，中国公民出境人次从 2001 年的 1 213 万人次增长到 2019 年 1.55 亿人次。从 2003 年起，中国出境旅游人数首次超过日本，成为亚洲最大的客源输出国。根据 UNWTO 统计数据显示，中国公民出境旅游花费居世界首位，中国已成为世界上最大的出境旅游国家。

On December 11, 2001, China officially became a member of the WTO, and the development of tourism faced new opportunities and challenges. On July 1, 2002, the Administrative Measures for Chinese Citizens' Traveling Abroad was formally implemented, which made the management of China's outbound tourism gradually step on a normal track.

2. 现状特征(Characteristics of Current Situation)

1)出境旅游人数增长迅猛,境外消费量日益增长

中国加入世界贸易组织为旅游业的发展注入了新的活力,中国现已成为亚洲第一大客源国和全球增长最快的新兴客源输出国。表 1-15 是 1995—2019 年中国出境旅游发展情况。

表 1-15 1995—2019 年中国出境旅游发展情况

年　份	出境人次/百万人次	增长率/(%)
1995	4.52	21.10
1996	5.06	12.00
1997	5.32	5.14
1998	8.43	58.46
1999	9.23	9.49
2000	10.47	13.43
2001	12.13	15.85
2002	16.60	36.85
2003	20.22	21.81
2004	28.85	42.68
2005	31.03	7.56
2006	34.52	11.25
2007	40.95	18.63
2008	45.84	11.94
2009	47.66	3.97
2010	57.39	20.42
2011	70.25	22.41
2012	83.18	18.41
2013	98.19	18.05
2014	107.28	9.26
2015	116.89	8.96
2016	122.03	4.40
2017	130.51	6.95
2018	149.72	14.72
2019	154.63	3.28

资料来源:根据历年文化和旅游部统计资料整理。

2004年是中国公民出境旅游增长最快的一年,出境旅游人数达到2 885万人次,较上年增长42.68%,是中国公民出境旅游目的地数量增加最多的一年。

2006—2009年中国公民出境旅游增长速度放缓,2010年又达到20.4%的增长速度,出境旅游人数达5 739万人次。2013年我国公民出境人数创下9 819万人次的新高,比上年增长18.0%。自2014年至2019年,从1亿零728万人次增加到1亿5 463万人次,再创新高。

中国不仅是亚洲出境旅游人数最多的国家,而且也是世界上出境旅游人均消费最高的国家之一。根据中国旅游研究院的统计,2013年中国出境游消费在境外已经达到1287亿美元。早在2012年,中国的出境消费就已经超过了德国和美国,成为世界第一,2013—2019年中国人出境旅游消费一直保持世界第一。国家外汇管理局的数据显示,2019年上半年,中国境外旅行支出1 275亿美元,超五成旅行支出发生在亚洲地区。根据UNWTO统计数据显示,2019年中国公民出境旅游花费为2 770美元。

正是由于中国公民出境旅游人数多、人均花费高,各旅游发达国家争相开发中国旅游市场,同时中国游客在国外受尊敬程度也与日俱增。

在国际贡献方面,根据世界旅游及旅行理事会的数据统计,2018年中国旅游业对全球GDP的综合贡献高达10.36万亿元(约合15 090亿美元),综合贡献居世界第二位;旅游业贡献的就业岗位数为7 991万个,稳居世界第一,但增长幅度较小。

China's joining WTO has injected new vitality into the development of tourism. It has become the largest tourist source nation in Asia and the fastest growing emerging tourist source nation in the world. China is the country with the largest amount of outbound tourists in Asia and the highest average consumption in the world. It is precisely because of the large amount of Chinese citizens traveling abroad and the high average consumption that developed countries are trying to develop China's tourism market. Meanwhile, Chinese tourists are being respected more and more in foreign countries.

2)出游目的地地域分布广泛,但仍以亚洲国家和地区为主

中国大陆居民从1983年开始可以到香港地区和澳门地区旅游,但是出境旅游一般来说以1990年政府允许居民自费前往新加坡、马来西亚和泰国旅游为正式开端。中国政府的出境旅游政策一直是"合理"地发展出境旅游市场,也就是"有计划、有组织和有控制地"发展出境旅游。

从2002年开始,中国明显加快了出境旅游目的地的开放步伐,到2014年4月,中国公民出国旅游的目的地国家和地区已经达150个。2019年中国游客出境游度假产品已到达全球158个国家和地区,可为中国公民办理免签的国家和地区达15个,落地签的国家和地区达44个,互免普通护照签证的国家达14个。

中国出境旅游目的地的选择虽然很多,但到周边近距离国家和地区的旅游者仍然占绝大多数,并集中在开放比较早、距离比较近的亚太地区国家和直接接壤的国家和地区。亚洲在中国出境旅游中占有75.9%的份额,远远超过占13.2%份额、排名第二的

欧洲。

In 2019, there are 158 countries and regions around the world available for Chinese outbound tourists, among which 15 countries and regions are visa-free, 44 countries and regions are visa-on-arrival, and 14 countries are mutual exemption of ordinary passport visas. Although there are many destinations for Chine's outbound travel, the majority of tourists go to neighboring countries and regions.

3）出境游游客主要来自中国东部地区

出境游游客在东中西三大地区间的比例大约为 6.2∶2.5∶1.3，长期处于三级阶梯状分布格局，继续呈现收敛趋势。

中国银联的数据显示，2019 年境外消费前十大客源省市为广东、上海、北京、江苏、浙江、四川、湖北、山东、福建、辽宁，其中 8 个为东部省市，2 个为中西部省市。

Outbound tourists are mainly from the east of China.

4）出境游游客的选择方式既"从众"也"由心"

"从众"表现在，初次出境旅游者众多，跟团游依然是许多人的心头好。"由心"表现在，越来越多的出境游游客倾向于自由行，与跟团游几乎势均力敌。自由行、新跟团游等出境游市场变迁和对应商业模式的创新正在从越来越多"小"的方面重塑当前的中国出境旅游业。

中国旅游研究院发布的《中国出境旅游发展年度报告 2019》显示，2018 年，通过团队形式进行出境旅游的游客比例达 55.24%，50.65% 的受访者表示在未来的出境旅游中愿意参加旅游团。与 2017 年的 72.1% 相比，有明显下降，但境外出游参团的游客仍占多数。

"Follow the herd" is manifested in the fact that the large number of first-time outbound tourists still love package tours. "Follow the heart" is reflected in the fact that more and more outbound tourists prefer to travel on their own, almost close to package tours.

5）银行卡消费仍是主要支付方式，移动支付比例快速提升

中国银联卡已成为中国人出境主流支付工具。为更好服务出境游客，银联国际加速受理环境建设。2019 年，境外已有 176 个国家和地区、2850 万商户支持银联卡，"云闪付"用户已可在境外 52 个国家和地区扫码支付。

中国移动支付在全球旅游市场不同区域呈现层次化发展趋势，其中在日韩、新马泰等中国游客热门出游国的渗透率或使用活跃度均较高。2019 年，中国游客境外平均每 10 笔消费中，就有 3.4 次通过移动支付实现，相比去年提升 6 个百分点。中国游客在境外当地通过手机支付的人均总金额相比 2018 年提升 18%，中国的移动支付系统在免税店、美妆店和大型促销零售店等境外旅游零售场景的高覆盖，也进一步强化了中国游客的移动支付使用深度。

China UnionPay card has become the mainstream payment tool for Chinese people going abroad. China's mobile payment develops at all levels in different regions of the global tourism market, among which the penetration rate or usage activity of Chinese tourists has developed relatively mature in popular Chinese tourist destinations such as Japan, South Korea, Singapore, Malaysia and Thailand.

中国出入境旅游市场的发展前景
（Development Prospect of China's Inbound and Outbound Tourism Market）

1. 战略目标(Strategic Objectives)

根据UNWTO最新公布的数据,2018年,中国入境旅游接待规模位居全球第四,排在法国、西班牙和美国之后。尽管中国目前外部环境相对复杂,内部资源也有待优化,但在文旅融合发展的新时期,随着各项政策的带动,中国入境旅游市场的发展前景良好,其增长趋势有望得到进一步稳固。

"十三五"期间中国旅游业提出,2020年旅游市场总规模达到67亿人次,旅游投资总额2万亿元人民币,旅游业总收入达到7万亿元。其中发展国际旅游的目标就是大大提高国际影响力,包括入境旅游持续增长,出境旅游健康发展,与旅游业发达国家的差距明显缩小。2020年是"十三五"规划的收官之年,我国已实现了当初的战略目标。"十四五"期间,我国旅游业发展环境总体上利大于弊,全面建成小康社会奠定了基本发展格局,高质量发展成为主线,消费持续升级,基础设施不断完善,科技迅速发展,生态文明建设迈上新台阶,这些都为旅游业发展创造了良好条件。"十四五"期间我国旅游消费将继续保持高于GDP的增长速度,出游更加理性、文明。国内四五线城市以及农村旅游市场开始兴起,旅游需求在继续朝大众化、品质化方面发展的同时更加多样化;入境旅游有所上升,新兴市场可望有较好表现,来华游客动机更加多元;出境旅游保持中高速度增长,出国比重进一步上升,我国将继续保持世界第一大出境旅游客源国的地位。

During the 13th Five-Year Plan period, China's tourism proposed that the total scale of tourism market would reach 6.7 billion tourists by 2020, the total tourism investment would reach 2 trillion yuan, and the total tourism revenue would reach 7 trillion yuan. The goal of developing international tourism is to greatly enhance the international influence, including the sustained growth of inbound tourism, the healthy development of outbound tourism, and the obvious reduction of the gap with the developed countries in tourism industry. 2020 is the closing year of the 13th Five-Year Plan, and China has achieved the original strategic goal. During the 14th Five-Year Plan period, the overall advantages of China's tourism development environment outweigh the disadvantages. Building a moderately prosperous society in all aspects has laid the basic development pattern. High quality development has become the main line. Consumption has been continuously upgraded. Infrastructure has been continuously improved. Science and technology have developed rapidly. The construction of ecological civilization has stepped up to a new stage. All these have created good conditions for the development of tourism. During the 14th Five-Year Plan period, China's tourism consumption will continue to maintain a growth rate higher than GDP, and travel will be more rational and civilized. The domestic tourism markets in fourth-and fifth-tier cities and rural areas will begin to rise, and the tourism demand will continue to develop towards popularization and quality while becoming more diversified; inbound tourism will increase, the emerging market is expected to have a better performance, and the motivation of tourists to China will become more diversified; outbound tourism will maintain a medium-to-high rate of growth, and the proportion of outbound tourism will increase. China will continue to maintain its position as the world's largest outbound tourist source country.

2. 前景展望(Prospect)

1)机遇(Opportunity)

(1)全球入境旅游市场持续繁荣,为中国入境旅游发展营造良好环境。

全球入境旅游自2010年从金融危机中恢复增长以来,到2019年已实现连续十年的不间断增长。全球入境旅游市场的繁荣意味着有更多的国际游客可能选择来华旅游,中国潜在的入境旅游市场规模更大。与此同时,中国公民出境旅游意愿更高,六成被访者计划在未来一年内开展出境旅游。

The boom of the global inbound tourism market means that more international tourists are likely to choose to visit China, and China's potential inbound tourism market will be larger.

(2)各级政府对提振入境旅游达成共识,政策支持力度加大。

从国家到地方都意识到提振入境旅游的重要性,提振入境旅游是中国实现从旅游大国到旅游强国目标的重要内容。入境旅游作为向世界人民展现中国文明文化,分享经济发展成果的重要媒介,也更加受到重视。在促进入境旅游发展的实践过程中,国家及地方政府继续在放宽签证、购物退税、对入境旅游服务商实施奖励等政策上不断探索创新,为中国入境旅游发展提供良好的政策环境。

国家和地方政府陆续出台促进入境旅游发展的意见、行动计划,凝聚社会各界发展入境旅游的共识,为入境旅游发展指明方向。如国务院办公厅于2019年8月份出台了《关于进一步激发文化和旅游消费潜力的意见》,各地也出台了相应的促进入境旅游发展的意见或计划,指明各自入境旅游的发展目标和重点工作任务。

The local and national governments have realized the importance of boosting inbound tourism, and it is an important part of China's goal of becoming a powerful tourism country from a big tourism country. The national and local governments have successively issued opinions and action plans to promote the development of inbound tourism, and to build the consensus of social public to develop inbound tourism and to point out the direction for the development of inbound tourism.

(3)文旅融合为中国入境旅游发展提供新动力。

2018年,国家文化和旅游部正式组建完成,随后省市县各级文化和旅游行政部门机构改革任务也基本完成。中央和地方各级政府根据"宜融则融、能融尽融"的总思路,秉持"以文促旅、以旅彰文"的理念,积极探索文旅融合发展的新道路。文旅融合发展在促进文化和旅游产业高质量发展,满足广大人民群众美好生活需要的同时,也正在为入境旅游发展凝聚新动力。一方面,文旅融合发展将直接丰富旅游供给,提升旅游服务和产品的品质,增加其文化特色和异域风情,更好地满足赴华入境游客,尤其是外国游客了解中国文化的需求。另一方面,在文旅融合发展的新时期,海外旅游目的地营销可以更好地整合海外文化和旅游机构的力量,丰富并创新海外旅游目的地营销推广活动,提升营销绩效。此外,文旅融合发展也将促进复合型人才的培养,并吸引一批优秀的人文艺术专家进入入境旅游市场,为入境旅游的持续、健康发展提供人才储备。

The integration of culture and tourism is promoting the high-quality development of culture and tourism and meeting the needs of the people for a better life. At the same time, it is also gathering new impetus for the development of inbound tourism.

(4)出入境游客证件便利化应用提升入境游客在华旅行便利度。

2019年5月,国家移民管理局联合15部委印发《关于推动出入境证件便利化应用的工作方案》,提出对港澳同胞和华侨提供互联网出入境证件身份认证服务,在2019年底实现港澳同胞和华侨的入境证件在交通运输、金融、通讯、医疗、住宿等公共服务领域的便利应用。港澳同胞和华侨可分别凭借港澳通行证和华侨护照,像本地居民使用身份证一样,线上进行机票、火车票预定、手机电话卡购买等业务,线下快速办理银行开户、住宿登记等业务。出入境证件便利化应用将直接促使部分入境游客率先实现"一部手机游中国"。虽然,互联网出入境证件身份认证和身份证件在公共领域服务的便利化应用仅限于港澳同胞和华侨,但这种便利化政策也意味着在条件成熟时应用于外国游客的可能性,这一实践经验也将为未来中国实行入境签证电子化及外国人证件在华便利化使用等提供宝贵经验。

The facilitation of passport will directly prompt some inbound tourists first achieve "Travelling China with one mobile phone", which is currently limited to Hong Kong and Macao compatriots and overseas Chinese, but the facilitation of policy also means that it is likely to foreign visitors when conditions are ripe enough. It also provides valuable experience for China to issue electronic visas and for foreigners to use their credentials easily in China.

2)挑战(Challenge)

与此同时,中国入境旅游也面临着严峻的挑战。

(1)国际政治经济形势存在不和谐、不稳定因素。

世界经济出现逆全球化趋势。2017年美国总统特朗普上台后,实行贸易保护主义,推崇"美国优先",逆全球化趋势进一步凸显,这也促使德国、法国、意大利等国不同程度地转向民粹,加之中东极端势力的干扰,各国逆全球化趋势更加明显。这一系列因素给中国的入境客源市场,特别是美国来华旅游市场带来负面影响。

The world economy is going against globalization. In particular, the US practices trade protectionism, and advocates "America First", which further highlights the anti-globalization trend, and has a negative impact on US tourism market to China to a certain extent.

(2)面临着周边旅游目的地国家对我国入境旅游的较强竞争压力。

距离相近、风土人情相似的周边国家作为一国入境旅游主要客源市场的同时,往往也是一国入境旅游最主要的竞争对手。根据中国旅游研究院与谷歌联合开展的入境游客行为和态度调查结果,受访者未来一年计划去的旅游目的中,中国与澳大利亚和加拿大排在第五位,排在前四位的客源国家中有中国周边的日本、韩国、新加坡和泰国,其中日本独占鳌头,排在首位。间接表明,这些中国周边的国家对全球主要客源市场具有较大的吸引力,是中国更强有力的客源竞争对手。

Japan, South Korea, Singapore, Thailand and other countries around China are highly attractive to the world's major tourist source. They are strong source competitors of China.

(3)旅游基础设施和便利化水平仍有待提升。

经过多年发展,中国旅游基础设施已有明显改善,但国际化程度、公共服务配套及便利化水平仍显不足,入境游客在中国旅游的便利度有待进一步提升。中国旅游研究院与谷歌联合开展的入境游客行为和态度调查结果显示,多数受访者(70%)认为交通和基础设施是其来华旅游的障碍。其中,超过三成的受访者对公共厕所卫生、住宿场所等设施及景点提出更高要求。

After years of development, China's tourism infrastructure has been significantly improved, but the degree of internationalization, public service supporting and facilitation is still underdeveloped, and the convenience of inbound tourists traveling to China needs to be further improved.

为此,我们必须抓住机遇,迎接挑战,重点做好六个方面的工作:一是要优化旅游大环境;二是要深入研究中国海外客源市场,加大旅游创新力度,不断推陈出新,改进老的旅游产品,开发新的旅游产品,推出旅游精品;三是要进一步改善旅游基础设施,加强科技的注入,提升旅游便利化水平;四是要加大管理力度,确保旅游服务质量上档次;五是要建立与国际旅游业相适应的管理体系,它是提高中国国际市场竞争力的内在保证;六是要加大投资力度,积极开展境外旅游促销,要采取灵活的宣传促销策略,增加促销经费,积极举办各种旅游展销会和国际会议,继续开展各种旅游主题活动等。自1992年以来,中国国家旅游局(今文化和旅游部)确定了一系列旅游主题活动,从2011年开始我国确定了每年5月19日为全国旅游日,并且每年确定一个旅游主题活动,由此,中国掀起了一个个旅游高潮。当前国家正在实施的"一带一路"倡议,也为开拓外国人入境旅游市场创造了新的平台、新的条件、新的渠道和新的机遇,同时我们要围绕坚持和完善"一国两制"方针,推进港澳台旅游交流合作,围绕建设新型国际关系、构建人类命运共同体推动形成旅游业的全面开放新格局。展望未来,中国出入境旅游市场前景一片光明,中国必将跻身于世界旅游强国之列。

We must seize the opportunities, meet the challenges, and focus on the six aspects: First, we should optimize the overall environment of tourism; Second, we should study the overseas tourist market in depth, strengthen tourism innovation, develop new travel products, and launch quality tourism products. Third, we should further improve the tourism infrastructure; Fourth, we should strengthen management to ensure the quality of tourism service; Fifth, we should establish a management system in line with international tourism. Finally, we should increase investment and actively promote overseas tourism. Looking forward to the future, China's inbound and outbound tourism market has a bright prospect, and China will surely become one of the world's tourism powers.

Sum up(本章小结)

1. 回顾了世界国际旅游业发展的历程,认为国际旅游业总体上呈增长趋势,国际旅游市场在不断向纵深发展,五大区域的旅游发展不平衡,已呈现欧洲、亚太和美洲三足鼎立的旅游格局。

2. 国际旅游的基本特点主要表现为世界各旅游区发展不平衡,亚太地区发展迅猛;全球旅游增长趋缓,但世界旅游经济总量仍很大。

3. 国际旅游业发展呈现七个基本趋势:旅游业继续保持世界上最大产业的地位;国际旅游区域的重心向东转移的速度加快;国际旅游客源市场趋向分散化;国际旅游消费需求向多元化方向发展;中远程旅游逐渐兴旺;国际旅游对旅游安全更为重视;支付方式将改变国际旅游者的旅行生活等。

4. 回顾了中国入境旅游的发展历史,从客源构成、客源市场和客源国特征等方面分析了中国入境旅游的现状特征。

5. 回顾了中国出境旅游的发展历史,中国出境旅游的现状特征主要表现为:出境旅游人数增长迅猛,境外消费量日益增长;出游目的地在地域上分布广阔,但仍以亚洲国家和地区为主;出境旅游游客主要来自东部地区;出境游客的选择方式既"从众"也"由心";银行卡消费仍是主要支付方式,移动支付比例快速提升。

6. 中国出入境旅游机遇与挑战并存,但发展前景良好,提出了进一步发展中国出入境旅游的六大措施。

Reviewing and Thinking(复习与思考)

1. 简述国际旅游业发展的基本格局。
2. 简述国际旅游业发展的基本趋势。
3. 简要分析中国入境旅游市场的现状特征。
4. 简要分析中国出境旅游市场的现状特征。

CHAPTER

2

The Asia Tourism Region
（亚洲旅游区）

◇ **LEARNING OBJECTIVES**(学习目标)

1. Understand the basic situation of the main tourist source and destination countries in Asia（了解亚洲主要客源国和目的地国的基本情况）.

2. Master the tourism market development and tourism resources characteristics of the main source and destination countries in Asia(掌握亚洲主要客源国和目的地国的旅游市场发展与旅游资源特点).

3. Design some classic tourist routes(设计一些经典旅游线路).

◇ **LEARNING CONTENTS**(学习内容)

1. Japan（日本）

2. South Korea(韩国)

3. Thailand(泰国)

4. The Philippines(菲律宾)

5. Singapore(新加坡)

6. Malaysia(马来西亚)

7. India(印度)

◇ **PROBLEM ORIENTATION**(问题导向)

Is Asia the most important source and destination market for China?（亚洲是中国最重要的客源地和目的地市场吗?）

Section 1　General Situation of Asia(亚洲概况)

区域概况(Regional Overview)

1. 地理位置及范围(Geographical Location and Scope)

亚洲旅游区位于东半球的东北部,北临北冰洋,南临印度洋,东临太平洋。亚洲与欧洲以乌拉尔山、乌拉尔河、高加索山、里海、黑海、土耳其海峡为界,与非洲则以红海、苏伊士运河为界。

亚洲旅游区面积约4 457万平方千米,几乎占世界陆地面积的三分之一,是世界第一大洲。按地理方位,通常把亚洲旅游区分为东亚、东南亚、南亚、中亚和西亚五个部分。

The Asia Tourism Region is located in the northeast of the eastern hemisphere. It

CHAPTER 2　The Asia Tourism Region(亚洲旅游区) | 39

亚洲地图 ASIA

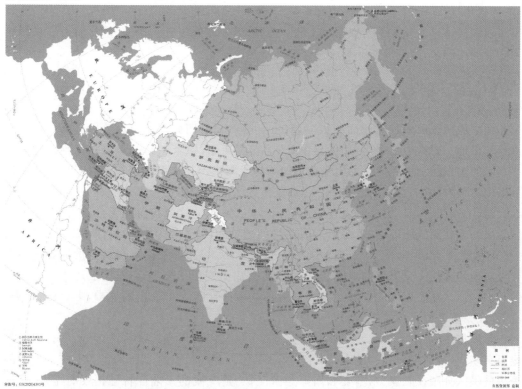

资料来源：标准地图服务网站，审图号：GS(2020)4393 号。

borders the Arctic Ocean in the north, the Indian Ocean in the south, the Pacific Ocean in the East. The Eurasia Tourism Region is bounded by the Ural Mountains, the Ural River, the Caucasus mountains, the Caspian Sea, the Black Sea and the Turkish Strait, while the Asia-Africa Tourism Region is bounded by the Red Sea and the Suez Canal.

Asian tourist area is the largest continent in the world, which covers an area of about 44.57 million km², accounting for almost one-third of the world's land area. According to geographical location, it is generally divided into four parts: East Asia, Southeast Asia, South Asia, Central Asia and West Asia.

东亚旅游区有中国、日本、朝鲜、韩国、蒙古5个国家。

东南亚旅游区有越南、老挝、柬埔寨、泰国、马来西亚、新加坡、菲律宾、印度尼西亚、缅甸、文莱、东帝汶等11个国家。

南亚旅游区有尼泊尔、不丹、印度、巴基斯坦、孟加拉国、斯里兰卡、马尔代夫等7个国家。

中亚旅游区有哈萨克斯坦、乌兹别克斯坦、土库曼斯坦、吉尔吉斯斯坦、塔吉克斯坦等5个国家。

西亚旅游区有阿富汗、伊朗、伊拉克、叙利亚、黎巴嫩、约旦、阿曼、阿拉伯联合酋长国、卡塔尔、巴林、也门、沙特阿拉伯、以色列、塞浦路斯、土耳其、阿塞拜疆、格鲁吉亚、亚美尼亚、科威特、巴勒斯坦等20个国家和地区。

亚洲旅游区的北部是俄罗斯领土的一部分,俄罗斯属于欧洲国家,其旅游市场主要集中在欧洲旅游区,故俄罗斯亚洲旅游区部分不在此讲述。

2. 自然风貌(Natural Features)

亚洲旅游区山地和高原面积很广,约占全区面积的四分之三。地势中部高,四周低。高原和山地主要集中在中部。"世界屋脊"的青藏高原、帕米尔高原和喜马拉雅山脉等世界著名的大山脉及世界最高的山峰珠穆朗玛峰雄踞中部。这里峻岭逶迤,冰川广布,是世界登山、探险旅游的热点地区之一。亚洲旅游区大陆四周多为中低山脉、丘陵和平原。大江大河(如长江、黄河、湄公河、恒河、印度河等)从中部呈放射状向四周分流,在上中游地区形成许多壮丽的峡谷,在下游形成许多广阔的冲积平原(如中国的长江中下游平原,南亚的印度河平原、恒河平原,西亚的美索不达米亚平原等)。平原地区多是世界著名的文化发源地和古代文化繁荣的地区,历史文物古迹旅游资源十分丰富,是开展历史文化旅游的理想之地。亚洲旅游区东部边缘众多的岛屿多处在地壳不稳定的地带,多火山、地震、温泉,成为著名的自然旅游资源之一。

亚洲旅游区地域广阔,南北跨寒、温、热三带,又因地形和距离海洋远近不同,因而气候复杂多样,特征明显。一是季风气候范围广(约占全区面积的25%),世界上唯一典型的季风气候区分布在东亚、东南亚和南亚旅游区;二是气候的大陆性特征比较明显;三是气候类型多样。中南半岛和印度半岛主要属于热带季风气候。马来半岛和马来群岛大部分属于热带雨林气候。东亚多属温带季风气候和亚热带季风气候。亚洲旅游区中部和西部多为干旱的温带大陆性气候。亚洲旅游区北部多属亚寒带针叶林气候。亚洲旅游区西南部多属热带沙漠气候,也有地中海气候。中部海拔较高的地区为高山气候。复杂多样的气候繁育着种类众多的动植物,生物旅游资源十分丰富。亚洲旅游区是世界难得的四季皆宜的旅游地区。

Asia tourism region has wide mountains and plateaus, with a vast area of about 8 000 km from east to west. From south to north it covers the cold, warm and hot zones. The climate is complex and diverse, and the biological tourism resources are very rich. Asia tourism region is one of the world's rare all-season destinations, and each country has an ideal tourist season.

3. 民族与宗教(Nationality and Religion)

亚洲旅游区是世界人口最多的旅游区,人口总数约为45.41亿人(2019年)。亚洲人口最多的国家是中国,其次是印度。

黄色人种是亚洲的主要人种,约占总人口的60%以上,其次是白色人种,还有少数棕色人种。亚洲旅游区有1 000多个民族,多数国家为多民族国家,民族民俗风情旅游资源丰富。亚洲旅游区是现代三大宗教——基督教、伊斯兰教和佛教起源地和最大的传播区，同时还有印度教、犹太教、道教等宗教，宗教文化旅游资源极具特色。

Asia tourism region is the most populous tourist area in the world. Most of the residents are yellow race. Asia tourism region is the birthplace and the largest spreading area of the three modern religions—Christianity, Islam, Buddhism and other religions such as Hinduism, Judaism and Taoism, and religious cultural tourism resources are very unique.

二 旅游业（Tourism）

1. 旅游资源（Tourism Resources）

亚洲旅游区是世界旅游资源最丰富的旅游区之一。自然、人文旅游资源丰富多彩，且具有古老性、独特性和稀有性，对旅游者有着很强的吸引力。

东亚旅游区海岸线曲折漫长，岛屿众多，有丰富的海滨和海岛旅游资源。东亚旅游区是世界上两大高山带和火山带汇合处，地形十分复杂，观光、登山、探险名山和火山旅游景观众多。东亚旅游区位于世界最大的大洲——亚洲和世界最大的大洋——太平洋的交接处，海陆热力差异大，属典型的季风气候，但热量带的纬度跨度大，气候复杂，生物旅游资源多样。东亚旅游区历史悠久，文化灿烂，名胜古迹众多，人文旅游资源以文物古迹、民俗风情和各种现代化建筑旅游景观为主。

东南亚旅游区特殊的地形结构造就了众多的寻幽猎奇、登山探险和休闲娱乐旅游景观。东南亚旅游区岛屿和半岛众多，形成了世界著名的海滨度假胜地和避寒胜地。东南亚属热带季风气候和热带雨林气候，热带生物旅游资源特别丰富。东南亚旅游区名胜古迹众多，佛教建筑如佛教寺庙、佛塔成为本区独具特色的人文景观。东南亚旅游区优越的区位条件为国际旅游业的发展提供了有利条件。

南亚旅游区地形多样，有名山大川。风景优美的海滩，印度半岛南部、斯里兰卡岛和马尔代夫群岛，为理想的度假和潜水运动场所。南亚旅游区气候多属热带季风气候，有丰富的热带季风雨林景观和动植物旅游资源。南亚旅游区有 8 000 多年的历史和光辉灿烂的文化，是印度教和佛教的发源地，宗教建筑和名胜古迹众多。

西亚沙漠广布，干谷纵横，是开展徒步探险旅游的理想之地。西亚有迷人的地中海沿岸风光和海滨旅游度假地。西亚是人类文明的摇篮之一，是三大宗教——伊斯兰教、基督教和犹太教的发源地，历史悠久，文化璀璨，历史文物古迹众多。麦加、麦地那、耶路撒冷等世界性的宗教圣地，每年都要接待大批的教徒和旅游者，是世界宗教旅游最密集的地区。

中亚旅游区地形复杂，以温带大陆性气候为主，草原风情游和沙漠探险是本区旅游的一大特色。中亚是古丝绸之路必经之地，清真寺、古城遗址和陵墓较多。

The Asia Tourism Region is one of the tourist areas with the most abundant tourist resources in the world. Both natural and cultural tourism resources are various. With obvious antiquity, uniqueness and rarity, it has a strong attraction to tourists.

The coastline of the East Asia Tourism Region is long and winding. There are numerous islands which are rich in seaside and island tourism resources. The East Asia Tourism Region is the confluence of two major alpine belts and volcanic belts in the world. The terrain is very complex. And there are a lot of sightseeing, mountains, and volcano tourism landscapes here.

The special topographic structure of the Southeast Asia Tourism Region has created a large number of tourism landscapes for seeking tranquility, climbing expedition, leisure and entertainment. There are many islands and peninsulas in this tourism area, forming a world-famous seaside resorts and cold refuges. Southeast Asia has a tropical monsoon climate and a tropical rain forest climate, and tropical bio-tourism resources are particularly rich. There are many places of interest in Southeast Asia Tourism Region. Buddhist architecture such as Buddhist temples and pagodas have become unique places of cultural interest in this area. The topography of the South Asia Tourism Region is diverse, with famous mountains and rivers. There are charming Mediterranean coastal scenery and seaside tourist resorts in West Asia, which is one of the cradles of human civilization and the birthplace of three major religions (Islam, Christianity and Judaism). It has a long history, splendid culture and numerous historical relics. The topography of the Central Asia Tourism Region is complex, with mainly temperate continental arid and semi-arid climates. Grassland-style tour and desert exploration are a major feature of this area. Central Asia is a must pass through the ancient Silk Road, with many mosques, ancient city sites and mausoleums.

2. 旅游经济(Tourism Economy)

亚洲旅游区多为发展中国家,近30多年来,政治形势相对稳定,经济持续高速发展,基础设施和旅游服务设施不断完善,人民生活水平迅速提高,闲暇时间不断增加,为旅游业发展奠定了良好的基础。亚洲旅游区虽然现代旅游业起步较晚,但30多年来旅游业发展十分迅速。亚洲旅游区国内旅游接待量和国际旅游收入在全世界所占的比重令人瞩目。同时,随着亚洲旅游区各国经济的迅速发展和居民收入水平的不断提高,中、短程国际旅游能力日益增强,出境旅游快速发展。

亚洲旅游区各国经济的多样性和互补性,促使该地区区域经济合作不断强化,并取得了喜人的成就。亚太经济合作组织(APEC)和东南亚国家联盟(ASEAN),对促进区域内经济、贸易、科技、文化、旅游等发展,都起到了积极的推动作用。

随着世界经济贸易的重心向亚太地区的扩展和亚洲旅游区各国政府对旅游业发展的高度重视,亚洲旅游业发展十分迅速。目前,亚洲旅游区无论是国际旅游接待量,还是国际旅游收入,都居世界第二位,而且每年旅游业发展增长的速度都超过了世界平均水平。其中东亚旅游区发展最快,东南亚次之。东亚旅游区和东南亚旅游区接待国际旅游者人数和所占市场份额,在亚洲旅游区中分别居第一位和第二位。随着全球经济重心逐渐从大西洋地区转移至太平洋地区,国际旅游市场的重心也将相应东移,亚洲旅游区将成为未来国际旅游市场的热点区域。

目前,从亚洲旅游区入境旅游市场的地区分布来看,以区域内游客、欧洲游客和北美洲游客为主。中国大陆居民出境旅游就是从新加坡、马来西亚、泰国旅游开始的,并以亚洲旅游区为主要出游目的地。区域内旅游目的地以中国和东盟国家为主。亚洲旅游区各国经济的快速发展,促进了该地区旅游资源的开发,提升了旅游服务设施水平,改善了旅游环境,加大了旅游宣传促销力度,增强了主旅游市场竞争力,国际旅游客流的重心正在向亚洲旅游区转移,亚洲将成为全球最具活力、发展最快的旅游区。不久的将来,亚洲旅游区有望成为世界最重要的旅游客源地和旅游目的地。

Although modern tourism in Asia tourism region started relatively late, the tourism industry has developed rapidly in the past 30 years. The volume of domestic tourism reception and international tourism revenue in the world has been growing steadily. At the same time, with the rapid economic development of Asian countries and the successive improvement of residents' income, the volume of trips to medium-and short-distance international destinations increased year on year, and the outbound tourism developed rapidly.

At present, according to the regional distribution of inbound tourism market in Asia tourism region, the tourists are mainly from Asia, Europe and North America. In the near future, Asia tourism region is expected to become the most popular tourist source and destination in the world.

Section 2 Japan(日本)

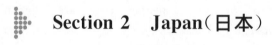

PART 1(第一部分)

1. 国土疆域(Territory)

日本位于太平洋西岸,西隔日本海、朝鲜海峡、黄海、东海,与朝鲜、韩国、中国、俄罗斯相望。日本国土陆地面积约37.8万平方千米,由北海道、本州、四国、九州四个大岛和其他6 800多个小岛组成。

Japan is located in the west coast of Pacific Ocean. It faces DPRK, South Korea and China across the sea of Japan, the Korean Strait, the Yellow Sea and the East China Sea in the west. The land area of Japan is about 378 000 km², which is composed of four islands, namely Hokkaido, Honshu, Shikoku and Kyushu, and more than 6 800 surrounding islands.

2. 自然风貌(Natural Features)

日本是个多山的国家,平原面积狭小,分布零散,是个地形地貌奇特的岛国。日本处于亚欧板块与太平洋板块的交界处、环太平洋火山地震带上,多火山和地震。有270多座火山(其中活火山100多座),有"火山国""地震国"之称。

日本地处东亚季风区,四面环海,故温带海洋性季风气候明显,具有四季分明、温和多雨的特征。

The Japanese landscape is mountainous, and the plains are small and dissected. Japan is located in the East Asian monsoon region. Surrounded by the sea, it has a typical temperate marine monsoon climate, with four distinct seasons, mild and rainy.

3. 人口民族(Population and Ethnicity)

日本总人口约1.25亿人(2021年),人口密度约为每平方千米332.33人。除东京圈(包括东京都及周边的琦玉县、千叶县、神奈川县)和冲绳外,日本各地的人口均在下降。其中,名古屋圈以及关西圈(京都府、大阪府、奈良县、兵库县)人口数量减少最多。日本老龄化程度居全球第一位,2020年厚生劳动省发布数据显示,日本65岁以上的老人总数首次超过3 610万人,占全国总人口28.7%。

日本的民族构成比较单一,主要民族为大和民族,此外还有阿依努人和琉球人。官方语言为日语,主要宗教为神道教和佛教。

Japan has a total population of about 127 million (2019), ranking 11th in the world, with a population density of 336.53 people per square kilometer. The main ethnic population is the Japanese.

4. 发展简史(Brief History of Development)

日本的历史可追溯到公元前1 000年前,但是直到第四世纪大和朝廷宣告成立,才奠定了日本的统一局面。公元645年,日本发生了大化革新,确立了以天皇为绝对君主的中央集权国家体制,但武士阶级把持着实际的控制权,各武士集团割据不断引发内战,皇帝逐步成了傀儡。因此可以说日本是在战乱之中摇摇晃晃地向前发展的。

19世纪末20世纪初,日本实施"明治维新",从此由封建社会向资本主义社会过渡。1905年后,日本的军国主义开始抬头,日本多次发动侵略战争,但最终遭受惨败。1946年,天皇正式宣布放弃神权。二战后,1945—1952年美国军队以"同盟国占领军"的名义,对日本实行军事占领,20世纪60年代末期,日本跃入世界经济强国之列。

Japan's history can be traced back to 1 000 BC, but it was not until the 4th century AD when the Yamato court proclaimed the unification of Japan. In the late 19th and the early 20th century, Japan implemented the "Meiji Restoration" and made the transition from a feudal society to a capitalist society. In the late 1960s, Japan leaped into one of the world's economic powers.

5. 政治经济(Politics and Economy)

日本首都为东京,国花为樱花,货币为日元。

日本虽然国土狭小,自然资源贫乏,但经济发达,是一个后起的高度发达的资本主义国家。日本工业高度发达,京滨、阪神、东京、北九州、北关东、千叶、濑户等是最重要的工业区。电子、汽车、钢材、船舶、家用电器、数控机床、化工产品等主要工业产品产量居世界首位或前列。日本农业现代化程度较高,但农业在国民经济中所占比重很小。

日本已经形成以海运为中心、公路为骨干,并与铁路、航空相配合的现代化运输网络,海、陆、空交通非常发达,具有运输线网密、衔接好、时速快和安全舒适等特点。

Although Japan is small in territory and poor in natural resources, it has a developed economy. It is an economic power in the world and a highly trending developed capitalist country.

6. 旅游市场(Tourism Market)

二战后,日本现代旅游业开始起步,并得到了长足的发展。特别是2003年日本政府实施"观光立国"政策,将旅游业作为支柱产业之一,并提出了旅游发展目标:2020年访日游客达到4 000万,2030年达到6 000万。

近年来,赴日外国游客数量稳步增长。日本国家旅游局发布的数据显示,2018年访日外国游客超过3 000万人次,2019年访日外国游客人数达到约3 188万人次,已连续7年破往期最高纪录。2019年,在日本的主要客源国中,中国人数最多,其次是韩国,第三是美国。日本出境旅游也发展较好,2019年日本出境旅游人数已超过1 600万人次。

随着中日关系的改善,中国游客访日人数不断上升,2018年中国游客访日人数达838万人次,2019年中国游客访日人数达959万人次;日本来华游客达268.97万人次,仅次于韩国。可见,日本是中国重要且比较稳定的客源国,也是中国重要的旅游目的地国之一。

Japan implements the tourism-based country strategy and regards the tourism industry as one of the pillar industries. The number of foreign tourists to Japan has grown steadily in recent years. Japan is China's important and relatively stable tourist source and destination country.

PART 2(第二部分)

Tourism Resources(旅游资源)

Japan attracted 1973 million international tourists in 2015. Japan has 16 World

Heritage Sites, including Himeji Castle and Historic Monuments of Ancient Kyoto. Popular foreigner attractions include Tokyo and Nara, Mount Fuji, ski resorts such as Niseko in Hokkaido, Okinawa, riding the Shinkansen and taking advantage of Japan's hotel and hotspring network.

日本有16处世界遗产,包括姬路城堡和古京都历史古迹。受外国人欢迎的景点包括东京、奈良、富士山、北海道滑雪胜地和冲绳岛等。日本的新干线、酒店和温泉也很受欢迎。

1. Tokyo(东京)

Tokyo (formerly known as Edo) is both the capital and largest city of Japan. The Greater Tokyo Area is the most populous metropolitan area in the world. It is the seat of the Emperor of Japan and the Japanese government. The city hosts 51 of the Fortune Global 500 companies, the highest number of any city in the world. Tokyo ranked third in the International Financial Centres Development Index. It ranked third in the Global Economic Power Index and fourth in the Global Cities Index. The city is also home to various television networks like Fuji TV, Tokyo MX, TV Tokyo, TV Asahi, Nippon Television, NHK and the Tokyo Broadcasting System.

Tokyo has many museums. In Ueno Park, there is the Tokyo National Museum, the country's largest museum and specializing in traditional Japanese art. Tokyo has many theatres for performing arts. These include national and private theatres for traditional forms of Japanese drama, such as the National Noh Theatre for noh and the Kabuki-za for kabuki.

东京(前称江户)是日本的首都和最大城市。大东京城市圈是世界上人口最多的大都市地区,是日本天皇和日本政府的所在地。这座城市拥有51家世界500强企业,是拥有世界500强企业数量最多的城市。东京在国际金融中心发展指数中排名第三。东京在全球经济实力指数中排名第三,在全球城市指数中排名第四。东京还拥有富士电视台、东京MX电视台、东京电视台、朝日电视台、日本电视台等各种电视网络。

东京有许多博物馆,其中东京国立博物馆,是日本最大的博物馆,专门研究日本传统艺术。东京有许多的剧院,包括日本传统戏剧形式的国立和私立剧院,如国立野剧院和歌舞伎剧院。

Asakusa Shrine (浅草神社 Asakusa-jinja), also known as Sanja-sama ("Shrine of the Three gods"), is one of the most famous Shinto shrines in Tokyo. Located in Asakusa, the shrine honors the three men who founded the Senso-ji. Asakusa Shrine is part of a larger group of sacred buildings in the area. It can be found on the east side of the Senso-ji down a street marked by a large stone torii.

Ueno Park (上野公園 Ueno Koen) is a spacious public park in the Ueno district of Taito, Tokyo. The park was established in 1873, on lands formerly belonging to the temple of Kan'ei-ji. Among the country's first public parks, it was founded following the western example as part of the borrowing and assimilation of international practices that characterize the early Meiji period. The home of a number of major museums, Ueno Park is also celebrated in spring for its cherry blossoms and hanami. The park and its attractions have drawn over ten million visitors a year, making it Japan's most popular city park.

浅草神社是日本东京最著名的神社之一,它是为了纪念 Senso-ji 的三位创始人而建。浅草神社是该地区神圣建筑群的一部分。

上野公园建于 1873 年,它是借鉴和吸收明治初期的国际惯例,仿效西方模式建立起来的。上野公园有许多大型博物馆,春天以樱花和"花见"闻名,它是日本最受欢迎的城市公园。

Ginza(銀座) is a district of Chuo, Tokyo. It is a popular upscale shopping area of Tokyo, with numerous internationally renowned department stores, boutiques, restaurants and coffee houses located in its vicinity. Ginza is recognized as one of the most luxurious shopping districts in the world, attracting visitors all around the world.

Tokyo Tower(東京タワー, Tokyo tawa) is a communication and observation tower located in the Shiba-koen district of Minato, Tokyo. At 332.9 metres high, it is the second-tallest building in Japan. The structure is an Eiffel Tower-inspired lattice tower that is painted white and international orange to comply with air safety regulations.

The Tokyo Imperial Palace (皇居 Kokyo, literally "Imperial Residence") is the primary residence of the Emperor of Japan. It is a large park-like area located in the Chiyoda ward of Tokyo and contains buildings including the main palace (宮殿, Kyuden), the private residences of the royal family, an archive, museums and administrative offices. It is built on the site of the old Edo Castle.

银座是东京一个很受欢迎的高档购物区,附近有许多国际知名的百货公司、精品店、餐厅和咖啡馆。银座被认为是世界上最豪华的购物区之一。东京塔高 332.9 米,是日本第二高的建筑。东京皇宫是日本天皇的主要居所。

2. Kyoto(京都)

Kyoto is a city located in the central part of the island of Honshu, Japan. It has a population close to 1.5 million. Kyoto is the former Imperial capital of Japan for more than one thousand years. Kyoto contains roughly 2000 temples and shrines. About 20% of Japan's National Treasures and 14% of Important Cultural Properties exist in the city. The UNESCO World Heritage Site Historic Monuments of Ancient Kyoto (Kyoto, Uji and Otsu Cities) includes 17 locations in Kyoto, Uji in Kyoto Prefecture, and Otsu in Shiga Prefecture.

Kinkaku-ji (金閣寺, "Temple of the Golden Pavilion"), officially named Rokuon-ji (鹿苑寺, "Deer Garden Temple"), is a Zen Buddhist temple in Kyoto. It is one of the most popular buildings in Japan, attracting a large number of visitors annually. It is designated as a National Special Historic Site and a National Special Landscape, and it is one of 17 locations comprising the Historic Monuments of Ancient Kyoto which listed as World Heritage Site.

Kiyomizu-dera（清水寺）, officially known as Otowa-san Kiyomizu-dera（音羽山清水寺）is an independent Buddhist temple in eastern Kyoto. The temple is part of the Historic Monuments of Ancient Kyoto（Kyoto, Uji and Otsu Cities）which listed as UNESCO World Heritage site.

The Kyoto Imperial Palace（京都御所, Kyoto-gosho）is the former ruling palace of the Emperor of Japan. The emperors have resided at the Tokyo Imperial Palace since 1869（Meiji Restoration）; the preservation of the Kyoto Imperial Palace was ordered in 1877. Today the grounds are open to the public, and the Imperial Household Agency hosts public tours of the buildings several times a day.

京都是一个位于日本本州岛中部的城市，是一千多年前日本帝国的首都。京都大约有2 000座寺庙和神社。约20%的日本国宝和14%的重要文化财产存在于市区。联合国教科文组织世界遗产地古京都历史古迹分布于17个地点，分别位于京都、京都县和大津市。

金阁寺，即鹿苑寺，是日本京都的一座禅宗佛教寺庙，它是日本最受欢迎的建筑之一。它被指定为国家特殊历史遗址和国家特殊景观，是古代京都世界遗产的17个历史遗迹之一。清水寺是京都东部的一个独立的佛教寺庙，也是古代京都世界遗产的17个历史遗迹之一。京都皇宫是前执政的日本天皇的皇宫。

3. Mount Fuji(富士山)

Mount Fuji, located on Honshu Island, is the highest mountain in Japan at 3 776.24 meters. An active stratovolcano that last erupted in 1707-1708, Mount Fuji lies about 100 kilometres（60 mi）south-west of Tokyo, and can be seen from there on a clear day. Mount Fuji's exceptionally symmetrical cone, which is snow-capped several months a year, is a well-known symbol of Japan and it is frequently depicted in art and photographs, as well as visited by sightseers and climbers.

Mount Fuji is one of Japan's "Three Holy Mountains" along with Mount Tate and Mount Haku. It is also a special place of scenic beauty and one of Japan's historic sites. It was added to the World Heritage List as a cultural site on June 22, 2013. As per UNESCO, Mount Fuji has "inspired artists and poets and been the object of pilgrimage for centuries". UNESCO recognizes 25 sites of cultural interest within the Mt. Fuji locality. These 25 locations include the mountain itself, Fujisan Hongu Sengen Shrine and six other Sengen shrines, two lodging houses, Lake Yamanaka, Lake Kawaguchi, the eight Oshino Hakkai hot springs, two lava tree molds, the remains of the Fuji-ko cult in the Hitoana cave, Shiraito Falls, and Miho no Matsubara pine tree grove.

富士山位于本州岛，是日本最高的山，海拔3 776.24米。富士山是一座活跃的火山，上一次喷发是在1707—1708年,富士山有着异常对称的圆锥体,每年有几个月被积雪覆盖,是日本的象征。

富士山与泰特山、白山并称日本"三大圣山",它是一个风景优美的地方,也是日本的历史遗址之一。2013年6月22日被列入《世界文化遗产名录》。联合国教科文组织确认富士山地区有25处文化名胜。

4. Osaka(大阪)

Osaka (大阪市, Osaka-shi) is a designated city in the Kansai region of Japan. It is the second largest metropolitan area in Japan and among the largest in the world with over 19 million inhabitants. Historically as a merchant city, Osaka has also been known as the "nation's kitchen" (天下の台所, tenka no daidokoro) and served as a center for the rice trade during the Edo period.

Osaka Castle (大坂城, Osaka-jo) is a Japanese castle in Chuo-ku, Osaka. The castle is one of Japan's most famous landmarks and it played a major role in the unification of Japan during the sixteenth century of the Azuchi-Momoyama period.

Shitennō-ji (四天王寺; also Arahaka-ji, Nanba-ji, or Mitsu-ji) is a Buddhist temple in Osaka. It is the first Buddhist and oldest officially administered temple in Japan, although the temple buildings have been rebuilt over the centuries.

大阪是一个日本关西地区的城市,是日本第二大都市圈,也是世界上最大的都市圈之一。在江户时代,大阪是一个商业城市,也被称为"国家的厨房"和大米贸易中心。大阪城堡是日本最著名的地标之一。

5. Hakone(箱根)

Hakone (箱根町, Hakone-machi) is a town in Ashigarashimo District in Kanagawa Prefecture, Japan. As of June 2012, the town had an estimated population of 13 492 thousand and a population density of 145 persons per kilometer. The total area was 92.82 kilometers. Hakone has been designated as a geopark by UNESCO.

箱根是神奈川县的一个小镇。箱根被联合国教科文组织指定为地质公园。

6. Nara (奈良)

Nara (奈良市, Nara-shi) is the capital city of Nara Prefecture located in the Kansai region of Japan. Eight temples, shrines and ruins in Nara remain: specifically Todai-ji, Saidai-ji, Kofuku-ji, Kasuga Shrine, Gango-ji, Yakushi-ji, Toshodai-ji, and the Heijo Palace, together with Kasugayama Primeval Forest, collectively form Historic Monuments of Ancient Nara, a UNESCO World Heritage Site.

Todai-ji (東大寺, Eastern Great Temple), is a Buddhist temple complex, that was once one of the powerful Seven Great Temples, located in the city of Nara. Its Great

Buddha Hall（大佛殿，Daibutsuden）houses the world's largest bronze statue of the Buddha Vairocana, known in Japanese simply as Daibutsu（大佛）. The temple also serves as the Japanese headquarters of the Kegon school of Buddhism. The temple is a listed UNESCO World Heritage Site as one of the Historic Monuments of Ancient Nara, together with seven other sites including temples, shrines and places in the city of Nara. Deer, regarded as messengers of the gods in the Shinto religion, roam the grounds freely.

Toshodai-ji（唐招提寺）is a Buddhist temple of the Risshu sect in the city of Nara, in Nara Prefecture. The Classic Golden Hall, also known as the kondo, has a single story, hipped tiled roof with a seven bay wide facade. It is considered the archetype of classical style. It was founded in 759 by the Chinese monk Jianzhen during the Nara period. Toshodai-ji is one of the places in Nara that UNESCO has designated as World Heritage Site—Historic Monuments of Ancient Nara.

奈良市的首都是奈良县，位于日本关西地区。奈良保留了8座寺庙、神社和遗址：东大寺、西大寺、Kofuku-ji、须贺神社、Gango-ji、药古寺、唐招提寺和Heijo宫，以及须古山原始森林，它们共同构成了"奈良古历史遗迹"，被联合国教科文组织列为世界遗产。

东大寺是佛教庙宇，佛陀大厅内拥有全世界最大的佛青铜雕像，在日本被称为大佛，寺庙也作为日本华严宗的总部。唐招提寺被认为是日本"古典风格"的原型，它是759年由唐代的中国僧人鉴真在奈良时期建立的。

7. Yakushima(屋久岛)

Yakushima（屋久岛）is one of the Osumi Islands belonging to Kagoshima Prefecture, Japan. Administratively, the whole island is the town of Yakushima. The majority of the island is within the borders of the Kirishima-Yaku National Park. In 1980 an area of 18 958 hectares was designated as a Man and the Biosphere Reserve by UNESCO. In 1993, 10 hectares of wetland at Nagata-hama was designated a Ramsar Site. It is the largest nesting ground for the endangered loggerhead sea turtle in the North Pacific. Yakushima's unique remnant of warm/temperate ancient forest has been a natural World Heritage Site since 1993. In the wilderness core area (12.19 square kilometres (3 010 acres) of the World Heritage Site, no record of past tree cutting can be traced. The island is visited by 300 000 tourists every year.

屋久岛的大部分都在雾岛屋久国立公园的边界内。1980年，18 958公顷的土地被联合国教科文组织列为人与生物圈保护区。1993年，长田滨的10公顷湿地被指定为拉姆萨尔湿地。它是北太平洋最大的濒危红海龟筑巢地。屋久岛独特的暖温带古老森林遗迹自1993年以来一直是世界自然遗产。

8. Himeji Castle(姬路城)

Himeji Castle（姬路城，Himeji-jo）is a hilltop Japanese castle complex located in

Himeji, in Hyogo Prefecture, Japan. The castle is regarded as the finest surviving example of prototypical Japanese castle architecture, comprising a network of 83 buildings with advanced defensive systems from the feudal period. The castle is frequently known as Hakuro-jo ("White Egret Castle") or Shirasagi-jo ("White Heron Castle") because of its brilliant white exterior and supposed resemblance to a bird taking flight.

Himeji Castle is the largest and most visited castle in Japan, and it was registered in 1993 as one of the first UNESCO World Heritage Sites in the country. The area within the middle moat of the castle complex is a designated Special Historic Site and five structures of the castle are also designated National Treasures. Along with Matsumoto Castle and Kumamoto Castle, Himeji Castle is considered one of Japan's three premier castles. In order to preserve the castle buildings, the restoration work has been proceeded for several years and reopened to the public on March 27, 2015. The work also removed decades of dirt and grime, restoring the formerly gray roof to its original brilliant white color.

姬路城被认为是现存最优秀的典型日本城堡建筑,由83座建筑组成,拥有封建时期的先进防御系统。这座城堡经常被称为"白鹭城",因为它有明亮的白色外观,像一只飞翔的鸟。

姬路城是日本最大、游客最多的城堡,1993年被联合国教科文组织列为日本首批世界遗产之一。姬路城和松本城、熊本城一样,被认为是日本三大主要城堡之一。

Section 3　South Korea(韩国)

PART 1(第一部分)

1. 国土疆域(Territory)

韩国位于亚洲旅游区东北部朝鲜半岛的南部,地处日本海与黄海之间,北与朝鲜接壤,南隔朝鲜海峡与日本相望。韩国国土面积约10.329万平方千米,海域岛屿星罗棋布,其中最大的岛屿是济州岛,还有巨济岛、江华岛、珍岛、南海岛等。海岸线较长,海岸多悬崖绝壁,港湾风光秀丽。

South Korea is located in the south of the Korean Peninsula in the northeast of the Asia Tourism Region. It is between the Sea of Japan and the Yellow Sea, bordering DPRK in the north and facing Japan across the Korean Strait in the south. South Korea covers an area of about 10.329 km², and sea islands are scattered all over the country.

The largest island is Jeju Island, as well as Juji Island, Jianghua Island, Zhendao Island and Nanhai Island. The coastline is long, with many steep precipices and cliffs and beautiful harbors.

2. 自然风貌(Natural Features)

韩国地势北高南低,东高西低,山地、丘陵面积较大,名山较多。太白山脉沿半岛东部海岸延伸,受到海浪冲击,形成悬崖峭壁海滨景观。雪岳山、五台山等山势雄伟,气象万千。平原主要分布于南部和西部。南部、西部岛屿多,海岸线曲折,形成许多著名的海滨、海岛游览地。

由于受海洋暖流及东南亚潮湿季风的影响,韩国具有海洋性气候和大陆性气候的双重特征。一年四季分明,春秋短,夏冬长。南部有海洋调节,具有温带海洋性气候特征。在韩国可以观赏到分属四季的美景,7—10月是旅游的黄金季节,8月是旅游最佳时间。

The landscape of South Korea is high in the north and low in the south, high in the east and low in the west, with a large part of mountains and hills and many famous mountains. South Korea's climate is characterized by both a marine climate and continental climate. July to October is the golden season and August is the best time to travel.

3. 人口民族(Population and Ethnicity)

韩国总人口约5200万(2021年),人口密度约为每平方千米527.3人,是世界人口密度最大的国家之一。韩国属于单一民族国家,绝大多数人口为朝鲜民族,占全国总人口的96.25%,只有少数华裔和日裔等。官方语言为朝鲜语(或称韩语)。主要宗教为基督新教、佛教和天主教。

South Korea has a total population of 52 million (2021), with a population density of about 527.3 people per square kilometer, making it one of the most densely populated countries in the world. The population of South Korea is highly homogeneous; almost the entire population is ethnically Korean. Its residents profess Protestantism, Buddhism, and Catholicism etc.

4. 发展简史(Brief History of Development)

大约公元前2333年,檀君王俭创建古朝鲜,之后先后建立了许多部落王国。公元前100年左右形成百济、高句丽、新罗三国鼎立的局面。公元676年,新罗统一了三国。公元918—1392年进入高丽时代。14世纪末建立了朝鲜王朝。1876年后韩国沦为日本的殖民地。第二次世界大战后日本投降,韩国彻底摆脱日本的统治,大韩民国诞生。

The Korean dynasty was established in the late 14th century. It became a colony of Japan after 1876. After World War II, Japan surrendered and South Korea was completely rid of Japan's rule, and the Republic of Korea was established.

5. 政治经济(Politics and Economy)

韩国首都为首尔,国花木槿花,货币韩元。

国家政体为总统内阁制,实行三权分立,立法机构是国会,司法机构是独立法院、检察院,行政权属于政府。主要政党:共同民主党、自由韩国党、正未来党等。

韩国近30年来经济发展较快,被国际社会称为亚洲"新兴工业化"地区之一和亚洲"四小龙"之一。钢铁、汽车、电子、造船、化学、纺织等工业发达。韩国是世界贸易大国之一,进出口总额占国民生产总值的50%左右。电子、纺织品、钢铁产品、化工、汽车、船舶、机械产品等出口量较大。

韩国海、陆、空交通均较发达,已形成铁路、公路、航空运输网络,铁路网稠密。高速公路可通往各大城市的旅游胜地。沿海地带有豪华旅游船,可供欣赏绮丽的海岸和岛屿景观。首尔、金浦、金海、济州等国际机场与韩国全国各地及世界各大城市之间均辟有航线,旅游交通十分便利。

In the past 30 years, the South Korea's economy grew rapidly and was recognized as one of the "newly industrialized" regions and one of the "four tigers" in Asia by international community. South Korea's transportation system is well developed with water, land and air transport network.

6. 旅游市场(Tourism Market)

韩国政府采取的一系列发展旅游的措施,吸引了来自世界各国的游客,给韩国旅游业带来了勃勃生机,旅游业成了韩国经济增长的新亮点。

据韩国文化体育观光部与韩国旅游发展局统计,2019年访韩外国游客数达1 750万人次,创历史新高;旅游收入达25.1万亿韩元,直接和间接产生的产值和就业人数分别达46万亿韩元和46万人。

韩国文化体育观光部十分重视中国市场,实施了简化签证申请手续的制度,放宽了中国收入较高地区游客多次出行的签证条件。截止到2019年11月,访韩的中国游客累计达551万人次,较上年同期增长26.1%。2019年来自美国的游客超过100万人次,因此,美国将成为继中国、日本之后,访韩游客超过100万人次的客源地。同时,韩国也一直是中国重要的客源国,中国文化和旅游部统计显示,2018年韩国来华游客达到419.18万人次,韩国已成为中国第一大客源国。

South Korea's tourism industry is well developed. In recent years, the South Korea government decided to take tourism as a strategic industry and actively encouraged and developed tourism. According to the statistics of China's Ministry of Culture and Tourism, the number of tourists from South Korea to China reached 4 191 800 in 2018, making South Korea the largest source of tourists to China.

PART 2(第二部分)

Tourism Resources(旅游资源)

In 2012, 11.1 million foreign tourists visited South Korea, making it the 20th most visited country in the world, and the 6th most visited country in Asia. Most tourists come from Japan, China. The recent popularity of Korean popular culture, often known as the "Korean Wave", has increased tourist arrivals. Seoul is the principal tourist destination for visitors; popular tourist destinations outside of Seoul include Seoraksan national park, the historic city of Gyeongju and subtropical Jeju Island. Traveling to North Korea is not normally possible without a special permission, but in recent years organized group tours have allowed groups of South Korean citizens to visit Mount Kumgang.

South Korea's historical tourist attractions include the ancient capitals of Seoul, Gyeongju and Buyeo. Some natural landmarks include the peaks of the Baekdudaegan, particularly Seoraksan and Jiri-san, of Danyang Ondal Cave and Hwanseongul Cave, and beaches such as Haeundaeand Mallipo. Except Jeju island, there are many smaller islands. Excursion ferries are quite common along the south and west coasts and also to Ulleung-do Island, off the east coast.

韩国国际游客主要来自日本和中国。首尔是游客的主要旅游目的地；首尔以外的热门旅游目的地包括雪岳山国家公园、历史名城庆州和亚热带济州岛。近年来，有组织的团体旅游已经允许韩国公民团体参观朝鲜金刚山。

韩国的历史旅游景点包括首尔、庆州和布约。一些自然地标包括白头大干山脉的山峰，尤其是雪岳山和智异山，丹阳洞和幻仙窟，以及海云台和万里浦等海滩。除了济州岛，还有许多较小的岛屿。

1. Seoul(首尔)

Seoul—officially the Seoul Special City—is the capital and largest metropolis of South Korea, forming the heart of the Seoul Capital Area, which includes the surrounding Incheon metropolis and Gyeonggi province. It is home to over half of all South Koreans along with 678 102 international residents. The Seoul Capital Area contains five UNESCO World Heritage Sites: Changdeok Palace, Hwaseong Fortress, Jongmyo Shrine, Namhansanseong and the Royal Tombs of the Joseon Dynasty. Seoul is surrounded by mountains, the tallest being Mount Bukhansan, the world's most visited national park per square foot. Modern landmarks include the iconic N Seoul Tower, the gold-clad 63 Building, the neo futuristic Dongdaemun Design Plaza, Lotte World—the world's second largest indoor theme park, Moonlight Rainbow Fountain—the world's longest bridge fountain and the Sevit Floating Islands. The birthplace of K-pop and the Korean Wave, Seoul received over 10 million international visitors in 2014, making it the world's 9th most visited city and 4th largest earner in tourism.

首尔是韩国的首都和最大的大都市。首尔首都地区有 5 处联合国教科文组织世界遗产:昌德宫、华城城堡、宗庙、南山城和朝鲜王朝的皇家陵墓。首尔四面环山,最高的是北汉山。现代地标包括标志性的首尔塔、镀金的 63 大厦、新未来主义的东大门设计广场、乐天世界、世界第二大室内主题公园、月光彩虹喷泉、世界最长的大桥喷泉和塞维特浮岛。首尔是韩国流行音乐和韩流的发源地。

Gyeongbokgung(景福宫), also known as Gyeongbokgung Palace or Gyeongbok Palace, was the main royal palace of the Joseon Dynasty. Built in 1395, it is located in northern Seoul, South Korea. The largest of the Five Grand Palaces built by the Joseon Dynasty, Gyeongbokgung served as the home of Kings of the Joseon Dynasty, the Kings' households, as well as the government of Joseon. It also houses the National Palace Museum of Korea and the National Folk Museum within the premises of the complex.

Changdeokgung(昌德宫) is set within a large park in Jongno-gu, Seoul, South Korea. It is one of the "Five Grand Palaces" built by the kings of the Joseon Dynasty (1392-1897). As it is located east of Gyeongbok Palace, Changdeokgung, along with Changgyeonggung, is also referred to as the "East Palace".

景福宫位于韩国首尔北部,建于 1395 年,是朝鲜王朝的皇宫。景福宫是由朝鲜王朝建造的五大宫殿中最大的一座,是朝鲜王朝国王、国王的家庭以及朝鲜政府的所在地。它拥有韩国国立古宫博物馆和国家民俗博物馆内的综合设施。

昌德宫是朝鲜王朝建造的"五大宫殿"之一。由于它位于景福宫以东,昌德宫和昌庆宫也被称为"东宫"。

Changdeokgung was the most favored palace of many Joseon princes and retained many elements dating from the Three Kingdoms of Korea period that were not incorporated in the more contemporary Gyeongbokgung. One such element is the fact that the buildings of Changdeokgung blend with the natural topography of the site instead of imposing themselves upon it. Like the other Five Grand Palaces in Seoul, it was heavily damaged during the Japanese occupation of Korea (1910-1945). Currently, only about 30% of the pre-Japanese buildings survive. Today there are 13 buildings remaining on the palace grounds and 28 pavilions in the gardens, occupying 110 acres (44 hectares) in all and the area is designated as Historical Site No. 122. Buildings of note include Donhwamun (built in 1412, rebuilt in 1607, with a copper bell weighing 9 short tons or 8 metric tons), Injeongjeon (main hall), Seongjeongjeon Hall(auxiliary office in the main hall), Huijeongdang (the king's private residence, later used as a conference hall), Daejojeon Hall (living quarters), and Nakseonjae Hall. The Palace chosen to worldwide travel expert evaluation and reader preferences is registered the world's 500 attractions in research.

The National Museum of Korea is the flagship museum of Korean history and art in South Korea, and is the cultural organization that represents Korea. Since its establishment in 1945, the museum has been committed to various studies and research activities in the fields of archaeology, history and art, continuously developing a variety of exhibitions and education programs.

昌德宫是许多朝鲜王子最喜欢的宫殿，保留了许多可以追溯到朝鲜三国时期的元素，这些元素没有被纳入更现代的景福宫。昌德宫的建筑与自然地形融为一体，它和首尔的其他五大宫殿一样，在日本占领朝鲜(1910—1945)期间遭到严重破坏，只有大约30%的建筑保存下来。

韩国国家博物馆是韩国历史和艺术的旗舰博物馆，也是代表韩国的文化组织。自1945年成立以来，博物馆一直致力于考古、历史、艺术等领域的各种研究活动，不断发展各种展览和教育项目。

Myeongdong is a dong in Jung-gu, Seoul, South Korea between Chungmu-ro, Eulji-ro, and Namdaemun-ro. It covers 0.99 km^2 with a population of 3 409 and is mostly a commercial area, being one of Seoul's main shopping and tourism districts. The area is known for its two historically significant sites, namely the Myeongdong Cathedral and the Myeongdong Nanta Theatre.

明洞是首尔主要的购物和旅游区之一。该地区以其两个具有历史意义的遗址而闻名，即明洞大教堂和明洞剧场。

2. Busan(釜山)

Busan is South Korea's second largest city after Seoul. Busan has Korea's largest beach and longest river, and is home to the world's largest department store, the Shinsegae Centum City. The major tourist destinations are Haeundae Beach, Beomeosa Temple, Haedong Yonggungsa Temple, Geumjeongsanseong Fortress, Dongnaeeupseong Fortress, Dongnae-hyangyo Confucian Academy and Chungnyeolsa Shrine.

Haeundae Beach is a beach in Busan, South Korea. Haeundae beach is 40 minutes away from Busan's main railway station (in the Downtown area), and less than one hour from Gimhae International Airport. Along the 12 km of coastline is Busan's most popular beach, and with Seogwipo's, it is one of the most famous beaches in South Korea. Because of its easy access from downtown Busan, the beach is busy year round with several kinds of beach festivals.

Beomeosa (Temple of the Nirvana Fish) is a head temple of the Jogye Order of Korean Buddhism in Cheongnyong-dong, Geumjeong-gu, Busan, South Korea. Built on the slopes of Geumjeongsan, it is one of the country's most known urban temples.

釜山是韩国第二大城市,仅次于首尔。釜山拥有韩国最大的海滩和最长的河流,也是世界上最大的百货商店"中原新天地"的所在地。主要旅游景点有海云台海滩、美美莎寺、海东龙公沙寺、金钟山城炮台、东 naeupseong 炮台、东 naehyangyo 儒家学院和忠陵寺。

3. Jeju Island(济州岛)

Jejudo (also known as Jeju Island) is the largest island off the coast of the Korean Peninsula, and the main island of Jeju Province. The island lies in the Korea Strait, southwest of South Jeolla Province. The island contains the natural World Heritage Site—Jeju Volcanic Island and Lava Tubes. Jejudo has a temperate climate; even in winter, the temperature rarely falls below 0°C. Manjanggul Lava Tube, 8 km long with a 1 km publicly accessible portion. The places of interest are Seongsan Ilchulbong or "Sunrise Peak"—a volcanic tuff cone and crater, Mount Hallasan—the island's central dominant peak, Seongeup Folk Village, Jeju Teddy Bear Museum.

济州岛是朝鲜半岛最大的岛屿,位于韩国海峡,全罗南道西南。岛上有世界自然遗产济州火山岛和熔岩管。旅游景点有"日出峰"(一个凝石锥和火山口)、Hallasan 山(岛的中心主峰)、Seongeup 民俗村、济州岛泰迪熊博物馆。

4. Gyeongju(庆州)

Gyeongju is a coastal city in the far southeastern corner of North Gyeongsang Province in South Korea. Gyeongju was the capital of the ancient kingdom of Silla (57 BC-935 AD) which ruled about twothirds of the Korean Peninsula between the 7th and 9th centuries. A vast number of archaeological sites and cultural properties from this period remain in the city. Gyeongju is often referred to as "the museum without walls". Among such historical treasures, Seokguram grotto, Bulguksa temple, Gyeongju Historic Areas and Yangdong Folk Village are designated as World Heritage Sites by UNESCO. The major historical sites have helped Gyeongju become one of the most popular tourist destinations in South Korea.

庆州是位于韩国庆尚北道东南角的一座沿海城市。庆州是古代新罗王国(公元前57年—公元935年)的首都,庆州经常被称为"没有墙的博物馆"。在这些历史瑰宝中,石窟庵、七宫寺、庆州历史遗址区和阳东民俗村是世界遗产。许多重要的历史遗迹使庆州成为韩国最受欢迎的旅游目的地之一。

Section 4　Thailand(泰国)

PART 1(第一部分)

1. 国土疆域(Territory)

泰国位于中南半岛中南部,东北部与老挝为邻,东南部与柬埔寨交界,南部与马来西亚接壤,西部与缅甸毗邻。国土面积约 51.31 万平方千米。

Thailand is located in the south-central Indo-China Peninsula, bordering Laos in the northeast, Cambodia in the southeast, Malaysia in the south, and Myanmar in the west. The land area is about 513 000 km².

2. 自然风貌(Natural Features)

泰国的领土南北距离约 1 600 千米,东西之间最宽距离为 780 千米。地势北高南低,山川纵列,平原居中。地形大体分为四部分:西北部山区,东北部高原,西南部为狭长的丘陵区,中部是平原区(其中湄南河流域是泰国农耕集中区)。

泰国地处热带,绝大部分地区属于热带季风气候,全年气温都比较高。全年月平均气温为 24~30 ℃。年降水量约 1 000 mm。全年分为热、雨、凉三季,全年皆宜旅游。

Located wholly within the tropical monsoon zone, Thailand encompasses diverse landscapes, including the mountainous areas of the northwest, the broad plateau of the northeast, the hilly areas along the narrow southwest, and the fields of the central plains. It is suitable for travel all year round.

3. 人口民族(Population and Ethnicity)

泰国人口约 6 900 万人(2021 年),人口密度约为每平方千米 134.5 人。全国共有 30 多个民族。泰族为主要民族,占人口总数的 75%。在泰华人约有 900 万,占全国人口的 14%,是除泰人之外最大的族群,其余为佬族、华族、马来族、高棉族等,泰语为国语。90% 以上的民众信仰佛教,马来族信奉伊斯兰教,还有少数民众信仰基督教、天主教、印度教和锡克教。

Thailand has a population of 69 million (2021), with a population density of about 134.5 people per square kilometer. The vast majority of the inhabitants of Thailand are Thai people, accounting for 75% of the total population. The vast majority of people in

Thailand are adherents of Buddhism, especially Theravada Buddhism.

4. 发展简史(Brief History of Development)

泰国原名暹罗,大约在 5 000 年前泰国所在的地区就有人类居住。公元 6 世纪时,中国南部的部分傣族人南迁至中南半岛,定居于湄公河流域,建立了一些小国家,这就是今天泰国的祖先。1238 年傣族人建立了一个独立的王朝——素可泰王朝。1350 年湄南河流域的乌通王在阿瑜陀耶建立了大城王朝。大城王朝历经 33 位君主,历时 417 年。1767 年大城王朝覆灭,出现了吞武里王朝。15 年后又出现咖达纳哥王朝,该王朝迁都曼谷,又称"曼谷王朝"。泰国逐步趋向安定。

Thailand has a history of over 700 years. The Kingdom of Sukhothai was founded in 1238, which began to form a relatively unified country. Thailand has experienced the Sukhothai period, the Ayutthayan period, the Thon Buri and early Bangkok period.

5. 政治经济(Politics and Economy)

国家政体为议会君主立宪制。国王为国家元首,总理为政府首脑。国家立法议会负责制定法律,行使国会和上、下两院职权。司法系统由宪法法院、司法法院、行政法院和军事法院构成。主要政党有为泰党、泰国民主党、自豪泰党等。

泰国原为典型农业国,经济结构单一。近 20 年来逐步向新兴工业国转变,主要工业部门是电子、汽车装配、建材和石化等。大米、橡胶、海产品出口量较大。泰国运输业以公路和空运为主。公路交通发达,城乡之间均有公路相通。国际国内航空以曼谷为中心,素方那普国际机场已成为东南亚重要的空中交通枢纽。

Thailand used to be a typical agricultural country with a single economic sector. The main industrial sectors are electronics, automobile assembly, building materials and petrochemicals, etc. The transportation industry is mainly road and air transport.

6. 旅游市场(Tourism Market)

泰国旅游业发展很快,已成为亚洲重要的旅游目的地国。泰国的入境旅游市场主要为东亚,其中,中国占 40%;其次是欧洲和美洲。国际旅游人数也不断增长,泰国体育旅游部的数据显示,2019 年赴泰国旅游的国际游客人数已从 2018 年的 3 800 万人次上升到 3 900 万人次,创下历史新高。2019 年前 11 月,泰国接待游客 3 587 万人次,同比增长 4.4%,旅游营业收入达 1.74 万亿泰铢,同比增长 3.67%。

泰国作为中国游客的热门旅游目的地,成为众多游客的首选旅游地之一。泰国一直是我国主要的目的地国和客源国之一。中国文化和旅游部的数据显示,2019 年中国赴泰国游客人数约为 1 098 万人次,2019 年中国接待泰国入境游客数量为 65.79 万人次。

With convenient transportation and rich tourism resources, Thailand has become an important tourist destination in Asia. Tourism industry developed rapidly in Thailand.

Thailand has always been one of the most popular destinations and tourist source to China.

PART 2(第二部分)

Tourism Resources(旅游资源)

Asian tourists primarily visit Thailand for Bangkok and the historical, natural, cultural sights in its vicinity. Western tourists not only visit Bangkok and its surroundings, but also travel to the southern beaches and islands. The north is the chief destination for trekking and adventure travel with its diverse ethnic minority groups and forested mountains. The region hosting the fewest tourists is Isan in the northeast.

Thailand's attractions include diving sites, sandy beaches, hundreds of tropical islands, nightlife, archaeological sites, museums, hill tribes, flora and bird life, palaces, Buddhist temples and several World Heritage Sites. Many tourists follow courses during their stay in Thailand. Popular classes in Thai are cooking, Buddhism and traditional Thai massage. Thai national festivals range from Thai New Year Songkran to Loy Krathong. Many localities in Thailand also have their own festivals. Among the best-known are the "Elephant Round-up" in Surin, the "Rocket Festival" in Yasothon and the "Phi Ta Khon" festival in Dan Sai. Thai cuisine has become famous worldwide with its enthusiastic use of fresh herbs and spices.

亚洲游客主要游览泰国曼谷及其附近的历史、自然和文化景点。而西方游客不仅游览曼谷及其周边地区,而且还前往南部的海滩和岛屿。泰国北部是徒步旅行和探险旅行的主要目的地,接待游客最少的地区是东北部的伊桑。

泰国的旅游项目包括潜水场所、沙滩、数百个热带岛屿、夜生活、考古遗址、博物馆、山地部落、植物和鸟类生活、宫殿、佛教寺庙和一些世界遗产。泰国受欢迎的课程有泰式烹饪、佛教和传统泰式按摩。泰国的国家节日从泰国新年宋干节到水灯节。许多地方也有自己的节日。泰国菜因其热衷使用新鲜香草和香料而闻名于世。

1. Bangkok(曼谷)

Bangkok is the capital and most populous city of Thailand. Bangkok is one of the world's top tourist destination cities. Bangkok's multi-faceted sights, attractions and city life appeal to diverse groups of tourists. Royal palaces and temples as well as several museums constitute its major historical and cultural tourist attractions. Shopping and dining experiences offer a wide range of choices and prices. The city is also famous for its dynamic nightlife. Although Bangkok's sex tourism scene is well known to foreigners, it is usually not openly acknowledged by locals or the government.

曼谷是泰国的首都和人口最多的城市，是世界上最好的旅游城市之一。曼谷的风景和城市生活吸引着不同的游客。皇家宫殿和寺庙以及一些博物馆构成了它的主要历史和文化旅游景点。这座城市也以其充满活力的夜生活而闻名。

Among Bangkok's well-known sights are the Grand Palace and major Buddhist temples, including Wat Phra Kaew, Wat Pho, and Wat Arun. The Giant Swing and Erawan Shrinedemonstrate Hinduism's deep-rooted influence in Thai culture. Vimanmek Mansion in Dusit Palace Park is famous as the world's largest teak building, while the Jim Thompson House provides an example of traditional Thai architecture. Other major museums include the Bangkok National Museum and the Royal Barge National Museum. Cruises and boat trips on the Chao Phraya River and Thonburi's canals offer views of some of the city's traditional architecture and ways of life on the waterfront.

Shopping venues, many of which are popular with both tourists and locals, range from the shopping centres and department stores concentrated in Siam and Ratchaprasong to the sprawling Chatuchak Weekend Market. Taling Chan Floating Market is among such markets in Bangkok. Yaowarat is known for its shops as well as street-side food stalls and restaurants, which are also found throughout the city. Khao San Road has long been famous as a backpackers' destination, with its budget accommodation, shops and bars attracting visitors from all over the world.

The Grand Palace is a complex of buildings at the heart of Bangkok, Thailand. The palace has been the official residence of the Kings of Siam (and later Thailand) since 1782. The palace is one of the most popular tourist attractions in Thailand.

曼谷的著名景点是大皇宫和佛教寺庙，包括玉佛寺、卧佛寺等。巨大的秋千和四面佛展示了印度教对泰国文化根深蒂固的影响。都实皇家公园的柚木宫是世界上最大的柚木建筑，而吉姆·汤普森故居则是泰国传统建筑的典范。主要的博物馆包括曼谷国家博物馆和皇家驳船国家博物馆。乘船游览湄南河和吞武里运河，可以欣赏到城市的一些传统建筑和滨水生活方式。

很多购物场所都很受游客和当地人的欢迎，如集中在暹罗和拉查帕森的购物中心和百货商店，以及庞大的乍都乍周末市场。

大皇宫是位于泰国曼谷市中心的建筑群。1782年以来，这座宫殿一直是暹罗国王的官邸，是泰国最受欢迎的旅游景点之一。

In shape, the palace complex is roughly rectangular and has a combined area of 218 400 square metres, surrounded by four walls. Rather than being a single structure, the Grand Palace is made up of numerous buildings, halls, pavilions set around open lawns, gardens and courtyards. Its asymmetry and eclectic styles are due to its organic development, with additions and rebuilding being made by successive reigning kings over 200 years of history. It is divided into several quarters: the Temple of the Emerald Buddha; the Outer Court, with many public buildings; the Middle Court, including the

Phra Maha Monthien Buildings, the Phra Maha Prasat Buildings and the Chakri Maha Prasat Buildings; the Inner Court and the Siwalai Gardens quarter. The Grand Palace is currently partially open to the public as a museum, but it remains a working palace, with several royal offices still situated inside.

宫殿建筑群的形状大致呈长方形,总面积为 218 400 平方米。大皇宫不是一个单一结构的建筑,而是由无数的建筑、大厅、亭台楼阁围绕着开放的草坪、花园和庭院组成。它的不对称和折中主义风格是在 200 多年的历史中由历代国王逐渐补充和重建而形成的。它分为几个部分:玉佛寺、外院、中庭、内院和西瓦莱花园区。大皇宫目前部分作为博物馆向公众开放。

Wat Phra Kaew is regarded as the most sacred Buddhist temple (wat) in Thailand. The Emerald Buddha housed in the temple is a potent religio-political symbol and the palladium (protective image) of Thai society. The main building is the central phra ubosot, which houses the statue of the Emerald Buddha. The Emerald Buddha, a dark green statue, is in a standing form, about 66 centimetres tall, carved from a single jade stone.

玉佛寺被认为是泰国最神圣的佛寺,寺庙里的祖母绿佛像是一个强有力的宗教政治象征,也是泰国社会的保护神。玉佛像是一尊深绿色的雕像,呈站立状,高约 66 厘米,由一块玉石雕刻而成。

Wat Pho, also spelt Wat Po, is a Buddhist temple complex in the Phra Nakhon District, Bangkok, Thailand. It is on Rattanakosin Island, directly south of the Grand Palace. The temple is first on the list of six temples in Thailand classed as the highest grade of the first-class royal temples. It is associated with King Rama Ⅰ who rebuilt the temple complex on an earlier temple site, and became his main temple where some of his ashes are enshrined. The temple was later expanded and extensively renovated by Rama Ⅲ. The temple complex houses the largest collection of Buddha images in Thailand, including a 46-meter long reclining Buddha. The temple was also the earliest center for public education in Thailand, and still houses a school of Thai medicine. It is known as the birthplace of traditional Thai massage which is still taught and practiced at the temple.

卧佛寺位于拉塔纳科辛岛上,大皇宫正南方。这座寺庙是泰国六座被列为一级皇家寺庙中等级最高的寺庙。拉玛一世在早期的寺庙遗址上重建了寺庙建筑群,并作为供奉其骨灰的主要寺庙。寺庙建筑群收藏了泰国最大的佛像,包括一尊 46 米长的卧佛。这里也是泰国传统按摩的发源地。

The National Museum in Thailand is the main museum on the history of the Thai culture. The main museum is located in Bangkok on Na Phrathat Road next to the Sanam Luang, not far from Wat Phra Kaew. The Bangkok National Museum is the main branch museum of the National Museums in Thailand and also the largest museum in Southeast

Asia. The museum was established and opened in 1874 by King Rama Ⅴ to exhibit relics from the rule of King Rama Ⅳ. Today the galleries contain exhibits covering Thai history back to Neolithic times. The collection includes The King Ram Khamhaeng Inscription, which was inscribed on UNESCO's Memory of the World Register in 2003 in recognition of its world significance.

曼谷国家博物馆是泰国国家博物馆的主要分馆,也是东南亚最大的博物馆。该博物馆于1874年由国王拉玛五世建立,以展示国王拉玛四世统治时期的文物。藏品包括国王拉姆·汉亨(Ram Khamhaeng)的题词,该题词于2003年被联合国教科文组织列入世界记忆名录。

2. Phuket(普吉岛)

Phuket is Thailand's largest island and nestles against the Indian Ocean Coast 870 kilometers south of Bangkok. Phuket derives its wealth from tin and rubber, is blessed with teeming marine life, and has enjoyed a rich and colorful history. Phuket is blessed with magnificent coves and bays, powdery, palm-fringed white beaches, sparkling island-dotted seas, sincerely hospitable people, comfortable accommodation, superb seafood, lushly forested mountains, lovely waterfalls and parks, and delightful turn-of-the-century Indo/Portuguese and Chinese-influenced architecture which create an enchanting ambiance perfectly suited to total relaxation.

普吉岛是泰国最大的岛屿,坐落在曼谷以南870千米处的印度洋。普吉岛盛产锡和橡胶,拥有丰富的海洋生物、丰富多彩的历史、美丽的海湾、粉状的白色沙滩、波光粼粼的大海、热情好客的人们、舒适的住宿、上佳的海鲜、郁郁葱葱的山脉、美丽的瀑布和公园。

3. Pattaya(芭堤雅)

Pattaya is a city in Thailand, a beach resort popular with tourists and expatriates. It is on the east coast of the Gulf of Thailand. It is known as the "Oriental Hawaii". The main sweep of the bay area is divided into two principal beachfronts. Pattaya Beach is parallel to city centre, and runs from Pattaya Nuea south to Walking Street. Along Beach Road are restaurants, shopping areas, and night attractions.

Popular activities include golf (21 golf courses within one hour of Pattaya), go-kart racing, and visiting different theme parks and zoos such as the Elephant Village, where demonstrations of training methods and ancient ceremonial re-enactments are performed daily. The private Sri Racha Tiger Zoo features tigers, crocodiles, and other animals in daily shows. The Vimantaitalay tourist submarine offers 30-minute trips underwater to see corals and marine life just a few kilometres offshore.

Other attractions in Pattaya include the Million Years Stone Park, Pattaya Crocodile

Farm, Pattaya Park Beach Resort Water Park, Funny Land Amusement Park, Siriporn Orchid Farm, Silverlake Winery, Underwater World Pattaya, the Thai Alangkarn Theater Pattaya (cultural show), Bottle Art Museum, Ripley's Believe It or Not Museum, and Underwater World, an aquarium with a collection of marine species from the Gulf of Thailand including sharks and stingrays. Khao Pratamnak or Khao Phra Bat is a small hill between south Pattaya and Jomtien Beach that provides a panoramic view of the city and its crescent bay. The hill is topped by Wat Khao Phra Bat, a temple, and the monument of Kromluang Chomphonkhetudomsak, who is regarded as the founding father of the modern Thai navy.

Thepprasit Market is the biggest and busiest market in Pattaya. It is open every Friday, Saturday, and Sunday evening on Thepprasit Road. It is known for selling pets, has many Thai food stalls including local specialities like fried insects and scorpions as well as branded clothing, shoes, and electronic goods.

芭堤雅是泰国的一个海滨度假城市，位于泰国湾的东海岸，被称为"东方夏威夷"，很受游客和外籍人士的欢迎。

这里受欢迎的活动包括高尔夫、卡丁车比赛，以及参观不同的主题公园和动物园，如大象村，那里每天都有训练方法的演示和古代仪式的重演。维曼塔塔莱旅游潜水艇可提供30分钟的水下旅行，可以在离岸几千米的地方观赏珊瑚和海洋生物。

芭堤雅的其他景点包括百万年石公园、芭堤雅鳄鱼农场、芭堤雅海滩度假水上公园、有趣的土地游乐园、诗丽波兰农场、银湖酿酒厂、水下世界芭堤雅、泰国阿朗甘剧院、瓶子艺术博物馆、雷普利的"信不信由你"博物馆和水下世界等。

Thepprasit 市场是芭堤雅最大、最繁忙的市场，以出售宠物而闻名。

4. Chiang Mai(清迈)

Chiang Mai is the largest and most culturally significant city in northern Thailand. Chiang Mai was one of two tourist destinations in Thailand on TripAdvisor's 2014 list of "25 Best Destinations in the World", where it ranks the 24th place. Chiang Mai has over 300 Buddhist temples ("wat" in Thai). These include:

Wat Phrathat Doi Suthep, the city's most famous temple, stands on Doi Suthep, a hill to the north-west of the city. The temple dates from 1383.

Wat Chiang Man, the oldest temple in Chiang Mai, dating from the 13th century. King Mengrai lived here during the construction of the city. This temple houses two important and venerated Buddha figures, the marble Phra Sila and the crystal Phra Satang Man.

Wat Phra Singh is within the city walls, dates from 1345, and offers an example of classic Northern Thai-style architecture. It houses the Phra Singh Buddha, a highly venerated figure brought here many years ago from Chiang Rai.

清迈是泰国北部最大、最具文化意义的城市。在 TripAdvisor 2014 年发布的"世界 25 个最佳旅游目的地"榜单中,清迈是泰国的两个旅游目的地之一,排名第 24 位。

清迈有 300 多座佛教寺庙。素贴寺,又称双龙寺,是这座城市最著名的寺庙,建于 1383 年。清曼寺是清迈最古老的寺庙,始建于 13 世纪。帕辛寺始建于 1345 年,是泰国北部经典建筑风格的典范,佛寺内供奉着多年前从清莱迁来的备受尊崇的佛陀帕辛。

5. Phi Phi Island(皮皮岛)

The Phi Phi Islands are in Thailand, between the large island of Phuket and the west Strait of Malacca coast of the mainland. Ko Phi Phi Don is the largest island of the group. The Islands are reachable by speedboats or long-tail boats most often from Krabi Town or from various piers in Phuket Province.

The islands feature beaches and clear water that have had their natural beauty protected by national park. Tourism on Ko Phi Phi has exploded since the filming of the movie The Beach. In the early 1990s, only adventurous travelers visited the island. Today, Ko Phi Phi is one of Thailand's most famous destinations for scuba diving and snorkeling, kayaking and other marine recreational activities.

The number of tourists visiting the island every year is so high that Ko Phi Phi's coral reefs and marine fauna have suffered a damage as a result.

There are no hotels or other type of accommodation on the smaller island Ko Phi Phi Lee. The only opportunity to spend the night on this island is to take a guided tour to Maya Bay and sleep in a tent.

皮皮岛位于普吉岛大岛和马六甲海峡西岸之间。大皮皮岛是该群岛中最大的岛屿。这些岛屿以海滩和清澈的海水为特色,其自然美景受到国家公园的保护。今天,大皮皮岛是泰国最著名的潜水、浮潜、皮划艇和其他海洋娱乐活动的目的地之一。

每年来岛上旅游的游客数量络绎不绝,导致大皮皮岛的珊瑚礁和海洋动物遭受了严重破坏。

Section 5　The Philippines(菲律宾)

PART 1(第一部分)

1. 国土疆域(Territory)

菲律宾位于亚洲旅游区东南部、南海与太平洋之间,北隔巴士海峡与中国的台湾地区相望，南部、西南部隔苏拉威西海、巴拉巴克海峡，与印度尼西亚、马来西亚相望。它由7 000多个大小岛屿组成，总面积约29.97万平方千米，其中吕宋岛、棉兰老岛、萨马岛等11个主要岛屿占全国总面积的96%左右。

The Philippines is located in the southeast of the Asian Tourism Region, between the South China Sea and the Pacific Ocean. It faces China's Taiwan Province across the Bashi Strait in the north, and Indonesia and Malaysia across the Sulawesi Sea and the Balabac Strait in the south and southwest. It consists of 7 107 islands with a total area of 299 700 km^2, of which 11 main islands, including Luzon Island, Mindanao Island, Samar Island, account for about 96% of the country's total area.

2. 自然风貌(Natural Features)

菲律宾是世界第三大群岛国家，素有"千岛乐园"之美誉。其中吕宋岛面积最大，棉兰老岛是全国第二大岛。全国地形崎岖不平，丘陵、山地、高原占75%以上，平原面积狭小。全国有200多座火山，其中有活火山20余座，火山遗迹旅游资源丰富。棉兰老岛东南部的阿波火山现已辟为国家公园。

菲律宾是位于赤道与北回归线之间的群岛国家，大部分地区属于热带雨林气候，高温多雨的气候使这里拥有热带植物一万余种，其中包括红木、乌木、棒木、檀木在内的珍贵树种达2 500多种。菲律宾有明显的旱季(3月至5月)、雨季(6月至10月)和凉季(11月至次年2月)，全年皆宜旅游，其中，凉季是最佳的旅游季节。

The Philippines, the third largest archipelagic country in the world, known as the "paradise of a thousand islands", of which Luzon Island is the largest. The landscape of the country is rugged, with more than 75% of the land surface consisting of hills, mountains and plateaus, and narrow coastal plains. The climate of the Philippines is tropical rainforest climate and is suitable for travel throughout the year.

3. 人口民族(Population and Ethnicity)

菲律宾人口约1.08亿(2021年)，人口密度约为每平方千米360人。主要民族为马来族，占全国人口的85%以上，还包括他加禄人、伊洛人、邦邦牙人、维萨亚人和比科尔人等；少数民族及外来后裔有华人、阿拉伯人、印度人、西班牙人和美国人等；菲律宾有70多种语言。国语为是菲律宾语，英语为官方语言。国民约85%信奉天主教，其他信奉伊斯兰教、独立教和基督教新教等，华人多信奉佛教。

The Philippines has a population of about 108 million (2021), with a population density of about 360 people per square kilometer. About 85 percent of Filipinos profess Catholicism.

4. 发展简史(Brief History of Development)

14世纪之前，菲律宾群岛上未形成国家，多以土著部落形式存在。1390年，苏门答腊岛移民米南加保人建立了菲律宾历史上第一个国家——苏禄苏丹国。1450年，阿拉伯商人赛义德·艾布伯克尔在菲律宾南部建立了伊斯兰政权。西班牙于1571年占领马尼拉，建立殖民统治。1898年，美西战争爆发，西班牙战败，与美国签署《巴黎和约》，菲律宾宣告独立，成立菲律宾共和国，但1899年菲律宾沦为美国的殖民地。第二次世界大战结束后，菲律宾再次沦为美国殖民地。1946年7月4日，菲律宾独立，但美国在菲律宾的经济和政治方面享有特权地位。

Spain occupied Manila and established colonial rule in 1571. In 1899, it became an American colony. The Philippines became independent in 1946, but the United States had a privileged economic and political status in the country.

5. 政治经济(Politics and Economy)

菲律宾首都马尼拉，国花茉莉花，货币菲律宾比索。

国家政体为总统制。总统是国家元首、政府首脑兼武装部队总司令。菲律宾议会称国会，是最高立法机构，由参、众两院组成。菲律宾司法权属最高法院和各级法院。主要政党有民主人民力量党、自由党、基督教穆斯林民主力量党等。

菲律宾经济是出口导向型经济，对外部市场依赖较大。第三产业在国民经济中的地位突出，农业和制造业也占相当比重。自20世纪60年代后期采取经济开放政策，积极吸引外资，经济取得较快的发展。外向型工业较发达，成衣、半导体、铜锭、椰油、香蕉等产品出口量较大。菲律宾是世界上最大的椰子出口国。1982年被世界银行列为"中等收入国家"。

菲律宾交通以公路和海运为主。铁路不发达，集中在吕宋岛。航空运输主要由菲律宾航空公司等航运企业经营，全国各主要岛屿间都有航班。

The Philippines' economy is largely based on agriculture, followed by services, manufacturing, and commerce. The transportation in the Philippines is mainly road and sea transport, and the tourism transportation is still convenient.

6. 旅游市场(Tourism Market)

菲律宾十分重视旅游业，国际旅游成为其外汇收入的重要来源之一。

菲律宾旅游部的数据显示，2019年菲律宾接待入境游客共826万人次，超过了820万的目标，比上一年增长15.2%。在菲律宾的客源国和地区排名中，韩国居首位，达198万人次，增长22.5%；中国大陆排名第二，达174万人次，增长近四成；美国第三，达106万人次。

菲律宾一直是我国比较稳定的目的地国和客源国之一。中国文化和旅游部统计数据显示,2018年菲律宾来华旅游人次达到120.30万人。

In 2019, South Korea topped the list of source of visitors to the Philippines, with 1.98 million visitors, up 22.5 percent. Mainland China ranked second with 1.74 million visitors. The United States is the third. The Philippines has always been one of China's relatively stable tourist destinations and sources.

PART 2(第二部分)

Tourism Resources(旅游资源)

Tourism is one of the major contributors to the economy of the Philippines. The country's rich biodiversity is the main tourist attraction. Its beaches, mountains, rainforests, islands and diving spots are among the country's most popular tourist destinations. The country's rich historical and cultural heritage is also one of the attractions of the Philippines.

As an archipelago consisting of about 7 000 islands, the Philippines has numerous beaches, caves and other rock formations. Tourist attractions in the country include the white sand beaches of Boracay, named as the best island in the world by Travel + Leisure in 2012, commercial shopping malls located in Manila including the SM Mall of Asia, Festival Supermall, etc., Banaue Rice Terraces in Ifugao, historic town of Vigan, Chocolate Hills in Bohol, Magellan's Cross in Cebu, Tubbataha Reef in Visayas and others in the rest of the country.

旅游业是菲律宾经济的主要贡献者之一。丰富的生态多样性对游客有很大吸引力,海滩、山脉、热带雨林、岛屿和潜水点是该国最受欢迎的旅游目的地,而丰富的历史和文化遗产造就了菲律宾的文化景观。

菲律宾是一个由7 000多个岛屿组成的群岛,拥有众多海滩、洞穴和多种岩层。长滩岛拥有白色沙滩,是世界上最好的岛屿。还有马尼拉的商业购物中心,包括SM亚洲购物中心、集会超市等。旅游景点还有伊富高省的巴纳韦梯田、维甘历史古城、波霍尔的巧克力山、宿务的麦哲伦十字架、维萨亚斯的图巴塔哈群礁等等。

1. Manila(马尼拉)

Manila is the capital city of the Philippines. It is the home to extensive commerce and seats the executive and judicial branches of the Filipino government. It also contains vast amount of significant architectural and cultural landmarks in the country. Metro Manila contains several notable attractions including a UNESCO World Heritage Site and 45 other cultural heritage landmarks. These cultural attractions are mostly concentrated in the City of Manila and offer a glimpse into the city's Malay, Spanish, and American origins. Popular sites include the Spanish colonial buildings in Intramuros, the World Heritage Site of San Agustin Church, Rizal Park, and a few Art Deco and Revival style buildings like Manila Metropolitan Theater and the National Museum of the Philippines. There are also modern attractions such as the Manila Ocean Park, the integrated resort complex of Resorts World Manila, and the newly opened Solaire Resort & Casino and City of Dreams Manila.

The most popular attractions are the Rizal Park, also called Luneta Park. It is the most popular landmark of Manila. The Monument of the Dr. Jose Rizal, the national hero of the country can be found in the park. Several areas such as the Japanese and Chinese Garden, the Open Auditorium and many more can also be found. A life size depiction of the execution scene of Dr. Rizal in the said park is also one of the attractions.

Intramuros—the 400-year-old fortress was the original "Manila" before the Americans expanded the city and made the fortress just one of the districts. Many historical places can be found inside the district such as the Plaza de Roma, the ruins of the Aduana Building, the Manila Cathedral, the Old Ayuntamiento de Manila, the Palacio del Gobernador, the Casa Manila, the Cuartel de Santa Lucia, San Agustin Church and many more.

Manila Ocean Park is an aquamarine park located in a reclaimed land adjacent to the Quirino Grandstand and Wallace Field. It houses different marine species such as sharks, sting rays, seals, etc.

Manila Chinatown is the oldest Chinatown in the world. It covers most part of the Binondo District. It houses many Chinese stores and boutiques where some are even a hundred-year old shops.

Baywalk is the most distinctive attraction that represents the city together with the Rizal Monument. Baywalk is long promenade along the Roxas Boulevard where the sunset can be seen with a perfect view.

Malacañang Palace is the where the president and his family lives.

马尼拉是菲律宾的首都，是菲律宾政府行政和司法机构的所在地，也是商业中心。这里有大量重要的建筑和文化地标，包括一处世界遗产和45个文化遗产地标。最受欢迎的景点包括西班牙殖民时期的建筑、世界遗产圣奥古斯丁教堂、黎刹公园，以及一些装饰艺术和复兴风格的建筑，如马尼拉大都会剧院和菲律宾国家博物馆。现代化的景点有马尼拉海洋公园、马尼拉云顶世界和新开业的太阳赌场度假村等。

最受欢迎的景点是黎刹公园，它是马尼拉最受欢迎的地标，国家英雄何塞·黎刹博士的纪念碑就在公园里，还有日本花园、中国花园、露天礼堂等。公园里逼真的黎刹博士行刑场景也是吸引游客的地方之一。

有400年历史的市中市要塞是最初的"马尼拉"。马尼拉有许多历史遗迹,如罗马广场、阿杜纳建筑遗址、马尼拉大教堂、马尼拉市政厅、马尼拉总督府、卡撒马尼拉博物馆、圣卢西亚教堂、圣奥古斯丁教堂等。

马尼拉海洋公园是一个海蓝宝石公园,这里有不同的海洋物种,如鲨鱼、刺鳐、海豹等。马尼拉唐人街是世界上最古老的唐人街。最独特的景点是海滨步道,它和黎刹纪念碑都是这座城市的代表,漫步海滨步道可以欣赏到日落的完美景色。

2. El Nido(爱妮岛)

El Nido is a first class municipality and managed resource protected area in the province of Palawan in the Philippines. According to CNNGo, it is the Best Beach and Island destination in the Philippines for its "extraordinary natural splendor and ecosystem". From the towering marble cliffs and enchanting lagoons to its 100 white sandy beaches, lush jungle and mangrove forest, prehistoric caves and waterfalls, El Nido is one of the top tourist destinations in Palawan, which is often referred to as the "Philippines' Last Frontier".

爱妮岛是菲律宾巴拉望省一级自治市和管理资源保护区。因为它"非凡的自然风光和生态系统",被誉为菲律宾最好的海滩和岛屿。爱妮岛有高耸的大理石悬崖、迷人的舄湖、100个白色沙滩、郁郁葱葱的丛林和红树林、史前洞穴和瀑布。爱妮岛是巴拉望的顶级旅游目的地之一,而巴拉望经常被称为"菲律宾最后的边境"。

3. Boracay(长滩岛)

Boracay is a small island in the Philippines located approximately 315 km south of Manila and 2 km off the northwest tip of Panay Island in the Western Visayas region of the Philippines. Boracay Island and its beaches have received awards from numerous travel publications and agencies. Apart from its white sand beaches, Boracay is also famous for being one of the world's top destinations for relaxation. It is also emerging among the top destinations for tranquility and night life.

长滩岛是菲律宾的一个小岛,位于马尼拉以南约315千米。长滩岛及其海滩曾获得许多旅游出版物和旅行社的推荐。除了白色的沙滩,长滩岛是世界上最著名的休闲胜地之一,也是宁静和夜生活的最佳目的地之一。

4. Cebu(宿务)

Cebu is one of the most developed provinces in the Philippines, with Cebu City as the main center of commerce, trade, education and industry in the Visayas. In a decade it has transformed into a global hub for furniture-making, tourism, business processing services, and heavy industry.

Cebu City is a significant cultural centre in the Philippines. The imprint of Spanish and Roman Catholic culture is evident. The city's most famous landmark is Magellan's Cross. This cross, now housed in a chapel, is reputed to have been planted by Ferdinand Magellan (Fernão Magalhães) when he arrived in the Philippines in 1521. Revered by Filipinos, the Magellan's Cross is a symbol of Catholicism in the Philippines.

A few steps away from the Magellan's Cross is the Basilica Minore del Santo Niño (Church of the Holy Child). This is an Augustinian church elevated to the rank of Basilica in 1965 during the 400th year celebration of Catholicism in the Philippines, held in Cebu. The church, which was the first to be established in the islands, is built of hewn stone and features the country's oldest relic, the figure of the Santo Niño de Cebu (Holy Child of Cebu).

宿务是菲律宾最发达的省份之一,是维萨亚地区的主要商业、贸易、教育和工业中心。在十年的时间里,它已经转变为一个全球家具制造、旅游、商业加工服务和重工业中心。

宿务市也是菲律宾重要的文化中心,随处可以看到西班牙和罗马天主教文化的印记。这座城市最著名的地标是麦哲伦十字。这个十字架现在被安置在一个小教堂里,受到菲律宾人的尊敬,麦哲伦十字架在菲律宾是天主教的象征。

离麦哲伦十字架几步之遥的是圣婴圣殿,这座教堂是岛上第一个建立起来的教堂,由凿成的石头建造,并以该国最古老的遗迹——宿务圣婴的雕像为特色。

5. The Tubbataha Reefs Natural Park(图巴塔哈群礁自然公园)

The Tubbataha Reefs Natural Park is a protected area of the Philippines located in the middle of Sulu Sea. In December 1993, the UNESCO declared the Tubbataha Reefs National Park as a World Heritage Site as a unique example of an atoll reef with a very high density of marine species; the North Islet serving as a nesting site for birds and marine turtles. The site is an excellent example of a pristine coral reef with a spectacular 100-meter perpendicular wall, extensive lagoons and two coral islands. In 1999, Ramsar listed Tubbataha as one of the Wetlands of International Importance. In 2008, the reef was nominated at the New 7 Wonders of Nature.

图巴塔哈群礁自然公园是菲律宾苏禄海中部的一个保护区。1993年12月,联合国教科文组织宣布图巴塔哈群礁国家公园为世界遗产,因为它是海洋物种密度非常高的环礁的一个特例;北岛是鸟类和海龟筑巢的地方。1999年,拉姆萨尔将图巴塔哈列为国际重要湿地之一。

6. Baroque Churches of the Philippines(菲律宾巴洛克式教堂)

The Baroque Churches of the Philippines is the official designation to a collection of four Spanish-era churches in the Philippines, upon its inscription to the UNESCO World

Heritage List in 2003. They are also one of the most treasured in the country.

The baroque churches in the Philippines are located in Bao'ai, Santa Maria, Manila and Miagao in Luzon. Among them, St. Augustine Church, La Noestra Señora de la Asuncion Parish Church, and Miagao Church Grounds are the most famous.

菲律宾的巴洛克式教堂有四座,是菲律宾西班牙时代的产物,2003年被联合国教科文组织列入世界遗产名录,它们也是这个国家最珍贵的文物之一。

菲律宾的巴洛克教堂位于菲律宾吕宋岛的巴奥艾、圣玛丽亚、马尼拉和米娅。其中,圣奥古斯丁教堂、奴爱斯特拉·塞纳拉·阿斯姆史奥教堂和比略奴爱巴教堂最为著名。

Section 6 Singapore(新加坡)

PART 1(第一部分)

1. 国土疆域(Territory)

新加坡(新加坡共和国的简称)位于东南亚旅游区马来半岛南端,地处太平洋与印度洋两大洋、亚洲与大洋洲两个旅游区之间的航运要冲,扼马六甲海峡进出口咽喉,是东南亚最繁忙的海陆交通枢纽,素有"东方十字路口"之称。新加坡由新加坡岛及附近63个小岛组成,国土面积724.4平方千米,有"袖珍王国"之称。

Singapore (short for the Republic of Singapore) is located at the southern tip of the Malay Peninsula of the southeast Asia Tourism Region. Singapore is located at the shipping hub between the Pacific Ocean and the Indian Ocean, the two tourism regions of Asia and Oceania. It is the throat of the import and export of the Strait of Malacca. It is the busiest land and sea transportation hub in Southeast Asia and is known as the "Oriental Crossroad". Singapore is composed of the island of Singapore and 63 small islands nearby, covering an area of 724.4 km^2. It is known as the "Pocket Kingdom".

2. 自然风貌(Natural Features)

新加坡地势平坦,起伏不大,平均海拔约15米。中部虽有一些丘陵,但最高的武吉知马山海拔也仅163米。新加坡岛以外的众多小岛,主要分布于北部和南部。其中较大的有德光岛、乌敏岛等。

新加坡属热带海洋气候,终年高温潮湿多雨,植物繁茂,终年常绿,热带植物种类繁多。这里有茂密的热带林、高大的棕榈、美丽的三叶花、世界上为数不多的大片椰林、大规模的兰花园和植物园等,是一个美丽的热带岛国。由于受海洋调节,气候不太炎热,年平均气温为 24~32 ℃,年降水量约 2 345 毫米,一年四季皆宜旅游。但 5—6 月和 9—12 月是两个旅游旺季,5 月和 9 月是旅游最佳时间。

The landscape of Singapore is flat with little ups and downs, with an average elevation of about 15 m. Timah Hill, the highest summit, has an elevation of only 163 m. Singapore is only 136.8 km away from the equator. Its climate is characterized by a tropical marine climate, and is suitable for tourism throughout the year.

3. 人口民族(Population and Ethnicity)

新加坡总人口约 570 万人(2019 年),人口密度每平方千米约 7 868.6 人,是世界上人口密度排名第二的国家。其中,华人占常住人口的 74% 左右,居首位;其次是马来人和印度人。马来语为国语,英语、华语、马来语、泰米尔语为官方语言。新加坡属多宗教国家,主要宗教为佛教、道教、伊斯兰教、基督教和印度教。

Singapore has a total population of about 5.7 million (2019), with Chinese accounting for about 74% of the resident population, ranking first. The population density is about 7 868.6 people per square kilometer, making it the second most densely populated country in the world. Singapore is a multi-religious country, and each ethnic group has its own religious affiliations.

4. 发展简史(Brief History of Development)

新加坡古称淡马锡,在公元 8 世纪之前,它只是个无名的海岛小渔村。8 世纪建国,属室利佛逝王朝。18—19 世纪是马来柔佛王国的一部分。1824 年至二战前沦为英国殖民地。1942 年被日本占领。1945 年日本投降后英国恢复殖民统治。1946 年划为英属殖民地。1959 年实行自治,成为自治邦。1963 年脱离英国管辖加入马来西亚。1965 年 8 月 9 日在李光耀的领导下,成立了新加坡共和国,成为一个总统制的主权独立国家。现在新加坡已成为经济发达的国家。

Singapore was founded in the 8th century AD and was part of the Johor Kingdom of Malaysia in the 18th and 19th centuries. It became a British colony since 1824. In 1963, Singapore seceded from Britain and joined the Federation of Malaysia. In 1965, the Republic of Singapore was founded.

5. 政治经济(Politics and Economy)

首都为新加坡市,国花为胡姬花,货币为新加坡元

新加坡实行议会共和制。总统为国家名义元首,由全民选举产生,任期 6 年。总统委任议会多数党领袖为总理。总统和议会共同行使立法权。议会称国会,实行一院制。议员由公民投票选举产生,占国会议席多数的政党组建政府。新加坡设最高法院和总检察

署。政党主要有人民行动党、新加坡工人党。

新加坡是一个发达的资本主义国家,被誉为"亚洲四小龙"之一,同时凭借着地理优势,成为亚洲重要的金融、服务和航运中心之一。新加坡十分重视绿化和环境卫生,故有"花园城市"的美称。新加坡是东南亚名副其实的区域中心。

新加坡传统经济以商业为主,包括转口贸易、加工出口和航运业等。进入20世纪90年代后,以服务业为发展重心,加速经济国际化、自由化和高科技化,经济得到较快发展。在保持原有的转口贸易、加工出口、航运等为主的经济特色的同时,大力发展制造业、服务业和旅游业,形成了运输、贸易、机械、旅游业和金融服务五大支柱,经济取得令世界瞩目的成就,位居亚洲四小龙之首。

新加坡海、陆、空交通运输十分活跃。新加坡海港是世界上最繁忙的港口之一,海运十分便利。新加坡樟宜国际机场是世界最繁忙的航空港之一,成为联系欧洲、美洲、大洋洲的航运中心。铁路和公路四通八达。

Singapore is a small country with few natural resources, but superior location. They have enhanced advantages and minimized disadvantages and built international trade ports, duty-free shopping centers, international financial centers, world-famous entrepots, trade centers, transportation centers, international conference centers and "garden cities", making the country a veritable regional center in Southeast Asia.

6. 旅游市场(Tourism Market)

新加坡政府十分重视旅游业的发展,20世纪60年代起,新加坡旅游业从无到有,在自身资源先天不足的情况下迅速发展成为亚洲乃至世界重要的旅游目的地之一。新加坡的十大客源市场为中国、印度尼西亚、印度、马来西亚、澳大利亚、日本、菲律宾、南非、美国和越南。

一直以来,新加坡都是中国游客心中广受好评的旅游目的地。2019年,中国赴新加坡旅客超360万人,以年均6.1%的增速,连续3年蝉联新加坡"最大入境客源国"榜首之位。仅2019年第一季度,由中国游客贡献的旅游收益就高达10.9亿新元(约合54.5亿元人民币),远超其他国家。新加坡也是中国的主要客源国之一,中国文化和旅游部的统计数据显示,2018年新加坡来华旅游人数达到97.80万人。

Singapore is one of the most popular tourist destinations in the world. The top ten tourist source markets are China, Indonesia, India, Malaysia, Australia, Japan, the Philippines, South Africa, the United States and Vietnam.

PART 2(第二部分)

Tourism Resources(旅游资源)

Tourism in Singapore is a major industry and contributor to the Singaporean economy, attracting 15 095 152 international tourists in 2014, over twice of Singapore's total population. It is also environmentally friendly, and maintains natural and heritage conservation programs. Along with this, it also has one of the world's lowest crime rates. As English is the dominant one of its four official languages, it is generally easier for tourists to understand when speaking to the local population of the country, for example, when shopping.

The Orchard Road district, which is dominated by multi-storey shopping centres and hotels, can be considered the center of tourism in Singapore. Other popular tourist attractions include the Singapore Zoo, River Safari and Night Safari, which allows people to explore Asian, African and American habitats at night without any visible barriers between guests and the wild animals. The Singapore Zoo has embraced the "open zoo" concept whereby animals are kept in enclosures, separated from visitors by hidden dry or wet moats, instead of caging the animals, while the River Safari, features 10 different ecosystems around the world, including the River Nile, Yangtze River, Mississippi, Amazon as well as the Tundraand has 300 species of animals, including numerous endangered species.

Jurong Bird Park is another zoological garden centred on birds, which is dedicated towards exposing the public to as much species and varieties of birds from around the world as possible, including a flock of one thousand flamingos. The tourist island of Sentosa, which attracts 19 million visitors in 2011, is located in the south of Singapore, consists of about 20-30 landmarks, such as Fort Siloso, which was built as a fortress to defend against the Japanese during World War Ⅱ. Among the latest tourists attractions built in Singapore includes the two integrated resorts which houses casinos, namely Marina Bay Sands and Resorts World Sentosa, a Universal Studios theme park and Gardens by the Bay.

旅游业是新加坡经济的主要产业和贡献者。新加坡还是世界上犯罪率最低的国家之一。

乌节路地区以购物中心和酒店为主，是新加坡的旅游中心。其他受欢迎的旅游景点包括新加坡动物园、河川生态园和夜间野生动物园。

新加坡裕廊飞禽公园是一个以鸟类为中心的动物园，它致力于向公众展示尽可能多的来自世界各地的鸟类和物种。圣淘沙岛位于新加坡南部，由20—30个标志性建筑组成。新加坡最新建成的旅游景点包括两个设有赌场的综合度假村，即滨海湾金沙和圣淘沙名胜世界。

1. Universal Studios Singapore(新加坡环球影城)

Universal Studios Singapore is a theme park located within Resorts World Sentosa on Sentosa Island, Singapore.

Universal Studios Singapore is 20 hectares in size, occupying the easternmost part of the 49-hectare (120-acre) Resorts World Sentosa. There are a total of 24 attractions, of which 18 are original or specially adapted for the park. The park consists of seven themed zones which surround a lagoon. They are Hollywood, New York, Sci-Fi city, Ancient Egypt, The Lost World, Far Far Away and Madagascar. Each zone is based on a blockbuster movie or a television show, featuring their own unique attractions, character appearances, dining and shopping areas. The park features the world's tallest pair of dueling roller coasters that are based on the popular television series, Battlestar Galactica; a castle from the world of Shrekand Monster Rock, a live musical show featuring the Universal Monsters. Universal Studios Singapore has over 30 restaurants and food carts, together with 20 unique retail stores and carts located around the park. Attractions premiering are marked "Premiere" and dining outlets that are certified Halal are marked with "Halal".

新加坡环球影城是一个主题公园，位于新加坡圣淘沙岛上的圣淘沙名胜世界。公园共有24处景点，其中18处是原址或专门为公园而建。该公园包括七个主题区，分别是好莱坞、纽约、科幻城市、古埃及、失落的世界、遥远之地和马达加斯加。每个区域都以一部大片或电视节目为基础，有自己独特的景点、人物形象、餐饮和购物区。

2. Sentosa(圣淘沙)

Sentosa is a relatively large island of Singapore located to its south. Along with a beach-front resort, the island's tourist attractions include Fort Siloso, its historical museum, the Underwater World aquarium and the Tiger Sky Tower. Singapore also features two casinos (integrated resorts), one is the Marina Bay Sands, the other is Resorts World Sentosa (home to Universal Studios Singapore). The proposal of building the integrated resorts was controversial.

圣淘沙岛是位于新加坡南部的一个相对较大的岛屿。除了海滨度假胜地，岛上的旅游景点还包括西乐索炮台、历史博物馆、水下世界水族馆和老虎天空塔。这里有赌场——圣淘沙名胜世界。

3. Clarke Quay(克拉码头)

Clarke Quay is a historical riverside quay in Singapore, located within the Singapore River Planning Area. During the colonial era, Boat Quay was the commercial centre where barge lighters would transport goods upstream to warehouses at Clarke Quay. At present, five blocks of restored warehouses house various restaurants and night clubs. There are also moored Chinese junks (tongkangs) that have been refurbished into floating pubs and restaurants. The Cannery is one of the anchor tenants of the place.

There are over 5 different concepts in one block. Another anchor tenant, The Arena, will be home to Singapore's First Permanent Illusion Show (starting August 2008) starring J C Sum and "Magic Babe" Ning. The G-MAX reverse bungee, the first in Singapore, is located at the entrance which opened in November 2003. Notable restaurants and nightclubs include Hooters and Indochine. River cruises and river taxis on the Singapore River can be accessed from Clarke Quay. One of its most popular attractions is its exciting host of CQ's signature events happening once every quarter.

克拉克码头是新加坡历史悠久的河边码头。在殖民时代,这里是商业中心,驳船将货物从上游运输到克拉克码头的仓库。这里有停泊的中国舢板船,经过整修后变成了漂浮的酒吧和餐馆;从克拉克码头可以到达新加坡河上的水上游船和水上出租车处。

4. Marina Bay Sands(滨海湾金沙)

Marina Bay Sands is an integrated resort fronting Marina Bay in Singapore. Developed by Las Vegas Sands, it is billed as the world's most expensive standalone casino property at $8 billion, including the land cost. Marina Bay Sands has three 55-story hotel towers which were topped out in July 2009. The three towers are connected by a 1 hectare roof terrace, Sands Sky Park.

In front of the three towers include a Theatre Block, a Convention and Exhibition Facilities Block, as well as the Casino Block, which have up to 1 000 gaming tables and 1 400 slot machines. The ArtScience Museum is constructed next to the three blocks and has the shape of a lotus. Its roof is retractable, providing a waterfall through the roof of collected rainwater when closed in the day and laser shows when opened at night. In front of the Event Plaza is Wonder Full, a light and water show that is the largest in Southeast Asia and was produced by Laservision.

The Sky Park has the world's longest elevated swimming pool, with a 146-meter vanishing edge, 191 meters above ground. The pools are made up of 422 000 pounds of stainless steel and can hold 376 500 gallons (1 424 cubic meters) of water. The SkyPark also has rooftop restaurants such as The Sky on 57 (by Justin Quek), nightclubs such as KU DÉTA, The Club facilities, gardens, hundreds of trees and plants, and a public observatory deck on the cantilever with 360-degree views of the Singapore skyline.

滨海湾金沙是一个综合度假胜地。滨海湾金沙拥有三座55层的酒店大楼,三座塔楼由1公顷的屋顶露台——金沙空中花园连接。

三座塔的前面包括一个剧院大楼、一个会议展览设施大楼,以及拥有多达1 000张赌桌和1 400台老虎机的赌场大楼。艺术科学博物馆建在三个街区的旁边,呈莲花的形状,屋顶是可伸缩的,白天关闭时,收集的雨水会形成瀑布,晚上打开时,就会出现激光。活动广场前有水幕灯光秀Wonder Full,是东南亚最大的水幕灯光秀。

空中花园拥有世界上最长的空中游泳池,游泳池由42.2万磅不锈钢组成,可容纳

1 424立方米的水。在悬臂上的公共观景台上,可以360度看到新加坡的天际线。

5. Singapore Botanic Gardens(新加坡植物园)

The Singapore Botanic Gardens is a 156-year-old tropical garden located at the fringe of the Singapore's main shopping belt. It is one of three gardens, and the only tropical garden, to be honored as a UNESCO World Heritage Site. Early in the nation's independence, Singapore Botanic Gardens' expertise helped to transform the island into a tropical Garden City, an image and moniker for which the nation is widely known. Singapore's Botanic Gardens is the only one in the world that opens from 5:00 a.m. to midnight every day of the year. More than 10 000 species of flora is spread over its 82-hectare area, which is stretched vertically; the longest distance between the northern and southern ends is 2.5 km. The Botanic Gardens receives about 4.5 million visitors annually.

National Orchid Garden is the main attraction within the Botanic Garden. Located on the mid-western side of the Garden, the hilly 3-hectare site has a collection of more than 1 000 species and 2 000 hybrids of orchids. The Singapore Botanic Gardens has a small tropical rainforest of around 6 hectares in size, which is older than the gardens themselves. Located next to the National Orchid Garden, this 1-hectare garden brings together members of the Zingiberaceae family. Jacob Ball as Children's Garden is located at the quieter northern end of the Botanic Gardens. It has its own visitor centre with a café. It opened on Children's Day, October 1, 2007. The National Parks Board claims it is Asia's first children's garden. There are play areas like the Water Play area, a small playground, tree-houses with slides, and a maze. There are also interactive exhibits that teach how photosynthesis takes place, and a mini-garden that showcases how plants may be used to make dyes and beverages, or as herbs.

新加坡植物园是一个有着156年历史的热带花园,位于新加坡主要购物区的边缘。作为三大花园之一,它是唯一一个被联合国教科文组织列为世界遗产的热带花园。园内有10 000多种植物,每年接待约450万游客。

国立胡姬花园是植物园的主要景点,有超过1 000个兰花品种和2 000种杂交兰花。新加坡植物园有一个大约6公顷的小热带雨林,比植物园本身还要古老。互动展览区展示光合作用的过程;迷你花园展示植物如何被用来制造染料、饮料或草药。

6. Merlion Park(鱼尾狮公园)

Merlion Park, a landmark of Singapore, is a major tourist attraction at One Fullerton, Singapore, near the Central Business District. Two structures of the Merlion are located at the park. The original merlion structure measures 8.6 metres tall, while a Merlion cub located near the original statue measures 2 metres tall.

鱼尾狮公园是新加坡的地标性建筑,位于新加坡中央商务区附近,是一个主要的旅游景点。

7. Jurong Bird Park in Singapore(新加坡裕廊飞禽公园)

Located in Jurong west, an area of 20.2 hectares. Keep the park has more than 400 kinds of birds, about 3 500 of which 20 percent are threatened. Park identified a wide range of birds from around the world, there are flamingo from Spain, cassowary from Guinea, colorful starlings, and Antarctic penguins and other birds knowledge. Other major attractions include the Museum, African Waterfall Aviary, Lory Loft, Southeast Asia aviary and award-winning African Wetlands. Here visitors can also visit the park behind the daily operations, how to look at the staff to take care of endangered bird chicks and abandoned eggs.

新加坡裕廊飞禽公园有超过400种鸟类,约3 500只,其中濒危鸟类占20%。例如,有来自西班牙的火烈鸟,来自几内亚的食火鸟,彩色的椋鸟,还有南极企鹅。游客还可以参观公园的日常操作场所,看看工作人员如何照顾濒临灭绝的雏鸟和遗弃的鸟蛋。

8. Singapore Zoo(新加坡动物园)

The Singapore Zoo, formerly known as the Singapore Zoological Gardens and commonly known as the Mandai Zoo, occupies 26 hectares on the margins of Upper Seletar Reservoir within Singapore's heavily forested central catchment area. It is operated by Wildlife Reserves Singapore, who also manage the neighbouring Night Safari, River Safari and the Jurong Bird Park. There are over 300 species of animals in the zoo, of which 34% are considered to be threatened species. The zoo attracts 1.9 million visitors each year.

From the beginning, Singapore Zoo followed the modern trend of displaying animals in naturalistic, open exhibits with hidden barriers, moats, and glass between the animals and visitors. It houses the largest captive colony of orangutans in the world.

新加坡动物园位于上Seletar水库的边缘。它由新加坡野生动物保护区运营。动物园里有300多种动物,其中34%是濒危物种。动物园以自然的方式展示动物,在动物和游客之间设置隐藏的屏障、护城河和玻璃。

9. Buddha Tooth Relic Temple(佛牙寺龙华院)

The Buddha Tooth Relic Temple is a Buddhist temple and museum complex located in the Chinatown district of Singapore. The temple is based on the Tang Dynasty architectural style and built to house the tooth relic of the historical Buddha. The ground breaking ceremony was conducted on March 13, 2005. Costing $62 million and two years later, a soft launch was held to coincide with the 2007 Vesak Day celebration. It is claimed that the relic of Buddha from which it gains its name was found in 1980 in a collapsed stupa in Myanmar. Since opening, the temple has become a popular attraction in Chinatown. Simple vegetarian fare is served in the basement of the temple, though donations are accepted.

佛牙寺龙华院是位于新加坡唐人街区的一座佛教寺庙和博物馆综合体。这座寺庙是为了存放佛牙舍利而根据唐代建筑风格建造的，自从开放以来，这座寺庙已经成为唐人街的热门景点。

10. Museum(博物馆)

Singapore has four major museums depicting the art and history of the country and of the region. The Asian Civilisations Museum specializes in the material history of China, Southeast Asia, South Asia and West Asia, from which the diverse ethnic groups of Singapore trace their ancestry, while the Peranakan Museum, the first of its kind in the world, explores Peranakan cultures in Singapore and other former Straits Settlements in Malacca and Penang, and other Peranakan communities in Southeast Asia. Singapore's National Museum of Singapore is the oldest museum in the country, with its history dating back to 1849, mainly showcases collections of nation-building and the history of Singapore from the 14th century in a story-telling approach, while the Singapore Art Museum is a contemporary art museum focusing on art practices in Singapore, Southeast Asia and Asia.

新加坡有四个主要的博物馆展示国家和地区的艺术和历史。亚洲文明博物馆专门研究中国、东南亚、南亚和西亚的历史；土生华人博物馆则是世界上第一个此类博物馆，展示的是新加坡土生华人的文化。新加坡国家博物馆是全国最古老的博物馆，展示了国家建设的成就和新加坡的历史；新加坡艺术博物馆是一个展示当代艺术的博物馆。

Section 7 Malaysia(马来西亚)

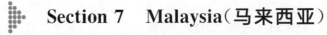

PART 1(第一部分)

1. 国土疆域(Territory)

马来西亚领土位于东南亚旅游区，地处太平洋与印度洋的交汇处，由马来半岛南部的西马来西亚(简称"西马")、婆罗洲北部的沙捞越与沙巴(简称"东马")两个部分组成。国土面积约 33 万平方千米。

Malaysia is located in the Southeast Asia Tourism Region, at the intersection of the Pacific and Indian Oceans. It consists of West Malaya in the southern part of the Malay Peninsula, Sarawak and Sabah (East Malaysia) in the northern part of Borneo. The land area is about 330 000 km².

2. 自然风貌(Natural features)

马来西亚西马地区地势北高南低,中部是山,向东西两侧逐渐降低,沿海为平原。马来西亚地形较复杂,自然旅游资源较丰富。特别是沙捞越森林覆盖面积占 90% 以上,显花植物达 9 000 种之多,占全世界的三分之一,是极佳的旅游胜地。

马来西亚位于赤道附近,属热带雨林气候,终年高温多雨,无四季变化,只存在旱、雨季的区别。沿海平原地区年平均气温在 25~28 ℃,山区年平均气温 22~28 ℃。马来西亚全年气候稳定,四季皆宜旅游。

The landscape of Western Malaysia region is high in the north and low in the south, mountains in the middle, decreasing gently to the east and west sides, and the coastal plains. Located in a low latitude area, Malaysia's climate is marine, and suitable for tourism throughout the year.

3. 人口民族(Population and ethnicity)

马来西亚人口约 3 275 万(2021 年),人口密度为每平方千米 99.24 人。主要民族为马来人、华人和印度人,其中马来人占 69%,华人占 23%。官方语言为马来语,英语为通用语,华语使用也较广泛。主要宗教为伊斯兰教(逊尼派),伊斯兰教为国教,其他宗教有佛教、印度教和基督教。

Malaysia has a population of about 32 750 000 (2021) with a population density of 99.24 persons per square kilometer, Malays 69% and Chinese 23%. The main population in Malaysia professes Islam, Buddhism, Hinduism and Christianity, with Islam as Malaysia's official religion.

4. 发展简史(Brief history of development)

公元前数百年,马来半岛就有一个叫吉打王国的国家。之后,马来半岛上的小王国一直处于分合不定的局面,不统一的分裂状态从公元 5 世纪一直延续到公元 1400 年。公元 1400 年,马来西亚的第一个封建王国马六甲王国开始出现。1511 年马来西亚沦为葡萄牙殖民地。1641 年马六甲被荷兰殖民者占领。1786 年,英国人开始对马来半岛进行长达 171 年的统治。二战期间,日本对婆罗洲的沙捞越与沙巴进行了 3 年多的统治。1957 年 8 月 31 日正式宣布独立,1963 年 9 月 16 日马来西亚成立。

In 1400 AD, the Kingdom of Malacca, the first feudal kingdom of Malaysia, began to emerge. In 1511, Malaysia became a colony of Portugal. Independence was officially declared on August 31, 1957 and Malaysia was founded on September 16, 1963.

5. 政治经济(Politics and economy)

首都为吉隆坡,国花为朱槿(又名扶桑),货币为马来西亚令吉。

马来西亚是君主立宪制国家,实行议会内阁制。国家最高法律是马来西亚联邦宪法。国家对内对外的最高代表被称为元首,君主即马来西亚最高元首,而政府首脑是总理,马来西亚内阁是联邦政府行政部门。国会,由上议院和下议院组成,是马来西亚最高立法机构。司法机构由联邦法院、伊斯兰法庭和特别军事法庭组成。政党有40多个,主要有希望联盟、国民阵线等。

马来西亚为亚洲新兴工业国之一。电子业、制造业、建筑业、石化、钢铁、纺织、加工业较发达。橡胶、棕油、胡椒产量居世界前列。锡产量长期居世界首位,有"锡和橡胶王国"的美誉。

高速公路网络比较发达,主要城市中心、港口和重要工业区都有高速公路连接。民航公司主要有马来西亚航空公司(马航)和亚洲航空公司(亚航)。该国共有25个机场,其中国际机场7个。

Malaysia is one of the emerging industrial countries in Asia. It is highly developed in electronics, manufacturing, construction, petrochemical, iron and steel, textile, processing industry. The output of rubber, palm oil and pepper all ranks first in the world. The production of tin has long been No. 1 in the world, so it has the reputation of "Tin and Rubber Kingdom".

6. 旅游市场(Tourism Market)

马来西亚独特的历史文化与自然资源,加上它地处东南亚中心地带,具有便利的海洋、航空运输条件,拥有相对完善的旅游服务配套设施,这些都为旅游业的发展奠定了良好基础。马来西亚十分重视发展旅游业,各州均设有旅游协会,大力发展旅行社,加快建设旅馆(现拥有世界一流的"希尔顿""美伦""联邦""总统"等高级大型酒店),加速建设旅游景点,积极开展宣传促销活动,旅游业发展迅速。

马来西亚实行以政府为主导的旅游业发展模式,旅游业已经成为马来西亚国民经济的三大支柱产业之一。旅游业收入不仅占到国内生产总值的15.2%,而且提供了23.5%的就业岗位。2018年,马来西亚接待游客2 583万人次。2019年马来西亚共接待国际游客2 610万人次,旅游外汇收入861.4亿令吉。新加坡、印尼、中国、泰国是马来西亚的主要旅游客源地。

中国是马来西亚第三大入境客源市场及第二大国际旅游收入来源国。2018年,马来西亚共接待290万中国游客,比2017年增长29%。2019年1月至9月,马来西亚接待中国游客达 240 万,增长 5.7%。

马来西亚一直是我国比较稳定的客源国之一,中国文化和旅游部的统计数据显示,2018 年,马来西亚来华旅游人次达到 129.07 万。2019 年前十个月,马来西亚来华游客 107.5 万,增长 7.9%。

Tourism is one of Malaysia's three pillar industries. Malaysia's main tourist sources are Singapore, Indonesia, China and Thailand. China is Malaysia's third largest inbound tourist market and second largest source of international tourism revenue.

PART 2(第二部分)

Tourism Resources(旅游资源)

Malaysia ranked 10th place in the world and 2nd place in Southeast Asia for tourist arrivals.

马来西亚的旅游人数在世界排名第十,在东南亚排名第二。

1. Kuala Lumpur(吉隆坡)

Kuala Lumpur is the national capital and most populous global city in Malaysia. The major tourist destinations in Kuala Lumpur include Petronas Twin Towers, the Merdeka Square, the House of Parliament, the Petaling Street, the National Palace (Istana Negara), the Kuala Lumpur Tower, the National Museum, the Central Market, Kuala Lumpur City Gallery, the National Monument, and religious sites such as the Jamek Mosque.

The Istana Negara (Malay for National Palace) is the official residence of the King of Malaysia. It is located at Jalan Duta. The palace complex has an area of 97.65 hectares, 22 domes.

吉隆坡是马来西亚的首都和全球人口最多的城市之一。吉隆坡的主要旅游目的地包括双子塔、独立广场、国会大厦、茨厂街、国家皇宫、吉隆坡塔、国家博物馆、中央市场、吉隆坡城市画廊、国家纪念碑和宗教场所,如占美清真寺。

马来西亚国家皇宫是马来西亚国王的官邸,位于吉隆坡大使路。宫殿建筑群占地 97.65 公顷,有 22 个圆顶。

The National Mosque of Malaysia is located in Kuala Lumpur. It has a capacity of 15 000 people and is situated among 53 000 m² of beautiful gardens. The mosque is a bold and modern approach in reinforced concrete, symbolic of the aspirations of a then newly independent Malaysia. Its key features are a 73-metre-high minaret and a 16-pointed star concrete main roof. The main roof is reminiscent of an open umbrella, the minaret's cap a folded one. The folded plates of the concrete main roof are a creative solution to achieving the larger spans required in the main gathering hall. Reflecting pools and fountains spread throughout the compound.

马来西亚国家清真寺位于吉隆坡,坐落在53 000平方米的美丽花园中,可容纳15 000人。这座清真寺采用钢筋混凝土建造,大胆而现代,象征着当时刚刚独立的马来西亚的愿景。清真寺的主要特点是73米高的尖塔和16个角的星形混凝土主屋顶。主屋顶像一把打开的雨伞,尖塔就像一个折叠的帽子。混凝土主屋顶的折板是一个创造性的方案,可以达到主聚会大厅所需的跨度。水池和喷泉遍布整个院落。

2. Sabah(沙巴)

Sabah is Malaysia's easternmost state, one of two Malaysian states on the island of Borneo. Sabah currently has six national parks. One of these, the Kinabalu National Park, was designated as a World Heritage Site in 2000. It is the first of two sites in Malaysia to obtain this status, the other being the Gunung Mulu National Park in Sarawak.

Sipadan Island is Malaysia's sole oceanic island, rising 600 m from the sea floor and only 40 000 m^2 in size. Surrounded by crystal clear waters, the island is a treasure trove of some of the most amazing species such as sea eagles, kingfishers, sunbirds, starlings, wood pigeons, coconut crab, turtles, bumphead parrotfish and barracudas.

The Tunku Abdul Rahman Marine Park comprises a cluster of five idyllic islands, Pulau Manukan, Pulau Mamutik, Pulau Sulug, Pulau Gaya and Pulau Sapi, spread over 4 929 hectares, of which two-thirds is sea. The islands have soft white beaches that are teeming with fish and coral, and are home to a variety of exotic flora and fauna such as the intriguing megapode (Burung Tambun), a chicken look-alike bird with large feet that makes a meowing sound like a cat.

沙巴是马来西亚最东端的一个州,是婆罗洲岛上的两个马来西亚州之一。沙巴目前有六个国家公园。其中京那巴鲁国家公园是世界遗产,另一个是沙捞越的姆鲁山国家公园。西巴丹岛是马来西亚唯一的海洋岛屿,海拔600米,面积只有4万平方米。东姑阿都拉曼海洋公园由五个田园诗般的岛屿组成,分别是玛奴观岛、玛木堤岛、苏禄岛、嘉亚岛和沙碧岛。这些岛屿有柔软的白色海滩,到处都是鱼类和珊瑚,是各种奇异动植物的家园。

3. Sarawak(沙捞越)

Sarawak is one of the two Malaysian states on the island of Borneo. Sarawak has an equatorial climate with tropical rainforests and abundant animal and plant species. The state has several prominent cave systems at Gunung Mulu National Park. Sarawak Museum is the oldest museum in Borneo. Cultural performances are also presented here. Sarawak Museum houses a collection of artefact such as pottery, textiles, and woodcarving tools from various ethnic tribes in Sarawak, and also ethnographic materials of local cultures. The museum building preserves its French architecture. Sarawak Cultural Village is located at the foot of Mount Santubong, Kuching. Known as the "living museum", it showcases the various ethnic groups carry out traditional activities in their respective traditional houses. Miri is a coastal city in northeastern Sarawak, Malaysia. Miri is the main tourist gateway to Gunung Mulu National Park, Loagan Bunut National Park, Lambir Hills National Park, Niah National Park and Miri-Sibuti Coral Reef National Park.

沙捞越是婆罗洲岛上两个马来西亚州之一。沙捞越属赤道气候,热带雨林和动植物种类丰富。该州在姆鲁山国家公园有几个著名的洞穴系统。沙捞越博物馆是婆罗洲最古老的博物馆,它收藏了来自沙捞越各民族部落的陶器、纺织品和木雕工具等文物,以及当地文化的民族志资料。

4. Malacca(马六甲)

Malacca City, formerly known as Kota Melaka, is the capital city of the Malaysian state of Malacca. It is one of the Malay's oldest cities. The Melaka Sultanate Palace was built to represent the Malay culture and Malaccan history during the sultanate era. The building was constructed without the using any nails. The city also includes a variety of other cultural attractions such as the Chinatown, Little India and Portuguese Settlement. The Cheng Ho Cultural Museum is the site where Zheng He, a famous Muslim Chinese voyager, was believed to have set up a large warehouse complex along the northern side of the Malacca River, while the Straits Chinese Jewellery Museum is a site where there has been a collection of Chinese jewellery design and motifs since the establishment of relations between Malacca and the Ming Dynasty of China. The Dutch Square is an area surrounded by Dutch buildings such as the Stadthuys, Christ Church, Queen Victoria's Fountain, and Chinese settlers structure of Clock Tower.

马六甲市是马来西亚马六甲州的首府。它是马来西亚最古老的城市之一。马六甲苏丹皇宫代表了马来文化和马六甲苏丹时期的历史,这座建筑没有使用任何钉子。郑和文化博物馆是中国著名的穆斯林航海家郑和在马六甲河北侧建造大型仓库的所在地,而中国珠宝博物馆则是马六甲与中国明朝建交以来收藏中国珠宝设计和图案的场所。

5. Gunung Mulu National Park(姆鲁山国家公园)

The Gunung Mulu National Park is a national park in Miri Division, Sarawak, Malaysia, it is a UNESCO World Heritage Site that encompasses caves and karst formations in a mountainous equatorial rainforest setting. The park is famous for its caves and the expeditions that have been mounted to explore them and their surrounding rainforest, most notably the Royal Geographical Society Expedition of 1977-1978, which saw over 100 scientists in the field for 15 months. This initiated a series of over 20 expeditions now drawn together as the Mulu Caves Project. The national park is named after Mount Mulu, the second highest mountain in Sarawak.

穆鲁山国家公园位于马来西亚沙捞越的美里区,被联合国教科文组织列入世界遗产,它包括赤道雨林山区的洞穴和喀斯特地貌,以开展洞穴和雨林的探险活动而闻名。

Section 8　India(印度)

PART 1(第一部分)

1. 国土疆域(Territory)

印度位于南亚次大陆,东北与中国、尼泊尔、不丹、孟加拉国接壤,东部与缅甸为邻,西北与巴基斯坦毗邻,东临孟加拉湾,西濒阿拉伯海,东南部与斯里兰卡隔海相望。面积约298万平方千米,是南亚面积最大的国家。

India is located in the South Asian subcontinent, adjacent to China, Nepal, Bhutan, Bangladesh in the northeast, Myanmar in the east, Pakistan in the northwest, bay of Bengal in the east, Arabian Sea in the west, Sri Lanka across the sea in the southeast. With an area of 2.98 million km^2, it is the largest country in South Asia.

2. 自然风貌(Natural Features)

印度地形大致可分为三部分:北部为高山区,有喜马拉雅山脉,高峰耸立,深谷幽邃,人烟稀少,交通不便;中部为平原区,印度河—恒河平原是世界古代文明的发祥地之一,开发历史悠久,历史文物古迹丰富;南部为高原区,德干高原构成印度半岛的主体。

印度地处低纬度,北回归线大致横贯中部,南临辽阔的热带海洋,北有高山阻挡冷空气的侵入,大部分地区属热带季风气候。

The landscape of India can be roughly divided into three parts: high mountains in the north, plains in the middle and plateaus in the south; The main rivers are the Indus and the Ganges; Located in low latitudes, India has a tropical monsoon climate.

3. 人口民族(Population and Ethnicity)

印度人口总数为13.24亿人(2021年),仅次于中国,位居世界第二,人口密度444.3

人/平方千米。

印度号称民族、宗教和语言的博物馆。印度有100多个民族,其中印度斯坦族人数最多,约占全国人口的46.3%;其他较大的民族为泰卢固族、马拉提族、泰米尔族、孟加拉族等。官方语言为印地语和英语。

宗教对印度社会有很深刻的影响,绝大部分居民信奉印度教,教徒占总人口的80.5%。其他宗教有伊斯兰教、基督教、锡克教、佛教和耆那教等。

India is the second-most populous country in the world (after China), with an estimated population of 1.324 billion people (in 2021). India is known as the museums of nationality, religion and language. Religion has a deep influence on Indian society, with about 80.5% of the population professing Hinduism.

4. 发展简史(Brief History of Development)

印度是历史悠久的文明古国之一。公元前2500年至公元前800年,雅利安人来到印度河流域,创造出前所未有的文明,这个时期史称"吠陀时期"。公元前6世纪,印度国内出现了十几个国家,进入列国纷争时期。公元前324年至公元前187年建立的孔雀王朝是印度历史上第一个统一的奴隶制国家,在阿育王统治时期达到全盛。公元320年,建立芨多王朝,其势力不断扩大,逐渐统一了印度。孔雀王朝和芨多王朝是印度人自己建立的王朝,它们是印度历史上的鼎盛时期。公元320年至公元606年,印度的封建制全面确立。16世纪,自称是英雄成吉思汗后裔的巴布儿打败德里的洛提王朝,宣布自己为印度斯坦大帝,建立了印度历史上的最后一个王朝——莫卧儿王朝。1757年印度逐步论为英国的殖民地。1849年,英国殖民者侵占全印度。1947年6月,英国通过《蒙巴顿方案》,实行印巴分治。8月15日,印度人民在民族英雄甘地的领导下,经过不懈的斗争,成立印度自治领,从而结束了英国在印度长达190年的殖民统治。1950年1月26日,印度宣布成立共和国,但仍为英联邦成员国。

From 2500 BC, to 800 BC the Aryans came to the Indus Valley, known as the Vedic period in the history. From 324 BC to 187 BC, the Maurya Dynasty was established; In 320, Gupta Dynasty was established. The Mughal Dynasty was established in the 16th century. After 1757, India gradually became a British colony. In June 1947, Britain put forward Mountbatten Plan and the Partition of India. On January 26, 1950, India was proclaimed a republic.

5. 政治经济(Politics and Economy)

首都为新德里。印度未正式确定国花,一般认为是莲花。货币为印度卢比。

印度是一个联邦制国家,总统是国家元首,但其职责是象征性的,实权由总理掌握。总统任期5年,由一个特设的选举机构间接选举产生。行政权力由以总理为首的部长会议行使。行政机构由总统、总理和各部部长组成。印度的立法权归议会所有,议会分为上下两院。最高法院是最高司法权力机关。主要政党有印度国民大会党和印度人民党。

印度是世界上经济发展最快的国家之一,已经建成较完整的工业体系,纺织、食品、精密仪器、汽车、医药、钢铁、船舶、电子、航空和空间技术等部门发展迅速,棉纱及棉制品、珠宝制品、成衣、医药及化工制品、皮革及制品、机械及五金制品、铁砂石出口量较大。印度是世界上公认的最大的软件供应国之一。印度农业和服务业是最大的经济部门。

India was one of the fastest growing major economy in the world. It has built a relatively complete industrial system. India is known publicly as one of the world's largest software suppliers, agriculture and services are the largest economic sectors.

6. 旅游市场(Tourism Market)

印度政府采取各种积极措施吸引国外旅游者。如在发展宗教文化旅游、历史文化旅游、观光旅游的同时,大力开发海滩旅游地和冒险旅游地,组织各种国际会议,组织到野生动物保护区游览;增建旅馆、改善条件、提高旅游设施标准,兼顾高档和廉价旅游市场等。

近年来,印度经济增长迅速,旅游业发展迅猛。2019 年 11 月,世界经济论坛(WEF)发布的《2019 年旅游业竞争力报告》显示,在全球 140 个国家和地区中,印度排名第 34 位,比 2017 年提升 6 位,上升势头明显。

印度旅游部的数据显示,2018 年,印度外国游客数量从 2017 年的 1 004 万人次增加到 2018 年的 1 056 万,增长率为 5.2%。旅游业作为国家的外汇创收部门继续发挥着重要作用,2017 年旅游外汇收入 273.1 亿美元,2018 年旅游外汇收入 285.9 亿美元,增长 4.7%。

2018 年印度在国际游客中的占比为 1.2%。2018 年抵达亚太地区的国际游客中有 5% 来自印度,排名第七。2018 年印度的前 15 大客源国是孟加拉国、美国、英国、斯里兰卡、加拿大、澳大利亚、马来西亚、中国、德国、俄罗斯、法国、日本、新加坡、尼泊尔和泰国。这 15 个国家的游客约占印度外国游客总数的 75.33%。

印度出境游发展也较快。印度旅游局的数据显示,2017 年印度出境游旅客为 2 394 万人,2018 年印度出境人数为 2 629 万人,增长 9.8%。

印度是中国极具潜力的目的地国和比较重要的客源国。1981 年,来自中国的入境人数仅为 1 371 人,2018 年增长到 281 768 人,复合年均增长率为 32.4%。在印度的旅游客源国中,中国排名第八,占其总入境人数的 2.67%。2018 年,印度来华旅游达到 86.33 万人次,增长较快。

The Indian government has taken various active measures to attract foreign tourists. For example, while developing religious culture tourism, historical culture tourism, and sightseeing tourism, the governments exploit more beach and adventure tourism destinations, organize various international conferences, visit wildlife reserves, build more hotels, improve conditions, raise the standard of tourism facilities, and give consideration to both high-end and low-cost tourism markets. While developing the surrounding tourism markets, they hope to attract more tourists from Western Europe, the United States, Japan, Australia and other countries. In 2018, China was the 8th largest tourist source market to India.

PART 2(第二部分)

Tourism Resources(旅游资源)

There are 38 World Heritage Sites in India that are recognized by UNESCO as of 2019. India's first two sites inscribed on the list at the Seventh Session of the World Heritage held in 1983 were the Agra Fort and the Ajanta Caves. Over the years, 36 more heritages have been inscribed, including 7 natural heritages, 30 cultural heritages and 1 mixed heritage of culture and nature, ranking sixth in the world in quantity. The cultural heritages in India are marked by their brilliant craftsmanship on stone. Most of the temples of India which are inscribed on this list are built in stone, without any mortar and with sculpture carved on it.

截至2019年,印度共有38处世界遗产。1983年被列入名单的两处遗址是阿格拉古堡和阿旃陀石窟。多年来,又增加了36处遗产,其中自然遗产7处,文化遗产30处,文化与自然混合遗产1处,数量居世界第六位。印度的文化遗产以其精湛的石头工艺而著称,列入世界遗产的大多数印度寺庙都是用石头建造的,没使用任何灰浆,上面雕刻着雕塑。

1. Red Fort Complex(红堡建筑群)

Red Fort Complex, also known as Lal Qila, is a palace fort built in the 17th century by Shah Jahan, the fifth Mughal emperor as part of his new capital city of Shahjahanabad. Located to the north of Delhi. It represents the glory of the Mughal rule and is considered the high point of Mughal architectural, artistic aesthetic creativity. The architectural design of the structures built within the fort represents a blend of Persian, Timuri and Indian architectural styles; Isfahan, the Persian Capital is said to have provided the inspiration to build the Red Fort Complex. The planning and design of this complex, in a geometrical grid plan with pavilion structures, was the precursor of several monuments which were built later in Rajasthan, Delhi, Agra and other places. The palace complex has been fortified by an enclosure wall built with red sand stone (hence the name Red Fort).

红堡建筑群位于德里北部,是17世纪由第五位莫卧儿皇帝沙·贾汗修建的宫殿式堡垒,是其新首都沙贾汗纳巴德的一部分,它代表了莫卧儿统治的荣耀,被认为是莫卧儿建筑、艺术和审美创造力的顶峰。堡垒内的建筑设计融合了波斯、蒙古和印度的建筑风格。红堡因宫殿建筑群周围有一道用红砂岩建造的围墙而得名。

2. Humayun's Tomb(胡马雍陵)

Humayun's Tomb, Delhi, the first tomb built with several innovations, set at the centre of luxurious gardens with water channels, was the precursor monument to the Taj Mahal (built a century later). It was built in 1570 and was inscribed as a UNESCO World Heritage Site in 1993 for its cultural importance. Its Mughal architectural style has been acclaimed as the "necropolis of the Mughal Dynasty" for its double domed elevation provided with chhatris. Apart from the tomb of Humayun, the funerary also has 150 tombs of various members of the royal family. The tomb is built with a char-bagh (fourfold) layout with two gates, one on the south and the other on the west. It has a number of water channels, a pavilion and a bath. The tomb set on an irregular octagonal plinth has a raised dome of 42.5 meters high, covered by marble slabs and decorated with chhatris.

位于德里的胡马雍陵墓建于1570年,坐落在有水道的豪华花园中心,是第一座有众多创新之处的陵墓,泰姬陵的前身就是这座陵墓。1993年它被联合国教科文组织列为世界文化遗产。其莫卧儿建筑风格被誉为"莫卧儿王朝的墓地"。

3. Ajanta Caves(阿旃陀石窟)

Ajanta Caves listed as a UNESCO World Heritage Site, are Buddhist caves that were built in two phases, the first phase was from the 2nd century BC. In the second phase, further additions were made during the 5th and 6th centuries AD of the Gupta period. The caves depict richly decorated paintings, frescoes, which are reminiscent of the Sigiriya paintings in Sri Lanka and sculptures. As a whole, there are 31 rock-cut cave monuments which are unique representations of the religious art of Buddhism.

阿旃陀石窟为佛教石窟,被联合国教科文组织列为世界文化遗产。石窟内有丰富的绘画、壁画和雕塑。石窟共有31处洞穴遗迹,是佛教艺术的独特代表。

4. Ellora Caves(埃洛拉石窟)

Ellora Caves also known as Ellora Complex are a cultural mix of religious arts of Buddhism, Hinduism and Jainism. These are 34 monasteries and temples sculpted contiguously into rock walls of a high basalt cliff, which are seen along a length of 2 kilometres. Dated to 600 to 1000 AD, they are a reflection of artistic creation of the ancient civilization of India. This cultural property has been inscribed under the UNESCO World Heritage List in 1983.

埃洛拉石窟,也叫埃洛拉石窟群,是佛教、印度教和耆那教宗教文化艺术的混合建筑群。1983年,它被列入联合国教科文组织世界遗产名录。

5. Elephanta Caves(埃勒凡塔石窟或象岛石窟)

The Elephanta Caves are a network of sculpted caves located on Elephant Island, or

Gharapuri (literally "the city of caves") in Mumbai Harbour, 10 kilometres to the east of the city of Mumbai. The island, located on an arm of the Arabian Sea, consists of two groups of caves—the first is a large group of five Hindu caves, the second, a smaller group of two Buddhist caves. The Hindu caves contain rock-cut stone sculptures, representing the Shaiva Hindu sect, dedicated to the god Shiva. The rock-cut architecture of the caves is dated to between the 5th and 8th centuries, although the identity of the original builders is still a subject of debate. The caves are hewn from solid basalt rock. Renovated in the 1970s, the caves were designated an UNESCO World Heritage Site in 1987 to preserve the artwork.

象岛石窟位于孟买港的大象岛，字面意思是"洞穴之城"，距离孟买市东部 10 千米。这些岩洞的建筑可以追溯到 5 世纪到 8 世纪，包括两个石窟群——5 个印度教洞穴和 2 个佛教洞穴，并于 1987 年被联合国教科文组织列为世界遗产。

6. Agra Fort(阿格拉古堡)

Agra Fort, also known as the Red Fort of Agra, which represented Mughal's opulence and power as the center piece of their empire was inscribed in the UNESCO World Heritage List in 1982. The fortress located on the right bank of the Yamuna River, built in red sandstone, covering a length of 2.5 kilometres and surrounded by a moat, encloses several palaces, towers and mosques. The impressive structures built within the precincts of the fort are the Khas Mahal, the Shish Mahal, Muhamman Burje (an octagonal tower), Diwan-i-Khas (1637), Diwan-i-Am, white marble mosque or the Pearl Mosque (built during 1646-1653) and the Nagina Masjid (1658-1707). These monuments are remarkable for the fusion of Persian art of the Timurid and the Indian art form. It is very close to the famous Taj Mahal with a buffer zone separating the two monuments.

阿格拉古堡作为莫卧儿帝国的中心，代表了帝国的财富和权力，1982 年被列入联合国教科文组织世界遗产名录。这座城堡位于穆纳河右岸，建在红色砂岩上，长 2.5 千米，周围有一条护城河，还有几座宫殿、塔楼和清真寺。

7. Taj Mahal(泰姬陵)

Taj Mahal, one of the Seven Wonders of the World is a mausoleum—a funerary mosque. It was built by Emperor Shah Jahan in memory of his second wife Mumtaz Mahal who had died in 1631. It is a large edifice made in white marble in typical Mughal architecture, a style that combines elements from Persian, Islamic and Indian architectural styles. It was inscribed in the UNESCO World Heritage List in 1983. It is set amidst vast Mughal Gardens, which cover 17 hectares of land on the right bank of the

Yamuna River. It has an octagonal layout marked by four exclusive minarets at four corners with a pristine elevation of a central bulbous dome below which the tombs are laid in an underground chamber. Calligraphic inscriptions in-crusted in polychromatic pierra dura, decorative bands and floral arabesques glorify the monument's graphic beauty and provide a perfect impression to the viewers.

世界七大奇迹之一的泰姬陵是一座陵墓,它是皇帝沙·贾汗为了纪念他的第二任妻子穆塔兹·马哈尔而建造的,穆塔兹·马哈尔于1631年去世。这是一座用白色大理石建造的大型建筑,有典型的莫卧儿建筑风格,结合了波斯、伊斯兰和印度的建筑艺术。1983年,它被列入世界遗产名录。

8. Buddhist Monuments at Sanchi(桑吉佛教古迹)

Buddhist Monuments at Sanchi, located 45 kilometres from Bhopal in the Indian state of Madhya Pradesh are a group of Buddhist monuments dated between 200 BC and 100 BC. The site, however, has been conjectured to have been developed in the 3rd century BC, when Emperor Ashoka of the Mauryan Empire ruled. The principal monument is Stupa 1 dated to the 2nd century and 1st century BC. These Buddhist sanctuaries were active Buddhist religious monuments, which flourished till the 12th century. The sanctuary has a plethora of monolithic pillars, palaces, temples and monasteries in different status of preservation. It was inscribed as a World Heritage Site by UNESCO on January 24, 1989 for its unique cultural importance. It was discovered only in 1818 in a deserted state of preservation. Archaeological excavations undertaken thereafter revealed 50 unique monuments.

桑吉佛教古迹位于距离印度中央邦博帕尔45千米的地方,是一组可以追溯到公元前200年到公元前100年的佛教建筑群。圣殿内有大量的单片柱、宫殿、寺庙和修道院。因其独特的文化性,1989年1月24日它被列入世界遗产名录。

 知识拓展2.1　金砖国家(见二维码)

Sum up(本章小结)

1.亚洲旅游区是世界上新开发的旅游区,进入21世纪,其国际旅游业发展迅猛,成为世界重要的旅游目的地和客源地。

2.本章从地理位置及范围、自然风貌、民族与宗教、旅游市场等方面介绍了亚洲旅游区的基本概况。

3.本章选取了日本、韩国、泰国、菲律宾、新加坡、马来西亚、印度七个国家进行介绍,它们是亚洲地区比较重要的目的地国和客源国。

4.每个国家的介绍分为两部分,第一部分介绍了各国的国土疆域、自然风貌、人口民族、发展简史、政治经济和旅游市场的基本概况,第二部分介绍了各国的旅游资源。

Reviewing and Thinking(复习与思考)

1.亚洲旅游区中哪些国家最有可能成为中国最主要的旅游客源国?为什么?

2.亚洲旅游区中哪些国家最有可能成为中国主要的旅游目的地国?为什么?

3.亚洲旅游区哪些宗教建筑景观最值得我们去游览?

4.亚洲旅游区哪些自然景观对你的吸引力最大,为什么?

5.试设计一条中国(广州)—泰国(曼谷、大成、芭堤雅)六日游旅游线路。

6.菲律宾旅游资源有何特色?最吸引中国游客的景点有哪些?

7.韩国与中国在人文旅游资源方面有何相似之处?

8.新加坡与中国在人文旅游资源方面有何相似之处?

9.新加坡、马来西亚和菲律宾有哪些著名的旅游城市和旅游景点?

10.马来西亚历史与新加坡历史有何渊源?

CHAPTER

3

The Europe Tourism Region
（欧洲旅游区）

CHAPTER 3 The Europe Tourism Region(欧洲旅游区)

◇ **LEARNING OBJECTIVES** (学习目标)

1. Understand the basic situation of the main tourist source and destination countries in Europe(了解欧洲主要客源国和目的地国的基本情况).

2. Master the tourism market development and tourism resources characteristics of the main source and destination countries in Europe(掌握欧洲主要客源国和目的地国的旅游市场发展与旅游资源特点).

3. Design some classic tourist routes(设计一些经典旅游线路).

◇ **LEARNING CONTENTS**(学习内容)

1. Britain(英国)
2. France(法国)
3. Germany(德国)
4. Italy(意大利)
5. Spain(西班牙)
6. Russia(俄罗斯)
7. Switzerland(瑞士)
8. Greece(希腊)

◇ **PROBLEM ORIENTATION**(问题导向)

Where is the most developed area of international tourism in the world? (世界上国际旅游业最发达的地区在哪里?)

Section 1 General Situation of Europe(欧洲概况)

区域概况(Regional Overview)

1. 地理位置及范围(Geographical Location and Scope)

欧洲旅游区位于亚欧大陆西部。北临北冰洋,西濒大西洋,南隔地中海与非洲相望,东以乌拉尔山脉、乌拉尔河、大高加索山脉、博斯普鲁斯海峡、达达尼尔海峡同亚洲分界。面积为1 016万平方千米,面积超过大洋洲,是世界第六大洲。

欧洲地图 EUROPE

资料来源：标准地图服务网站，审图号：GS(2020)4390 号。

欧洲旅游区有 45 个国家和地区。按照地理方位，我们通常把欧洲旅游区分为北欧、南欧、西欧、中欧和东欧五个部分。北欧旅游区指日德兰半岛、斯堪的纳维亚半岛一带。包括冰岛、法罗群岛（丹）、丹麦、挪威、瑞典和芬兰 6 个国家和地区。南欧旅游区指阿尔卑斯山脉以南的巴尔干半岛、亚平宁半岛、伊比利亚半岛和附近岛屿，包括罗马尼亚、保加利亚、塞尔维亚、黑山、克罗地亚、斯洛文尼亚、波斯尼亚和黑塞哥维那、马其顿、阿尔巴尼亚、希腊、意大利、圣马力诺、梵蒂冈、西班牙、葡萄牙、安道尔，马耳他等 17 个国家和地区。西欧旅游区包括英国、爱尔兰、荷兰、比利时、卢森堡、法国和摩纳哥等 7 个国家和地区。中欧旅游区包括波兰、捷克、斯洛伐克、匈牙利、德国、奥地利、瑞士、列支敦士登等 8 个国家和地区。东欧旅游区包括爱沙尼亚、拉脱维亚、立陶宛、白俄罗斯、乌克兰、摩尔多瓦和俄罗斯等 7 个国家和地区。

The Europe Tourism Region is located in the west of Eurasia. It is adjacent to the Arctic Ocean in the north, the Atlantic Ocean in the west. It faces Africa across the Mediterranean Sea. It is bounded by the Ural Mountains, the Ural River, the great Caucasus Mountains, the Bosporus Strait and the Dardanelles Strait in the East. It covers an area of 10 160 000 km², and is larger than Oceania, making it the sixth largest continent in the world.

  There are 45 countries and regions in the Europe Tourism Region. According to the geographical location, the Europe Tourism Region is usually divided into five parts: Northern Europe, Southern Europe, Western Europe, Central and Eastern Europe. The northern Europe Tourism Region refers to the area of Jutland Peninsula and Scandinavia, including Iceland, the Faroe Islands (Denmark), Denmark, Norway, Sweden and Finland. The southern Europe Tourism Region refers to the Balkans Peninsula, Apennine Peninsula, Iberian Peninsula and nearby islands on the south of Alps. The Mediterranean Sea and the Black Sea are on the south and east, and the Atlantic Ocean on the west. It includes 17 countries and regions—Romania, Bulgaria, Serbia, Montenegro, Croatia, Slovenia, Bosnia and Herzegovina, Macedonia, Albania, Greece, Italy, San Marino, Vatican, Spain, Portugal, Andorra, Malta. The western Europe Tourism Region includes the United Kingdom, Ireland, the Netherlands, Belgium, Luxembourg, France and Monaco. The central Europe Tourism Region includes 8 countries and regions—Poland, Czech Republic, Slovakia, Hungary, Germany, Austria, Switzerland and Liechtenstein. There are seven countries and regions in the eastern Europe Tourism Region—Estonia, Latvia, Lithuania, Belarus, Ukraine, Moldova and Russia.

2. 自然风貌(Natural Features)

  欧洲旅游区的地形特点是以平原为主,冰川地貌分布较广,高山峻岭汇集于欧洲南部,海拔 200 m 以下的平原约占全区面积的 60%。欧洲平原西起大西洋岸,东至乌拉尔山,绵延数千千米,形成横贯欧洲的大平原。阿尔卑斯山脉横亘欧洲南部,是欧洲最大的山脉。东南部大高加索山脉的主峰厄尔布鲁士山,海拔 5 642 米,为欧洲最高峰。北部斯堪的纳维亚山脉地势比较平缓,沿岸多深入内陆、两岸陡峭的峡湾。其中阿尔卑斯山成为登山、滑雪、探险、避暑、疗养的旅游胜地。

  欧洲旅游区的河流分布很均匀,河网稠密,水量较充足,多短小而水量充沛的河流。河流大多发源于欧洲中部,分别流入大西洋、北冰洋、里海、黑海和地中海。欧洲最长的河流是伏尔加河,长 3 692 千米。多瑙河为第二大河,长 2 850 千米。欧洲是一个多小湖群的大洲,湖泊多为冰川作用形成,如芬兰有"千湖之国"的之称,全境大小湖泊有 6 万多个。阿尔卑斯山麓地带分布着许多较大的冰碛湖和构造湖,山地河流多流经湖泊,湖泊地区如日内瓦湖区成为著名的游览地,而伏尔加河、莱茵河、多瑙河是欧洲著名的水上旅游线。

  欧洲旅游区大部分地区地处北温带,气候温和湿润。西部大西洋沿岸夏季凉爽,冬季温和,是典型的温带海洋性气候。东部因远离海洋,属温带大陆性气候。南部地中海沿岸地区冬季温和多雨,夏季炎热干燥,属地中海气候。夏季是欧洲旅游区的最佳旅游季节,但每个国家的最佳旅游时间有所不同。

The general landscape of Europe tourism region are mainly plains, widely distributed glaciers, and converging mountain ranges in the south of Europe. The rivers are evenly distributed, with the dense river network and adequate water, and many of the rivers are short and abundant in water. Most of the region is located in the northern temperate zone, and the climate is mild and humid. Summer is the best season for visitors in Europe.

3. 民族与宗教（Nationality and Religion）

欧洲旅游区现有人口约 7.45 亿（2021 年），人口密度约为每平方千米 70 人。欧洲旅游区绝大部分居民是白种人（欧罗巴人种），种族构成相对比较单一。欧洲主要语言有英语、俄语、法语、德语、意大利语、西班牙语等。居民多信奉天主教和基督教。位于意大利首都罗马市西北角的城中之国梵蒂冈,是世界天主教中心。

The current population of Europe tourism region is about 745 million (2021), with about 70 people per square kilometer. Europe tourism region has an ethnically homogeneous population, which is heavily concentrated in Caucasian. The majority of residents profess Catholicism and Christianity.

知识拓展 3.1　欧洲的"世界之最"（见二维码）

旅游业（Tourism）

欧洲旅游区经济发达,工业、交通、商贸、金融保险、旅游业等在世界上占有举足轻重的地位,是世界旅游业最发达的地区。

欧洲旅游区中的西欧地区，是世界旅游业发展最早、最快的地区。自19世纪中叶起，欧洲大陆的旅游活动就非常活跃，西欧的许多国家便成为主要的旅游接待国和客源输出国。法国、瑞士、奥地利和意大利等国修建了一批旅游设施并相继成立了旅行社、旅游俱乐部和旅游联合会。然而，第二次世界大战却使正在兴起的旅游活动中断了。二战后，特别是20世纪60—70年代后，处于世界六大旅游区领先地位的欧洲旅游区（主要是西欧地区），因其经济发达、国民收入高、旅游资源丰富、旅游业发展历史长、出国旅游盛行，成为全世界最大的旅游客源市场，也是世界最发达的旅游市场，平均每年有1亿8千万人出国旅游，占全世界国际旅游人数的70%以上，其旅游收入占世界旅游收入的50%以上。自1985年6月14日，德国、法国、荷兰、比利时和卢森堡五国在卢森堡的边境小镇申根签署申根协定以来，申根协议国不断增加，使欧洲各国的出入境旅游更为方便。

欧洲旅游区是世界各国最重要的客源地，也是中国主要的客源市场，其中以俄罗斯、英国、德国、法国来华人数最多，均属中国十大客源国之列，意大利、荷兰、西班牙、瑞典、奥地利、瑞士等来华旅游人数次之，也是中国比较重要的客源市场。

欧洲旅游区是世界上最受欢迎的旅游目的地，其国际游客主要来自欧洲内部各国，约占总人数的80%，其余游客多来自北美、日本。从入境游客数量来看，2018年欧洲旅游区共接待了7.10亿入境游客，同比增长5%。从国际旅游收入来看，2018年欧洲旅游区的国际旅游收入为570亿美元，同比增长5%，是全球国际旅游增长的主要动力。

目前，欧洲已成为中国重要的旅游目的地，欧洲绝大部分国家和地区已对中国公民开放，其中欧盟27个国家已经全部成为中国公民出国旅游目的地，一些国家对中国游客入境提供便利。

2018年是中欧旅游年，中国公民赴欧洲游表现抢眼。在目的地选择方面，传统热门国家人气不减，意大利、法国、英国、德国、西班牙、希腊等国依然领跑，这些目的地也更受90后群体的欢迎，成为他们第一次前往欧洲的目的地选择。而出境游经验较为丰富、有一定经济基础的80后则渐渐倾向于选择新兴国家，其中，爱沙尼亚、保加利亚、克罗地亚、拉脱维亚、斯洛文尼亚等小众目的地热度上升。中国旅游研究院公布的数据显示，2018年中国赴欧洲旅游人数超过600万人次，中国主要旅游目的地国家Top20中，欧洲国家占四分之一。随着赴欧签证、航班、汇率、消费服务等方面的政策利好，2019年中国赴欧洲旅游继续保持增长趋势，2019年上半年，中国赴欧洲旅游人数达到300万人次，增长7.4%。

Europe tourism region has highly developed economy, with industry, transportation and trade, finance and insurance, tourism, etc, occupying a dominant position in the world, and it is the most developed region in world tourism. Among them, Western Europe is the earliest and fastest growing major tourism region. Europe tourism region is the most popular source of tourists to each country in the world. Its international tourists are mainly from the internal countries, the rest are mostly from North America and Japan. Europe is a major source market and tourist destination to China.

知识拓展 3.2　欧盟简介（见二维码）

 知识拓展 3.3　申根签证（见二维码）

Section 2　Britain（英国）

PART 1（第一部分）

1. 国土疆域（Territory）

英国是由大不列颠岛、爱尔兰岛东北部及附近许多岛屿组成的岛国，它位于欧洲旅游区西部，东临北海，与比利时、荷兰、德国、丹麦、挪威等国相望；南隔英吉利海峡与法国为邻；西邻爱尔兰共和国，横隔大西洋与美国、加拿大遥遥相对；北过大西洋可达冰岛。

英国国土面积约为24.41万平方千米（包括内陆水域）。其中英格兰13.04万平方千米，苏格兰7.88万平方千米，威尔士2.08万平方千米，北爱尔兰1.41万平方千米。海岸线总长11 450千米。

The United Kingdom (Britain) is an island country composed of the island of Great Britain, the northeast of Ireland and many nearby islands. It is located in the west of the Europe tourist region. It borders the North Sea on the east, and it is adjacent to Belgium, the Netherlands, Germany, Denmark, Norway. It faces France across the English Channel in the south. The Republic of Ireland is in its west. It faces the United States and Canada across the Atlantic Ocean. Iceland can be reached across the Atlantic Ocean in the north.

The land area of the United Kingdom is 244 100 km^2 (including inland waters). Among them, England is 130 400 km^2, Scotland is 78 800 km^2, Wales is 20 800 km^2 and Northern Ireland is 14 100 km^2. The total length of coastline is 11 450 km.

2. 自然风貌(Natural Features)

英国境内多低山和丘陵，海拔大都在500 m以下。苏格兰和威尔士以丘陵为主，英格兰以平原为主，北爱尔兰以高原和平原为主。整体地势西北高、东南低。

英国大部分位于50°～60°N，常年受西风和北大西洋暖流的影响，属于典型的温带海洋性气候，其特点是湿润、温和，季节间的温度变化很小，多雾，日照时数少。全年雨天较多，年降水量丰富。伦敦成为世界著名的雾都。

英国的主要河流有泰晤士河，全长346千米，流经牛津、伦敦等重要城市，注入北海，它是英国风光最美丽的河流。另外一条主要河流为塞文河，长354千米。

英国湖泊较多，北爱尔兰的内伊湖最大；英格兰西北部的湖区有大小湖泊20多个，总面积2 243平方千米，大部分湖泊为山谷冰川融化而成。

The landscape of the UK is low mountainous and hilly, with the elevation of mostly 500 m below; It belongs to the typical temperate marine climate. The main rivers are the Thames and Severn; There are many lakes in the United Kingdom, among which Lough Neagh in Northern Ireland is the largest lake. Most of the lakes are melted from valley glaciers.

3. 人口民族(Population and Ethnicity)

英国人口约6 679.68万(2019)，其中英格兰人占80%以上。英国是一个人口稠密的国家，人口密度约为每平方千米273.65人，但人口分布极不均匀，80%以上的人口居住在城市。

英国主要有四个民族，即英格兰人、苏格兰人、威尔士人、爱尔兰人。这些民族都带有凯尔特人的血统,融合了日耳曼人的成分。官方语言为英语,威尔士北部还使用威尔士语,苏格兰西北高地及北爱尔兰部分地区仍使用盖尔语。居民多信奉基督教新教,主要分英格兰教会(亦称英国国教、圣公会)和苏格兰教会(亦称长老会)。另有天主教会及伊斯兰教、印度教、锡克教、犹太教和佛教等较大的宗教社团。

The UK has a population of 66 796 800 (2019), which more than 80% is English. The UK is a densely populated country, with more than 80% of the population living in cities. There are four main ethnic groups in the UK, namely English, Scottish, Welsh and Irish. Most of the residents profess Protestantism.

4. 发展简史(Brief History of Development)

在不列颠群岛上很早就有人类活动。英国历史是一部征服与合并的历史。公元1至5世纪,大不列颠岛东南部受罗马帝国统治。后盎格鲁、撒克逊、朱特人相继入侵。7世纪开始形成封建制度。公元829年英格兰统一,史称"盎格鲁-撒克逊时代"。1066年诺曼底公爵威廉渡海征服英格兰,建立诺曼底王朝。1536年英格兰与威尔士合并。1640年爆发资产阶级革命,1649年5月19日宣布成立共和国。1660年王朝复辟。1688年发生"光荣革命",确立了君主立宪制。1707年英格兰与苏格兰合并。1801年又与爱尔兰合并。18世纪60年代至19世纪30年代成为世界上第一个完成工业革命的国家。1914年占有的殖民地面积比本土面积大111倍,是第一殖民大国,自称"日不落帝国"。1921年爱尔兰南部26郡成立"自由邦",北部6郡仍归英国。第一次世界大战后,英国开始衰落,其世界霸权地位逐渐被美国取代。第二次世界大战严重削弱了英国的经济实力。随着1947年印度和巴基斯坦相继独立,英殖民体系开始瓦解。目前,英在海外仍有13块领地。1973年1月英国加入欧共体(今欧盟),2020年1月退出欧盟。

The history of England is full of conquest and amalgamation. The UK was the first colonial power, and the colonies occupied in 1914 were 111 times larger than the mainland of the UK, calling itself the "Empire on which the sun never sets". With the independence of India and Pakistan in 1947, the British colonial system began to collapse.

5. 政治经济(Politics and Economy)

首都为伦敦,国花为玫瑰,国鸟为红胸鸲,货币为英镑。

英国实行君主立宪制。国王是世袭的国家元首、立法机关的组成部分、最高司法长官、武装部队总司令和英国国教的世俗领袖。议会是英国最高立法机构,由国王、上院(贵族院)、下院(众议院)组成。每届议会大选后,首相由多数党领袖担任,并由英王任命。

英国是世界经济发达国家之一,是世界第五大经济体。英国是老牌的工业发达国家,但第二次世界大战后,英国工业发展缓慢。目前的工业部门有采矿、冶金、化工、机械、电子、电子仪器、汽车、航空、食品、饮料、烟草、轻纺、造纸、印刷、出版、建筑等。生物制药、航空和国防是英国工业研发的重点,也是英国最具创新力和竞争力的行业。农业在英国国民经济中不占重要地位。英国的交通十分发达,设施完备,为旅游业的发展提供了条件。

The UK is a unitary state with a constitutional monarchy. Britain is one of the economically developed countries in the world. Its highly developed transportation and complete facilities provide convenience for the development of tourism.

6. 旅游市场(Tourism Market)

英国是近代旅游业的发源地,一直是欧洲重要的旅游市场,也是世界重要的旅游目的地国。英国旅游业收入居世界第五,从业人员约 300 万,占就业人口的 10%。

虽然政治的不确定性和脱欧可能给英国的经济带来不良影响,但是英国旅游业在过去几年表现良好。据世界旅游组织统计,2019 年英国接待国际旅游者总数为 3 630 万人次,次于法国、西班牙、美国、中国、意大利、土耳其、墨西哥、德国和泰国,居世界第 10 位;英国国际旅游收入达 519 亿美元,仅次于美国、西班牙、法国、泰国,居世界第 5 位。2019年英国出境旅游消费总额为 760 亿美元,居世界第 4 位。

英国是中国重要的旅游客源国之一,2018 年来华旅游人数达 60.80 万人次,十年增长 15%。

英国也是中国重要的旅游目的地国。英国旅游局的数据显示,2019 年上半年,英国接待的中国游客和游客消费金额双双创下历史纪录,2019 年 1 月至 6 月间来英国的中国游客比 2018 年同期增加了 1%,游客消费金额达 2.57 亿英镑,增长 14%。

As the birthplace of modern tourism, the UK has always been an important tourist market in Europe and an important tourist destination in the world. The UK is an important tourist source destination to China.

PART 2(第二部分)

Tourism Resources(旅游资源)

1. Tourist Attractions(旅游名胜)

England has some unique natural environments, and has a significant ecotourism industry.

1)The Eden Project in Cornwall(康沃尔郡的伊甸园工程)

The Eden Project is a tourist attraction in Cornwall, England. Inside the two biomes are plants that are collected from many diverse climates and environments. The project is located in a reclaimed kaolinite pit, located 2 kilometers from the town of St. Blazey and 5 kilometres from the larger town of St. Austell, Cornwall.

The complex is dominated by two huge enclosures consisting of adjoining domes that house thousands of plant species, and each enclosure emulates a natural biome. The domes consist of hundreds of hexagonal and pentagonal, inflated, plastic cells supported by steel frames. The first set of domes simulates a tropical environment and the second, a Mediterranean environment. The attraction also has an outside botanical garden which is home to many plants and wildlife native to Cornwall and the UK in general; it also has many plants that provide an important and interesting backstory, for example, those with a prehistoric heritage.

英国自然环境独特,有着重要的生态旅游产业。

康沃尔郡的伊甸园工程是英国康沃尔郡的一个旅游景点,建在一个采掘陶土遗留下来的巨坑上。该工程由穹顶建筑组成,里面容纳了数千种植物,每个穹顶都模拟了一个自然生物群落。穹顶由数百个六角形和五角形的膨胀塑料单元组成,由钢架支撑。第一组穹顶建筑模拟了热带环境,第二组穹顶建筑模拟了地中海环境。

2) The Lake District(湖区)

The Lake District, also known as The Lakes or Lakeland, is a mountainous region in northwest England. As a popular holiday destination, it is famous for its lakes, forests and mountains (or falls) and its associations with the early 19th century writings of William Wordsworth and the other Lake Poets.

Historically split between Cumberland, Westmorland and Lancashire, the Lake District is now entirely in Cumbria. The land in England higher than 910 meters above sea level lies within the National Park, including Scafell Pike, the highest mountain in England. It also contains the largest lake in England—Windermere.

湖区是英格兰西北部的一个山区。它以湖泊、森林和山脉(或瀑布)而闻名。英格兰所有海拔超过910米的地方都位于湖区国家公园内。湖区拥有英格兰最高的山峰斯科菲峰和英格兰最大的湖泊温德米尔湖。

3) The Peak District National Park(峰区国家公园)

The Peak District is an upland area in England, most of which lies in northern Derbyshire but also includes parts of Cheshire, Greater Manchester, Staffordshire and Yorkshire.

The Peak District National Park became the first national park in the United Kingdom in 1951. With its proximity to the cities of Manchester and Sheffield and easy access by road and rail, it attracts millions of visitors every year.

峰区是英格兰的一个高地地区。1951年,峰区国家公园成为英国第一个国家公园。

4) Dartmoor and Exmoor(达特穆尔和埃克斯穆尔)

Dartmoor is an area of moorland in southern Devon, England. Protected by National Park status as Dartmoor National Park, it covers 953 square kilometres. It is a popular tourist destination.

Exmoor is loosely defined as an area of hilly open moorland in west Somerset and north Devon in Southwest England. It is named after the River Exe, the source of which is situated in the center of the area.

达特穆尔是英格兰德文郡南部的一片荒地，是一个受保护的国家公园，是一个受欢迎的旅游目的地。埃克斯穆尔是位于英格兰西南部萨默塞特郡西部和北德文郡的一个多山的开放式荒地。

5) The New Forest(新森林)

The New Forest is an area of southern England which includes one of the largest remaining tracts of unenclosed pastureland, heathland and forest in the heavily populated southeast of England. The name also refers to the New Forest National Park which has similar boundaries.

新森林是英格兰南部的一个地区，有英格兰最大的无围栏牧场、石楠丛和森林。

6) The Jurassic Coast(侏罗纪海岸)

The Jurassic Coast is a World Heritage Site on the English Channel coast of southern England. Chartered in 2001, the Jurassic coast was the second wholly natural World Heritage Site to be designated in the United Kingdom. The site was featured on the television programme Seven Natural Wonders as one of the wonders of the southwest of the UK, and in a 2005 poll of Radio Timesreaders, the Jurassic Coast was named as the fifth-greatest natural wonder in Britain.

侏罗纪海岸是位于英格兰南部、英吉利海峡沿岸的世界遗产。它曾被电视节目评为英国西南部的七大自然奇观之一，也被称为英国第五大自然奇观。

7) The Broads in Norfolk(诺福克湿地公园)

The Broads are a network of mostly navigable rivers and lakes in the English counties of Norfolk and Suffolk. The lakes, known locally as broads, were formed by the flooding of peat workings. The Broads, and some surrounding land, were constituted as a special area with a level of protection equivalent to a national park by the Norfolk and Suffolk Broads Act 1988.

The total area is 303 square kilometres, most of which is in Norfolk, with over 200 kilometres of navigable waterways.

这里拥有英国诺福克郡和萨福克郡的主要通航河流和湖泊网络。这些湖泊在当地被称为广阔的湖泊，是由泥炭矿床的洪水形成的。

8) The National Forest(国家森林)

The National Forest is an environmental project in central England run by The National Forest Company. Areas of north Leicestershire, south Derbyshire and southeast Stafford shire, square kilometers are being planted, in an attempt to blend ancient woodland with new plantings to create a new national forest.

国家森林是英格兰中部的一个环境项目,由国家森林公司经营,这里种植了520平方千米的植物。

2. Tourist Cities(旅游城市)

England's long history and pervasive culture spread worldwide through the English language and colonialism make England a popular tourist destination, particularly in London.

Heritage Cities in England:

Bath(巴斯): A spa town, famous for its Georgian architecture and crescents, and also for its Roman baths.

Brighton(布莱顿): Brighton is a seaside resort which includes two piers, West Pier and Brighton Pier, and is home to the Royal Pavilion.

Bristol(布里斯托尔): Brunel's The Clifton Suspension Bridge is a famous landmark, and the ship, the SS Great Britain is another of Brunel's famous constructions, which is now in dry dock in Bristol.

Cambridge(剑桥): A famous university town.

Canterbury(坎特伯雷): Renowned for its cathedral.

Chester(切斯特): Important Roman and medieval walled city with an amphitheatre and 11th century Benedictine Abbey, now the cathedral. Renowned for its covered medieval shop rows, race course and Chester Zoo.

Dover(多佛): A major port with access to the continent. Dover Castle is also well known for its white cliffs and to a lesser extent for its castle.

Durham(达勒姆): A famous university town, also renowned for its cathedral and castle.

Exeter(埃克塞特): City home to Exeter Cathedral and Rougemont Castle.

Haworth(哈沃斯): where the Brontë Sisters lived, is very popular with Japanese tourists, as Wuthering Heights has a cult following in Japan.

Lincoln(林肯): A medieval city, home to the very ornate Lincoln Cathedral and to Lincoln Castle, where a copy of the Magna Carta is kept.

Liverpool(利物浦): The 2008 European Capital of Culture, a major commercial port and World Heritage Site, home to two cathedrals, the Royal Liverpool Philharmonic Orchestra and a strong theatrical tradition. It has more listed buildings, registered historic parks, museums and art galleries than any other city in the UK outside of London. The home of two Premier League football clubs, they are Liverpool and Everton. It is the first city in the world to be linked by passenger railway (with Manchester). It is also famous for The Grand National, and its musical, maritime and literary heritage.

Norwich(诺里奇): City renowned for its castle and cathedral. The latter has the second-tallest spire in the country.

Nottingham(诺丁汉): The city and Nottingham Castle are famed worldwide for their links with the legend of Robin Hood. Sherwood Forest is nearby.

Oxford(牛津): A city known for its university, the University of Oxford.

Plymouth(普利茅斯): A naval dockyard, with a listed heritage area, the Barbican, which includes the National Marine Aquarium and the Mayflower Steps. Also home to Smeaton's Tower, a former lighthouse now used as a viewpoint.

Portsmouth(朴次茅斯): Portsmouth is also a naval dockyard, and has some famous ships on display, including the Mary Rose, and HMS Victory, all within its Historic Dockyard. Also home to Gunwharf Quays retail center, with its iconic Spinnaker Tower.

Salisbury(索尔兹伯里): Salisbury Cathedral is very well known, and has the tallest spire in the country. Nearby is the pre-historic site of Stonehenge, which is administered by English Heritage.

Shrewsbury(什鲁斯伯里): Medieval walled town situated within a loop of the Severn River. It is famous for many timber framed buildings, churches, stone bridges and as the birthplace of Charles Darwin.

Stratford-upon-Avon(斯特拉福德): The birthplace of William Shakespeare is probably the most visited place in Stratford. It had more than 805 000 visitors in 2011.

York(约克): Famous for the York Minster cathedral. Also there are the National Railway Museum and a wealth of preserved medieval streets and buildings, such as the Merchant Adventurers' Hall and the Shambles.

Other places in England are also of historical interest. The city of Manchester is the second most visited city in England after London (in a survey from 2002). Many foreign tourists also visit the neighboring countries Scotland and Wales.

Domestic tourists, and foreign tourists who have specific interests in art, music, history etc., also visit the following cities:

Birmingham(伯明翰): A major city, with an orchestra, major exhibition venues (NEC, ICC) and art galleries. Of historical interest for its significant role in the industrial revolution, the childhood home and inspiration of Tolkien, noted for its shopping and boasting the longest stretch of nightclubs in England.

Hadrian's Wall(哈德良长城): The Roman wall built in Northumberland by order of the Emperor Hadrian.

Hereford(赫里福德): A cathedral city, famous for the chained library in the cathedral, and the Mappa Mundi.

Manchester(曼彻斯特): A culturally pre-eminent city, once famous for its industry. It is known for the Hallé orchestra and many museums, art galleries and its Victorian and Edwardian era architecture. The city was host of the 2002 Commonwealth Games and is home to two Premier League football clubs. Manchester is also known for being the world's first industrialized city, and is well noted for its shopping, cuisine, music, media, social history and nightlife.

Winchester(温彻斯特)：A cathedral city, also famous for its castle, which has a depiction of King Arthur's Round Table in the Great Hall.

英国悠久的历史和文化通过英语和殖民主义传播到世界各地,使英国,特别是伦敦,成为一个受欢迎的旅游目的地。遗产城市主要包括巴斯、布莱顿、布里斯托尔、剑桥、坎特伯雷、切斯特、多佛、达勒姆、埃克塞特、哈沃斯、林肯、利物浦、诺里奇、诺丁汉、牛津、普利茅斯、朴次茅斯、索尔兹伯里、什鲁斯伯里、斯特拉福德、约克、伯明翰、哈德良长城、赫里福德、曼彻斯特、温彻斯特等。

Section 3　France(法国)

PART 1(第一部分)

1. 国土疆域(Territory)

法国位于欧洲旅游区的最西端,整个国土形状略呈六边形。其国土三面临海,三面靠陆,西濒大西洋的比斯开湾,西北隔英吉利海峡与英国相望,东南临地中海。东、东北与摩纳哥、意大利、瑞士、德国、卢森堡、比利时相接,西南同西班牙、安道尔接壤。国土面积约55万平方千米。国境线长5 695千米,其中海岸线长约2 700千米。这种地理位置使其对外联系极为方便,无任何天然障碍,来往畅通无阻。

France is located in the westernmost point of the Europe tourism region. The whole territory is in the shape of a little hexagon. It faces the sea on three sides and land on three sides. It borders the Bay of Biscay in the Atlantic Ocean to the west, and faces the United Kingdom across the English Channel to the northwest. It faces the Mediterranean Sea in the southeast. The east and northeast are bordered by Monaco, Italy, Switzerland, Germany, Luxembourg, and Belgium, and the southwest by Spain and Andorra. The land area is 5 500 million km². The total length of the border line is 5 695 km, and the coastline is about 2 700 km. This geographical location makes it very convenient to contact with the outside world, free from any natural obstacles and unimpeded communication.

2. 自然风貌(Natural Features)

法国地理风貌多姿多彩,它以独特的魅力吸引着世界各地的旅游者。

法国的地形主要以平原和丘陵为主,地势东南高、西北低。全国分为三大地形区:一是东南部山地区。包括比利牛斯山脉、中央高原、阿尔卑斯山、汝拉山和孚日山。东南部沿岸平原狭窄,风景秀丽,是著名的旅游区。二是西北部盆地丘陵区,包括巴黎盆地、卢瓦尔河下游平原。三是罗纳谷地,索恩-罗纳河谷介于中央高原和阿尔卑斯山之间,南北狭长,宽仅20～30 km,是法国南北交通的天然走廊。

法国优越的地理位置和有利的地形决定了它得天独厚的气候特点,全年适宜旅游,最佳的季节是春夏之季。1月平均气温北部为1～7 ℃,南部为6～8 ℃;7月平均气温北部为16～18 ℃,南部为21～24 ℃。降水量由西向东逐渐减少。西部为温带海洋性气候,中部和东部地为温带大陆性气候,南部为地中海气候。

法国河流众多,水量丰富,其中大部分河流发源于中央高原,并向西北和东南方向呈扇形分布,分别注入大西洋和地中海。其中最著名的四大河流是卢瓦尔河、罗纳河、塞纳河、加龙河。卢瓦尔河是法国第一大河,全长1 012千米,流域面积121 000平方千米,源于中央高原南部的塞文山脉,向北流经法国中部地区的肥田沃土,穿越莽莽森林区,注入比斯开湾。卢瓦尔河流域气候温和,树木茂盛,风光秀丽,河流两岸有众多的城堡、葡萄园和公园,是最具有法国特色的地方。塞纳河是法国北部的一条大河,全长约776千米,流域面积约78 000平方千米,发源于法国东部的朗格勒高原,向西北横贯巴黎盆地,注入英吉利海峡。它像一条玉带,静静地流过巴黎市区,乘塞纳河的游船欣赏两岸的名胜,别有一番情趣。

法国境内点缀着大大小小的湖泊,似繁星散落,其中最大最著名的是位于瑞士与法国边界的美丽的日内瓦湖。

The landscape of France is mainly plains and hills. The whole country is divided into three topographic areas: the southeast mountainous area in the southeast, the basin hilly area in the northwest, and the Rhone valley. The west area has a temperate marine climate, a temperate continental climate in the center and east area, and a Mediterranean climate in the south coastal region of the Mediterranean. In France there are many rivers with abundant water, among which the most famous four rivers are Loire, Rhone, Seine and Garonne. The largest and most famous lake in France is the beautiful Lake Geneva on the border between Switzerland and France.

3. 人口民族(Population and Ethnicity)

法国总人数约6 706万人(2020年),人口密度约为每平方千米121.93人。法国是一个以法兰西民族为主体的国家,法兰西人占全国总人口的83%,少数民族有阿尔萨斯人、布列塔尼人、科西嘉人等,大约占人口总数的7.9%,还有约8%的人口来自非洲和欧洲其他国家的移民。

法语属印欧语系罗曼语族,是联合国工作语言之一,它以其准确、严谨、优雅,成为世界上最优美的语言。目前使用人口超过1亿。

法国的主要宗教是天主教,据统计,约有90%的人信奉天主教,但只有15%的人经常参加宗教活动。

France has a total population of about 67 060 000 (2020), with a population density of 121.93 people per square kilometer. France is a country ethnically dominated by French, and Catholicism is the main religion.

4. 发展简史(Brief History of Development)

法国古称高卢,高卢人是古代世界中最骁勇好战的民族之一,曾经征服过中欧大部分地区,但高卢人并非一个整体,从未形成过一个国家。公元5世纪法兰克人移居这里,公元843年,法国成为独立的国家,国名也由高卢改为法兰克。1337年英王觊觎法国王位,爆发"百年战争",后法国人民进行反侵略战争,于1453年结束百年战争。15世纪末到16世纪初形成中央集权国家。17世纪中叶,君主专制制度达到顶峰。随着资产阶级力量的发展,1789年法国爆发大革命,废除君主制,并于1792年9月22日建立第一共和国。1799年11月9日(雾月18日),拿破仑·波拿巴夺取政权,1804年称帝,建立第一帝国。1848年2月爆发革命,建立第二共和国。1851年路易·波拿巴总统发动政变,翌年12月建立第二帝国。1870年在普法战争中战败后,于1870年9月成立第三共和国直到1940年6月法国贝当政府投降德国,至此第三共和国覆灭。1871年3月18日,巴黎人民举行武装起义,成立巴黎公社。同年5月底,被法国军队残酷镇压。第二次世界大战期间法国遭德国侵略。1944年6月宣布成立临时政府,戴高乐担任首脑,1946年通过宪法,成立第四共和国。1958年9月通过新宪法,第五共和国成立,同年12月戴高乐当选总统。

France was called Gaul in ancient times, and Gaul was one of the most valiant people in ancient world. The Franks settled here in the 5th century. France became an independent country in 843, changing its name from Gaul to Franks. From the late 15th century to the early 16th century, a centralized state was founded. France was invaded by Germany during World War II.

5. 政治经济(Politics and Economy)

法国是半总统半议会制的共和国政体,议会是国家最高权力机构。总统为国家元首和武装部队统帅,总统任免总理并批准总理提名的部长,主持内阁会议,有权解散议会。议会由国民议会和参议院组成,拥有制定法律、监督政府、通过预算、批准宣战等权力。

法国是以工业为主导,工、农业都很发达的先进国家,也是欧洲经济联盟的主要发起国和成员国。法国的工业部门齐全,以机械、冶金、电子电器、纺织、服装、化妆品和食品等部门最为著名,核能、石化、海洋开发、军火、宇航事业发展迅速,位居世界前列。法国的农业十分发达,是世界著名的农产品出口大国,其中谷物、乳肉、甜菜、葡萄等的出口量均位居世界前列。法国的交通运输是世界上最发达的国家之一,公路网是世界上最密集、欧盟国家中最长的,总长度超过 100 万千米,其中高速公路 11 465 千米。法国的铁路网也很密集,拥有高速铁路 2 024 千米。法国享有"空中中转站"的美称,航班通达 134 个国家和地区的 529 个城市。

France is a multi-party, semi-presidential and semi-parliamentary republic. France is an advanced country dominated by industry, with both highly developed industry and agriculture. It is also the main initiator and member state of the European Economic Union. France's industrial sectors are completely developed, among which machinery, metallurgy, electronic appliances, textiles, clothing, cosmetics and food sectors are the most famous. Agriculture is well developed. France is the world's famous agricultural products export country. Transportation is one of the most developed countries in the world, and the road network is one of the most dense and diversified in the world.

6. 旅游市场(Tourism Market)

法国经济发达,人民生活富裕,基础设施和旅游设施完备,旅游业十分发达。旅游业是法国的重要产业,是法国营业额最高、收益最好、创造就业机会最多的行业之一,是世界最重要旅游目的地国。

近几年来,法国国际旅游业发展势头良好,2017 年是法国旅游业的强势复兴之年,2018 年、2019 年法国旅游业继续向好。据 UNWTO 统计,2019 年法国接待国际游客达 8 940 万人次,居世界第一位;国际旅游收入 673 亿美元,仅次于美国和西班牙,排名世界第三,比上一年增加 5%,达到历史最高水平。法国是中国重要的旅游目的地之一,2018 年有 220 万中国游客到法国旅游,平均停留天数 6 天;中国游客在法国总共消费 40 多亿欧元。

法国也是世界最重要的旅游客源国之一。据 UNWTO 统计,2019 年法国国际旅游支出达到 480 亿美元,居世界五位。法国是中国比较重要的旅游客源国,2018 年来华旅游人数达 50 万人次,十年增长 18%。

Tourism is an important industry in France. It is one of the industries with the highest turnover, the biggest benefit and the largest job opportunities in France. France is the world's most important tourist destination and one of the world's most important tourist sources.

PART 2(第二部分)

Tourism Resources(旅游资源)

1. Tourist Attractions(旅游名胜)

France has 37 sites inscribed in UNESCO's World Heritage List and features cities of high cultural interest (Paris being the foremost, but also Toulouse, Strasbourg, Bordeaux, Lyon, and others), beaches and seaside resorts, ski resorts, and rural regions that many enjoy their beauty and tranquillity. Small and picturesque French villages of quality heritage (such as Collonges-la-Rouge or Locronan) are promoted through the association Les Plus Beaux Villages de France (The Most Beautiful Villages of France). The "Remarkable Gardens" label is a list of the over two hundred gardens classified by the French Ministry of Culture. This label is intended to protect and promote remarkable gardens and parks.

法国有37处遗址被联合国教科文组织列入世界遗产名录,并以具有高度文化价值的城市为特色(巴黎是最重要的城市,还包括图卢兹、斯特拉斯堡、波尔多、里昂和其他城市)。法国还拥有海滩和海滨胜地、滑雪胜地以及许多以其美丽和宁静而著称的乡村地区。"法国最美村庄"协会致力于推广法国美丽乡村的优质遗产(如 Collonges-la-Rouge 或 Locronan)。

1) Collonges-la-Rouge(科隆热拉鲁格)

Collonges-la-Rouge is a commune in the Corrèze department in the Limousin region of France. Collonges-la-Rouge is entirely built with red sandstone. Its existence is proven since the 8th century thanks to the donation of the count of Limoges of the parish to the monastery of Charroux.

The village is a member of the Les Plus Beaux Villages de France (The Most Beautiful Villages of France) association, and is actually where this association was created. Its one of the most visited sites in the Limousin.

科隆热拉鲁格是法国利穆赞大区的一个村庄。它的最早可追溯到公元8世纪,它完全是用红色砂岩建造的。该村庄是"法国最美村庄"协会的成员之一,是利穆赞最受欢迎的景点之一。

2) Locronan(洛克罗南)

Locronan is a commune in the Finistère department of Brittany in northwestern France, with a population of 800. Locronan is a member of the Les Plus Beaux Villages de France ("The most beautiful villages of France") association.

洛克洛南是法国西北部布列塔尼的一个村庄,是"法国最美村庄"协会的成员。

3) French Riviera (the Côte d'Azur)法国里维埃拉(蓝色海岸)

With more than 10 million tourists a year, the French Riviera (or Côte d'Azur), in southeastern France, is the second leading tourist destination in the country, after the Parisian region. According to the Côte d'Azur Economic Development Agency, it benefits from 300 days of sunshine per year, 115 kilometres of coastline and beaches, 18 golf courses, 14 ski resorts and 3 000 restaurants. Each year the Côte d'Azur hosts 50% of the world's superyacht fleet, with 90% of all superyachts visiting the region's coast at least once in their lifetime.

位于法国东南部的里维埃拉,这里每年 300 天有阳光,有 115 千米的海岸线和海滩、18 个高尔夫球场、14 个滑雪胜地和 3 000 家餐馆。

4)Loire Valley(卢瓦尔河谷)

Another major destination are the Châteaux of the Loire Valley, this World Heritage Site is noteworthy for the quality of its architectural heritage, in its historic towns such as Amboise, Angers, Blois, Chinon, Nantes, Orléans, Saumur, and Tours, but in particular for its castles (châteaux), such as the Châteaux d'Amboise, de Chambord, d'Ussé, de Villandry and Chenonceau, which illustrate to an exceptional degree the ideals of the French Renaissance.

卢瓦尔河谷风景迷人,拥有一些世界遗产,历史城镇有昂布瓦斯、布洛瓦、南特、奥尔良等,城堡有香波城堡、舍农索城堡等。

2. Tourist Cities(旅游城市)

France, especially Paris, has some of the world's largest and renowned museums, including the Louvre, which is the most visited art museum in the world, the Musée d'Orsay, mostly devoted to impressionism, and Beaubourg, dedicated to contemporary art. Disneyland Paris is Europe's most popular theme park, with 15 million combined visitors to the resort's Disneyland Park and Walt Disney Studios Park in 2009.

法国,尤其是巴黎,拥有世界上最大和最著名的博物馆,包括卢浮宫,这是世界上参观人数最多的艺术博物馆;奥赛博物馆,主要致力于印象主义;博堡,致力于当代艺术。巴黎迪士尼乐园是欧洲最受欢迎的主题公园。

1)Paris(巴黎)

Paris, the capital city, is the third most visited city in the world. Paris has some of the world's largest and renowned museums, including the Louvre, which is the most visited art museum in the world, but also the Musée d'Orsay, mostly devoted to impressionism, and Beaubourg, dedicated to contemporary art. Paris hosts some of the world's most recognizable landmarks such as the Eiffel Tower, which is the most-visited paid monument in the world, the Arc de Triomphe, the cathedral of Notre Dame or the Sacré Cœur. The Cité des Sciences et de l'Industrie is the biggest science museum in Europe. Located in Parc de la Villette in Paris, France, it is at the heart of the Cultural Center of Science, Technology and Industry (CCSTI), a center promoting science and science culture. Near Paris is the Palace of Versailles, the former palace of the kings of France, now a museum.

首都巴黎是世界第三大旅游城市。巴黎拥有世界上最大和最著名的博物馆,如卢浮宫、奥赛博物馆、博堡等;巴黎附近的凡尔赛宫,以前是法国国王的宫殿,现在是一座博物馆。巴黎拥有世界著名的地标建筑,如埃菲尔铁塔、凯旋门、巴黎圣母院和圣心大教堂等。

2) Provence(普罗旺斯)

A large part of Provence is designed as the 2013 European Capital of Culture. Numerous of famous natural sites can be found in the region, as the Gorges du Verdon, the regional natural park of Camargue, the Calanques National Park and the typical landscape of Luberon. Provence hosts dozens of renowned historical sites like the Pont du Gard, the Arles' Roman Monuments or the Palais des Papes in Avignon. Several cities also attract a lot of tourists, like Aix-en-Provence, Marseille or Cassis, on the Mediterranean Sea coastline.

普罗旺斯是欧洲文化之都,该地区有许多著名的自然景点,如韦尔东峡谷、卡马尔格自然公园、卡朗格国家公园和吕贝隆的风景。普罗旺斯有几十个著名的历史景点,如加尔桥、阿尔勒罗马纪念碑和阿维尼翁的教皇宫。

3) Bordeaux(波尔多)

Bordeaux is classified "Town of Art and History". The city is home to 362 historical monuments (only Paris has more in France) with some buildings dating back to Roman times. Bordeaux has been inscribed on UNESCO World Heritage List as "an outstanding urban and architectural ensemble". Bordeaux is home to one of Europe's biggest 18th-century architectural urban areas, making it a sought-after destination for tourists and cinema production crews. It stands out as one of the first French cities, after Nancy, to have entered an era of urbanism and metropolitan big scale projects, with the team Gabriel father and son, architects for King Louis XV.

波尔多被列为"艺术和历史之城"。这座城市有362座历史古迹,其中一些建筑可以追溯到罗马时代。波尔多被联合国教科文组织列入世界遗产名录,拥有"杰出的城市和建筑群"。波尔多是18世纪欧洲最大的建筑城区之一,是游客和电影制作团队的热门目的地。

4) Lyon(里昂)

The historical centre of Lyon was designated a UNESCO World Heritage Site in 1998. In its designation, UNESCO cited the "exceptional testimony to the continuity of urban settlement over more than two millennia on a site of great commercial and strategic significance." The specific regions composing the Historic Site include the Roman district and Fourvière, the Renaissance district (Vieux Lyon), the silk district (slopes of Croix-Rousse), and the Presqu'île, which features architecture from the 12th century to modern times.

里昂的中心地区于1998年被联合国教科文组织列为世界遗产。被联合国教科文组织评价为"在具有重大商业和战略意义的遗址上,两千多年来城市居住区的连续性的特殊证明"。

5) Marseille(马赛)

Marseille is known for the Calanques National Park, the new MuCEM, the Basilica of Notre Dame de la Garde, the Stade Vélodrome, the Palais Longchamp or the Vieux-Port de Marseille.

马赛以卡朗格国家公园、欧洲与地中海文明博物馆、圣母加德大教堂、隆尚宫、马赛旧港等而闻名。

6) Metz(梅茨)

Metz possesses one of the largest urban conservation area in France and more than 100 buildings of the city are classified on the Monument Historique list. Because of its historical and cultural background, Metz benefits from its designation as "Town of Art and History". The city features noteworthy buildings such as the Gothic Saint-Stephen Cathedral, the Basilica of Saint-Pierre-aux-Nonnains, its Station Palace, or its Opera House, the oldest one working in France. Metz is home to some world-class venues including the Arsenal Concert Hall and the Centre Pompidou-Metz Museum, the most visited art venue in France outside Paris.

梅茨拥有法国最大的城市保护区之一,该市有100多座建筑被列入历史古迹名录。梅茨因其深厚的历史和文化背景,被誉为"艺术和历史之城"。

7) Strasbourg(斯特拉斯堡)

Strasbourg's historic city center, the Grandeîle (Grand Island), was classified a World Heritage Site by UNESCO in 1988, the first time such a honour was placed on an entire city center. Strasbourg is immersed in the Franco-German culture and although violently disputed throughout history, has been a bridge of unity between France and Germany for centuries, especially through the University of Strasbourg, currently the second largest in France, and the coexistence of Catholic and Protestant culture.

斯特拉斯堡历史悠久的市中心——大岛于1988年被联合国教科文组织列为世界遗产。斯特拉斯堡沉浸在法德文化中,几个世纪以来,斯特拉斯堡一直是法德之间团结的桥梁。

8) Toulouse(图卢兹)

Toulouse has two UNESCO World Heritage Sites, the Canal du Midi and the largest Romanesque building in the Europe, the Saint-Sernin Basilica. The city historic center also hosts the 13th century gothic monastery Ensemble conventuel des Jacobins (burial place of Saint Thomas Aquinas) and the 16th century bridge Pont Neuf.

图卢兹有两处被联合国教科文组织列入世界遗产,米迪运河和欧洲最大的罗马式建筑圣塞尔南大教堂。

Section 4　Germany(德国)

PART 1(第一部分)

1. 国土疆域(Territory)

德国位于欧洲的心脏地带,与9个国家毗邻。东部与波兰、捷克接壤,西部与荷兰、比利时、卢森堡、法国相邻,南部与奥地利和瑞士为界,北临北海和波罗的海,与丹麦毗邻。边界线全长3 876千米,海岸线长2 389千米,全国面积约357 582平方千米。它是东西欧之间和斯堪的纳维亚与地中海地区之间的交通枢纽,其间水、陆、空条条道路经过德国,被称为"欧洲的走廊"。

Germany is located in the heart of Europe, adjacent to nine countries. It borders Poland and the Czech Republic in the east, the Netherlands, Belgium, Luxembourg and France in the west, Austria and Switzerland in the south, the North Sea, the Baltic Sea and Denmark in the north. The total length of the boundary line is 3 876 km. The length of the coastline is 2 389 km. The land area is 357 582 km^2. It is the transportation hub between East and West Europe and between Scandinavia and the Mediterranean region, in which water, land and air roads pass through Germany, known as the "corridor of Europe".

2. 自然风貌(Natural Features)

德国北自北海和波罗的海沿岸,南至阿尔卑斯山,整个地势南高北低,可分为5个地形区:北部的北海沿岸多沙丘和沼泽,波罗的海沿岸沙地、岩石各半,沙嘴、潟湖众多;北德平原,位于北海、波罗的海沿岸和中部山地之间;中德山地,是北德平原以南、多瑙河以北的中部山地;西南部莱茵河断裂谷地区;南部巴伐利亚高原和阿尔卑斯山区为德国最高峰。

风景如画的波罗的海海滨是著名的度假胜地,这里海洋性气候温和宜人,大大小小的岛屿、潟湖、浅湾星罗棋布,它们时而陡峭,时而平缓,纵横交错,形成了变化万千的海岸风光。其中浅海湾和潟湖上巨大的芦苇在欧洲独一无二。这里有未遭破坏的自然环境,众多宁静而安逸的浴场隐蔽在原始的自然景色之中。波罗的海海滨以其特有的魅力,每年都吸引着众多旅游者到此度假休闲。

阿尔卑斯山是欧洲第一大名山,一眼望去,蜿蜒起伏的山峦、白雪皑皑的山峰、郁郁葱葱的松林、波光粼粼的湖泊纵横交错,山谷中的村庄、峰巅上的古堡教堂隐现在云雾之中。

其变幻莫测的迷人景色使之成为德国最著名的旅游胜地。

德国属温带气候,1月平均气温为−5~1 ℃,7月平均气温为14~19 ℃,年降水量500~1 000毫米,山地可达1 800 mm。但其内部还有一定差异,其中西北一带为温带海洋性气候,往东往南逐渐过渡到温带大陆性气候。

德国境内河流很多,主要河流有莱茵河、易北河、奥得河、多瑙河、威悉河。除多瑙河由西向东流入黑海外,其余河流均由南向北注入北海或波罗的海。德国的河流景色优美,特别是莱茵河沿岸如诗如画的中世纪古罗马风格城镇、碧绿的葡萄园、傲然屹立的古城堡令人目不暇接。莱茵河发源于瑞士中南部的阿尔卑斯山脉北麓,为西欧第一大河,是德国境内最大的河流,它是德国的摇篮。多瑙河发源于德国西南部,是欧洲第二长河,也是一条国际性河流。德国较大的湖泊有博登湖、基姆湖、阿莫尔湖等。

莱茵河是欧洲一条著名的国际性河流。莱茵河流经德国的部分长865千米,流域面积占德国总面积的40%,是德国文化的摇篮。从美因茨到科布伦茨的近200千米的河段是莱茵河景色最美的一段,这里河道蜿蜒曲折,河水清澈见底。人们坐在白色的游艇之上,极目远望,碧绿的葡萄园层次有序地排列在两岸,一座座以桁架建筑而引人注目的小城和50多座古堡、宫殿遗址点缀在青山绿水之中。一段段古老的传说把人们的思绪带向遥远的过去,人们深深地陶醉在这充满浪漫情趣的多姿多彩的莱茵美景之中。

The landscape of Germany is high in the south and low in the north. It can be divided into five topographical divisions: the coastal area of the North Sea and the Baltic Sea in the north; the North German Plains; the Central German mountains; the Rhine river valley in the southwest; the Bavarian plateaus and the Alps.

Germany has a temperate climate, a temperate maritime climate for the northwest area, and a gradual transition to a temperate continental climate.

There are many rivers in Germany, including Rhine, Elbe, Oder, Danube, Weser, etc.

3. 人口与民族(Population and Ethnicity)

德国人口约为8 319万(2021年),人口密度为每平方千米233人,是欧洲人口最稠密的国家之一。城市人口占总人口的85%以上。

德国是一个单一民族的国家,德意志人占90%以上。此外,还有少数的丹麦人、索布族人、犹太人和吉卜赛人。外籍人口1 091.54万,占人口总数的12.2%,其中土耳其人最多,约147.64万。

德语为官方语言。它属于印欧语系中的日耳曼语族,它与丹麦语、挪威语、瑞典语、荷兰语及英语均为亲属语言。标准德语称为高地德语,北德人讲标准德语,而南德人讲施瓦本德语,与标准德语有较大的差别。世界上有1亿多人以德语为母语,除德国外,还有奥地利、列支敦士登、瑞士的绝大部分、意大利的南蒂罗尔等地使用德语。

大部分居民信奉基督教,其中新教和天主教两派教徒的人数各占30%。

Germany has a population about 83.19 million (2020), with a population density of

233 people per square kilometer. Germany is basically a homogenous country, with the German people making up more than 90%. The majority of the population is Christian, in which Protestants and Catholics are about 30% respectively.

4. 发展简史(Brief History of Development)

来到德国的柏林墙遗址前,遥想东西德分割的时代,使我们不得不思考德国不平常的历史。看过《第三帝国的兴亡》一书的人都知道,德国历史上先后出现过三个帝国,弄清三个帝国的来龙去脉,也就弄清了德国历史的轮廓。

公元962年建立德意志民族的神圣罗马帝国。1871年建立统一的德意志帝国。1914年挑起第一次世界大战。1919年建立魏玛共和国。1939年发动第二次世界大战。战后被美、英、法、苏联四国占领。1949年5月23日西部颁布《基本法》,建立德意志联邦共和国。同年10月7日东部成立德意志民主共和国。1990年10月3日,民主德国正式加入联邦德国,德国实现统一。

The Holy Roman Empire of the German nation was founded in 962 AD. A unified German Empire was founded in 1871. World War Ⅰ was started in 1914. The Weimar Republic was established in 1919. World War Ⅱ was launched in 1939. The Federal Republic of Germany was founded on May 23, 1949. The German Democratic Republic was established in the east on October 7 of the same year. On October 3, 1990, Germany was unified.

5. 政治经济(Politics and Economy)

首都为柏林,国花为矢车菊,国鸟为白鹳,货币为欧元。

德国是一个由拥有一定立法、行政和司法自治权的各州联合组成的联邦制共和国。国家元首是总统。总统只是国家权力的象征性代表,其职权主要是礼节性的。联邦政府,即内阁为国家最高行政机构,联邦总理握有实权。

德国是高度发达的工业国。经济总量位居欧洲首位,世界第四。同时,它还是G7(七国集团)成员和欧盟的创始国之一。德国雄居前茅的经济实力决定了它具有举足轻重的地位,它的一举一动对欧洲乃至世界经济都具有重要影响。工业是德国的经济支柱,其中重工业处于支配地位,钢铁、机械、化工、电气和汽车等部门特别发达,占全部工业产值的40%以上。采煤、造船以及战后新兴的石油加工、电子、核能利用、航天、信息技术等部门也很发达。德国农业发达,机械化程度高。德国交通运输业十分发达。公路、水路和航空运输全面发展。特别是公路密度为世界之最。德国的航空运输业发达,法兰克福机场是世界主要航空港之一,汉莎航空公司是国际上经营最好的航空公司之一。德国内河运输十分发达。杜伊斯堡的内河港口是世界上最大的内河港。德国的海洋运输业也很发达,在集装箱船及装船运输方面居世界领先地位。

Germany is a federal republic of states. Germany is a highly developed industrial nation, and its economic volume ranks first in Europe. Industry is the mainstay of Germany's economy. Agriculture is highly developed with high level of mechanization. The transportation industry is very developed, and the highway, waterway and air transportation are fully developed, especially the highway density is the highest in the world.

6. 旅游市场(Tourism Market)

德国经济发达,旅游基础好,旅游业发达。德国人热爱旅游,据德国旅游中心提供的数据,七成以上的德国人每年至少外出长途旅游一次,其中65%以上是出国旅游。德国人每年用于旅游的支出占其总支出的15%到20%,而来自世界各地的游客每年在德国的总消费额也高达200亿欧元。正因为如此,德国的旅游服务业高度发达,同业间的竞争也十分激烈。

德国是世界重要的旅游目的国,德国传统的五大国际客源市场是荷兰、瑞士、美国、英国和奥地利。世界旅游组织的数据显示,2019年德国接待过夜游客人数约3 956万,国际旅游收入为582亿美元。目前,中国前往德国旅游的人数约150万,只占中国出境旅游人数的1%,德国还未进入中国前十五位出境旅游目的地国的行列。

德国也是世界重要的旅游客源国之一。世界旅游组织的数据显示,2018年德国出境人数达1.08亿人,国际旅游项目支出达998.65亿美元。

德国是中国重要的旅游客源国,2018年来华旅游人数达64.30万人次,十年增长24%。

Germany's developed economy has laid a good foundation for tourism. Germany is an important tourist destination in the world, and its five traditional international tourist source markets are the Netherlands, Switzerland, the United States, the United Kingdom and Austria. Germany is one of the most important tourist sources in the world and also to China.

知识拓展 3.4 展览会的王国(见二维码)

知识拓展 3.5　德国慕尼黑啤酒节(见二维码)

PART 2(第二部分)

Tourism Resources(旅游资源)

Germany is well known for its diverse tourist routes, such as the Romantic Road, the Wine Route, the Castle Road, the Timber-Frame Road and the Avenue Road. There are 39 UNESCO World Heritage Sites in Germany, including the old town cores of Regensburg, Bamberg, Lübeck, Quedlinburg, Weimar, Stralsund and Wismar. Germany's most-visited landmarks include Neuschwanstein Castle, Cologne Cathedral, Berlin Bundestag, Hofbräuhaus Munich, Heidelberg Castle, Dresden Zwinger, Fernsehturm Berlin and Aachen Cathedral. The Europa-Park near Freiburg is Europe's second most popular theme park resort, following Disneyland Paris. Its nature-protected national parks, biosphere reserves and other nature parks are popular destinations for ecotourism.

德国以其多样化的旅游路线而闻名,如浪漫之路、葡萄酒之路、城堡之路、木架之路和大道之路。德国有39处联合国教科文组织世界遗产,包括雷根斯堡、班贝格、吕贝克、奎德林堡、魏玛、施特拉尔松德和维斯马等古城。德国参观人数最多的地标建筑包括新天鹅堡、科隆大教堂、国会大厦、慕尼黑皇家啤酒馆、海德堡城堡、德累斯顿的茨威格宫、柏林电视塔和亚琛大教堂。弗赖堡附近的欧罗巴公园是欧洲第二受欢迎的主题公园,仅次于巴黎的迪士尼乐园。其国家公园、生物圈保护区和其他自然公园是生态旅游的热门目的地。

1. Tourist Attractions(旅游名胜)

1)Neuschwanstein Castle(新天鹅堡)

Neuschwanstein Castle (New Swanstone Castle) is a nineteenth-century Romanesque

Revival palace on a rugged hill above the village of Hohenschwangau near Füssen in southwest Bavaria, Germany. The palace has appeared prominently in several movies and was the inspiration for Disneyland's Sleeping Beauty Castle and later, similar structures.

新天鹅堡是一座 19 世纪罗马复兴式宫殿,位于德国巴伐利亚州西南部富森附近的霍恩施万高村的崎岖山丘之上。这座宫殿曾出现在多部电影中,也是迪士尼睡美人城堡以及后来类似建筑的灵感来源。

2)Europa-Park(欧罗巴公园)

Europa-Park is the largest theme park in Germany and the second most popular theme park resort in Europe, following Disneyland Paris. It is located in Rust, in southwestern Germany, between Freiburg and Strasbourg, France. The park is home to twelve roller coasters, the oldest being the Alpenexpress Mine Train, where a powered coaster speeds through a diamond mine, and the newest coaster being Arthur, a suspended indoor and outdoor powered roller coaster and dark ride combination.

欧罗巴公园是德国最大的主题公园,也是继巴黎迪士尼乐园之后欧洲第二受欢迎的主题公园。它位于德国西南部的鲁斯特,在弗赖堡和法国斯特拉斯堡之间。

3)Heidelberg Castle(海德堡城堡)

Heidelberg Castle is a famous ruin in Germany and landmark of Heidelberg. The castle ruins are among the most important Renaissance structures north of the Alps. It is located 80 meters up the northern part of the Königstuhl hillside, and thereby dominates the view of the old downtown. It is served by an intermediate station on the Heidelberger Bergbahnfunicular railway that runs from Heidelberg's Kornmarkt to the summit of the Königstuhl.

海德堡城堡是德国著名的遗址,也是海德堡的标志性建筑。城堡遗址是阿尔卑斯山北部文艺复兴时期最重要的建筑之一。它位于王座山山坡北部 80 米处,可以俯瞰老市中心。

4)Cologne Cathedral(科隆大教堂)

Cologne Cathedral is a Roman Catholic cathedral in Cologne, Germany. It is the seat of the Archbishop of Cologne, currently, since his 2014 transfer from Berlin, Rainer Maria Cardinal Woelki, and of the administration of the Archdiocese of Cologne. It is a renowned monument of German Catholicism and Gothic architecture and is a World Heritage Site. It is Germany's most visited landmark, attracting an average of 20 000 people a day.

科隆大教堂是位于德国科隆的罗马天主教大教堂,是德国天主教和哥特式建筑的著名历史遗迹,是世界遗产,也是德国游客最多的旅游胜地。

2. Tourist City(旅游城市)

1)Berlin(柏林)

Berlin grew out of the historical city center, the Nikolai quarter, its sister town of Cölln, the settlements founded by the Elector, such as Dorotheenstadt or Friedrichstadt and finally the creation of Greater Berlin in 1920, when the hitherto independent towns of Spandau, Charlottenburg or Cöpenick were merged with the old Berlin to form a city of four million inhabitants. This decentralised historical development has resulted in a plethora of sights in Berlin today—not just in the center of the city, but also in the outlying boroughs.

For various reasons the main symbol of the city is the Brandenburg Gate; its unmissable landmarks are the Berlin TV tower in Mitte and the broadcasting tower on exhibition land in Westend.

柏林有众多的景观,不仅分布在城市中心,而且遍布在外围行政区。这座城市的主要标志是勃兰登堡门,其他不容错过的地标主要有米特的柏林电视塔和韦斯特展览区的广播塔。

2)Munich(慕尼黑)

Munich is the capital and largest city of the German state of Bavaria. It is the third largest city in Germany, after Berlin and Hamburg. Munich is home to many national and international authorities, major universities, major museums and theaters. Its numerous architectural attractions, international sports events, exhibitions, conferences and Oktoberfest attract considerable tourists. Munich is a center of finance, publishing, and advanced technologies. Munich is one of the most prosperous and fastest growing cities in Germany, and the seat of numerous corporations and insurance companies. The Deutsches Museum or German Museum, located on an island in the River Isar, is the largest and one of the oldest science museums in the world. The city has several important art galleries.

慕尼黑是德国巴伐利亚州的首府和最大城市,也是德国第三大城市,仅次于柏林和汉堡,是许多国家和国际权威机构、主要大学、主要博物馆和剧院的所在地。其众多的旅游景点、举办的国际体育赛事、展览、会议和啤酒节吸引了大量的旅游者。

3)Hamburg(汉堡)

A typical Hamburg visit includes a tour of the city hall and the grand church St. Michaelis (called the Michel), and visiting the old warehouse district (Speicherstadt) and the harbour promenade (Landungsbrücken). Sightseeing buses connect these points of interest. As Hamburg is one of the world's largest harbor, many visitors take one of the harbor and canal boat tours which start from the Landungsbrücken. Major destinations also include museums. The Beatles had stints on the Reeperbahn early in their careers.

Others prefer the laid-back neighbourhood Schanze with its street cafés, or a barbecue on one of the beaches along the river Elbe. Hamburg's famous zoo, the Tierpark Hagenbeck, was founded in 1907 by Carl Hagenbeck as the first zoo with moated, barless enclosures.

典型的汉堡之旅包括参观市政厅、圣米迦勒教堂、旧仓库区和海港长廊。汉堡是世界上最大的港口之一,许多游客乘坐从靠岸栈桥出发的船游览。

4)Regensburg(雷根斯堡)

Regensburg is a city in southeast Germany. The medieval center of the city is a UNESCO World Heritage Site and a testimony of the city's status as cultural center of southern Germany in the Middle Ages. In 2014, Regensburg was among the top sights and travel attractions in Germany.

雷根斯堡是德国东南部的一座城市。中世纪的市中心被联合国教科文组织列入世界遗产,是中世纪德国南部文化中心的见证。

Section 5　Italy(意大利)

PART 1(第一部分)

1. 国土疆域(Territory)

意大利地处欧洲南部、地中海北岸,其领土包括亚平宁半岛、西西里岛、撒丁岛及其他小岛。亚平宁半岛像一只巨大的长筒靴伸入蔚蓝色的地中海。意大利北部与法国、瑞士、奥地利、斯洛文尼亚接壤,东、西、南三面临海,东面临亚得里亚海,南临爱奥尼亚海,西临第勒尼安海。在意大利境内还有两个独立的国家:一个是地处东北部的圣马力诺共和国,它是欧洲最古老的共和国;另一个是梵蒂冈,它位于意大利的首都罗马,是罗马天主教会的中心。意大利的国土面积约为 301 333 平方千米,海岸线长约 7 200 千米。

Italy is located on the northern coast of the Mediterranean Sea in southern Europe. Its territory includes the Apennine Peninsula, Sicily, Sardinia and other small islands. The Apennine Peninsula is like a giant boot stretching into the blue Mediterranean Sea. Italy's continental boundary is adjacent to France, Switzerland, Austria and Slovenia in the north; it faces the sea in the east, west and south, the Adriatic Sea in the east, the Ionian Sea in the east, and the Tiereni Sea in the west. There are also two independent countries in Italy: one is the Republic of San Marino in the northeast, which is the oldest republic in Europe; the other is the Vatican, which is located in Rome, the capital of Italy and the center of the Roman Catholic Church. Italy's territory area is about 301 333 km², and its coastline is 7 200 km.

2. 自然风貌(Natural Features)

意大利是一个多山的国家,自然景色优美。北部是阿尔卑斯山脉,沿着亚平宁半岛走向的是亚平宁山脉,两山交接处以东是著名的波河平原。火山是意大利重要旅游资源之一,主要分布在亚平宁半岛和西西里岛等地。维苏威火山是世界著名的活火山,它位于那不勒斯市东南,海拔1 281米。公元79年,它发生大爆发,将附近的庞贝城埋在厚厚的火山灰和浮石之下。进入20世纪后它又几次喷发,分别为1906年、1929年和1944年。埃特纳火山是欧洲最高大、最活跃的火山,位于西西里岛东岸,海拔3 323 m。活火山的奇景、积雪的山峰、山坡的森林、山麓的葡萄园和橘子林等,给当地的旅游业增添了活力。

意大利南部半岛和岛屿地区是典型的地中海气候,冬季不冷且多雨,夏季炎热又干燥。1月平均气温为2~10 ℃,7月平均气温为23~26 ℃,大部分地区年降雨量在500~1 000毫米。

意大利充分利用海滨优势和地中海气候,在海岸带建起了长达数百千米的海滨旅游基地,包括6 000多个海滨浴场、150多个旅游港口、500多个海滨旅游中心,游乐设施非常齐全。

意大利的河流很多,但大多短小流急,春冬流量大,夏秋流量小。波河是意大利最大的河流,全长652千米,发源于阿尔卑斯山,向东流入亚得里亚海。台伯河是流经罗马的主要河流。

Italy is a mountainous country with beautiful natural scenery. The Alps are in the north; the Apennines Mountains goes along with the Apennines Peninsula, the famous Po River plain lies in the west of two mountains' junction; volcano is one of the important tourism resources in Italy. The peninsula and islands of southern Italy have a typical Mediterranean climate. There are many rivers in Italy, but most of them are short and have swift water current. The Po River is the largest river in Italy.

3. 人口与民族(Population and Ethnicity)

意大利人口约为5 926万(2021年)人口密度为每平方千米196.66人。在意大利的民族构成中,95%以上是意大利人,基本上是单一民族的国家。

意大利的官方语言是意大利语,它属于印欧语系罗曼语族。意大利语还是圣马力诺、梵蒂冈的官方语言,也是瑞士四种正式语言之一。

意大利是一个信奉天主教的国家,90%以上的居民信奉天主教。

Italy has a population of about 59.26 million (2021) with a population density of 196.66 people per square kilometer. Italy is basically a homogeneous country with more than 95% Italian. It is a Catholic country with more than 90% adherents.

4. 发展简史(Brief History of Development)

意大利是欧洲的文明古国,古往今来,许多文人赞颂过意大利,把它描绘成"欧洲的天堂和花园"。

公元前2000年,在意大利开始出现定居居民,他们属于拉丁民族。公元前754年罗马建城,从此,拉丁人开始被称为罗马人,罗马也就成为今日意大利的一种象征。

古罗马从公元前753年开始,直至公元476年西罗马帝国灭亡,前后共1 229年的漫长历史。公元962年受神圣罗马帝国统治。11世纪诺曼人入侵意大利南部并建立王国。12—13世纪又分裂成许多王国、公国、自治城市和小封建领地。

在14世纪和15世纪,在地中海沿岸的某些城市开始出现资本主义萌芽。从16世纪到18世纪中叶,专制主义制度在意大利各城市国家确立,1861年3月建立意大利王国。1870年9月20日,意大利军队占领罗马,实现了统一。

意大利统一后,资本主义经济得以迅速发展,20世纪初,进入帝国主义阶段并开始殖民扩张。1922年墨索里尼上台,同德国、日本结成同盟,实行了长达20余年的法西斯统治。1946年6月2日,废除君主制,成立意大利共和国。

Ancient Rome had a long history of 1 229 years from 753 BC until the fall of the Western Roman Empire in 476 AD. It was ruled by the Holy Roman Empire in 962 AD. The Kingdom of Italy was established in March 1861. On September 20, 1870, the Italian army captured Rome, and finally achieved unification.

5. 政治经济(Politics and Economy)

首都为罗马。国花是雏菊,又名五月菊。货币为欧元。

意大利政体是议会共和制,实行两院制议会和内阁负责制。总统是国家元首和民族统一的象征,无行政权,不设副总统。总理由总统任命,对议会负责。议会拥有立法权和决定国家重大政治问题的权力。立法权由参众两院集体行使。

意大利发达的资本主义国家,属于西欧四大强国之一。意大利南北经济发展不平衡,北方的工农业、商业发达,人们的生活水平较高;南方的工业较落后,以农业为主。经过政府的努力,这种不平衡状态已有很大的改观。意大利的工业在国民经济中占重要地位。由于国内自然资源贫乏,原料和能源主要依赖进口,因此意大利工业具有明显的以加工业出口为主的特点。其主要工业部门有机械工业、食品工业、纺织、服装、制鞋、皮革业等。意大利是军火生产大国,是世界上仅次于美、俄、法的第四大军火出口国。

意大利的农业也很发达。农业产值占国内生产总值的3.5%,农业人口占全国的10%。小麦是最重要的农作物,蔬菜在意大利农业生产和出口中占有重要地位,是欧洲最大园圃蔬菜生产国之一。意大利号称"橄榄王国",种植历史达3 000年之久。意大利的葡萄和葡萄酒享誉世界。

意大利的交通运输业相当发达。自古就有"条条大路通罗马"之说。全国共有机场96座。海运业非常发达,共有325个港口,主要有热那亚、那不勒斯、威尼斯等。意大利铁路和公路交通也十分便利。

The Italian government is a parliamentary republic. Italy is a developed capitalist country in the world, which is one of the four great powers in Western Europe. The economic development is unbalanced between the north and the south of Italy. The industrial, agricultural and commercial development in the north of Italy is developed, while industry in the south is backward. Italy's transport industry is quite developed, aviation, railway and road traffic are very convenient.

6. 旅游市场(Tourism Market)

意大利旅游资源丰富,旅游业发达,旅游收入是弥补国家收支逆差的重要来源。意大利是世界旅游大国,世界旅游业理事会(WTTC)的数据显示,意大利最重要的客源市场是德国,占所有国际入境旅客的20%,美国和法国均排在第二位,占8%,英国排在第三位,占6%。

据世界旅游组织统计,2019年,意大利接待的国际旅游者为6 451万人次,国际旅游收入496亿美元。2019年,旅游业为意大利创造了近350万个工作岗位,占该国总劳动力的14.9%;旅游业还创造了2 329亿欧元的GDP,占意大利经济的13%。

近年来,中国人赴意大利旅游发展迅猛,2019中国赴意大利旅游人数达600万人次,比2018年增加100万。

意大利是中国极具潜力的旅游客源国,2018年意大利来华旅游人数达27.80万人次,十年增长45%。

Italy has rich tourism resources and developed tourism industry. Tourism income is a great source to make up the deficit of national income and expenditure. Italy's most important source markets are Germany, the United States, France and the UK. Italy is a potential tourist source for China.

PART 2(第二部分)

Tourism Resources(旅游资源)

People mainly visit Italy for its rich art, cuisine, history, fashion and culture, its beautiful coastline and beaches, its mountains, and priceless ancient monuments. Italy has 51 total sites inscribed on the list, making it the country with most World Heritage Sites. Out of Italy's 51 heritage sites, four are shared with other countries in 2015. Four World Heritage Sites in Italy are of the natural type, all others are cultural sites (47). Therefore, Italy has the largest number of world cultural heritage sites followed by Spain with 39 cultural sites.

人们游览意大利主要是因为它拥有丰富的艺术、美食、历史、时尚和文化、美丽的海岸线和海滩、群山和珍贵的古代遗迹。2015年,意大利共有51处遗址上榜,成为世界遗产最多的国家。在意大利的51处遗产中,有4处与其他国家共享。意大利有4处世界遗产属于自然类型,其他都是文化遗产(47处)。因此,意大利是世界文化遗产最多的国家,其次是西班牙,共有39处文化遗产。

1. Tourist Attractions(旅游名胜)

1)Dolomites(多洛米蒂山)

The Dolomites are a mountain range located in northeastern Italy. One national park and many other regional parks are located in the Dolomites. In August 2009, the Dolomites were declared a UNESCO World Heritage Site. A tourist mecca, the Dolomites are famous for ski in the winter months and mountain climbing, hiking, cycling, and base jumping, as well as paragliding and hang gliding in summer, late spring and early autumn. Free climbing has been a tradition in the Dolomites since 1887.

多洛米蒂山是位于意大利东北部的山脉,这里有一个国家公园和许多区域公园。2009年8月,多洛米蒂山被联合国教科文组织列入世界遗产。

2)Monte San Giorgio(圣乔治山)

Monte San Giorgio is a wooded mountain (1 096 m above sea level) of the Lugano Prealps, overlooking Lake Lugano in Switzerland. It lies in the southern part of the canton of Ticino, between the municipalities of Brusino Arsizio, Riva San Vitale and Meride. Monte San Giorgio became a UNESCO World Heritage Sites in 2003, because "it is the single best known record of marine life in the Triassic Period, and records important remains of life on land as well". The Italian region west of Poncione d'Arzo (Porto Ceresio) was added as an extension to the World Heritage Site in 2010.

圣乔治山海拔1 096米,是一座树木繁茂的山,这里可以俯瞰瑞士的卢戈诺湖。圣乔治山在2003年被联合国教科文组织列入世界遗产,它记录了三叠纪时期最著名的海洋生物,同时也记录了陆地上重要的生物遗迹。

3)Mount Etna(埃特纳火山)

Mount Etna is an active stratovolcano on the east coast of Sicily, Italy. Mount Etna is one of the most active volcanoes in the world and is in an almost constant state of activity. The fertile volcanic soils support extensive agriculture, with vineyards and orchards spread across the lower slopes of the mountain and the broad Plain of Catania to the south. Due to its history of recent activity and nearby population, Mount Etna has been designated a Decade Volcano by the United Nations. In June 2013, it was added to the list of UNESCO World Heritage Sites.

埃特纳火山是意大利西西里岛东海岸的一座活火山,它是世界上最活跃的火山之一。肥沃的火山土壤有利于农业发展,葡萄园和果园散布在较低的山坡和广阔的卡塔尼亚平原。2013年6月,埃特纳火山被教科文组织列入世界遗产名录。

4) Isole Eolie (Aeolian Islands)伊索莱·约里(伊奥利亚群岛)

The Aeolian Islands are avolcanic archipelago in the Tyrrhenian Sea north of Sicily, named after the demigod of the winds Aeolus. The locals residing on the islands are known as Aeolians. The Aeolian Islands are a popular tourist destination in the summer, and attract up to 200 000 visitors annually. The Aeolian Islands are listed by UNESCO as World Heritage Sites.

伊奥利亚群岛是位于西西里岛以北的一座火山群岛,它是夏季旅游胜地,被联合国教科文组织列为世界遗产。

5) Gran Paradiso National Park(大帕拉迪索国家公园)

Gran Paradiso National Park is an Italian national park in the Graian Alps, between the Aosta Valley and Piedmont regions. The park is named after Gran Paradiso Mountain, which is located in the park, and is contiguous with the French Vanoise National Park. The land the park encompasses was initially protected in order to protect the Alpine ibex from poachers, as it was a personal hunting ground for King Victor Emanuel II, but now also protects other species.

大帕拉迪索国家公园位于格雷晏阿尔卑斯山,公园以位于大帕拉迪索山命名,与法国的瓦努瓦斯国家公园毗连。

2. Tourist City(旅游城市)

1) Rome(罗马)

Rome is one of the most important tourist destinations of the world, due to the incalculable immensity of its archaeological and art treasures, as well as for the charm of its unique traditions, the beauty of its panoramic views, and the majesty of its magnificent "villas" (parks). Among the most significant resources: plenty of museums (Capitoline Museums, the Vatican Museums, Galleria Borghese, and a great many others), aqueducts, fountains, churches, palaces, historical buildings, the monuments and ruins of the Roman Forum, and the Catacombs. Rome is the third most visited city in the EU. Rome is the city with the most monuments in the world.

罗马是世界上最重要的旅游目的地之一,因为它拥有数不清的考古和艺术珍宝、独特的传统魅力、全方位的美景和宏伟的建筑。最重要的旅游资源包括大量的博物馆、引水渠、喷泉、教堂、宫殿、历史建筑、古罗马广场的纪念碑和废墟,以及地下墓穴。罗马是欧盟第三大旅游城市。

2) Milan(米兰)

Milan is one of EU's most important tourist destinations, and Italy's second. The city boasts several popular tourist attractions, such as the city's Duomo and Piazza, the Teatro alla Scala, the San Siro Stadium, the Vittorio Emanuele Ⅱ Gallery, the Sforza Castle, the Pinacoteca di Brera and the Via Monte Napoleone. Most tourists visit sights such as Milan Cathedral, the Sforza Castle and the Teatro alla Scala, however, other main sights such as the Basilica of Sant'Ambrogio, the Navigli and the Brera district are less visited and prove to be less popular. The city also has numerous hotels, including the ultra-luxurious Town House Galleria, which is the world's first seven-star hotel, ranked officially by the Société Générale de Surveillance, and one of the leading hotels of the World.

米兰是欧盟最重要的旅游目的地之一,也是意大利第二大旅游目的地。著名的旅游景点有城市的大教堂和广场、斯卡拉剧院、圣西罗体育场、伊曼纽尔二世拱廊、斯福尔扎城堡、布雷拉美术馆和蒙特拿破仑街。大多数游客参观的景点包括米兰大教堂、斯福尔扎城堡和斯卡拉剧院等。

3) Florence(佛罗伦萨)

Florence is famous for its history: a center of medieval European trade and finance and one of the wealthiest cities of the time, it is considered the birthplace of the Renaissance, and has been called "the Athens of the Middle Ages". The Historic Center of Florence attracts millions of tourists each year. It was declared a World Heritage Site by UNESCO in 1982. The city is noted for its culture, Renaissance art, architecture and monuments. The city also contains numerous museums and art galleries, such as the Uffizi Gallery and the Palazzo Pitti, and still exerts an influence in the fields of art, culture and politics. Due to Florence's artistic and architectural heritage, it has been ranked by Forbes as one of the most beautiful cities in the world. Florence is an important city in Italian fashion, being ranked in the top 51 fashion capitals of the world; furthermore, it is a major national economic center, as well as a tourist and industrial hub.

佛罗伦萨以其历史而闻名,它是中世纪欧洲贸易和金融中心,是文艺复兴的发源地,被称为"中世纪的雅典"。佛罗伦萨以其文化、文艺复兴时期的艺术、建筑和历史遗迹而闻名。佛罗伦萨历史中心在1982年被联合国教科文组织列为世界遗产,被福布斯评为世界上最美丽的城市之一。

4) Bologna(博洛尼亚)

Bologna is home of the first university in the Western world. This city has a rich history and culture. Bologna is well known for its cuisine.

博洛尼亚是西方世界第一所大学的所在地。这个城市有着丰富的历史和文化,同时,它以美食而闻名。

5)Genoa(热那亚)

Genoa (Genova) was one of the most important medieval maritime republics. It is a very wealthy and diverse city. Its port brings in tourism and trade, along with art and architecture. Genoa is birthplace of Columbus and jeans.

热那亚是中世纪最重要的海上共和国之一,是一个非常富有和多样化的城市。它的港口带来了旅游业和贸易,也带来了艺术和建筑。热那亚是哥伦布和牛仔裤的诞生地。

6)Naples(那不勒斯)

Naples (Napoli) is one of the oldest cities of the Western world, with a historic city center that is a UNESCO World Heritage Site. Naples is also near the famous volcano Vesuvius and the ruins of the ancient Roman towns of Pompeii and Ercolano.

那不勒斯是西方世界最古老的城市之一,其历史悠久的市中心被联合国教科文组织列入世界遗产,它附近还有著名的维苏威火山及古罗马城镇庞贝和埃尔科拉诺的遗址。

7)Pisa(比萨)

Pisa is one of the medieval maritime republics. It has lots of medieval palaces and squares. It is home to the unmistakable image of the Leaning Tower of Pisa. It is a very touristy city. It is famous too for the Advanced Normal School of Pisa.

比萨是中世纪的海上共和国之一。这是一个典型的旅游城市,有许多中世纪的宫殿和广场,是比萨斜塔的所在地,以比萨高等师范学校而闻名。

8)Turin(都灵)

Turin (Torino) is the first capital of Italy, after being the capital of Kingdom of Sardinia (actually Piedmont-centred), what had promoted national reunification. It is home of the FIAT, the most important industry in Italy. Turin is a well-known industrial city, based on the aerospace industry and, of course, automobile industry.

都灵是意大利的第一个首都,是撒丁王国的首都。都灵是著名的工业城市,以航空航天工业和汽车工业为基础,是意大利著名汽车公司菲亚特的故乡。

9)Venice(威尼斯)

Venice (Venezia) is known for its history (the most important, beside Genoa and Pisa, of the medieval maritime republics), art, and world famous canals. It is one of the most beautiful cities in Italy; it is home to Island of Murano, which is famous for its hand-blown glass. St. Mark's Square is where most of the tourists converge and it can get very crowded in the summer time.

威尼斯是中世纪最重要的海上共和国,以其历史、艺术和世界著名的运河而闻名。它是意大利最美丽的城市之一,也是以手工吹制玻璃闻名的穆拉诺岛的所在地。

Section 6　Spain(西班牙)

PART 1(第一部分)

1. 国土疆域(Territory)

西班牙东临地中海,北濒比斯开湾,东北同法国、安道尔接壤,西邻葡萄牙,南隔直布罗陀海峡与非洲的摩洛哥隔海相望,扼地中海和大西洋航路的咽喉,被称为通往欧洲、非洲、中东和拉丁美洲的"桥梁"。西班牙总面积50.6万平方千米,海岸线长约7 800千米。

Spain is adjacent to the Mediterranean Sea in the east, Biscay Bay in the north, France and Andorra in the northeast, and Portugal in the west. The Strait of Gibraltar in the south faces Morocco in the African continent across the sea, which is the throat of the Mediterranean and Atlantic routes. It is known as the "bridge" to Europe, Africa, the Middle East and Latin America. Its area is 506 000 km^2, its coastline is about 7 800 km.

2. 自然风貌(Natural Features)

西班牙是一个多山的国度,坎塔布里亚山脉、比利牛斯山脉、戈列多山脉、安达卢西亚山脉、瓜达拉玛等山脉形成了西班牙复杂奇特的地形。

北部山地区,绵亘着东西走向的比利牛斯山脉和坎塔布利亚山脉,海拔达2 000 m以上,山地林木茂盛,景色迷人,其间许多宽广的河谷置于其间,湖水清澈如镜,落差不一的飞瀑不胜枚举。中部梅塞塔中央高原区,约占全国面积的60%,平均海拔600~800 m。这里居住着西班牙人中的1/3以上,历来是西班牙重要的工业、农业和旅游区。东北部是阿拉贡平原区,该区位于比利牛斯山脉东南面的坎布罗河流域,是一个大致呈三角形的波状平原。这里是西班牙的天然粮仓,也是重要的葡萄、柑橘等水果产地。地中海沿岸山地区,从东南部安达卢西亚至东北部的加泰卢尼亚,蜿蜒曲折,跨度达1 500 km有余。安达卢西亚山脉的最高峰穆拉森山海拔3 478 m,是伊比利亚半岛的最高点,号称西班牙"民族的脊梁"。南部安达卢西亚平原,位于摩莱纳山脉和安达卢西亚山脉之间,这里一马平川,坦坦荡荡。那加利群岛是由火山喷发而成,它由13个火山岛组成,总面积为7 273 km^2。

西班牙本土大体上位于36°~43°N,受地中海、大西洋,以及复杂地形的影响,大部分地区属温带,同时呈现多样性,总体特征是温和少雨、干燥多风,一年四季分明。最冷月为1~2月,平均气温是:东部、南部为8~13 ℃;北部2~10 ℃。最热月是8月,平均气温是:东部、南部为24~36 ℃;北部为16~21 ℃。最低气温达-25 ℃,最高气温可达40 ℃。中部梅塞塔高原为大陆性气候,冬夏温差大。北部和西北部为温带海洋性气候,冬夏温差不大,南部和东南部为地中海式气候,夏季酷热,冬暖多雨。大自然赋予西班牙适宜的气候,使其成为世界著名的旅游王国。

西班牙河流众多,纵横交错,萦回百折,但大多数河流水流量不大,大部分河段不利于航行。主要河流有埃布罗河(全长 927 千米)、杜埃罗河(长 780 千米)、塔霍河(长 910 千米)、瓜的亚纳河(长 820 千米)和瓜达基维尔河(长 560 千米)等,这些河流分别向西、南、东三个方向注入大西洋和地中海。

Spain is a mountainous country. The mountains of Cantabria, Pyrenees, Gorrido, Andalusia, Guadarama and so on form the complex and unique landscape of Spain.

Most parts of Spain lie in the temperate zone, the overall characteristics of the climate is mild, less rain, dry, windy, and four distinct seasons.

Spain has many rivers, but most of them are not very rich in water flow. The main rivers are the Ebro River, the Duero River and so on.

3. 人口民族(Population and Ethnicity)

西班牙人口约 4 710 万(2020 年),人口密度为每平方千米 93.08 人。西班牙是一个多民族国家,主体民族是卡斯蒂利亚人(即西班牙人),占总人口的 80%以上,少数民族有加泰罗尼亚人、加里西亚人和巴斯克人。

西班牙语即卡斯蒂利亚语,为西班牙的官方语言。西班牙语是世界上的一个大语种,是国际通用语言和联合国使用的六种语言之一。目前,全世界有 3 亿人口使用西班牙语,仅次于汉语和英语。西班牙是一个以天主教为主的国家,有 96%的居民信奉天主教,其圣城圣地亚哥被称为欧洲的"朝圣之路"。

Spain has a population of about 47.10 million (2020) with a population density of 93.08 people per square kilometer. Spain is a multi-ethnic country, and the main ethnic group is Castilian, that is, the Spanish people. Spain is a Catholic country, with 96% of its residents professing Catholicism.

 知识拓展 3.6　西班牙的吉卜赛人(见二维码)

4. 发展简史(Brief History of Development)

西班牙是一个历史悠久、文明古老的国家。公元 8 世纪起,西班牙先后遭外族入侵,西班牙人民为反对外族侵略,进行了长达 800 年的斗争,终于在 1492 年赶走了摩尔人,取得了"光复运动"的胜利,建立了统一的封建王朝。同年航海家哥伦布发现了西印度群岛,此后,西班牙逐渐成为海上强国,对外进行扩张,在欧、美、非、亚四大洲均有殖民地。1580 年西班牙征服葡萄牙,成为欧洲最大的国家。1588 年西班牙"无敌舰队"被英国击溃,西班牙开始衰落。1873 年 2 月 11 日爆发资产阶级革命,建立第一共和国。西班牙在第一次世界大战中宣布中立,这使西班牙有机会同交战双方进行贸易和劳务出口,因此大力推动了西班牙资本主义的发展。1931 年 4 月 12 日,西班牙再次爆发革命,建立第二共和国。1936 年 7 月佛朗哥发动叛乱,并得到希特勒和墨索里尼的支持,经过 3 年内战,于 1939 年夺取政权,开始实行长达 36 年的独裁统治。1975 年 11 月 20 日,佛朗哥去世,胡安·卡洛斯继承王位。胡安·卡洛斯一世国王继位后,西班牙开始走上民主改革的道路。1978 年 12 月 29 日,西班牙宣布实行议会君主立宪制。

Since the 8th century, Spain has been invaded by foreign nations. In 1492, a unified feudal dynasty was established. Later, Spain gradually became a maritime power. In 1580, Spain conquered Portugal and became the most powerful nation in Europe. In 1588, the Spanish Armada was defeated by the British and Spain began to decline. On December 29, 1978, Spain was declared a parliamentary constitutional monarchy.

5. 政治经济(Politics and Economy)

首都为马德里,国花为石榴花,货币为欧元。

西班牙是社会民主法治国家,实行两院议会君主制。国王为国家元首和武装部队最高统帅,是国家的象征。

西班牙是一个中等发达的资本主义国家,经济总量居欧盟第五位、世界第十三位。西班牙是一个后进的工业国,工业产值占国内生产总值的比例较高。西班牙的工业分布很不平衡,主要集中在马德里、加泰罗尼亚、巴克斯、瓦伦西亚、安达卢西亚和卡斯蒂亚莱昂地区。汽车工业在西班牙起步较晚,是西班牙的支柱产业之一,位居欧盟第二、世界第八。西班牙的制鞋业也很发达,阿利坎被誉为"制鞋王国",是世界产鞋中心之一。

西班牙是一个传统的农业国,农产品基本自给,有些农产品还可供出口。西班牙素有"橄榄王国"之称。它也是世界上最大的葡萄酒生产国之一,葡萄酒产量仅次于意大利和法国,居世界第三位。

西班牙的交通运输非常发达。全国有机场 105 个,主要机场有马德里巴拉哈斯机场、帕尔马·德马略卡机场和巴塞罗那机场。西班牙三面环海,港口体系完善。西班牙的铁路建设较早,有 160 多年的历史。有三条过境铁路,一条通往葡萄牙,另两条经法国通往欧洲其他国家。西班牙国内运输以公路为主,公路密如蛛网,遍布全国。

Spain is a social democracy under the rule of law. Spain is a moderately developed capitalist country. Its economy ranks 5th place in EU and 13th place in the world. Spain is a backward industrial country, and the industrial output value accounts for a large proportion of GDP. Spain is a traditional agricultural country, and agricultural products are virtually self-sufficient. Spain's transportation is developed, with perfect aviation, railway highway transport.

6. 旅游市场(Tourism Market)

西班牙号称"旅游王国",它和法国、美国并称世界三大旅游国,世界旅游组织总部就设在西班牙首都马德里。旅游业是西班牙经济的重要支柱和外汇的主要来源之一,是世界最具竞争力的旅游国家。

到西班牙旅游的外国游客中有80%仍来自欧洲国家,主要是英国人和德国人,他们主要到西班牙享受海滩和阳光。据UNWTO统计,2019年西班牙入境旅游人数达8 370万人次,居世界第二位;入境旅游收入达923.37亿美元,居世界第二位。近年来,欧洲经济复苏缓慢,欧洲游客人数减少,但在西班牙旅游部门的努力宣传下,亚洲游客的人数保持增长。2018年中国游客数量增长了约26%,较2017年增加约13.42万人;日本游客数量增长约23.8%,人数增加约10.6万人。其中,中国游客到西班牙旅游人数增长较快,西班牙国家统计局的数据显示,2017年到西班牙旅游的中国游客人数仅为51.47万人,2018年升至59.7万人。

出国旅游,特别是近距离出国旅游在西班牙人的生活中占有越来越重要的位置。西班牙人出国旅游的目的主要是度假,其次是商务、探亲访友和其他私人性质的旅游。但出境旅游市场相对较小,出国旅游的目的地主要是欧盟国家,约占85%,依次为法国、葡萄牙、意大利、奥地利,其次是拉丁美洲国家(约占4%)和远东国家(约占4%)。目前,西班牙还未成为中国重要的客源国,近年来,西班牙来华旅游增长缓慢。据文化和旅游部统计,2014年中国旅行社接待西班牙来华旅游者为14.10万人次,2019年为17.13万人次。

西班牙国内旅游市场相对较小,但发展迅速。国内度假旅游者大多数去海岸目的地,但也有少数人到巴利阿里群岛和加那利群岛。其中阿扎哈海岸、布兰卡海岸和安达卢西亚海岸是最受欢迎的旅游目的地,西班牙的北部海岸也十分受游人喜爱。

Spain is known as the "Kingdom of Tourism". Tourism is a major pillar of the Spanish economy and one of the main sources of foreign exchange. It is one of the world's top three tourism powers and has become the world's most competitive tourism country. Eighty percent of foreign visitors to Spain are still from European countries, mainly English and German; The outbound tourism destinations are mainly EU nations; The domestic tourism market is relatively small, but it is growing rapidly.

PART 2(第二部分)

Tourism Resources(旅游资源)

The climate of Spain, its geographic location, popular coastlines, diverse landscapes, historical legacy, vibrant culture and excellent infrastructure, has made Spain's international tourist industry among the largest in the world. In the last five decades, international tourism in Spain has grown to become the second largest in the world in terms of spending.

西班牙的气候、地理位置、受欢迎的海岸线、多样的景观、历史遗产、充满活力的文化和优良的基础设施,使西班牙的国际旅游业跻身世界前列。在过去的五十年里,西班牙已发展成为世界第二大旅游消费国。

1. Tourist Attractions(旅游名胜)

Spain is the fourth largest country in Europe, and has a diverse landscape and, as a result, is often called "a miniature continent". Many indigenous and endemic species owe their current situation to the existence of protected areas with which they try to avoid their decline or extinction. To date, Spain has a total of 15 national parks, of which 10 are on the mainland, 1 in the Balearic Islands and 4 in the Canary Islands. Spain's most visited national park is the Teide National Park in the Canary Islands and crowned with the third largest Volcano in the world from its base, the Teide, with 3 718 meters above the sea level (also the highest point in Spain). The Teide also has the distinction of being the most visited national park in Europe and second in the world.

The mild climate during the whole year and the extensive sandy beaches of the Mediterranean and Atlantic Ocean as well as of its two archipelagoes (the Balearic Islands and the Canary Islands respectively) have been attracting tourists from Northern Europe for decades. The most popular Spanish mainland coasts are on its Mediterranean side. Spain's two archipelagoes, the Balearic Islands off the mainland coast in the Mediterranean and the volcanic Canary Islands in the Atlantic, are both very popular destinations with Spaniards and Europeans.

西班牙是欧洲第四大国家,拥有多样化的景观,被称为"微型大陆"。迄今为止,西班牙共有 15 个国家公园,其中 10 个在大陆,1 个在巴利阿里群岛,4 个在加那利群岛。西班牙游客最多的国家公园是加那利群岛的泰德国家公园,泰德火山是世界第三大火山,海拔 3 718 米。

全年温和的气候、地中海和大西洋广阔的沙滩以及地中海的两个群岛(分别是巴利阿里群岛和加那利群岛),一直吸引着西班牙人和欧洲人,这两个群岛是他们非常喜欢的旅游目的地。

1) Teide National Park(泰德国家公园)

Teide National Park is a national park located in Tenerife (Canary Islands, Spain). It is centered on Mount Teide, the highest mountain of Spain (3 718 metres high) and the islands of the Atlantic (it is the third largest volcano in the world from its base on the ocean floor). It is the largest national park in Spain and an important part of the Canary Islands. The park has an area of 18 990 hectares and was named a World Heritage Site by UNESCO on June 28, 2007. Since the end of 2007, it has also been one of the 12 Treasures of Spain. On a ridge, to the east of Teide, are the telescopes of the Observatorio del Teide. Territorially, it belongs to the municipality of La Orotava. The Teide is the most famous natural icon not only of Tenerife, but also of all the Canary Islands.

泰德国家公园是位于西班牙加那利群岛的国家公园,是西班牙最大的国家公园,也是加那利群岛的重要组成部分。泰德山是西班牙最高的山,高3 718米,是世界第三大火山。2007年6月28日它被联合国教科文组织列为世界遗产。

2) Doñana National Park(多尼亚纳国家公园)

Doñana National Park consists of the delta region where the Guadalquivir River reaches the Atlantic Ocean. It is home to a diverse variety of biotopes, such as lagoons, marshlands, dunes, and maquis. The park is one of the largest heronries in the Mediterranean region and holds more than 500 000 water fowl during the winter.

多尼亚纳国家公园由瓜达尔基维尔河进入大西洋的三角洲地区组成,这里潟湖、沼泽和沙丘遍布。它是各种生物群落的家园,是地中海地区最大的海鸟公园之一,冬季拥有超过50万只水禽。

3) Plaza de Espana(西班牙广场)

Plaza de Espana is a lovely plaza just out of the center of town, where many of the main roads in Barcelona. It is also home to Barcelona's old bull-fighting ring which is now nothing but a shell, albeit quite a beautiful one. The main draw to Plaza de Espana is the Palau Nacional which is the Museum of Catalan art. It's stunning and there is never a better time to see it than when it is lit up at night with the Magic Fountain in front. The Magic Fountain is a free music and light show.

位于巴塞罗那市中心的西班牙广场是一个迷人的广场,是巴塞罗那古老的斗牛场的所在地。加泰罗尼亚艺术博物馆、夜晚魔法喷泉是它最吸引人的地方。

4) Port Olímpic(奥林匹克港)

The Port Olímpic is a marina located in Barcelona, Catalonia. Located east of the Port of Barcelona, it hosted the sailing events for the 1992 Summer Olympics. The venue was opened in 1991.

奥林匹克港是位于巴塞罗那市加泰罗尼亚的一个码头。这里举办了1992年夏季奥运会的帆船比赛。

5)Columbus Monument(哥伦布纪念碑)

The Columbus Monument is a 60m tall monument to Christopher Columbus at the lower end of La Rambla, Barcelona, Catalonia, Spain. It was constructed for the Exposición Universal de Barcelona (1888) in honor to Columbus, first voyage to the America. The monument serves as a reminder that Christopher Columbus reported to Queen Isabella Ⅰ and King Ferdinand Ⅴ in Barcelona after his first trip to the new continent.

哥伦布纪念碑高60米,建于1888年,纪念哥伦布的第一次美洲之旅。

6)Casa Milà(米拉之家)

Casa Milà, popularly known as La Pedrera, is a modernist building in Barcelona, Catalonia, Spain. It was the last civil work designed by Catalan architect Antoni Gaudí, built between the years 1906 and 1912. It was commissioned in 1906 by businessman Pere Milà i Camps and his wife Roser Segimon. At the time, it was controversial because of the undulating stone facade and twisting wrought iron balconies and windows designed by Josep Maria Jujol. Architecturally it is considered structurally innovative, with a self-supporting stone front and columns, and floors free of load bearing walls. Also innovative is the underground garage.

In 1984 it was declared a World Heritage Site by UNESCO. Currently, it is the headquarters of the Catalunya La Pedrera Foundation, which manages the exhibitions, activities and public visits at Casa Milà.

米拉之家是西班牙巴塞罗那的一座现代主义建筑,建于1906年至1912年间。它在建筑结构上有许多创新之处,建筑物的重量完全由柱子承受,地板没有承重墙,有着起伏的石头立面、扭曲的铁艺阳台和窗户。1984年它被联合国教科文组织列为世界遗产。

2. Tourist Cities(旅游城市)

As a crossroad of several civilizations, Spain offers a number of historical cities and towns. Major destinations include Spain's two largest cities: Madrid and Barcelona, which stand as two of the leading city destinations in Europe. Both offer a matchless number of attractions and their importance in commerce, education, entertainment, media, fashion, science, sports and arts contribute to their status as two of the world's major global cities. Thirteen Spanish cities have been declared World Heritage Cities by the UNESCO: Alcalá de Henares, Ávila, Cáceres, Córdoba, Cuenca, Ibiza, Mérida, Salamanca, San Cristóbal de la Laguna, Santiago de Compostela, Segovia, Tarragona and Toledo. As of June 2013, Spain has 44 total sites inscribed on the list, third only to

Italy (49 sites) and China (45 sites). Other first-class destinations are Seville, Granada, Santander, Oviedo, Gijón, Bilbao and San Sebastián.

Spain is heterogeneous in Europe and the Arab moors to the ancient city of Spain brought colors of Islamic civilization. In Barcelona, you can see Gaudi, Picasso and Dali. Crazy Spaniard to Madrid to watch is Goya and Murillo. In Andalusia of southern Spain, you can see a true Spaniard—sunny, warm and optimistic. You can see flamenco dance in Seville, in grana of Alhambra.

作为几个文明的十字路口,西班牙拥有许多历史悠久的城镇。主要旅游目的地包括西班牙的两个最大的城市:马德里和巴塞罗那,这是欧洲两个主要的旅游目的地城市,它们在商业、教育、娱乐、媒体、时尚、科学、体育和艺术方面的重要性,也使它们成为世界上两个重要的全球性城市。13 个西班牙城市已被联合国教科文组织列为世界遗产城市。截至 2013 年 6 月,西班牙共有 44 处景点上榜,仅次于意大利(49 处)和中国(45 处)。

1)Madrid(马德里)

Madrid is a southwestern European city, the capital of Spain, and the largest municipality of the Community of Madrid. While Madrid possesses modern infrastructure, it has preserved the look and feel of many of its historic neighbourhood and streets. Its landmarks include the Royal Palace of Madrid; the Royal Theatre with its restored 1850 Opera House; the Buen Retiro Park, founded in 1631; the 19th-century National Library building (founded in 1712) containing some of Spain's historical archives; a large number of national museums, and the Golden Triangle of Art, located along the Paseo del Prado and comprising three art museums: Prado Museum, the Reina Sofía Museum, a museum of modern art, and the Thyssen-Bornemisza Museum, which completes the shortcomings of the other two museums. Cibeles Palace and Fountain have become the monument symbol of the city.

马德里是欧洲西南部的一个城市,是西班牙的首都,也是马德里自治区最大的自治市。虽然马德里拥有现代化的基础设施,但它保留了许多历史街区和街道。它的地标包括马德里皇家宫殿、皇家剧院和 1850 年重修的歌剧院、建于 1631 年的布恩雷蒂罗公园、建于 1712 年的国家图书馆、大量的国家博物馆和艺术金三角等。

2)Barcelona(巴塞罗那)

Besieged several times during its history, Barcelona has a rich cultural heritage and is today an important cultural center and a major tourist destination. Particularly renowned are the architectural works of Antoni Gaudí and Lluís Domènech i Montaner, which have been designated UNESCO World Heritage Sites. The headquarters of the Union for the Mediterranean is located in Barcelona. The city is known for hosting the 1992 Summer Olympic Games as well as world-class conferences and expositions and also many international sport tournaments. Barcelona is one of the world's leading tourist, economic, trade fair and cultural centers, and its influence in commerce, education, entertainment, media, fashion, science, and the arts all contribute to its status as one of the world's major global cities.

巴塞罗那拥有丰富的文化遗产,是一个重要的文化中心和重要的旅游目的地。特别著名的是安东尼·高迪和路易·多梅内克·蒙塔内尔的建筑作品,它们已被联合国教科文组织列入世界遗产。地中海联盟的总部设在巴塞罗那。巴塞罗那是世界著名的旅游、经济、贸易博览会和文化中心之一,以主办1992年夏季奥运会、世界级会议和博览会以及许多国际体育赛事而闻名。

3) Toledo(托莱多)

Toledo is a municipality located in central Spain, 70 km south of Madrid. It was declared a World Heritage Site by UNESCO in 1986 for its extensive cultural, monumental heritage and historical coexistence of Christian, Muslim and Jewish cultures.

Toledo is known as the "Imperial City" for having been the main venue of the court of Charles I, and as the "City of the Three Cultures", having been influenced by a historical coexistence of Christians, Muslim and Jewish cultures. In 1085, the city fell to Alfonso VI of Castile as the first major city in the Christian Reconquista. Toledo has a history in the production of bladed weapons, which are now popular souvenirs of the city.

托莱多是西班牙中部的一个直辖市,位于马德里以南70千米。1986年,因其文化和纪念性遗产,以及基督教、穆斯林和犹太文化的历史共存,被联合国教科文组织列入世界遗产。托莱多被称为"帝国之城"。这里曾是查理一世宫廷的所在地,是"三种文化之城",历史上一直受基督教、穆斯林和犹太文化共存的影响。

Section 7　Russia(俄罗斯)

PART 1(第一部分)

1. 国土疆域(Territory)

俄罗斯也称俄罗斯联邦,位于欧洲的东部和亚洲的北部,领土面积约1 709.82万平方千米,是世界上面积最大的国家。俄罗斯东濒太平洋,西临波罗的海,西南连黑海,北靠北冰洋。俄罗斯横跨欧亚大陆,东西最长9 000千米,南北最宽4 000千米。邻国西北面有挪威、芬兰,西面有爱沙尼亚、拉脱维亚、立陶宛、波兰、白俄罗斯,西南面是乌克兰,南面有格鲁吉亚、阿塞拜疆、哈萨克斯坦,东南面有中国、蒙古和朝鲜。东面与日本和美国隔海相望。

Russia is also called the Russian Federation. It is located in the east of Europe and the north of Asia, with the territory area of 17 098 200 km^2. It is the largest country in the world. Russia borders the Pacific Ocean in the east, the Baltic Sea in the west, the Black Sea in the southwest and the Arctic Ocean in the north. Russia straddles Eurasia, with the longest distance of 9 000 km from east to west and the widest distance of 4 000 km from north to south. Neighboring countries include Norway and Finland in the northwest, Estonia, Latvia, Lithuania, Poland and Belarus in the west, Ukraine in the southwest, Georgia, Azerbaijan and Kazakhstan in the south, and China, Mongolia and North Korea in the southeast. It faces Japan and the United States across the sea to the east.

2. 自然风貌(Natural Features)

俄罗斯的自然风貌在世界上享有盛名,山川湖岛众多,景色优美,每年吸引着无数游人。

俄罗斯地形复杂多样,整个地形犹如阶梯,从西往东逐渐升高。西部主要是辽阔的东欧平原和西西伯利亚平原,东部是中西伯利亚高原和远东山地,西南部为大高加索山脉。乌拉尔山介于东欧平原和西西伯利亚平原之间,是欧亚两洲的交界处。大高加索山脉是俄罗斯西南部最主要的山脉,位于黑海和里海之间,主峰厄尔布鲁士山海拔5 642米,峰顶终年白雪皑皑。

俄罗斯大部分地区处于北温带,以大陆性气候为主,温差普遍较大,1月平均气温为−5~−40 ℃,7月平均气温为11~27 ℃;年平均降水量为150~1 000毫米,冬季,俄罗斯全境几乎都降雪,积雪期和积雪的厚度随纬度增高而增加,冰雪旅游资源丰富。

黑海沿岸一带为地中海气候,旅游业极为兴盛,最大的海滨疗养胜地索契就坐落在黑海之滨;西伯利亚地区十分寒冷,奥伊米亚康被称为"北半球的寒极",对敢于冒险的旅游者有极大的吸引力;北冰洋沿岸为极地气候,白熊、海象、极昼、极夜的自然奇观同样对旅游者有很大的诱惑力。

俄罗斯河流众多,最长的是西伯利亚的鄂毕河,连同支流额尔齐斯河总长度为5 410千米,叶尼塞河是俄罗斯水量最大的河流;伏尔加河是欧洲最长的河流,全长3 692千米,流域面积138万平方千米,被誉为俄罗斯的"母亲河"。

俄罗斯境内多湖泊,有20多万个。位于东西伯利亚的贝加尔湖是俄罗斯最大的湖泊,也是世界上最深的淡水湖,最深处为1 637米。贝加尔湖长为636千米,平均宽度为48千米,湖面面积3.15万平方千米,蓄水量为23万亿立方米。

The landscape of Russia is complex and diversified. The whole landform is like a ladder rising gradually from west to east. The broad eastern European Plain and the western Siberian plain are in the west, the central Siberian plateau and the far eastern mountains are in the east, and the great Caucasus mountains are in the southwest.

Russia, the world's largest country by area, its most areas are located in high latitudes, with temperate continental climate.

Russia has many rivers. The longest river is Ob in Siberia, and the largest one is Yenisei.

Russia has more than 200 000 lakes. Lake Baikal, located in eastern Siberia, is the largest lake in Russia and also the deepest and largest freshwater lake of all lakes in the world.

3. 人口民族(Population and Ethnicity)

俄罗斯人口约1.46亿(2020年),人口密度约每平方千米8.54人。俄罗斯有194个民族,其中俄罗斯人约占总人口的77.7%,主要少数民族有鞑靼、乌克兰、楚瓦什、巴什基尔、白俄罗斯、摩尔多瓦、亚美尼亚、阿瓦尔、哈萨克等。

俄语是俄罗斯联邦全境内的官方语言。主要宗教为东正教,其次为伊斯兰教。

Russia has a population of about 146 million (2020), with a population density of about 8.54 people per square kilometer. Russia has 194 ethnic groups, among which Russians account for about 77.7% of total population. The main religion is Orthodox.

4. 发展简史(Brief History of Development)

俄罗斯是一个古老的国家,其祖先为东斯拉夫人。

15世纪末至16世纪初,以莫斯科大公国为中心,逐渐形成多民族的封建国家。1547年,伊凡四世(伊凡雷帝)改大公称号为沙皇。1721年,彼得一世(彼得大帝)改国号为俄罗斯帝国。1861年废除农奴制。19世纪末至20世纪初成为军事封建帝国主义国家。1917年2月,资产阶级革命推翻了专制制度。1917年11月7日(俄历10月25日)十月社会主义革命,建立了世界上第一个社会主义国家政权——俄罗斯苏维埃联邦社会主义共和国。1922年12月30日,俄罗斯联邦、外高加索联邦、乌克兰、白俄罗斯成立苏维埃社会主义共和国联盟(后扩至15个加盟共和国)。1990年6月12日,俄罗斯苏维埃联邦社会主义共和国最高苏维埃发表《国家主权宣言》,宣布俄罗斯联邦在其境内拥有"绝对主权"。1991年8月,苏联发生"8·19"事件。9月6日,苏联国务委员会通过决议,承认爱沙尼亚、拉脱维亚、立陶宛三个加盟共和国独立。12月8日,俄罗斯联邦、白俄罗斯、乌克兰三个加盟共和国的领导人在别洛韦日签署《独立国家联合体协议》,宣布组成"独立国家联合体"。12月21日,除波罗的海三国和格鲁吉亚外的苏联11个加盟共和国签署《阿拉木图宣言》和《独立国家联合体协议议定书》。12月26日,苏联最高苏维埃举行最后一次会议,宣布苏联停止存在。至此,苏联解体,俄罗斯联邦成为完全独立的国家,并成为苏联的唯一继承国。1993年12月12日,经过全民投票通过了俄罗斯独立后的第一部宪法,规定国家名称为"俄罗斯联邦"。

From the end of the 15th century to the beginning of the 16th century, a multi-ethnic feudal state gradually formed with the Grand Duchy of Moscow as the center. From the end of the 19th century to the beginning of the 20th century, it became a military feudal imperialist country. On November 7, 1917 (Russian calendar October 25) October socialist revolution established the world's first socialist state regime—the Russian Soviet Federal Socialist Republic. The former Soviet Union disintegrated in 1991, and the Russian Federation became fully independent. On December 12, 1993, the first constitution of Russia was passed by referendum, which proclaimed the name "the Russian Federation".

5. 政治经济(Politics and Economy)

首都为莫斯科。国花为葵花,国树为白桦树。货币为卢布。

俄罗斯为总统制的联邦国家。总统为俄罗斯国家元首兼武装部队最高统帅,享有国家最高行政领导权。俄罗斯由22个共和国、46个州、9个边疆区、4个自治区、1个自治州、3个联邦直辖市组成。

俄罗斯是一个工农业、交通运输、科学技术都比较发达的国家。俄罗斯工业发达,部门齐全,以机械、钢铁、冶金、石油、天然气、煤炭、森林工业及化工等为主,木材和木材加工业也较发达,但民用工业落后状况尚未根本改变。

俄罗斯的农业远不如工业发达,但由于土地面积大,农产品产值并不低。农牧业并重,主要农作物有小麦、大麦、燕麦、玉米、水稻和豆类;经济作物以亚麻、向日葵和甜菜为主;畜牧业主要为养牛、养羊、养猪业。

俄罗斯交通运输以铁路为主导。公路在交通中占重要地位。航空运输以客运为主,与80多个国家的航线相通。在俄罗斯的交通工具中,最令人赞叹的是地铁,其运行准时、安全。其中以莫斯科地铁最负盛名,它是举世公认的最漂亮、最繁华的地铁,运营长度居世界第五位。对来自世界各地的旅游者来说,它不仅是交通工具,更是一座座各具特色、魅力无穷的地下艺术宫殿。

Russia is a presidential federal republic. Russia is developed in industrial and agricultural production, transportation, science and technology. Russia has developed industry and complete departments. Agriculture is far less developed than industry, but because of the vast land area, the output value of agricultural products is not low. Transportation is dominated by railway transport, road transport also occupies an important position, and air transport is mainly passenger transport.

6. 旅游市场(Tourism Market)

俄罗斯的旅游业为新兴经济部门,近年来发展较快。俄罗斯接待的海外旅游者四分之三来自原独联体国家,其他主要客源国为波兰、蒙古、中国、德国、美国和英国。据

UNWTO 统计，2018 年俄罗斯接待入境旅游者达 2 455 万人。近年来中国赴俄旅游增长较快，中国已成为赴俄罗斯旅游人数最多的国家。

俄罗斯人最喜欢去的度假旅游目的地是土耳其、波兰和中国；商务旅游目的地是德国、中国和芬兰等；探亲访友等旅游目的地是芬兰、德国、意大利和土耳其。近年来俄罗斯出境游市场稳定上升，俄罗斯联邦统计局的数据显示，2019 年上半年俄罗斯居民出境旅游 1 989 万人次，同比增长 6%。俄罗斯也是国际旅游开支最大的国家之一，UNWTO 的数据显示，2019 年俄罗斯的国际旅游开支为 406 亿美元。

俄罗斯是中国重要的旅游客源国，中俄有漫长的边境线，随着中俄经济的发展，边境旅游发展迅速。2018 年，俄罗斯成为中国第六大旅游客源国，仅次于缅甸、越南、韩国、日本、美国，俄罗斯赴华旅游 241.50 万人次，同比增长 2.5%。2019 年俄罗斯首站到访中国的游客 108 万人次，同比增长达 19%。

国内旅游业占俄罗斯旅游业的比重较大，且保持平稳的发展势头。在俄罗斯人的生活中，度假旅游是不可缺少的。一般而言，俄罗斯人的度假方式有三种：一是平常度假，在春夏之季的周末，俄罗斯人或去别墅，或全家带着食物外出郊游，冬天去滑雪，秋天喜欢去森林中采蘑菇；二是近距离度假，俄罗斯人把每年的 6~8 月称为度假的黄金季节；三是旅游度假，俄罗斯人可利用假期到国内的休养所、疗养院、旅游点、度假村、乡村休养，也可以参加旅行团欣赏祖国的自然景观。

Russia's tourism industry is an emerging economic sector and has developed rapidly in recent years. Three-quarters of Russia's overseas tourists come from the former CIS. The other major sources are Poland, Mongolia, China, Germany, the United States and the United Kingdom. Russia's favorite holiday destinations are Turkey, Poland and China; Business destinations are Germany, China, Finland, etc.

Russia is a popular tourist source for China. With the economic development of China and Russia, border tourism develops rapidly. In 2018, Russia became the sixth largest source of tourists to China.

PART 2(第二部分)

Tourism Resources(旅游资源)

Tourism in Russia has seen rapid growth, first inner tourism and then international tourism as well. Rich cultural heritage and great natural variety place Russia among the most popular tourist destinations in the world. The country contains 23 UNESCO World Heritage Sites, while many more are on UNESCO's tentative lists.

Major tourist routes in Russia include a travel around the Golden Ring of ancient cities, cruises on the big rivers including the Volga, and long journeys on the famous Trans-Siberian Railway. Diverse regions and ethnic cultures of Russia offer many different food and souvenirs, and show a great variety of traditions, including Russian banya, Tatar Sabantuy, or Siberian shamanist rituals.

俄罗斯的旅游业发展迅速,首先是国内旅游业,然后是国际旅游业。丰富的文化遗产和自然多样性使俄罗斯成为世界上最受欢迎的旅游目的地之一。该国有 23 处联合国教科文组织世界遗产,还有许多在联合国教科文组织的暂定名单上。

俄罗斯的主要旅游线路包括环绕古老城市的金环旅行,包括伏尔加河在内的大河巡游,以及在著名的跨西伯利亚铁路上长途旅行。俄罗斯不同的地区和民族文化提供了许多不同的食物和纪念品,并展示了各种各样的传统,包括俄式桑拿浴,鞑靼萨班节,或西伯利亚萨满教仪式。

1. Tourist Attractions(旅游胜地)

The warm subtropical Black Sea coast of Russia is the site for a number of popular sea resorts, including Crimea and Sochi, known for their beaches and wonderful nature. At the same time, Sochi can boast a number of major ski resorts, such as Krasnaya Polyana; the city is the host of 2014 Winter Olympic Games. The mountains of the Northern Caucasus contain many other popular ski resorts, such as Dombay in Karachay-Cherkessia.

The most famous natural tourist destination in Russia is Lake Baikal, named the Blue Eye of Siberia. This unique lake, oldest and deepest in the world, has crystal-clean waters and is surrounded by taiga-covered mountains.

Other popular natural destinations include Kamchatka with its volcanoes and geysers, Karelia with its many lakes and granite rocks, Altai with its snowy mountains and Tyva with its wild steppes.

黑海海岸因温暖的亚热带气候而成为俄罗斯受欢迎的海滨胜地,包括克里米亚和索契,以其海滩和自然环境而闻名。索契和北高加索山脉拥有许多滑雪胜地。

俄罗斯最著名的自然旅游目的地是贝加尔湖,被称为"西伯利亚的蓝眼",它是世界上最古老、最深的湖,湖水清澈如水晶,四周群山环绕。其他受欢迎的目的地包括堪察加半岛的火山和间歇泉、卡累利阿的湖泊和花岗岩、阿尔泰的雪山和图瓦的野生草原。

1)Crimea(克里米亚)

The development of Crimea as a holiday destination began in the second half of the 19th century. The development of the transport networks brought masses of tourists from central parts of the Russian Empire. At the beginning of the 20th century, a major development of palaces, villas, and dachas began, most of which remain. These are some of the main attractions of Crimea as a tourist destination. There are many Crimean legends about famous tourist places, which attract the attention of tourists.

克里米亚作为度假胜地始于 19 世纪下半叶。20 世纪初,宫殿、别墅和乡间别墅开始大规模开发,其中大部分保留了下来,成为吸引游客的主要景点。

2) Sochi(索契)

With the Alpine and Nordic events held at the nearby ski resort of Roza Khutor in Krasnaya Polyana, Sochi hosted the XXII Olympic Winter Games and XI Paralympic Winter Games in 2014, as well as the Russian Formula 1 Grand Prix from 2014 until at least 2020. It is also be one of the host cities for the 2018 FIFA World Cup.

索契2014年举办了第22届冬奥会和第11届冬季残奥会,举办了2014年到2020年的俄罗斯一级方程式大奖赛,它也是2018年世界杯的主办城市之一。

3) Lake Baikal(贝加尔湖)

Lake Baikal is a rift lake in Russia. It is the largest freshwater lake by volume in the world, containing roughly 20% of the world's unfrozen surface fresh water. With a maximum depth of 1 637 m, Baikal is the world's deepest lake. It is considered among the world's clearest lakes and is considered the world's oldest lake—at 25 million years. Baikal is home to thousands of species of plants and animals, many of which exist nowhere else in the world. The lake was declared a UNESCO World Heritage Site in 1996.

贝加尔湖是俄罗斯的一个裂谷湖,是世界上体积最大的淡水湖。贝加尔湖是世界上最深的湖,最大深度为1 637米,被认为是世界上最清澈的湖泊之一,也是世界上最古老的湖泊,有2 500万年的历史。1996年,该湖被联合国教科文组织列为世界遗产。

2. Tourism Cities(旅游城市)

The most popular tourist destinations in Russia are Moscow and Saint Petersburg, the current and the former capital of the country and great cultural centers, recognized as World Cities. Moscow and Saint Petersburg feature such world-renowned museums as Hermitage and Tretyakov Gallery, famous theaters including Bolshoi and Mariinsky, ornate churches such as Saint Basil's Cathedral, Cathedral of Christ the Saviour, Saint Isaac's Cathedral and Church of the Savior on Blood, impressive fortifications such as Moscow Kremlin, Peter and Paul Fortress, beautiful squares such as Red Square and Palace Square, and streets such as Tverskaya and Nevsky Prospect. Rich palaces and parks of extreme beauty are found in the former imperial residencesin suburbs of Moscow (Kolomenskoye, Tsaritsyno) and Saint Petersburg (Peterhof, Strelna, Oranienbaum, Gatchina, Pavlovsk Palace, Tsarskoye Selo). Moscow contains a great variety of impressive Soviet era buildings along with modern skyscrapers, while Saint Petersburg, nicknamed Venice of the North, boasts of its classical architecture, many rivers, channels and bridges.

Kazan, the capital of Tatarstan, shows a unique mix of Christian Russian and Muslim Tatar cultures. The city has registered a brand The Third Capital of Russia, though a number of other major Russian cities compete for this status, including Samara, Novosibirsk, Yekaterinburg and Nizhny Novgorod, all being major cultural centers with rich history and prominent architecture. Veliky Novgorod, Pskov, Dmitrov and the cities of Golden Ring (Vladimir, Yaroslavl, Kostroma and others) have at best preserved the architecture and the spirit of ancient and medieval Rus, and also are among the main tourist destinations. Many old fortifications (typically Kremlins), monasteries and churches are scattered throughout Russia, forming its unique cultural landscape both in big cities and in remote areas.

俄罗斯最受欢迎的旅游目的地是圣彼得堡和莫斯科,它们是现在和以前俄罗斯的首都和文化中心,被公认为世界城市。莫斯科和圣彼得堡有世界闻名的艾尔米塔什博物馆和特列季亚科夫画廊;著名的剧院有莫斯科大剧院和马林斯基剧院;华丽的教堂有圣瓦西里大教堂、基督救世主大教堂、圣以撒大教堂和基督喋血教堂;防御工事有克里姆林宫、彼得和保罗要塞;美丽的广场有红场和冬宫广场;还有非常美丽的宫殿和公园。而圣彼得堡,被称为"北方威尼斯",以其古典建筑、众多的河流、水渠和桥梁而闻名。

喀山是鞑靼斯坦共和国的首都,是一个独特的混合了基督教文化和穆斯林鞑靼文化的城市。萨马拉、新西伯利亚、叶卡捷琳堡和下诺夫哥罗德都是拥有深厚历史和杰出建筑的重要文化中心。

1)Saint Petersburg(圣彼得堡)

Saint Petersburg is often described as the most Westernized city of Russia, as well as its cultural capital. The historic centre of Saint Petersburg and related groups of monuments constitute a UNESCO World Heritage Site. Saint Petersburg is home to The Hermitage, one of the largest art museums in the world. The city has 221 museums, 2 000 libraries, more than 80 theaters, 100 concert organizations, 45 galleries and exhibition halls, 62 cinemas and around 80 other cultural establishments. Every year the city hosts around 100 festivals and various competitions of art and culture, including more than 50 international ones.

The museum world of Saint Petersburg is incredibly diverse. The city is not only home to the world-famous Hermitage Museum and the Russian Museum with its rich collection of Russian art, but also the palaces of Saint Petersburg and its suburbs, so-called small town museums and others like the museum of famous Russian writer Dostoyevsky; Museum of Musical Instruments, the museum of decorative arts and the museum of professional orientation.

The musical life of Saint Petersburg is rich and diverse, with the city now playing host to a number of annual carnivals. Ballet performances occupy a special place in the cultural life of Saint Petersburg. The Petersburg School of Ballet is named as one of the best in the world.

圣彼得堡经常被描述为俄罗斯最西方化的城市,是俄罗斯的文化首都。圣彼得堡的历史中心和相关古迹群是世界遗产。该市有221个博物馆,2 000个图书馆,80多个剧院,100个音乐会组织,45个画廊和展览厅,62个电影院和大约80个文化机构,有世界上最大的艺术博物馆之一的艾尔米塔什博物馆。每年,这座城市都会举办100多个节日以及各种艺术和文化比赛,其中包括50多个国际比赛。

圣彼得堡有各种各样的博物馆。这座城市有世界著名的艾尔米塔什博物馆和俄罗斯博物馆,收藏了丰富的俄罗斯艺术作品。

圣彼得堡的音乐生活是丰富多样的。芭蕾舞表演在圣彼得堡的文化生活中占有特殊的地位,彼得斯堡芭蕾舞学校是世界上最好的芭蕾舞学校之一。

2)Moscow(莫斯科)

Moscow is the northernmost and coldest megacity and metropolis on Earth. It is home to the Ostankino Tower, the tallest free standing structure in Europe; the Federation Tower, the tallest skyscraper in Europe; and the Moscow International Business Center. The city is well known for its architecture, particularly its historic buildings such as Saint Basil's Cathedral with its brightly colored domes. With over 40 percent of its territory covered by greenery, it is one of the greenest capitals and major cities in Europe and in the world. Moscow is considered the center of Russian culture, having served as the home of Russian artists, scientists and sports figures and because of the presence of museums, academic and political institutions and theaters. The Moscow Kremlin and Red Square are also one of several World Heritage Sites in the city.

The Moscow Kremlin, usually referred to as the Kremlin, is a fortified complex at the heart of Moscow, overlooking the Moskva Riverto the south, Saint Basil's Cathedral and Red Square to the east, and the Alexander Garden to the west. The kremlin includes five palaces, four cathedrals, and the enclosing Kremlin Wall with Kremlin towers. The complex serves as the official residence of the President of the Russian Federation.

Red Square is a city square (plaza) in Moscow, Russia. It separates the Kremlin, the former royal citadel and currently the official residence of the President of Russia, from a historic merchant quarter known as Kitai-gorod. Red Square is often considered the central square of Moscow since Moscow's major streets, which connect to Russia's major highways, originate from the square.

莫斯科是地球上最北最冷的大城市。这座城市以其建筑而闻名,有欧洲最高的独立建筑奥斯坦金诺电视塔、欧洲最高的摩天大楼联邦大厦和莫斯科国际商务中心。这里的历史建筑十分漂亮,如圣瓦西里大教堂,有着色彩鲜艳的圆顶。

莫斯科超过40%的地域被绿色植物覆盖,它是欧洲和世界上最环保的首都和主要城市之一。莫斯科是俄罗斯文化的中心,是众多俄罗斯艺术家、科学家和体育人物的故乡,有众多博物馆、学术和政治机构以及剧院。

克里姆林宫和红场是莫斯科的世界遗产。克里姆林宫是俄罗斯联邦总统的官邸,它是一个防御森严的建筑群,俯瞰着莫斯科河、圣瓦西里大教堂、红场和亚历山大花园。克里姆林宫包括五个宫殿、四座大教堂，以及由克里姆林宫塔楼环绕的克里姆林宫墙。红场是莫斯科的一个城市广场，也是莫斯科的中心广场，因为莫斯科连接俄罗斯主要高速公路的主要街道都从红场开始。

Section 8　Switzerland(瑞士)

PART 1(第一部分)

1. 国土疆域(Territory)

瑞士是位于中欧的内陆国。与奥地利、列支敦士登、意大利、法国和德国接壤。瑞士面积约41 284平方千米。

Switzerland is a landlocked country in central Europe. It borders Austria, Lichtenstein, Italy, France and Germany. Switzerland covers an area of 41 284 km^2.

2. 自然风貌(Natural Features)

巍峨的高山、壮观的冰川、迷人的瀑布、秀丽的湖泊，以及茂密的森林和幽深的峡谷，使瑞士成为一个令人梦回萦绕的国度。

瑞士地形可概括为"六、三、一"三个字，即南部的阿尔卑斯山区占总面积的60％，中部高原占30％，西北部的汝拉山脉占10％。因为多山，全国地势较高，最低处也极少在海拔300米以下，大部分都在海拔900米以上。全境有多座海拔4 200米以上的山峰。阿尔卑斯山系有1/5在瑞士境内，整个瑞士的南部几乎都是阿尔卑斯山区，可以说，没有阿尔卑斯山便没有瑞士，它对瑞士的历史、社会、经济、政治等各方面都产生了极为重要的影响。

瑞士地处北温带，受海洋性和大陆性气候交替影响，年平均温度9 ℃。

瑞士多山，雨雪充沛，所以水资源丰富，江河湖泊众多。欧洲有3条著名的大河都与瑞士有关，它们是莱茵河、罗纳河和多瑙河。瑞士的湖泊大都出现于冰河时期。瑞士的大湖都在汝拉山脚下或中部高原上，其中日内瓦湖、苏黎世湖和博登湖以环境优美著称于世，成为旅游胜地。

The landform of Switzerland can be summarized as "six, three, one", that is, the Alps account for 60％ of the total area, the central plateau accounts for 30％, and the Jura Mountain accounts for 10％. Switzerland is a country with temperate marine climate and continental climate, abundant rain and snow, water resources, and numerous rivers and lakes. There are three famous rivers in Europe, Rhine, Rhone and Danube, all connected with Switzerland. Most of lakes appeared during the Ice Age, among which Lake Geneva, Lake Zurich and Lake Boden are famous for their beautiful scenery.

3. 人口民族(Population and Ethnicity)

瑞士人口约 860.6 万(2019 年)，人口密度约为每平方千米 208.46 人。外籍人约占总人口的 25%。德语、法语、意大利语及拉丁罗曼语 4 种语言均为官方语言，居民中讲德语的约占 62.8%，法语 22.9%，意大利语 8.2%，拉丁罗曼语 0.5%，其他语言 5.6%。信奉天主教的居民占 37.2%，新教 25.0%，其他宗教 7.4%，无宗教信仰 24.0%。

Switzerland has a population of about 8 606 000 (2019), with a population density of about 208.46 people per square kilometer. Foreigners account for 25% of the population, and its residents are mainly Catholic and Protestant.

4. 发展简史(Brief History of Development)

如今的瑞士，最早是凯尔特族人的聚居之地。公元前 100 年，罗马人率领大军占领此地，并阻止凯尔特人南下，所以他们便逐渐被罗马的文化所同化，并享受到罗马帝国时期的昌盛繁荣。直至中世纪来临，罗马帝国崩溃。1291 年 8 月 1 日，乌里、施维茨和下瓦尔登三个州在反对哈布斯堡王朝的斗争中秘密结成永久同盟，此即瑞士建国之始。1815 年维也纳会议确认瑞士为永久中立国。1848 年制定宪法，设立联邦委员会，成为统一的联邦制国家。瑞士在两次世界大战中均保持中立。战后，瑞士加入了一些国际组织。

In 100 BC, the Romans occupied the country and it enjoyed the prosperity of the Roman Empire until its collapse in the Middle Ages. Switzerland was founded on August 1, 1291. Vienna conference confirmed Switzerland as a permanent neutral state in 1815. It remained neutral in both world wars.

5. 政治经济(Politics and Economy)

首都为伯尔尼，国花为火绒草，货币为瑞士法郎，也可以使用欧元。

瑞士为联邦制国家，采取议会制。联邦议会是最高立法机构，联邦委员会是国家最高行政机构。有 14 个全球性组织的总部设在瑞士。

瑞士是高度发达的工业国，是世界上最富裕的国家之一。它实行自由经济政策，政府尽量减少干预。对外主张自由贸易，反对贸易保护主义政策，为欧洲贸易中心。瑞士工业高度发达，在国民经济中占主导地位。机械、化工、纺织、钟表、食品是瑞士的五大支柱产业。所产钟表驰名世界，瑞士素有"钟表王国"之称，它所生产的钟表由于计时准确、品种款式多、工艺水平高而畅销世界。瑞士所有已开发的农田都能地尽其用，畜牧业亦十分发达，主要农作物有小麦、燕麦、马铃薯和甜菜。肉类基本自给，奶制品自给有余。瑞士的交通运输以公路和铁路运输为主。铁路密度居世界前列，公路网四通八达、遍及全国。主要国际机场有苏黎世机场和日内瓦机场。

Switzerland is a federal state, and a highly developed industrial country. Machinery, chemicals, textiles, clocks and watches, and food are the five pillars of Swiss industry. Animal husbandry is also very developed, and the main crops are wheat, oats, potatoes and sugar beets. Transportation is dominated by road and railway transportation, the density of railway ranks the top in the world, and the road network extends to all directions.

6. 旅游市场(Tourism Market)

瑞士旅游业已有 200 多年的历史,瑞士旅游业十分发达,是仅次于机械制造和化工医药的第三大创汇行业。

瑞士有丰富而高质量的山地景观和冬季体育运动旅游资源。夏季和冬季是瑞士的两个旅游旺季,但全年旅游都不清淡。

瑞士入境旅游人数逐年增加,但因费用高,游客停留时间都很短,一般 2~5 天。瑞士旅游对德国依赖程度较高,还吸引来自欧洲北部和南欧的旅游者。

瑞士每年的游客达 6 500 万人次,其中外国游客逾 1 300 万人次。2019 年,瑞士的旅游业收入达 472.51 亿美元,相较于 2018 的 482.53 亿美元有所下降。瑞士虽是一个小国,却是世界旅游大国之一,旅游竞争力一直保持世界前列。2019 年,瑞士旅游竞争力排在全球第十位。UNWTO 的数据显示,2019 年瑞士接待过夜客 1 181 万人次。

瑞士是深受中国人喜爱的旅游目的地国。瑞士旅游局的数据显示,中国游客在瑞士酒店过夜人数 2013 年为 110 万人次,2018 年为 170 万人次,5 年间增幅为 54.5%,位居瑞士主要客源国第三位,其主要客源国是德国、美国、中国、英国、比利时、荷兰、卢森堡。中国游客人均每天消费 380 瑞郎(合人民币 2 694 元),2018 年中国游客在瑞士的消费额达到6.56亿瑞郎(合人民币 46.51 亿元)。

瑞士的出境旅游人数较多,每年约有 620 万人次到国外旅游。出境旅游者绝大多数是到地中海国家旅游。受欧债危机的影响,瑞士来华旅游增长缓慢,甚至有所下降,2014 年来华旅游人数为 7.95 万人次,2018 年来华旅游人数为 7.40 万人次。

瑞士是个富裕的国家,许多人非常喜欢度假旅游。国内旅游市场很大,国内旅游的人数约 230 万人,约占全国人口的 27%。国内旅游者大多数选择提供自助饮食的住宿地,如农舍小屋、野营地或公寓等。

Switzerland's tourism industry is very developed. It is the third largest export industry after machinery and chemicals in Switzerland. Its main tourist sources are Germany, the United States, China, the United Kingdom, Belgium, the Netherlands, Luxembourg and so on. Switzerland is an economically wealthy country, and the vast majority of outbound tourists are to European Mediterranean countries.

知识拓展 3.7　钟表王国（见二维码）

 知识拓展 3.8　奇特而有趣的国家（见二维码）

PART 2（第二部分）

Tourism Resources（旅游资源）

Tourists are drawn to Switzerland's Alpine climate and landscapes, in particular for ski and mountaineering. The most visited Swiss tourist attractions are first, the Rhine Falls, second, the Berne Bear exhibit (both for free), and third, with over 1.8 million paid entries: Zoo Basel.

来瑞士的游客大多被瑞士的高山气候和景观，尤其被滑雪和登山所吸引。参观人数最多的瑞士旅游景点：第一是莱茵瀑布；第二是伯尔尼熊展（均为免费）；第三是游客超过180万人的付费景点，即巴塞尔动物园。

1. Natural Tourism Resources（自然旅游资源）

1）Matterhorn—Symbol for Switzerland（马特洪峰——瑞士的象征）

The Matterhorn and Switzerland are inseparably linked to each other. The pyramid shaped colossus of a mountain, which is very difficult to climb, is said to be the most photographed mountain in the world. The Klein-Matterhorn ("Little Matterhorn"), which can be reached via a funicular, lies adjacent to the Matterhorn. Sometimes referred to as the Mountain of Mountains, the Matterhorn has become an iconic emblem of the Swiss Alps and the Alps in general. Since the end of the 19th century, when railways were built in the area, it has attracted increasing numbers of visitors and climbers. Each year a large number of mountaineers try to climb the Matterhorn from the Hörnli Hut via the northeast Hörnli ridge, the most popular route to the summit, with a large number of trekkers as well, undertaking the 10-day long circuit around the mountain. The Matterhorn is part of the Swiss Federal Inventory of Natural Monuments since 1983.

马特洪峰和瑞士密不可分。这座金字塔形的巨山很难攀登，据说是世界上拍照最多的山。马特洪峰有时被称为"群山之山"，它已成为瑞士阿尔卑斯山和整个阿尔卑斯山的标志性象征。自1983年以来，马特洪峰一直是瑞士联邦自然遗迹名录的一部分。

2）The Rhine Falls（莱茵河瀑布）

The Rhine Falls is the largest plain waterfall in Europe. The falls are located on the High Rhine in northern Switzerland. They are 150 m wide and 23 m high. The falls cannot be climbed by fish, except by eels that are able to worm their way up over the rocks. Boat trips can be taken up the Rhine to the falls and the Rheinfallfelsen. There are also viewing platforms with a spectacular view of the falls built on both sides of the Rhine. To stand high above Europe's largest waterfall, feeling the roar and vibration of the water over one's entire body—this can be experienced at the Rhine Falls near Schaffhausen.

莱茵河瀑布是欧洲最大的平原瀑布。瀑布位于瑞士北部的莱茵河上游，宽150米，高23米。站在欧洲最大的瀑布之上，能感受到水在全身上下的轰鸣和震动。

3）Creux du Van—Natural Spectacle（马蹄谷——自然奇观）

Creux du Van, a natural rock arena of immense proportions, is located at the border of the cantons of Neuenburg and Vaud. Impressive 160 m high vertical rock faces surround a 4 km long and over 1 km wide valley basin.

马蹄谷是一个巨大的天然岩石竞技场，160米高的垂直岩面围绕着一个4千米长、1千米多宽的山谷盆地。

4) Ruinaulta—Switzerland's Grand Canyon(瑞士大峡谷)

Ruinaulta is a canyon at Reichenau, eastern Switzerland. It is sometimes known as the Rhine Canyon, or Swiss Grand Canyon (more for its size than any resemblance to the Grand Canyon). Protected by cliffs several hundred metres high, the area is forested and a haven for wildlife. It is easily accessible only by the Ruinaulta line of Rhaetian Railways, and is a popular location for rafting.

瑞士大峡谷是瑞士东部的一个峡谷,有时也被称为莱茵峡谷。这个地区被几百米高的悬崖保护着,森林茂密,是野生动物的天堂,也是漂流的热门地点。

5) Aletsch—the Region Surrounding the Largest Alpine Glacier(阿莱奇——最大的阿尔卑斯冰川地区)

The Aletsch Glacier or Great Aletsch Glacier is the largest glacier in the Alps. The Aletsch Glacier is composed of four smaller glaciers converging at Concordia. The area of the Aletsch Glacier and some surrounding valleys is on the UNESCO World Heritage list, thus it is protected and the facilities are mostly restricted to the external zones. The region between Belalp, Riederalp and Bettmeralp (which is called Aletsch Region) in Valais gives access to the lower part of the glacier. The Bettmerhorn and Eggishorn are popular view points and are accessible by cable car. The Massa River can be crossed since 2008 by a suspension bridge, thus allowing hikes between the left and the right part of the glacier.

阿莱奇冰川是阿尔卑斯山最大的冰川,由四个较小的冰川组成。阿莱奇冰川和周围的一些山谷被联合国教科文组织列入世界遗产名录,因而受到保护。

6) The Gotthard Pass (哥达山口)

The Gotthard Pass or St. Gotthard Pass is a mountain pass in the Alps, connecting northern to southern Switzerland. The region of the Gotthard Pass is an important north-south axis in Europe and is crossed by three major traffic tunnels, each being the world's longest at the time of their construction: the Gotthard Rail Tunnel (1882), the Gotthard Road Tunnel (1980) and the Gotthard Base Tunnel (2016).

哥达山口是阿尔卑斯山脉的一个山口,连接着瑞士的南北。圣哥达山口地区是欧洲重要的南北轴线,有三条主要的交通隧道穿过,每一条隧道都是当时世界上最长的,包括哥达铁路隧道(1882 年)、哥达公路隧道(1980 年)和哥达基础隧道(2016 年)。

2. Cultural Tourism Resources(人文旅游资源)

1) Zurich(苏黎世)

Zürich or Zurich is the largest city in Switzerland. Many museums and art galleries can be found in the city, including the Swiss National Museum and the Kunsthaus. Schauspielhaus Zurich is one of the most important theatres in the German-speaking world. Most of Zurich's sites are located within the area on either side of the Limmat, between the main railway station and Lake Zurich. The churches and houses of the old town are clustered here, as are the most expensive shops along the famous Bahnhofstrasse. The Lindenhof in the old town is the historical site of the Roman castle, and the later Carolingian Imperial Palace.

苏黎世是瑞士最大的城市,城市里有很多博物馆和美术馆,包括瑞士国家博物馆和苏黎世美术馆。苏黎世的大部分景点都位于火车站和苏黎世湖之间。老城区的教堂和房屋,以及著名的班霍夫大街上最昂贵的商店都聚集在这里。老城区的林登霍夫是罗马城堡的历史遗址,后来成为加洛林王朝的皇宫。

(1) Swiss National Museum(瑞士国家博物馆)

The Swiss National Museum (German: Landesmuseum)—part of the Musée Suisse Group, itself affiliated with the Federal Office of Culture—is one of the most important art museums of cultural history in Europe. It is located in the city of Zurich. The exhibition tour takes the visitor from prehistory through ancient times and the Middle Ages to the 20th century (classic modern art and art of the 16th, 17th and 18th century is settled mainly in the Kunsthaus Museum in a different part of the city of Zurich). There is a very rich section with gothic art, chivalry and a comprehensive collection of liturgical wooden sculptures, panel paintings and carved altars. Zunfthaus zur Meisen near Fraumünster church houses the porcelain and faience collection of the Swiss National Museum. There are also a Collections Gallery, a place where Swiss furnishings are being exhibited, an Armoury Tower, a diorama of the Battle of Murten, and a Coin Cabinet showing 14th, 15th, 16th century Swiss coins and even some coins from the Middle Ages.

瑞士国家博物馆位于苏黎世市,是欧洲最重要的文化历史艺术博物馆之一。展览将带领游客从史前穿越古代和中世纪,再到20世纪的现代艺术。

(2) Kunsthaus Zurich(苏黎世美术馆)

The Kunsthaus Zurich is an art gallery in the Swiss city of Zurich. It houses one of the most important art collections in Switzerland, assembled over the years by the local art association called Zurcher Kunstgesellschaft. The collection spans from the Middle Ages to contemporary art, with an emphasis on Swiss art.

苏黎世美术馆收藏了从中世纪到当代最重要的艺术品,以瑞士艺术为主。

(3) Zurich's Old Town(苏黎世老城)

Zurich's medieval houses, contorted, narrow lanes and guild and town halls from the Renaissance period offer an attractive backdrop for world-class entertainment. A tour of the Old Town let visitors experience Zurich's multifaceted past. The double towers of the Grossmünster (Great Minster) are Zurich's landmark. Further sights worth seeing include the Peterskirche (Peter's Church), which has Europe's largest clockface, and the

Fraumünster (Minster of Our Lady), which is known for its stained glass windows by Giacometti and Chagall.

苏黎世中世纪时期的房屋、弯曲狭窄的小巷、文艺复兴时期的行会和市政厅,都营造出一种极具吸引力的一流娱乐消遣氛围。大教堂的双塔是苏黎世的地标。值得一看的景点包括圣彼得教堂,它拥有欧洲最大的钟面;圣母大教堂,它以彩绘玻璃窗而闻名。

2) Bern(伯尔尼)

The city of Bern or Berne is the capital of Switzerland. With a population of 142 900 (September 2020), Bern is the fifth most populous city in Switzerland. Bern is home to 114 Swiss heritage sites of national significance. It includes the entire Old Town, which is also a UNESCO World Heritage Site, and many sites within and around it. Some of the most notable in the Old Town include the Cathedral which was started in 1421 and is the tallest cathedral in Switzerland, the Zytglogge and Käfigturm towers, which mark two successive expansions of the Old Town, and the Holy Ghost Church, which is one of the largest Swiss Reformed churches in Switzerland. Within the Old Town, there are eleven 16th century fountains, most attributed to Hans Gieng, that are on the list.

伯尔尼是瑞士的首都。伯尔尼有114处国家文化遗产,整个老城区是联合国教科文组织世界遗产。老城区最著名的建筑包括1421年建成的大教堂,是瑞士最高的教堂;时钟塔和监狱塔,以及圣灵教堂。在老城区内,有11座16世纪的喷泉。

3) Geneva(日内瓦)

Geneva is the second most populous city in Switzerland and is the most populous city of Romandy, the French-speaking part of Switzerland. Geneva is a global city, a financial center, and worldwide center for diplomacy due to the presence of numerous international organizations, including the headquarters of many of the agencies of the United Nations and the Red Cross. Geneva is the city that hosts the highest number of international organizations in the world. It is also the place where the Geneva Conventions were signed, which chiefly concern the treatment of wartime non-combatants and prisoners of war. There are 82 buildings or sites in Geneva that are listed as Swiss heritage site of national significance, and the entire old city of Geneva is part of the Inventory of Swiss Heritage Sites.

日内瓦是一座全球性城市,是一个金融中心,也是世界范围内的外交中心。日内瓦是世界上拥有最多国际组织的城市,包括联合国机构和红十字会的总部,它是《日内瓦公约》的签署地。日内瓦有82座建筑和遗址被列为国家级文化遗产,整个日内瓦古城也被列入瑞士文化遗产名录。

4) Lausanne(洛桑)

Lausanne is a city in the French-speaking part of Switzerland. Lausanne is a focus of international sport, hosting the International Olympic Committee (which recognizes the city as the "Olympic Capital" since 1994), the Court of Arbitration for Sport and some 55 international sport associations. It lies in a noted wine-growing region. The city has a 28 station metro system, making it the smallest city in the world to have a rapid transit system.

洛桑是瑞士法语区的一个城市,是国际体育的中心城市,被国际奥委会确立为"奥林匹克之都"。这里有体育仲裁法庭和约 55 个国际体育协会。这座城市有 28 个地铁站,是世界上最小的拥有快速交通系统的城市。

5) Sion—Valais, Tourbillon, Old Town(锡永-瓦莱州,陶鲁比永城堡,老城)

Sion's history dates back to the Stone Age, as demonstrated by 5 000 year old stone menhirs and one of Switzerland's largest celtic necropolises. The hill of Valère with its basilica was named after the mother of a Roman city prefect. The foundations of the collegiate church, which was mentioned in historical documents for the first time 1 000 years ago, were already laid in Celtic times. The church is home to an organ from the 15th century. The ruins of the erstwhile bishop's castle from the 13th century lie on the adjacent hill of Tourbillon. Further attractions in the medieval Old Town include the Cathedral of Notre-Dame-du-Glarier (which dates back to the 15th century) and the Witches' Tower, which was part of the old city fortifications.

锡永的历史可以追溯到石器时代,有 5 000 年历史的巨大石柱和瑞士最大的凯尔特人墓地都印证着锡永悠久的历史。瓦莱山和它的长方形教堂是以罗马城执政官的母亲的名字命名的。这座教堂里有一架 15 世纪的管风琴。13 世纪的前主教城堡遗址座落在陶鲁比永城堡旁边的山丘之上。中世纪古城的其他景点还包括圣母院大教堂和女巫塔,它们是古城防御工事的一部分。

6) Chapel Bridge and Water Tower(卡佩尔廊桥和水塔)

Lucerne is divided by the river Reuss into an Old Town and a New Town. The two districts are connected by what is among other things the world's oldest covered wooden bridge, the Chapel Bridge, which dates back to the year 1332. The bridge was rebuilt true to the original after the fire of 1993 and leads to the actual landmark of Lucerne, the octagonal Water Tower. Like the over 500-year-old Musegg Wall with its turrets, the bridge and water tower were part of the city fortifications. At the outflow of the river Reuss, a historic needle dam, built in 1860, regulates the water level of the lake. The nearby Old Town boasts a town hall which dates back to the Late Renaissance as well as a Jesuit church, Switzerland's oldest Baroque church.

琉森被罗伊斯河分为旧城和新城。这两个城区被世界上最古老的木制廊桥——卡佩尔桥连接起来。这座桥建于 1332 年,1993 年火灾后重建,并通往琉森的地标——八角形水塔。这座桥和水塔也是城市防御工事的一部分。

7)Chillon Castle(西庸古堡)

Chillon Castle is located on a rock on the banks of Lake Geneva. The water castle is the most visited historic building in Switzerland. Chillon was made popular by Lord Byron, who wrote the poem *The Prisoner of Chillon* (1816) about François de Bonivard. Byron also carved his name on a pillar of the dungeon. Chillon is currently open to the public for visits and tours. According to the castle website, Chillon is listed as "Switzerland's most visited historic monument". There is a fee for entrance and there are both parking spaces and a bus stop nearby for travel. Inside the castle there are several recreations of the interiors of some of the main rooms including the grand bedroom, hall, and cave stores. Inside the castle itself there are four great halls, three courtyards, and a series of bedrooms open to the public. One of the oldest is the Camera domini, which was a room occupied by the Count of Savoy—it is decorated with 14th Century medieval murals.

西庸古堡建在日内瓦湖岸边的一块巨大岩石上,它是瑞士参观人数最多的历史建筑。城堡内部有四个大厅、三个庭院和一系列向公众开放的卧室。其中最古老的一个房间是萨瓦伯爵居住的房间,里面装饰着14世纪的中世纪壁画。

(3)Swiss Museum of Transportation(瑞士交通博物馆)

The Swiss Museum of Transportation, which was opened in 1959, is Switzerland's most popular museum. The history of mobility and communication is documented in exhibitions and theme parks, with simulations, interactive stations and films.

瑞士交通博物馆于1959年开放,是瑞士最受欢迎的博物馆。通过模拟、互动、电影,以及展览和主题公园的方式记录了交通和通讯的历史。

知识拓展 3.9　洛桑酒店管理学院(见二维码)

Section 9　Greece(希腊)

PART 1(第一部分)

1. 国土疆域(Territory)

希腊王国,简称希腊,位于欧洲东南部的巴尔干半岛南端,北部与保加利亚、马其顿、阿尔巴尼亚接壤,东北与土耳其的欧洲部分接壤,西南濒爱奥尼亚海,东临爱琴海,南隔地中海与非洲大陆相望。希腊全国总面积约131 957平方千米,其中15%为岛屿。海岸线长约15 021千米,领海宽度为6海里。

The Kingdom of Greece, or Greece for short, is located in the south end of Balkan Peninsula in southeast Europe, bordering Bulgaria, Macedonia and Albania in the north, the European part of Turkey in the northeast, the Ionia Sea in the southwest, the Aegean Sea in the east. It faces the African continent across the Mediterranean Sea in the south. The total area of Greece is 131 957 square kilometers, of which 15% are islands. The coastline is about 15 021 km long and the territorial sea is 6 nautical miles wide.

2. 自然风貌(Natural Features)

希腊境内多山,四分之三均为山地,沿海有低地平原。奥林匹斯山在希腊神话中被认为是诸神寓居之所,海拔2 917米,是希腊最高峰。品都斯山脉纵贯希腊西部,中部为色萨利盆地。希腊多半岛、岛屿,最大的半岛是伯罗奔尼撒半岛,最大的岛屿为克里特岛。

希腊南部地区及各岛屿属于地中海气候,全年气温变化不大,冬季平均气温0~13 ℃,夏季平均气温23~41 ℃,夏季较长,阳光强烈。

希腊大陆部分三面临海,河流短急,海岸多曲折港湾。

Greece is mountainous, with three-quarters of its land comprised of hills and mountains. There are lowland plains along the coast. The southern part of Greece and the islands have a Mediterranean climate. Part of the Greek mainland is seaward on three sides, with short rivers and twisty bays.

3. 人口民族(Population and Ethnicity)

希腊总人口约1112.8万(2019年),人口密度约每平方千米84.33人。其中约98%为希腊人。东正教为国教。

Greece has a population of about 11.128 million (2019), with a population density of about 84.33 people per square kilometer. Orthodoxy is the national religion.

4. 发展简史(Brief History of Development)

古希腊是西方文明的发源地,拥有悠久的历史,创造过灿烂的古代文明,并对欧、亚、非三大洲的历史产生了深远影响。公元前3000年,爱琴文明繁荣。后因北方落后部落侵入,爱琴文明衰落。公元前8世纪起,希腊各地先后建立起数以百计的奴隶制城邦。公元前5世纪希波战争后,希腊城邦进入繁荣时期,经济贸易兴盛,文化成就卓越。伯罗奔尼撒战争后,走向衰落。公元前4世纪希腊半岛被马其顿王国征服,公元前2世纪归罗马帝国统治。1453年东罗马帝国灭亡。1460年,希腊被兴起于亚洲西部的伊斯兰教封建军事帝国奥斯曼帝国统治。

1821年希腊爆发独立战争,1832年成立希腊王国。1924年,希腊成立第二共和国,后又复辟。1967年4月希腊建立了军人独裁政权。1973年,在军政府所主导的公投下,王室被废除,确立共和制。1974年7月,希腊军政府垮台,举行公民投票,有69%的民众赞成终止君主制度,确立国家政体为共和制,希腊王国至此宣告灭亡。此后由新民主党和泛希腊社会主义运动党(简称泛希社运)轮流执政。

Ancient Greece is known as the birthplace of Western civilization. In 3000 BC, the Aegean civilization flourished. By 800 BC, hundreds of independent city-states had formed. Greece reached its peak in the 5th century BC. It was ruled under the Roman Empire by 200 BC and ruled by Ottoman Empire in 1460. Greece declared its independence on March 25, 1821.

5. 政治经济(Politics and Economy)

首都为雅典。国歌为《自由颂》,国花为橄榄,货币为欧元。

首都雅典,雅典是世界上最古老的城市之一,有记载的历史就长达3 000多年。

希腊是一个实行议会共和制的欧洲国家。总统为国家元首,任期5年,可连任一次;立法权属议会和总统,行政权属总理,司法权由法院行使。希腊议会为一院制。执政党为新民主党,主要在野党为泛希社运、希腊共产党、左翼激进联盟党。

希腊属欧盟经济中等发达国家之一,经济基础较薄弱,工业制造业较落后。希腊经济的两大支柱产业是海运业和旅游业。农业较发达,工业主要以食品加工和轻工业为主。服务业是希腊经济的重要组成部分,2018年服务业占国内生产总值的81.01%。

Greece is a parliamentary republic and one of the moderately developed countries in European Union, with a weak economic foundation. The two pillar industries are shipping and tourism industry. Agriculture is relatively developed, while industrial manufacturing is relatively underdeveloped, predominantly food processing and light industry. The services is a major economic sector.

6. 旅游市场(Tourism Market)

希腊有 18 处世界文化遗产,其中包括 16 处文化遗产和 2 处文化和自然混合遗产,在拥有世界遗产的国家中排名第 16 位。

希腊的国际旅游者主要分两部分,一部分为传统的欧美国家的游客(如英、法、德、美等),另一部分为新兴国家的游客(如中国、俄罗斯、印度等)。传统国家的游客出行旅游相对而言比较有计划,时间集中在旅游旺季 6~8 月,以休闲度假为主,也有观光旅游。新兴国家的游客以观光旅游为主。发展中国家的游客呈现增长态势。

旅游业是希腊经济的支柱产业,虽然近年来受金融危机和欧债危机的影响,希腊社会治安恶化,经济低迷,但是希腊得天独厚的旅游与环境优势,以及欧元汇率的持续走低还是吸引了大量游客。虽然传统国家的游客在明显递减,但新兴国家的游客依然在增加,每年增长速度为 15%~20%,新兴国家的旅游人数弥补了传统国家旅游人数的短缺。近年来,希腊旅游业的发展极为迅速。2019 年,到访希腊的游客达到 3 660 万人次,同比增长 5.2%;旅游收入 181.79 亿欧元,同比增长 13.0%。

中国游客在蓬勃发展的希腊旅游业中占有重要地位,据希腊旅游部统计,2019 年前往希腊旅游的中国游客数量比 2018 年翻一番,超过 18 万人次。

世界经济论坛发布的 2019 年旅游业竞争力报告显示,希腊旅游业在 140 个国家中排名第 25 位。

Tourism is an important pillar industry. Since the financial crisis and the European debt crisis, Greece's social security has deteriorated and its economy has been in a downturn. However, Greece's unique advantages of tourism and environment, as well as the sustained decline of the euro exchange rate and other factors, still attract a large number of international travelers to this beautiful country.

International tourists to Greece are mainly divided into two parts: tourists from traditional European and American countries (such as the UK, France, Germany, the United States, etc.), and tourists from emerging countries (such as China, Russia, India, etc.).

 知识拓展 3.10　奥林匹克运动会(见二维码)

PART 2(第二部分)

Tourism Resources(旅游资源)

Tourism in Greece has been a key element of the economic activity in the country, and is one of the country's most important sectors. Greece has been a major destination and attraction since antiquity, for its rich history, as well as for its long coastline, many islands and beaches. Athens, Santorini, Myconos, Rhodes, Corfu and Crete are Greece major tourist destinations.

The most visited region of Greece is that of central Macedonia in northern Greece, near some of the most popular attractions in the country such as Halkidiki, Mount Olympus, Pella, the birthplace of Alexander the Great, and Greece's second largest city, Thessaloniki.

希腊旅游业一直是该国最重要的经济部门之一。自古以来,希腊就以其深厚的历史、漫长的海岸线、众多的岛屿和海滩成为重要的旅游目的地,其中雅典、圣托里尼、米克诺斯、罗德岛、科孚岛和克里特岛是希腊主要的旅游目的地。

希腊游客最多的地区位于希腊北部、靠近马其顿,那里一些最受欢迎的景点,如哈尔基迪基、奥林匹斯山、亚历山大大帝诞生地佩拉和希腊第二大城市塞萨洛尼基。

1. Tourism Attractions(旅游胜地)

1)Mykonos(米克诺斯)

Mykonos, a Greek island, is one of the top tourist destinations in Europe. It belongs to the Cyclades group and it is located between Tinos, Syros, Paros and Naxos. With a surface area of 86 km^2 and a population of approximately 6 200 (2002) inhabitants, it is considered one of the smallest islands of the group. Mykonos, except for being the most famous island of Greece, is also the most expensive one. It is the favorite destination of Greeks from all over the country, of tourists from all around the world and of celebrities. The island gets overcrowded during peak season, and it is an ideal destination for those who enjoy crowds, fun and night-long entertainment. The island is very beautiful with a wonderful mountainous landscape, clear waters, long sandy organized beaches, churches, chapels and windmills.

希腊的米克诺斯岛是欧洲顶级旅游目的地之一。米克诺斯岛除了是希腊最著名的岛屿外,也是最昂贵的岛屿,有着美丽的山地景观、清澈的海水、长长的沙滩、教堂、小教堂和风车,它是希腊人、世界各地的游客和名人最喜欢的目的地。

2) Paros(帕罗斯)

The island of Paros is the fourth largest of the Cyclades cluster. Its area is 185 km² and the population is about 9 000 people. The island consists mainly of large valleys, while mountains occupy its central part. Paros is one of the most modern tourist resorts of the Aegean. Due to its size, the island meets any visitor's needs, whether looking for relaxation or adventurous holidays. It is a typical Cycladic island with traditional villages full of whitewashed houses, narrow paved streets, flowered balconies, churches and many beautiful beaches. Parikia is the capital, the main port and the biggest settlement of the island of Paros with 3 000 inhabitants. Despite the quick development over the last decades, Parikia kept its traditional beauty. Built amphitheatrically around the port with whitewashed and flat roofed houses, wooden colored doors and windows, separated by narrow white alleys forming a labyrinth, it is the cultural and commercial center of Paros.

Historically, Paros was known for its fine white marble, which gave rise to the term "Parian" to describe marble or china of similar qualities. Today, abandoned marble quarries and mines can be found on the island, but Paros is primarily known as a popular tourist spot.

帕罗斯岛是基克拉泽斯群岛第四大岛,是爱琴海最现代化的旅游胜地之一。这是一个典型的基克拉泽斯岛,传统的村庄里到处都是粉刷过的房子、狭窄的铺砌街道、鲜花盛开的阳台、教堂和美丽的海滩。

帕罗奇亚是帕罗斯岛的首都、主要港口和最大的定居点。帕罗奇亚是帕罗斯的文化和商业中心,是一个受欢迎的旅游胜地。

2. Tourism Cities(旅游城市)

1) Athens(雅典)

Athens is the capital and largest city of Greece. Athens dominates the Attica region and is one of the world's oldest cities, with its recorded history spanning around 3 400 years, and the earliest human presence around the 11th-7th centuries BC. Classical Athens was a powerful city-state that emerged in conjunction with the seagoing development of the port of Piraeus. A centre for the arts, learning and philosophy, home of Plato's Academy and Aristotle's Lyceum, it is widely referred to as the cradle of Western civilization and the birthplace of democracy, largely because of its cultural and political impact on the European continent and in particular the Romans. In modern times, Athens is a large cosmopolitan metropolis and central to economic, financial, industrial, maritime, political and cultural life in Greece.

Athens is recognized as a global city because of its geo-strategic location and its importance in shipping, finance, commerce, media, entertainment, arts, international trade, culture, education and tourism. It is one of the biggest economic centres in southeastern Europe, with a large financial sector, and its port Piraeus is the largest port in Greece.

The heritage of the classical era is still evident in the city, represented by ancient monuments and works of art, the most famous of all being the Parthenon, considered a key landmark of early Western civilization. The city also retains Roman and Byzantine monuments, as well as a smaller number of Ottoman monuments.

Athens is home to two UNESCO World Heritage Sites, the Acropolis of Athens and the medieval Daphni Monastery. Landmarks of the modern era, dating back to the establishment of Athens as the capital of the independent Greek state in 1834, include the Hellenic Parliament (19th century) and the Athens Trilogy, consisting of the National Library of Greece, the Athens University and the Academy of Athens. Athens was the host city of the first modern Olympic Games in 1896, and 108 years later it welcomed home the 2004 Summer Olympics. Athens is home to the National Archeological Museum, featuring the world's largest collection of ancient Greek antiquities, as well as the new Acropolis Museum.

雅典是希腊的首都和最大的城市,是世界上最古老的城市之一,最早的人类出现在公元前11至7世纪。古典时期的雅典是一个强大的城邦,作为艺术、学习和哲学的中心,它是柏拉图学院和亚里士多德学园的所在地,它被称为西方文明的摇篮和民主的诞生地。现代雅典是一个大都市,是希腊经济、金融、工业、海事、政治和文化生活的中心。

雅典被认为是一个全球性城市,这得益于它的战略地理位置,以及它在航运、金融、商业、媒体、娱乐、艺术、国际贸易、文化、教育和旅游方面的重要性。它是欧洲东南部最大的经济中心之一,拥有庞大的金融部门,港口比雷埃夫斯是希腊最大的港口。

这座城市仍然保留着古典时期的遗产,以古代历史遗迹和艺术作品为代表,其中最著名的是帕特农神庙,它被认为是早期西方文明的重要里程碑。这座城市还保留了罗马和拜占庭时期的历史遗迹,以及少量的奥斯曼帝国的历史遗迹。

雅典有两处联合国教科文组织世界遗产:雅典卫城和中世纪的达芙妮修道院。现代地标包括19世纪的希腊议会和由希腊国家图书馆、雅典大学和雅典学院组成的"雅典三部曲"。雅典是1896年第一届现代奥运会的举办城市,也是2004年夏季奥运会的举办城市。

(1)Acropolis of Athens(雅典卫城)

The Acropolis of Athens is an ancient citadel located on a high rocky outcrop above the city of Athens and contains the remains of several ancient buildings of great architectural and historic significance, the most famous being the Parthenon. The word acropolis comes from the Greek words ἄκρον (akron, "edge, extremity") and πόλις (polis, "city"). Although there are many other acropolis in Greece, the significance of the Acropolis of Athens is that it is commonly known as "The Acropolis" without qualification.

Every four years, the Athenians held a festival called the Panathenaea that rivaled the Olympic Games in popularity. During the festival, a procession (believed to be depicted on the Parthenon frieze) traveled through the city via the Panathenaic Way and culminated on the Acropolis. There, a new robe of woven wool (peplos) was placed on either the statue of Athena Polias in the Erechtheum (during a regular Panathenaea) or on the statue of Athena Parthenos in the Parthenon (during the Great Panathenaea, held every four years).

雅典卫城是一座古老的要塞,坐落在雅典市中心的卫城山丘上,城内有几座具有重要建筑和历史意义的古建筑遗迹,其中最著名的是帕特农神庙。

雅典人每四年举行一次"泛雅典娜节",其受欢迎程度可与奥运会相媲美。在节日期间,一个游行队伍通过泛雅典之路穿过城市,并在卫城达到高潮。

(2) Olympia(奥林匹亚)

Olympia, a sanctuary of ancient Greece in Elis on the Peloponnese Peninsula, is known for having been the site of the Olympic Games in classical times. The Olympic Games were held every four years throughout Classical Antiquity, from the 8th century BC to the 4th century AD. The first Olympic Games were in honor of Zeus.

The sanctuary, known as the Altis, consists of an unordered arrangement of various buildings. Enclosed within the temenos (sacred enclosure) are the Temple of Hera, the Temple of Zeus, the Pelopion, and the area of the altar, where the sacrifices were made.

To the north of the sanctuary can be found the Prytaneion and the Philippeion, as well as the array of treasuries representing the various city-states. The Metroon lies to the south of these treasuries, with the Echo Stoa to the east. The hippodrome and later stadium were located east of the Echo Stoa. To the south of the sanctuary is the South Stoa and the Bouleuterion, whereas the Palaestra, the workshop of Pheidias, the Gymnasion, and the Leonidaion lie to the west.

Olympia was also known for the gigantic ivory and gold statue of Zeus that used to stand there, sculpted by Pheidias, which was named one of the Seven Wonders of the Ancient World by Antipater of Sidon. Very close to the Temple of Zeus which housed this statue, the studio of Pheidias was excavated in the 1950s. Evidence found there, such as sculptor's tools, corroborates this opinion. The ancient ruins sit north of the Alfeios River and south of Mount Kronos (named after the Greek deity Kronos). The Kladeos, a tributary of the Alfeios, flows around the area.

奥林匹亚是古希腊在伯罗奔尼撒半岛埃利斯的一个避难所,因古典时期举办奥运会而闻名。从公元前8世纪到公元4世纪,奥林匹克运动会每四年举办一次。第一届奥林匹克运动会是为了纪念宙斯。

这个被称为避难所的地方由各种建筑无序排列而成。在神圣围地内有赫拉神庙、宙斯神庙、佩洛普斯神庙和祭坛区域。

奥林匹亚因曾经矗立在那里的巨大的象牙和黄金宙斯雕像而闻名,这座雕像由菲迪亚斯雕刻,是古代世界七大奇迹之一。

(3) Temple of Zeus(宙斯神庙)

The massive temple of Zeus, the most important building in the Altis, standing in its very centre, is the largest temple in the Peloponnese, considered by many to be the perfect example of Doric architecture. It was built by the Eleans from the spoils of the Triphylian war and dedicated to Zeus. Construction began 470 BC and was completed before 456 BC, when an inscribed block was let into the east gable to support a gold shield dedicated by the Spartans in commemoration of their victory at Tanagra.

In the temple the statue portrayed Zeus enthroned, holding a sceptre in his left hand and a winged Victory in his right. The undraped parts of the statue were of ivory, while the robe and throne, the latter decorated with relief mythological scenes, were of gold. The temple's opulent sculptural decoration is a fine example of the Severe Style. The east pediment depicted the chariot race between Pelops and Oinomaos, presided by Zeus, master of the sanctuary, whose figure dominated the composition. The west pediment depicted the battle of the Lapiths and Centaurs, arranged round the central figure of Apollo. The twelve metopes, six at each end over the entrance to the pronaos and the opisthodomos, depicted the Labours of Hercules, mythical son of Zeus.

巨大的宙斯神庙是阿尔提斯最重要的建筑,是伯罗奔尼撒最大的神庙,被许多人认为是多立克式建筑的完美典范。神庙建于公元前 470 年,在公元前 456 年之前完工。

在神庙中,宙斯的雕像坐在王位上,左手拿着权杖,右手托着一尊胜利女神像。雕像未经修饰的部分是象牙制成的,而长袍和宝座是金色的。

(4) Byzantine and Christian Museum(拜占庭和基督教博物馆)

The Byzantine and Christian Museum is situated at Vassilissis Sofias Avenue in Athens, Greece. It was founded in 1914 and houses more than 25 000 exhibits with rare collections of pictures, scriptures, frescoes, pottery, fabrics, manuscripts and copies of artifacts from the 3rd century AD to the late medieval era. It is one of the most important museums in the world in Byzantine Art. In June 2004, in time for its 90th anniversary and the 2004 Athens Olympics, the museum reopened to the public after an extensive renovation and the addition of another wing.

拜占庭和基督教博物馆位于雅典,建于 1914 年,有 25 000 多件展品,珍藏了从公元 3 世纪到中世纪晚期的图片、经文、壁画、陶器、织物、手稿和文物复制品。它是世界上最重要的拜占庭艺术博物馆之一。

2) Thessaloniki(塞萨洛尼基)

Thessaloniki is a popular tourist destination in Greece. Thessaloniki is the second largest city in Greece. Thessaloniki is Greece's second major economic, industrial, commercial and political centre, and a major transportation hub for the rest of southeastern Europe; its commercial port is also of great importance for Greece and the southeastern European hinterland. The city is renowned for its festivals, events and vibrant cultural life in general, and is considered to be Greece's cultural capital. Events such as the Thessaloniki International Trade Fair and the Thessaloniki International Film Festival are held annually, while the city also hosts the largest bi-annual meeting of the Greek diaspora. Thessaloniki is the 2014 European Youth Capital.

Thessaloniki is home to numerous notable Byzantine monuments, including the Paleochristian and Byzantine monuments of Thessaloniki, a UNESCO World Heritage Site, as well as several Roman, Ottoman and Sephardic Jewish structures.

塞萨洛尼基是希腊第二大城市,也是希腊著名的旅游胜地,是希腊第二大经济、工业、商业和政治中心,也是东南欧主要交通枢纽。这座城市以节日、活动和充满活力的文化生活而闻名,是希腊的文化之都。

塞萨洛尼基是众多著名的拜占庭遗迹的所在地,包括早期基督教和拜占庭古迹,以及一些罗马、奥斯曼和西班牙系犹太人的建筑。

3)Nafplion(纳夫普利翁)

Nafplion, in the Peloponnese in Greece, is a seaport town that has expanded up the hillsides near the north end of the Argolic Gulf (Argolikos Bay). The town was the capital of Greece from 1829 to 1834. Nafplion is since 2011 the seat of the municipality of Nafplion.

位于希腊伯罗奔尼撒半岛的纳夫普利翁是一个港口城市,1829年到1834年,该市曾是希腊的首都。

Sum up(本章小结)

1.欧洲旅游区是世界上国际旅游最发达的地区,不仅是世界最重要的客源地,也是世界主要的旅游目的地。

2.本章从地理位置及范围、自然风貌、民族与宗教、旅游市场等方面介绍了欧洲旅游区的基本概况。

3.本章选取了英国、法国、德国、意大利、西班牙、俄罗斯、瑞士、希腊八个国家进行介绍,它们是中国在欧洲比较重要的目的地国和客源国。

4.每个国家的介绍分为两部分,第一部分介绍了各国的国土疆域、自然风貌、人口民族、发展简史、政治经济和旅游市场的基本概况,第二部分介绍了各国的旅游资源。

Reviewing and Thinking(复习与思考)

1. 简要分析法国、德国、西班牙、英国、意大利成为世界旅游大国的原因。
2. 欧洲各国主要的旅游城市有哪些？试列举其著名的旅游景点。
3. 试设计几条欧洲经典旅游线路。

CHAPTER

4

The North America Tourism Region
（北美洲旅游区）

CHAPTER 4　The North America Tourism Region(北美洲旅游区)

◇ **LEARNING OBJECTIVES(学习目标)**

1. Understand the basic situation of the major tourist source and destination countries in North America(了解北美洲主要客源国和目的地国的基本情况).

2. Master the tourism market development and tourism resources characteristics of the main source and destination countries in North America(掌握北美洲主要客源国和目的地国的旅游市场发展与旅游资源特点).

3. Design some classic tourist routes(设计一些经典旅游线路).

◇ **LEARNING CONTENT(学习内容)**

1. America(美国)

2. Canada(加拿大)

◇ **PROBLEM ORIENTATION(问题导向)**

Why can the United States become the most developed tourist country in the world?(为什么美国能成为世界上旅游业最发达的国家?)

Section 1　General Situation of North American (北美洲概况)

北美旅游区位于西半球大陆北部,北濒北冰洋,东西分别临辽阔的大西洋和太平洋,南以巴拿马运河同南美旅游区分界。包括加拿大、美国、墨西哥以及中美洲、西印度群岛上的国家,总面积2 422.8万平方千米。

The North America tourism region is located in the northern part of the western hemisphere, bordering the Arctic Ocean in the north, facing the vast Atlantic Ocean and the Pacific Ocean in the east and west respectively, and bordering the South American tourism region with the Panama Canal in the south. It includes Canada, the United States, Mexico and countries in Central America and the West Indies, with a total area of 24.228 million km^2.

北美旅游区地形呈明显的三个南北纵列带。西部是高大的科迪勒拉山系,国家公园、大峡谷多,山水旅游景观丰富;东部为低缓的山地、高原(包括古老的阿巴拉契亚山地和拉布拉多高原等),自然旅游资源和人文旅游资源兼备。中部是起伏平缓的低高原和平原,自然旅游资源丰富。中美洲和加勒比海地区海岸线漫长曲折,热带海岛多,阳光明媚,碧海银滩,景色迷人,是游泳、日光浴和泛舟的理想之地,是世界上最受欢迎的海滨旅游度假

北美洲地图 NORTH AMERICA

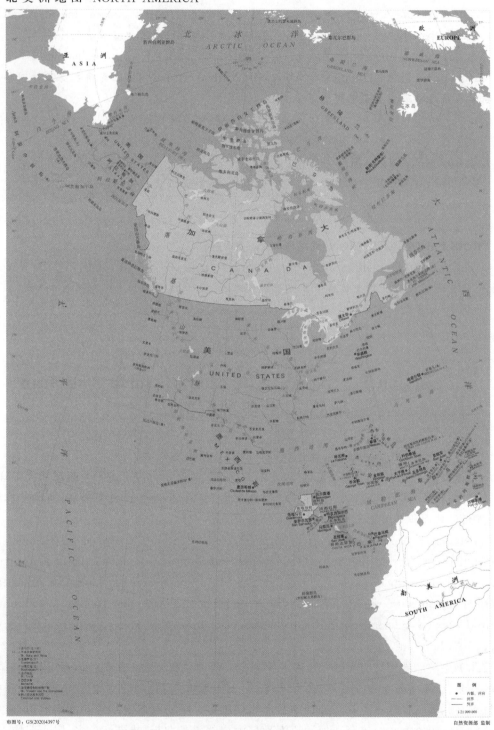

资料来源：标准地图服务网站，审图号：GS(2020)4397号。

胜地之一。

北美旅游区气候类型多样,拥有热带、寒带和温带的各种气候类型。大部分地区位于温带,气候具有显著的大陆性,以温带大陆性气候为主,生物旅游资源丰富。南部终年适合旅游。北部现代冰川分布广,冰雪旅游景观丰富,是冰雪旅游和探险旅游的最佳去处。

北美旅游区人口约5.37亿(2019年),但分布很不均衡,绝大部分人口分布在大陆东南部地区,其中以美国大西洋沿岸、五大湖周围、太平洋沿岸和墨西哥城周围人口密度最大。广大的北部地区和西部内陆地区人口稀少,有的地方甚至无人居住。民族成分复杂,主要以欧裔白种人为主。土著居民主要是印第安人和因纽特人。

北美旅游区是现代世界资本主义的主要中心之一,是世界经济发展水平最高的地区。北美旅游资源比较丰富,又由于其雄厚的经济基础、完备的旅游基础设施和服务设施,旅游业发达。长期以来,无论是接待国际游客量,还是国际旅游收入,北美旅游区均在世界前列。美国、加拿大、墨西哥均是全球15大国际旅游接待国和国际旅游收入国。美国、加拿大均为15个最大国际旅游消费支出国之一。

The landscape of North America tourism region shows three distinct north-south longitudinal belts. In the west is the high Cordillera mountain ranges, in the east is the low mountains and plateaus, and the low plateaus and plain belts are in the middle.

North America tourism region has a variety of climates, from tropical and cold zone to temperate zone. The climate is mainly temperate continental climate.

North America tourism region is one of the main centers of modern world capitalism and the most developed in the world. The United States, Canada and Mexico are among the top 15 international tourism destinations and international tourism revenue. Both the United States and Canada are among the top 15 international tourism consumption.

Section 2　The United States(美国)

PART 1(第一部分)

1. 国土疆域(Territory)

美国(全称美利坚合众国)位于北美旅游区中部,还包括北美旅游区西北端的阿拉斯加和太平洋中部的夏威夷群岛。北与加拿大相邻,南接墨西哥,西濒太平洋,东临大西洋,总面积约937万平方千米,仅次于俄罗斯、加拿大和中国,居世界第四位。

The United States is located in the middle of the North American tourism region, including Alaska at the northwest and the Hawaiian Islands in the middle of the Pacific

Ocean. It is adjacent to Canada in the north, Mexico in the south, the Pacific Ocean in the west and the Atlantic Ocean in the east. The total area is 9.37 million km², ranking fourth in the world after Russia, Canada and China.

2. 自然风貌(Natural Features)

美国本土地形大致可分为东部低山高原区、西部高山高原区和中部平原区。东部低山高原区有古老的拉布拉多高原和阿巴拉契亚山地,植被茂密,环境清幽;北段为游览和避暑胜地;南段多溶洞景观和急流瀑布风景水体景观,佛罗里达半岛的大沼泽地国家公园里是著名的风景名胜。西部高山高原区,落基山脉、内华达山脉及科罗拉多高原,山峰高峻、怪石嶙峋、风光壮丽,充满神奇色彩,黄石国家公园、科罗拉多大峡谷等许多举世闻名的旅游胜地分布在这里。西部的太平洋沿岸,海岸曲折萦回,阳光明媚,为理想的观光旅游胜地。中部平原区自然、人文景观丰富。五大湖区旅游景观丰富,著名的尼亚加拉瀑布每年吸引大量的旅游者。

美国地域广阔,地形复杂,气候类型多样,生物旅游资源丰富,各地的旅游景观各具特色,国家公园分布广,游客可选择的旅游目的地多,全年适宜旅游的时间长。

The landscape of the United States can be roughly divided into the eastern lowland plateaus, the western highland plateaus, and the central plains.

The United States has a vast area, complex landform, diverse climate type, rich biological tourism resources, and various tourism landscapes with their own characteristics. With a wide distribution of national parks, there are many tourist destinations for visitors to choose and a long time for tourism throughout the year.

3. 人口民族(Population and Ethnicity)

美国的人口约3.33亿(2021年),人口密度约为每平方千米35.54人。美国是移民国家,居民绝大部分是欧洲白色人种移民的后裔,有色人种有黑人、印第安人,此外华人、华侨也较多。美国是个民族成分多元化的国家,素有"民族熔炉"之美称,100多个民族的人来到美国共同生活,形成了特有的美利坚民族。不同民族、不同信仰的居民在友好共处中,又各自保留着自己的传统,使美国的人文景观更加丰富多彩。其中非拉美裔白人占60.1%,拉美裔占18.5%,非洲裔美国人占13.4%,亚裔占5.9%,混血占2.8%,印第安人和阿拉斯加原住民占1.3%,夏威夷原住民或其他太平洋岛民占0.2%(少部分人在其他族群内被重复统计)。官方语言为英语。人口中约46.5%信仰基督教,20.8%信仰天主教,1.9%信仰犹太教,0.5%信仰东正教,0.7%信仰佛教,0.9%信仰伊斯兰教,1.2%信仰其他宗教,22.8%无宗教信仰(少部分人群属于多宗教信仰被重复统计)。

The population of the United States is about 333 million (in 2021), with a population density of 35.54 people per square kilometer. The United States is a country of immigrants, and most of the residents are the descendants of European white immigrants. The residents mainly profess Protestantism and Catholicism.

4. 发展简史(Brief History of Development)

早在欧洲殖民者踏上美洲大陆之前,印第安人世代在这块土地上繁衍生息。1492 年哥伦布到达美洲后,欧洲殖民主义国家开始不断向北美移民。1733 年,英国在北美东部相继建立了 13 个殖民地。1775 年,爆发了反对英国殖民统治的独立战争。1776 年 7 月通过《独立宣言》,成立联邦共和国。乔治·华盛顿当选为第一任总统。

独立后,美国北方资本主义经济获得了迅速发展,而南方保持了奴隶制农业经济。1861 年反对黑奴制度的林肯就任美国总统,南部发动了叛乱,爆发了南北战争。1865 年战争以北方胜利而告终,从而为资本主义在全国的迅速发展扫清了障碍。之后美国资本主义经济得到迅速发展。

美国虽然只有 200 多年的历史,却是一个重视历史、尊重文化遗产的国家,相关历史遗迹都被精心地保护起来,不但众多的历史文物古迹保存完好,而且建有许多国家历史、文化、艺术、美术、科技博物馆,为旅游业的发展提供了十分有利的条件。

After Columbus arrived in America in 1492, European colonial countries began to continue to immigrate to North America. In 1733, the UK established 13 colonies in the eastern part of North America. In 1775, the Revolutionary War broke out. In July 1776, the United States passed the Declaration of Independence and founded a federal republic. The Civil War broke out in 1861. Since then, the American capitalist economy has developed rapidly.

5. 政治经济(Politics and Economy)

首都为华盛顿,国花为玫瑰花,货币为美元。

美国的国家政体为联邦总统制,实行立法、司法和行政三权分立,即立法权、行政权和司法权分别由国会、总统和联邦最高法院行使。三个部门行使权力时,彼此互相牵制,以达到权力平衡。国会有立法权,总统对国会通过的法案有权否决,国会又有权在一定条件下推翻总统的否决;总统有权任命高级官员,但须经国会认可,国会有权依法弹劾总统和高级文官;最高法院法官由总统任命并经国会认可,最高法院又可对国会通过的法律以违宪为由宣布无效。总统执掌行政权,既是国家元首,又是政府首脑;总统不对国会负责,直接对选民负责。

美国是一个经济高度发达的国家,国民生产总值长期居世界第一位。美国是世界最大的工业国,具有庞大完整的工业体系,生产能力和出口量都很大。农业高度发达,机械化程度高,粮食总产量约占世界的五分之一,出口量居世界前列。美国拥有完整而便捷的交通运输网络,旅游基础设施完备,旅游业相当发达。

The United States is a federal presidential state. It is a highly developed country with a GDP ranking first in the world for a long time. The United States is the world's largest industrial country with a huge and complete industrial system. Agriculture is highly developed with a high degree of mechanization. The total grain output accounts for about one-fifth of the world's total, and its export volume ranks among the highest in the world. The United States has a complete and convenient transportation network, complete tourism infrastructure and developed tourism industry.

6. 旅游市场(Tourism market)

美国经济实力雄厚,科学技术先进,旅游交通便利,服务设施完善,管理水平较高,旅游资源丰富,客源市场稳定,旅游业发达。

美国旅游资源丰富多样。自然旅游资源千姿百态,黄石国家公园、大峡谷、猛犸洞穴、夏威夷火山国家公园、尼亚加拉瀑布、威基基海滩等迷人的山色、湖光、悬崖、峡谷、瀑布、海滩,可供人们观光、度假、疗养。人文旅游资源丰富多彩,古今名胜、文化艺术、游乐园、博物馆遍布全国。纽约自由女神像的庄严、大都会艺术博物馆的豪华、影城好莱坞的浪漫、迪士尼乐园的欢乐、纽约的繁华和少数民族的民俗风情等深深地吸引着游人。美国已形成三大都市旅游带的发展格局:以纽约为中心的波士顿—华盛顿大都市旅游带(分布于美国东北部大西洋沿岸平原)、以芝加哥为中心的芝加哥—匹兹堡都市旅游带(分布于美国中部五大湖沿岸地区)和以洛杉矶为中心的圣地亚哥—旧金山城市群(分布于美国西南部太平洋沿岸)。三大都市旅游带具有发达的基础设施网络,一般都拥有大的港口,沿长轴呈带状扩展。

美国已成为世界最发达的旅游国,是世界最大的国际旅游客源地和接待地,在全部旅游收入中,约有70%来自国内旅游,国内旅游仍是旅游业的主要收入来源。

美国的主要旅游客源国是加拿大、墨西哥、日本、法国、德国、英国、西班牙、葡萄牙、意大利、荷兰、韩国、澳大利亚等。国际旅游收入、国际旅游接待量和国际旅游消费水平均居世界前列。据UNWTO统计,2019年国际旅游者人数为7 925万人次,居世界第三位,次于法国和西班牙;国际旅游收入为2 334亿美元,居世界第一位。

中国公民自2000年以来赴美国旅游的人数逐年增加。据麦肯锡咨询公司(McKinsey & Company)统计,2000年至2010年,中国赴美游客人数从24.9万人增长到80.2万人,2015年又增长了三倍,2017年超过300万人,中国游客人数在当年赴美外国游客总人数中排名第五,前四位依次是加拿大、墨西哥、英国和日本。2008年到2016年,中国游客在美消费总额增长了6倍,接近189亿美元。但是近年来,由于中美贸易争端等原因导致中国赴美游客人数下降,2018年为290万人,下降5.7%。

美国公民的主要旅游目的国是加拿大、墨西哥及西欧、东北亚、东南亚、北非一些国家,美国是仅次于中国的旅游支出最大的国家,2019年为1 823亿美元。美国一直是中国比较稳定的客源国,2018年美国公民来华旅游人数达248.36万人,十年增长45%,是我国第六位客源国。

The United States has become the world's most developed tourism country, is the world's largest source and reception of international tourism. Canada, Mexico, Japan,

France, Germany, the United Kingdom, Spain, Portugal, Italy, the Netherlands, South Korea, Australia and so on are the main sources of tourists to the United States. International tourism revenue, international tourism reception and international tourism consumption all rank among the top in the world. The main destinations for US citizens are Canada, Mexico and some countries in Western Europe, Northeast Asia, Southeast Asia and North Africa. The United States has always been a relatively stable source of tourists for China.

PART 2(第二部分)

Tourism Resources(旅游资源)

Tourism in the United States is a large industry that serves millions of international and domestic tourists yearly. Tourists visit the US to see natural wonders, cities, historic landmarks, and entertainment venues. Americans seek similar attractions, as well as recreation and vacation areas.

美国的旅游业是一个庞大的产业,每年为数以百万计的国际和国内游客提供服务。游客到美国去参观自然奇观、城市、历史地标和娱乐场所。同样,美国人喜爱寻求类似的景点、娱乐项目和度假区。

1. Natural Tourism Resources(自然旅游资源)

1)Grand Canyon National Park(大峡谷国家公园)

Grand Canyon National Park is the United States' 15th oldest national park. Named a UNESCO World Heritage Site in 1979, the park is located in Arizona. The park's central feature is the Grand Canyon, a gorge of the Colorado River, which is often considered one of the Seven Natural Wonders of the World. The park covers 1 217 262 acres of unincorporated area in Coconino and Mohave counties.

大峡谷国家公园是美国第15古老的国家公园。该公园位于美国亚利桑那州,1979年被联合国教科文组织列为世界遗产。该公园的特色是科罗拉多河大峡谷,是世界七大自然奇观之一。

2)Niagara Falls(尼亚加拉大瀑布)

Niagara Falls is the collective name for three waterfalls that straddle the international border between Canada and the United States; more specifically, between the province of Ontario and the state of New York. They form the southern end of the Niagara Gorge.

From largest to smallest, the three waterfalls are the Horseshoe Falls, the American Falls and the Bridal Veil Falls. The Horseshoe Falls lie mostly on the Canadian side and the American Falls entirely on the American side, separated by Goat Island. The smaller Bridal Veil Falls are also located on the American side, separate from the other waterfalls by Luna Island. The international boundary line was originally drawn through Horseshoe Falls in 1819, but the boundary has long been in dispute due to natural erosion and construction.

Located on the Niagara River, which drains Lake Erie into Lake Ontario, the combined falls form the highest flow rate of any waterfall in the world, with a vertical drop of more than 50 m. Horseshoe Falls is the most powerful waterfall in North America, as measured by vertical height and also by flow rate. The falls are located 27 km north-northwest of Buffalo, New York and 121 km south-southeast of Toronto, between the twin cities of Niagara Falls, Ontario, and Niagara Falls, New York.

While not exceptionally high, the Niagara Falls is very wide. The Niagara Falls is renowned both for their beauty and as a valuable source of hydroelectric power.

尼亚加拉瀑布横跨加拿大和美国之间的国界,是三个瀑布的总称:马蹄瀑布,美国瀑布和新娘面纱瀑布。马蹄瀑布主要位于加拿大一侧,美国瀑布完全位于美国一侧,被山羊岛隔开。较小的新娘面纱瀑布也位于美国一侧,与其他瀑布相隔月神岛。

瀑布位于尼亚加拉河上,是世界上流量最大的瀑布,垂直落差超过50米。以垂直高度和流速来衡量,马蹄瀑布是北美最壮观的瀑布。尼亚加拉瀑布虽然不是特别高,但是很宽,以其美丽和宝贵的水力发电资源而闻名。

3) Yellowstone National Park(黄石国家公园)

Yellowstone National Park is a national park located primarily in the U. S. state of Wyoming, although it also extends into Montana and Idaho. It was established by the U. S. Congress and signed into law by President Ulysses S. Grant on March 1, 1872. Yellowstone, widely held to be the first national park in the world, is known for its wildlife and its many geothermal features. It has many types of ecosystems, but the subalpine forest is most abundant. It is part of the South Central Rockies forests ecoregion. Native Americans have lived in the Yellowstone region for at least 11 000 years. Hundreds of structures have been built and are protected for their architectural and historical significance, and researchers have examined more than 1 000 archaeological sites.

Yellowstone National Park spans an area of 8 983 km^2, comprising lakes, canyons, rivers and mountain ranges. Yellowstone Lake is one of the largest high-elevation lakes in North America and is centered over the Yellowstone Caldera, the largest super volcano on the continent. The caldera is considered an active volcano. It has erupted with tremendous force several times in the last two million years. Half of the world's geothermal features are in Yellowstone, fueled by this ongoing volcanism. Lava flows and rocks from volcanic eruptions cover most of the land area of Yellowstone. The park is the centerpiece of the Greater Yellowstone Ecosystem, the largest remaining nearly-intact ecosystem in the Earth's northern temperate zone.

Hundreds of species of mammals, birds, fish and reptiles have been documented, including several that are either endangered or threatened. The vast forests and grasslands also include unique species of plants. Yellowstone Park is the largest and most famous megafauna location in the Continental United States. Forest fires occur in the park each year. Yellowstone has numerous recreational opportunities, including hiking, camping, boating, fishing and sightseeing. Paved roads provide close access to the major geothermal areas as well as some of the lakes and waterfalls. During the winter, visitors often access the park by way of guided tours that use either snow coaches or snowmobiles.

黄石国家公园主要位于美国怀俄明州,并延伸到蒙大拿州和爱达荷州。黄石国家公园是世界上第一个国家公园,以其野生动物和许多地热特征而闻名。它有许多类型的生态系统,其中亚高山森林最为丰富。美洲原住民已经在黄石地区生活了至少11 000年。数百座建筑因其建筑和历史意义而被保护。

黄石国家公园占地8 983平方千米,由湖泊、峡谷、河流和山脉组成。黄石湖是北美最大的高海拔湖泊之一,位于北美洲最大的超级火山——黄石火山口的中心,这是一座活火山,在过去的两百万年里,它以巨大的力量喷发了好几次。世界上一半的地热资源都在黄石国家公园,火山喷发产生的熔岩流和岩石覆盖了黄石公园的大部分陆地区域。该公园是大黄石生态系统的中心,大黄石生态系统是地球北温带现存的最大的完整的生态系统。这里有数百种哺乳动物、鸟类、鱼类和爬行动物,其中包括一些濒临灭绝或受到威胁的物种。黄石公园是北美洲最大、最著名的巨型动物保护区。黄石公园有许多娱乐项目,包括徒步旅行、露营、划船、钓鱼和观光等。

4)Big Basin Redwoods State Park(大盆地红杉州立公园)

Big Basin Redwoods State Park is a state park in the U. S. state of California, located in Santa Cruz County, about 36 km northwest of Santa Cruz. The park contains almost all of the Waddell Creek watershed, which was formed by the seismic uplift of its rim, and the erosion of its center by the many streams in its bowl-shaped depression. Big Basin is California's oldest State Park, established in 1902, earning its designation as a California Historical Landmark. Its original 15 km^2 have been increased over the years to over 73 km^2. It is part of the Northern California coastal forests ecoregion and is home to the largest continuous stand of ancient coast redwoods south of San Francisco. It contains 44 km^2 of old-growth forest as well as recovering redwood forest, with mixed conifer, oaks, chaparral and riparian habitats. Elevations in the park vary from sea level to over 600 m. The climate ranges from foggy and damp near the ocean to sunny, warm ridge tops.

The park has over 130 km of trails. Some of these trails link Big Basin to Castle

Rock State Park and the eastern reaches of the Santa Cruz range. The Skyline-to-the-Sea Trail threads its way through the park along Waddell Creek to Waddell Beach and the adjacent Theodore J. Hoover Natural Preserve, a freshwater marsh. The park has a large number of waterfalls, a wide variety of environments (from lush canyon bottoms to sparse chaparral-covered slopes), many animals (deer, raccoons, an occasional bobcat) and abundant bird life—including Steller's jays, egrets, herons and acorn woodpeckers.

大盆地红杉州立公园是美国加利福尼亚州的一个州立公园，位于圣克鲁斯县，在圣克鲁斯西北约 36 千米处。大盆地公园是加州最古老的州立公园，建于 1902 年，为加州历史地标。它是北加州海岸森林生态区的一部分，是旧金山南部最大的连续古老海岸红杉的家园。它包括 44 平方千米的原始森林和正在恢复的红杉森林，还有针叶树、橡树、灌木丛等。

公园的步道长度超过 130 千米。公园内有大量的瀑布，有多种多样的环境（从郁郁葱葱的峡谷底部到稀疏的灌木覆盖的山坡），有许多动物和鸟类，如鹿、浣熊、山猫、虎头松鸦、白鹭、苍鹭和橡子啄木鸟。

5) Hawaii Volcanoes National Park(夏威夷火山国家公园)

Hawaii is the 50th and most recent U.S. state to join the United States. Hawaii is the only U.S. state located in Oceania and the only one composed entirely of islands. Hawaii is the only U.S. state not located in the America. The state encompasses nearly the entire volcanic Hawaiian archipelago, which comprises hundreds of islands spread over 2 413 kilometers. Hawaii's diverse natural scenery, warm tropical climate, abundance of public beaches, oceanic surroundings, and active volcanoes make it a popular destination for tourists, surfers, biologists, and volcanologists. Because of its central location in the Pacific and 19th-century labor migration, Hawaii's culture is strongly influenced by North American and Asian cultures, in addition to its indigenous Hawaiian culture. Hawaii has over a million permanent residents, along with many visitors and U.S. military personnel. Its capital is Honolulu on the island of O'ahu.

Hawaii Volcanoes National Park, established in 1916, is a United States National Park located in the U.S. State of Hawaii, on the island of Hawaii. It encompasses two active volcanoes: Kilauea, one of the world's most active volcanoes, and Mauna Loa, the world's most massive subaerial volcano. The park gives scientists insight into the birth of the Hawaiian Islands and ongoing studies into the processes of vulcanism. For visitors, the park offers dramatic volcanic landscapes as well as glimpses of rare flora and fauna.

In recognition of its outstanding natural values, Hawaii Volcanoes National Park was designated as an International Biosphere Reserve in 1980 and a World Heritage Site in 1987. In 2000 the name recommended to be changed by the Hawaiian National Park Language Correction Act of 2000 observing the Hawaiian spelling, but that bill died. In 2012 the Hawai i Volcanoes National Park was honored on the 14th quarter of the

America the Beautiful Quarters.

夏威夷是美国第 50 个、也是最近一个加入美国的州,是美国唯一一个位于大洋洲的州,是唯一一个不在美洲的州,也是唯一一个完全由岛屿组成的州。夏威夷州几乎囊括了整个火山群岛,由数百个岛屿组成,绵延 2 413 千米。夏威夷多样的自然风光、温暖的热带气候、丰富的公共海滩、海洋环境和活火山使它成为游客、冲浪者、生物学家和火山学家到访的热门目的地。首都是瓦胡岛上的火奴鲁鲁。

夏威夷火山国家公园位于美国夏威夷州的夏威夷岛上。它包括两座活火山:基拉韦厄火山是世界上最活跃的火山之一;冒纳罗亚火山是世界上最大的陆地火山。

夏威夷火山国家公园于 1980 年被纳入国际生物圈保护区,并于 1987 年被列入世界遗产。

2. Cultural Tourism Resources(人文旅游资源)

1)The Statue of Liberty(自由女神像)

The Statue of Liberty is a colossal neoclassical sculpture on Liberty Island in New York Harbor in New York City, in the United States. The copper statue, designed by Frédéric Auguste Bartholdi, a French sculptor, was built by Gustave Eiffel and dedicated on October 28, 1886. It was a gift to the United States from the people of France.

The statue is of a robed female figure representing Libertas, the Roman goddess, who bears a torch and a tabula ansata (a tablet evoking the law) upon which is inscribed the date of the American Declaration of Independence, July 4, 1776. A broken chain lies at her feet. The statue is an icon of freedom and of the United States, and was a welcoming sight to immigrants arriving from abroad.

Bartholdi was inspired by French law professor and politician Édouard René de Laboulaye, who is said to have commented in 1865 that any monument raised to American independence would properly be a joint project of the French and American peoples. He may have been minded to honor the Union victory in the American Civil War and the end of slavery. Due to the troubled political situation in France, work on the statue did not commence until the early 1870s. In 1875, Laboulaye proposed that the French finance the statue and the Americans provide the site and build the pedestal. Bartholdi completed the head and the torch-bearing arm before the statue was fully designed, and these pieces were exhibited for publicity at international expositions. The torch-bearing arm was displayed at the Centennial Exposition in Philadelphia in 1876, and in Madison Square Park in Manhattan from 1876 to 1882. Fundraising proved difficult, especially for the Americans, and by 1885 work on the pedestal was threatened due to lack of funds. Publisher Joseph Pulitzer of the New York World started a drive for donations to complete the project that attracted more than 120 000 contributors, most of whom gave less than a dollar. The statue was constructed in France, shipped overseas in crates, and assembled on the completed pedestal on what was then called Bedloe's Island. The statue's completion was marked by New York's first ticker-tape parade and a dedication ceremony presided over by President Grover Cleveland.

自由女神像是一座巨大的新古典主义雕塑,位于美国纽约市纽约港的自由岛上。这座铜像由法国雕刻家弗雷德里克·奥古斯特·巴托尔迪设计、古斯塔夫·埃菲尔建造,并于1886年10月28日落成。是法国人民送给美国的礼物。

这座雕像是一个身穿长袍的女性形象,代表罗马女神利伯塔斯,她手持火炬和一块白板,上面刻着美国独立宣言起草的日期——1776年7月4日,脚下有一条断了的链子。这座雕像是自由和美国的象征。

雕像是在法国建成,历经磨难,装箱运至纽约,于1886年10月28日在美国纽约市纽约港的自由岛上落成。

2)Disneyland Park(迪士尼乐园)

Disneyland Park, originally Disneyland, is the first of two theme parks built at the Disneyland Resort in Anaheim, California, opened on July 17, 1955. It is the only theme park designed and built under the direct supervision of Walt Disney. It was originally the only attraction on the property; its name was changed to Disneyland Park to distinguish it from the expanding complex in the 1990s. Walt Disney came up with the concept of Disneyland after visiting various amusement parks with his daughters in the 1930s and 1940s. He initially envisioned building a tourist attraction adjacent to his studios in Burbank to entertain fans who wished to visit; however, he soon realized that the proposed site was too small. After hiring a consultant to help him determine an appropriate site for his project, Walt bought a 160-acre site near Anaheim in 1953. Construction began in 1954 and the park was unveiled during a special televised press event on the ABC Television Network on July 17, 1955.

Since its opening, Disneyland has undergone a number of expansions and major renovations, including the addition of New Orleans Square in 1966, Bear Country (now Critter Country) in 1972, and Mickey's Toontown in 1993. Opened in 2001, Disney California Adventure Park was built on the site of Disneyland's original parking lot. Disneyland has a larger cumulative attendance than any other theme park in the world, with over 650 million guests since it opened. In 2013, the park hosted approximately 16.2 million guests, making it the third most visited park in the world that calendar year. According to a March 2005 Disney Company report, 65 700 jobs are supported by the Disneyland Resort, including about 20 000 direct Disney employees and 3 800 third-party employees (independent contractors or their employees).

世界上第一家迪士尼乐园是在加利福尼亚州阿纳海姆建造的两个主题公园中的一个,于1955年7月17日开放。它是唯一一个在沃尔特·迪士尼直接监督下设计和建造的主题公园。该公园于1954年开始建设,并于1955年7月17日在美国广播公司电视网的一次特别电视新闻发布会上揭幕。

　　自开放以来,迪士尼乐园经历了多次扩建和重大翻修。迪士尼乐园的累计上座率超过了世界上其他任何主题公园,每年都吸引数以亿计的游客。

　　3)Mount Rushmore National Memorial(拉什莫尔山国家纪念公园)

　　Mount Rushmore National Memorial is a sculpture carved into the granite face of Mount Rushmore (Lakota Sioux name: Six Grandfathers) near Keystone, South Dakota, in the United States. Sculpted by Danish-American Gutzon Borglum and his son, Lincoln Borglum, Mount Rushmore features 18 m sculptures of the heads of four United States presidents: George Washington (1732-1799), Thomas Jefferson (1743-1826), Theodore Roosevelt (1858-1919), and Abraham Lincoln (1809-1865). The entire memorial covers 5.17 km^2 and is 1 745 m above sea level. South Dakota historian Doane Robinson is credited with conceiving the idea of carving the likenesses of famous people into the Black Hills region of South Dakota in order to promote tourism in the region. Robinson's initial idea was to sculpt the Needles; however, Gutzon Borglum rejected the Needles site because of the poor quality of the granite and strong opposition from Native American groups. They settled on the Mount Rushmore location, which also has the advantage of facing southeast for maximum sun exposure. Robinson wanted it to feature western heroes like Lewis and Clark, Red Cloud, and Buffalo Bill Cody, but Borglum decided the sculpture should have a more national focus and chose the four presidents whose likenesses would be carved into the mountain. After securing federal funding through the enthusiastic sponsorship of "Mount Rushmore's great political patron", U. S. Senator Peter Norbeck, construction on the memorial began in 1927, and the presidents' faces were completed between 1934 and 1939. Upon Gutzon Borglum's death in March 1941, his son Lincoln Borglum took over construction. Although the initial concept called for each president to be depicted from head to waist, lack of funding forced construction to end in late October 1941. Mount Rushmore has become an iconic symbol of the United States, and has appeared in works of fiction, and has been discussed or depicted in other popular works. It attracts over two million people annually.

　　拉什莫尔山国家纪念雕像是雕刻在拉什莫尔山花岗岩表面的雕塑,位于美国南达科他州的楔石附近。由丹麦裔美国人格曾·鲍格勒姆和他的儿子林肯·鲍格勒姆雕刻而成。拉什莫尔山上雕刻有四座18米高的美国前总统头像:乔治·华盛顿(George Washington,1732-1799)、托马斯·杰斐逊(Thomas Jefferson,1743-1826)、西奥多·罗斯福(Theodore Roosevelt,1858-1919)和亚伯拉罕·林肯(Abraham Lincoln,1809-1865)。

　　整个纪念馆占地5.17平方千米,海拔1 745米。纪念馆于1927年开始建造,总统的头像在1934年到1939年间完成。拉什莫尔山已经成为美国的一个标志性象征。

4) Headquarters of the United Nations(联合国总部)

The Headquarters of the United Nations is a complex in New York City. The complex has served as the official headquarters of the United Nations since its completion in 1952. It is located in the Turtle Bay neighborhood of Manhattan, on spacious grounds overlooking the East River. Its borders are First Avenue on the west, East 42nd Street to the south, East 48th Street on the north and the East River to the east. The term "Turtle Bay" is occasionally used as a metonym for the UN headquarters or for the United Nations as a whole.

The United Nations has three additional, subsidiary, regional headquarters, or headquarters districts. These were opened in Geneva (Switzerland) in 1946, Vienna (Austria) in 1980, and Nairobi(Kenya) in 2011. These adjunct offices help represent UN interests, facilitate diplomatic activities, and enjoy certain extraterritorial privileges, but only the main headquarters in New York City contains the seats of the principal organs of the UN, including the General Assembly and Security Council. All fifteen of the United Nations' specialized agencies are located outside New York City at these other headquarters or in other cities.

Although it is situated in New York City, the land occupied by the United Nations Headquarters and the spaces of buildings that it rents are under the sole administration of the United Nations and not the U.S. government. They are technically extra territorial through a treaty agreement with the U.S. government. However, in exchange for local police, fire protection and other services, the United Nations agrees to acknowledge most local, state, and federal laws. The United Nations Headquarters complex was constructed in stages with the core complex completed between 1948 and 1952. The Headquarters occupies a site beside the East River, on between 17 and 18 acres of land purchased from the real estate developer, William Zeckendorf, Sr. Nelson Rockefeller arranged this purchase, after an initial offer to locate it on the Rockefeller family estate of Kykuit was rejected as being too isolated from Manhattan. The US $8.5 million (adjusted by inflation US $83.4 million) purchase was then funded by his father, John D. Rockefeller, Jr., who donated it to the city. The Rockefeller family owned the Tudor City Apartments across First Avenue from the slaughter houses Wallace Harrison, the personal architectural adviser for the Rockefeller family and brother-in-law to a Rockefeller daughter, served as the Director of Planning for the United Nations Headquarters. His firm, Harrison and Abramovitz, oversaw the execution of the design.

联合国总部是位于纽约市的一座综合大楼,它位于曼哈顿的海龟湾社区,可以俯瞰东河,西临第一大道,南临东42街,北临东48街,东临东河。该建筑群自1952年竣工以来一直是联合国的官方总部。

联合国还有三个附属的区域总部或总部区。这些区域总部 1946 年在日内瓦（瑞士）开放，1980 年在维也纳（奥地利）开放，2011 年在内罗毕（肯尼亚）开放。所有 15 个联合国专门机构都位于纽约市以外的这些区域总部或其他城市。

虽然联合国总部位于纽约市，但联合国总部所占用的土地和它所租用的建筑物是由联合国单独管理的，而不是由美国政府管理。通过与美国政府签订条约，它们在技术上属于额外的领土。然而，为了换取当地警察、消防和其他服务，联合国承认美国大多数地方、州和联邦的法律。

5) The White House（白宫）

The White House is the official residence and principal workplace of the President of the United States, located at 1600 Pennsylvania Avenue NW in Washington, D.C. It has been the residence of every U.S. president since John Adams in 1800.

The house was designed by Irish-born James Hoban and built between 1792 and 1800 of white-painted Aquia Creek sandstone in the neoclassical style. When Thomas Jefferson moved into the house in 1801, he (with architect Benjamin Henry Latrobe) expanded the building outward, creating two colonnades that were meant to conceal stables and storage. However, in 1814, during the War of 1812, the mansion was set a blaze by the British Army in the Burning of Washington, destroying the interior and charring much of the exterior. Reconstruction began almost immediately, and President James Monroe moved into the partially reconstructed Executive Residence in October 1817. Construction continued with the addition of the South Portico in 1824 and the North in 1829.

The modern-day White House complex includes the Executive Residence, West Wing, East Wing, the Eisenhower Executive Office Building—the former State Department, which now houses offices for the President's staff and the Vice President—and Blair House, a guest residence. The Executive Residence is made up of six stories—the Ground Floor, State Floor, Second Floor, and Third Floor, as well as a two-story basement. The term White House is often used as a metonym for the Executive Office of the President of the United States and for the president's administration and advisers in general, as in "The White House has decided that...". The property is a National Heritage Site owned by the National Park Service and is part of the President's Park. In 2007, it was ranked second on the American Institute of Architects list of "America's Favorite Architecture".

白宫位于华盛顿特区宾夕法尼亚大道西北角 1600 号，是美国总统的官邸和主要办公场所。自 1800 年约翰·亚当斯总统入住以来，白宫一直是美国历届总统的住所。

这座建筑由爱尔兰裔詹姆斯·霍班设计，建于 1792 年至 1800 年间，由新古典主义风格的白色阿基亚溪砂岩建造。然而，在 1814 年，它被英国军队放火烧毁。重建工作几乎立即开始,1824年增建南门廊,1829年增建北门廊。

现代的白宫包括行政官邸、西翼、东翼、艾森豪威尔行政办公楼和布莱尔公馆。

6)Universal Studios Hollywood(好莱坞环球影城)

Universal Studios Hollywood is a film studio and theme park in the unincorporated Universal City community of the San Fernando Valley region of the city of Los Angeles, California, United States. It is one of the oldest and most famous Hollywood film studios still in use. Its official marketing headline is "The Entertainment Capital of LA". It was initially created to offer tours of the real Universal Studios sets and is the first of many full-fledged Universal Studios Theme Parks located across the world. Woody Woodpecker is the mascot for Universal Studios Hollywood.

Outside the theme park, a new, all-digital facility near the Universal Studios backlot was built in an effort to merge all of NBC Universal's West Coast operations into one area. As a result, the current home for KNBC, KVEA and NBC Newswith Telemundo Los Angeles Bureaus with new digital facility is on the Universal lot formerly occupied by Technicolor SA. Universal City includes hotels Universal Hilton & Towers, the Sheraton Universal Hotel, the multi-screen Globe Theatre, often used for banquets and receptions and Universal City Walk, which offers a collection of shops and restaurants. In 2013, the park hosted 6,148,000 guests, placing it 17th in the world and 9th among North American parks.

好莱坞环球影城是位于美国加利福尼亚州洛杉矶市圣费尔南多谷地区的一个电影工作室和主题公园。它是至今仍在使用的最古老、最著名的好莱坞电影制片厂之一。它最初是为了让游客参观真正的环球影城场景,是世界第一个成熟的环球影城主题公园。啄木鸟伍迪是好莱坞环球影城的吉祥物。

除主题公园外,环球影城外景场附近还新建了一个全数字设施。环球影城内有希尔顿酒店、喜来登环球酒店、多屏幕的环球剧院以及环球城市大道。

7)Broadway(百老汇)

Broadway is a road in the U.S. state of New York. Perhaps best known for the portion that runs through the borough of Manhattan in New York City, it actually runs 21 km through Manhattan and 3.2 km through the Bronx, exiting north from the city to run an additional 29 km through the municipalities of Yonkers, Hastings-On-Hudson, Dobbs Ferry, Irvington, and Tarrytown, and terminating north of Sleepy Hollow in Westchester County.

It is the oldest north-south main thoroughfare in New York City, dating to the first New Amsterdam settlement. The name Broadway is the English literal translation of the Dutch name, Breede weg. Broadway is known widely as the heart of the American theatre industry.

百老汇是美国纽约州的一条公路,它最著名的部分贯穿纽约曼哈顿岛。它是纽约市最古老的南北向主干道,最早可以追溯到新阿姆斯特丹建立第一个定居点时期。百老汇这个名字是荷兰语"Breede weg"的英文直译。百老汇被认为是美国戏剧业的心脏。

8)Silicon Valley(硅谷)

Silicon Valley is a nickname for the southern portion of the San Francisco Bay Area, which is located in the part of the U.S. state of California known as Northern California. It is home to many of the world's largest high-tech corporations, as well as thousands of tech startup companies. The word "valley" refers to the Santa Clara Valley where the region has traditionally been centered, which includes the city of San Jose and surrounding cities and towns. The word "silicon" originally referred to the large number of silicon chip innovators and manufacturers in the region. The term "Silicon Valley" eventually came to refer to all high tech businesses in the area, and is now generally used as a metonym for the American high-technology economic sector. Silicon Valley is a leading hub and startup ecosystem for high-tech innovation and development, accounting for one-third of all of the venture capital investment in the United States. Geographically, Silicon Valley is generally thought to encompass all of the Santa Clara Valley, the southern half of the Peninsula and southern portions of the East Bay.

It was in Silicon Valley that the silicon-based integrated circuit, the microprocessor, and the microcomputer, among other key technologies, were developed.

硅谷是旧金山湾区南部的一个昵称,它位于美国加利福尼亚州的北加州部分。它是许多世界高科技公司及数千家科技初创公司的所在地。硅谷是世界领先的高科技创新和发展中心,以及创业中心,占美国所有风险投资的三分之一。正是在硅谷,硅基集成电路、微处理器和微型计算机以及其他关键技术被开发出来。

  知识拓展 4.1　哥伦布日(见二维码)

知识拓展 4.2　美国旅游须知(见二维码)

Section 3　Canada(加拿大)

PART 1(第一部分)

1. 国土疆域(Territory)

加拿大位于北美旅游区北部,东濒大西洋,西临太平洋,南接美国,北靠北冰洋,西北与美国的阿拉斯加州接壤。海岸线长约 24 万千米,是世界上海岸线最长的国家。总面积约 998 万平方千米。

Canada is located in the north of the North American Tourism Region, bordering the Atlantic Ocean in the east, the Pacific Ocean in the west, the United States in the south, the Arctic Ocean in the north, Alaska in the northwest. The coastline is about 240 000 km, making it the country with the longest coastline in the world. The total area is 9.98 million km^2.

2. 自然风貌(Natural Features)

加拿大地形大致分为三部分:西部是科迪勒拉山系;东部是古老的拉布拉多高原,高原景观丰富;中部是广阔的平原,冰碛湖广布,五大湖区瀑布等水体景观十分有名。

加拿大位于北半球中高纬度地区,全国有 1/5 的地区在北极圈内,寒冷是气候的突出特点。冬季全国大部分地区有积雪,冰雪旅游资源十分丰富。

到加拿大旅游的最佳季节是5月到10月,在这段时间内可以感受加拿大独特的清凉夏季和枫叶艳红的秋季。

The terrain of Canada is roughly divided into three parts: the Cordillera Mountains in the west, the ancient Labrador Plateau in the east, and the vast plains in the middle.

Canada is located in the middle and high latitudes of the Northern Hemisphere. Cold is a prominent feature of the climate. It is rich in snow and ice tourism resources. The best season for tourism is from May to October.

3. 人口民族(Population and Ethnicity)

加拿大的总人口约3 800万(2020年)。加拿大是移民国家,居民主要为英、法等欧洲后裔,土著居民约占3%,其余为亚洲、拉美、非洲裔等。英语和法语同为官方语言。居民中信奉天主教的占总人口的45%,信奉基督教的占36%。

The total population of Canada is about 38 000 000 (2020). Canada is a country of immigrants, mainly are the European descendants of British and French, etc. Most residents profess Catholicism and Protestantism.

4. 发展简史(Brief History of Development)

加拿大原为印第安人和因纽特人的居住地。17世纪初沦为法国殖民地,后割让给英国。1867年加拿大成为英国最早的自治领。1926年加拿大获得外交上的独立。1931年,加拿大成为英联邦成员国。加拿大现仍为英联邦成员国。

Canada was originally inhabited by the Indians and the Inuit. It became a British colony in the 18th century. Canada gained diplomatic independence in 1926, but remained a member of the Commonwealth of Nations.

5. 政治经济(Politics and Economy)

首都为渥太华,国花为枫叶,货币为加元。

加拿大的国家政体为联邦议会制。英国女王是加拿大的国家元首。由女王任命的总督代行职权。总督由总理提名,女王任命。加拿大实行"三权分立",立法机构由加拿大议会——参议院和众议院组成;行政机构由总理及其内阁组成;司法机构由联邦、省和地方法院组成。

加拿大是西方七大工业国家之一。制造业和高科技产业较发达,资源工业、初级制造业和农业也是国民经济的主要支柱。加拿大以贸易立国,对外贸依赖较大,经济上受美国影响较深。

加拿大是一个农业高度发达的国家,是世界上最大的粮食生产国之一,也是世界上最大的渔产品出口国之一。

加拿大工业发达,在原子能和水力发电、通信和空间技术、石油化工、地球物理勘探、纸浆造纸、客运车辆制造等方面拥有先进技术和设备。

　　加拿大工业以采矿业、能源工业和制造业为主要部门。矿产和森林资源丰富。

　　加拿大交通运输业十分发达,已建起由铁路、公路、水运、航空和管道组成的现代化交通运输网络,旅游交通便利。

　　Canada is a federal parliamentary state. It is one of the seven industrialized powers in the West, with mining, energy and manufacturing as the main sectors. Canada's transportation industry is very developed. It has built up a modern transportation network composed by railway, highway, water transport, aviation and pipeline.

6. 旅游市场(Tourism market)

　　加拿大旅游业十分发达,2020年前三季度旅游业产值约175亿加元。主要旅游城市有温哥华、渥太华、多伦多、蒙特利尔、魁北克城等。

　　加拿大是世界重要的旅游客源国和国际旅游消费国之一,主要旅游客源国是美国、英国、法国等,2019年到访加拿大的国际过夜游客达到2 113万人次,连续第三年创历史新高。加拿大的主要旅游目的地国是美国、环地中海国家、东北亚和东南亚国家,是国际旅游支出最重要的国家之一,2019年国际旅游支出为353亿美元。

　　加拿大是中国重要的旅游客源国之一,2018年加拿大公民来华旅游人数达84.99万人次,十年增长54%。目前,加拿大已成为中国重要的旅游目的地国,2019年中国访加游客数量占访加游客总数的6%,位居第九。

　　Canada has a very developed tourism industry and is one of the world's important tourist source countries and international tourist consumers. The main tourist sources are the United States, the United Kingdom, France, etc. The main tourist destinations are the United States, some countries around the Mediterranean Sea, Northeast Asia and Southeast Asia.

　　Canada is one of the important tourist source of China and an important tourist destination to China in recent years.

PART 2(第二部分)

Tourism Resources(旅游资源)

　　Canada has a large domestic and foreign tourism industry. As the second largest country in the world, Canada's incredible geographical variety is a significant tourist attractor. Much of the country's tourism is centered on Canada's four largest metropolitan areas, Toronto, Montreal, Vancouver, and Ottawa, well known for their culture, diversity, as well as the many national parks and historic sites.

加拿大拥有庞大的国内外旅游市场。作为世界上面积第二大国家,其地理多样性是吸引游客的重要因素。加拿大的旅游业主要集中在多伦多、蒙特利尔、温哥华和渥太华这四个大都会地区,这些地区以其文化、多样性以及众多的国家公园和历史遗迹而闻名。

1. Natural Tourism Resources(自然旅游资源)

1)Stanley Park(斯坦利公园)

Designated a national historic site of Canada, Stanley Park is a magnificent green oasis in the midst of the heavily built urban landscape of Vancouver in British Columbia, Canada.

The park has a long history and was one of the first areas to be explored in the city. It was named after Lord Stanley, a British politician who had recently been appointed governor general. Unlike other large urban parks, Stanley Park is not the creation of a landscape architect, but rather the evolution of a forest and urban space over many years. Most of the manmade structures we see today were built between 1911 and 1937 under the influence of then superintendent W. S. Rawlings. Additional attractions, such as a polar bear exhibit, aquarium, and miniature train, were added in the post-war period. Much of the park remains as densely forested as it was in the late 19th century, with about a half million trees, some of which stand as tall as 76 metres and are up to hundreds of years old.

Significant effort was put into constructing the near-century-old Vancouver Seawall, which can draw thousands of residents and visitors to the park every day. The park also features forest trails, beaches, lakes, children's play areas, and the Vancouver Aquarium, among many other attractions. On June 18, 2014 Stanley Park was named "top park in the entire world" by TripAdvisor.

斯坦利公园是加拿大国家历史遗址,是加拿大不列颠哥伦比亚省温哥华城市景观中一片美丽的绿洲。

该公园历史悠久,以加拿大总督英国政治家斯坦利勋爵的名字命名。与其他大型城市公园不同的是,斯坦利公园并不是景观设计师设计的,而是森林和城市空间经过多年的演变形成的。公园的大部分森林仍然像19世纪末那样茂密,公园里大约有50万棵树,其中一些树高达76米,树龄数百年。公园内有森林小径、海滩、湖泊、儿童游乐区和温哥华水族馆等众多景点。

2)Niagara Falls(尼亚加拉瀑布)

Niagara Falls is a Canadian city on the western bank of the Niagara River in the Golden Horseshoe region of Southern Ontario. The municipality was incorporated on 12 June 1903. Across the Niagara River is Niagara Falls, New York.

The city is dominated by the Niagara Falls, a world-famous set of three large waterfalls on the Niagara River. Both the American and Horseshoe falls can be best seen from the Canadian side of the river, so the city has one of the major tourist attractions of the world. The natural spectacle attracts millions of tourists yearly. This area, which stretches along the Niagara Parkway and tourist promenade, is particularly concentrated at the brink of the falls. Apart from the natural attractions along the river, it includes observation towers, high-rise hotels, souvenir shops, casinos and theatres, mostly with colourful neon billboards and advertisements, and sufficient parking to accommodate visitors. Further to the north or south, golf courses are operated alongside historic sites from the War of 1812.

尼亚加拉瀑布市位于加拿大安大略省尼亚加拉河西岸,尼亚加拉河对面是美国的尼亚加拉瀑布。

尼亚加拉瀑布由尼亚加拉河上著名的三大瀑布组成。无论是美国瀑布,还是马蹄瀑布都可以从尼亚加拉河的加拿大一侧看到,是世界主要旅游景点之一。

3) Granville Island(格兰维尔岛)

Granville Island is a peninsula and shopping district in Vancouver, British Columbia, Canada. It is located across False Creek from Downtown Vancouver, under the south end of the Granville Street Bridge. The peninsula was once an industrial manufacturing area, but today it is now a hot spot for Vancouver tourism and entertainment. The area has received much acclaim in recent years for its buildings and shopping experience. The area was named after Granville Leveson-Gower, 2nd Earl Granville.

格兰维尔岛是位于加拿大不列颠哥伦比亚省温哥华市的一个半岛和购物区。它位于温哥华市中心佛斯河对面、格兰维尔街大桥南端,以格兰维尔第二伯爵格兰维尔的名字命名。半岛曾经是一个工业制造区,现在是温哥华旅游和娱乐的热点地区。

4) English Bay(英吉利湾)

English Bay is located in Vancouver, British Columbia, Canada, west of the downtown peninsula, which separates the bay from Burrard Inlet connecting to the northwest, and False Creek to the southeast. Point Grey on the south and Point Atkinson on the north form the bay's entrance from the Strait of Georgia.

英吉利湾位于加拿大不列颠哥伦比亚省温哥华市中心半岛以西,该半岛将该湾与连接西北部的巴拉德湾和东南部的佛斯河隔开。南部的格雷角和北部的阿特金森角构成了从乔治亚海峡进入海湾的入口。

5) Bow Falls(弓河瀑布)

Bow Falls is a major waterfall on the Bow River, Alberta just before the junction of it and the Spray River. The falls are located near the Banff Springs Hotel and golf course on the left-hand side of River Road. The falls are within walking distance of both Banff and the Banff Springs Hotel so they are visited by a large number of tourists despite their relatively small size. The 1953 Marilyn Monroe film *River of No Return* featured the falls.

弓形瀑布是弓形河上的一个主要瀑布,瀑布位于班夫温泉旅馆和高尔夫球场附近,在河道的左侧。1953年玛丽莲·梦露的电影《大河东去》就是以此瀑布为外景地拍摄的。

6)Lake Louise(路易斯湖)

Lake Louise, named Lake of the Little Fishes by the Stoney Nakota First Nations people, is a glacial lake within Banff National Park in Alberta, Canada. It is located 5 km west of the Hamlet of Lake Louise and the Trans-Canada Highway (Highway 1).

Lake Louise is named after the Princess Louise Caroline Alberta (1848-1939) the fourth daughter of Queen Victoria and the wife of the Marquess of Lorne, who was the Governor General of Canada from 1878 to 1883.

The emerald color of the water comes from rock flour carried into the lake by meltwater from the glaciers that overlook the lake. The lake has a surface of 0.8 km^2 and is drained through the 3 km long Louise Creek into the Bow River.

Fairmont's Chateau Lake Louise, one of Canada's grand railway hotels, is located on Lake Louise's eastern shore. It is a luxury resort hotel built in the early decades of the 20th century by the Canadian Pacific Railway.

Moraine Lake and Lake Agnes are also accessible from Lake Louise.

路易斯湖是加拿大阿尔伯塔省班夫国家公园内的一个冰川湖,位于路易斯湖小村庄和加拿大横贯公路以西5千米处。

路易斯湖是以路易斯·卡罗琳·阿尔伯塔公主(1848—1939)的名字命名的,她是维多利亚女王的第四个女儿,也是罗恩侯爵的妻子,罗恩侯爵曾于1878年至1883年担任加拿大总督。

湖水的翡翠色来自岩石粉,这些岩石粉是由俯瞰湖面的冰川融水带入湖中的。湖面面积为0.8平方千米,通过长3千米的路易斯河汇入弓河。

7)Columbia Icefield(哥伦比亚冰川)

The Columbia Icefield is the largest ice field in the Rocky Mountains of North America Located in the Canadian Rockies astride the Continental Divide along the border of British Columbia and Alberta, Canada, the ice field lies partly in the northwestern tip of Banff National Park and partly in the southern end of Jasper National Park.

哥伦比亚冰川是北美落基山脉最大的冰川,位于加拿大落基山脉,横跨不列颠哥伦比亚省和加拿大阿尔伯塔省边界的大陆分水岭,冰川部分位于班夫国家公园的西北端,部分位于贾斯珀国家公园的南端。

2. Cultural Tourism Resources(人文旅游资源)

1)CN Tower(加拿大国家电视塔)

The CN Tower is a 553.33 meter-high concrete communications and observation tower in downtown Toronto, Ontario, Canada. Built on the former Railway Lands, it was completed in 1976, becoming the world's tallest free-standing structure and world's tallest tower at the time. It held both records for 34 years until the completion of Burj Khalifa and Canton Tower in 2010. It remains the tallest free-standing structure in the Western Hemisphere, a signature icon of Toronto's skyline, and a symbol of Canada, attracting more than two million international visitors annually.

Its name "CN" originally referred to Canadian National, the railway company that built the tower. Following the railway's decision to divest non-core freight railway assets, prior to the company's privatization in 1995, it transferred the tower to the Canada Lands Company, a federal Crown corporation responsible for real estate development. Since the name CN Tower became common in daily usage, the abbreviation was eventually expanded to Canadian National Tower or Canada's National Tower. However, neither of these names is commonly used.

In 1995, the CN Tower was declared one of the modern Seven Wonders of the World by the American Society of Civil Engineers. It also belongs to the World Federation of Great Towers, where it holds second-place ranking.

加拿大国家电视塔是位于加拿大安大略省多伦多市中心的一座高553.33米的混凝土通信和观测塔。它建于1976年,是当时世界上最高的独立式建筑,也是当时世界上最高的高塔,现在仍然是西半球最高的独立式建筑,也是加拿大的象征。

它的名字"CN"是指加拿大国家铁路公司,该公司建造了这座塔。1995年,加拿大国家电视塔被美国土木工程师协会列为"世界七大工程奇迹之一"。

2)Chinatown(唐人街)

Chinatown is an ethnic enclave in Downtown Toronto, Ontario, Canada, with a high concentration of ethnic Chinese residents and businesses extending along Dundas Street West and Spadina Avenue west of the centre of the city. A second area known as East Chinatown, extends along both streets from the intersection of Broadview Avenue and Gerrard Street. First developed in the late 19th century, the main Chinatown is now one of the largest Chinatowns in North America and one of several major Chinese-Canadian communities in the Greater Toronto Area. There are approximately six Chinatowns in Greater Toronto, including in the municipalities of Markham and Mississauga.

唐人街位于加拿大安大略省多伦多市中心的一块飞地,华裔居民和企业在此高度集中。唐人街始建于19世纪末,现在是北美最大的唐人街之一,也是大多伦多地区几个主要的加拿大华人社区之一。大多伦多约有六个唐人街。

3) Toronto University(多伦多大学)

Toronto University is a public research university in Toronto, Ontario, Canada, situated on the grounds that surround Queen's Park. It was founded by royal charter in 1827 as King's College, the first institution of higher learning in the colony of Upper Canada. Originally controlled by the Church of England, the university assumed the present name in 1850 upon becoming a secular institution. As a collegiate university, it comprises twelve colleges that differ in character and history, each retaining substantial autonomy on financial and institutional affairs. It has two satellite campuses located in Scarborough and Mississauga.

Academically, the University of Toronto is noted for influential movements and curricula in literary criticism and communication theory, known collectively as the Toronto School. The university was the birthplace of insulin and stem cell research, and was the site of the first practical electron microscope, the development of multi-touch technology, the identification of Cygnus X-1 as a black hole, and the theory of NP-completeness. By a significant margin, it receives the most annual scientific research funding of any Canadian university. It is one of two members of the Association of American Universities located outside the United States.

多伦多大学是加拿大安大略省多伦多市的一所公立研究型大学,位于皇后公园周围。1827 年,皇家特许成立国王学院,这是上加拿大殖民地的第一所高等学府。这所大学由 12 个学院组成,还有两个卫星校区位于士嘉堡和密西沙加。

学术上,多伦多大学以具有影响力的运动、文学批评和传播学理论而闻名,被统称为"多伦多学派"。这所大学是胰岛素和干细胞研究的发源地,也是第一台实用电子显微镜、多点触控技术、天鹅座 X-1 黑洞的鉴定以及 NP 完全性理论的诞生地。

4) The Vancouver Convention Center(温哥华会议中心)

The Vancouver Convention Center (formerly known as the Vancouver Convention & Exhibition Centre, or VCEC), is a convention centre in Vancouver, British Columbia, Canada; it is one of Canada's largest convention centers. With the opening of the new West Building in 2009, it now has 43 340 m^2 of meeting space. It is owned by the British Columbia Pavilion Corporation, a crown corporation owned by the government of British Columbia.

温哥华会议中心是加拿大不列颠哥伦比亚省温哥华市的一个会议中心,也是加拿大最大的会议中心之一。2009 年新西楼启用后,它现在有 43 340 平方米的会议空间。

5) The Royal Ontario Museum(皇家安大略博物馆)

The Royal Ontario Museum (ROM) is a museum of art, world culture and natural history in Toronto, Canada. It is one of the largest museums in North America, the largest in Canada, and attracts over one million visitors every year, the second most for a

Canadian art museum. The museum is north of Queen's Park, in the University of Toronto district, with its main entrance on Bloor Street West. The museum subway station is named after the ROM, and since 2008, it is decorated to resemble the institution's collection.

皇家安大略博物馆位于多伦多大学区皇后公园以北,主入口位于布鲁尔街以西,是加拿大多伦多的艺术、世界文化和自然历史博物馆。它是北美最大的博物馆之一,也是加拿大最大的博物馆。

6) Casa Loma(卡萨罗马古堡)

Casa Loma (Spanish for Hill House) is a Gothic Revival style house and gardens in midtown Toronto, Ontario, Canada, that is now a museum and landmark. It was originally a residence for financier Sir Henry Mill Pellatt. Casa Loma was constructed over a three-year period from 1911-1914. The architect of the mansion was E. J. Lennox, who was also responsible for the designs of several other city landmarks. Casa Loma is situated at an altitude of 140 m.

卡萨罗马古堡是加拿大安大略省多伦多市中心一座哥特式复兴风格的房子和花园,现在是一座博物馆和多伦多的地标。它最初是金融家亨利·米尔·柏拉特爵士的住所。

7) Parliament Hill(国会山)

Parliament Hill, colloquially known as The Hill, is an area of Crown land on the southern banks of the Ottawa River in downtown Ottawa, Ontario. Its Gothic revival suite of buildings serves as the home of the Parliament of Canada and contains a number of architectural elements of national symbolic importance. Parliament Hill attracts approximately 3 million visitors each year.

Originally the site of a military base in the 18th and early 19th centuries, development of the area into a governmental precinct began in 1859, after Queen Victoria chose Bytown as the capital of the Province of Canada. Following a number of extensions to the parliament and departmental buildings and a fire in 1916 that destroyed the Center Block, Parliament Hill took on its present form with the completion of the Peace Tower in 1927. Since 2002, an extensive $1 billion renovation and rehabilitation project has been underway throughout all of the precinct's buildings; work is not expected to be complete until after 2020.

国会山位于安大略省渥太华市中心渥太华河南岸的一片王室领地。它的哥特式复兴建筑群是加拿大议会的所在地,包含了许多具有国家象征意义的建筑元素。

它最初是18世纪和19世纪初的军事基地所在地。1859年维多利亚女王选择拜镇作为加拿大省首府后,该地区开始发展成为政府管辖区。国会山经过多次扩建之后,呈现出现在的样貌。

知识拓展 4.3　郁金香节的来历

 知识拓展 4.4　枫叶之国——加拿大

 Sum up(本章小结)

1. 北美旅游区是世界经济发展水平最高的地区,也是世界上国际旅游发达的地区,既是世界重要的客源地,也是世界重要的旅游目的地。

2. 本章从地理位置及范围、自然风貌、民族与宗教、旅游市场等方面介绍了北美旅游区的基本概况。

3. 本章选取了美国和加拿大两个国家,其中美国是世界头号的旅游强国,加拿大是世界重要的旅游目的地国和客源国。

4.每个国家的介绍分为两部分,第一部分介绍了各国的国土疆域、自然风貌、人口民族、发展简史、政治经济和旅游市场的基本概况,第二部分介绍了各国的旅游资源。

Reviewing and Thinking(复习与思考)

1. 试比较北美与西欧的旅游资源有何差异?
2. 试述美国、加拿大成为世界旅游强国的原因。
3. 为什么美国、加拿大是中国重要的旅游客源国?
4. 美国、加拿大有哪些著名的旅游城市和旅游景点?
5. 试设计一条中国—美国十日精品游旅游线路。
6. 试设计一条中国—加拿大七日精品游旅游线路。

CHAPTER 5

The South America Tourism Region
(南美洲旅游区)

◇ **LEARNING OBJECTIVES**(学习目标)

1. Understand the basic situation of the major tourist source and destination countries in South America(了解南美洲主要客源国和目的地国的基本情况).

2. Master the tourism market development and tourism resources characteristics of the main source and destination countries in South America(掌握南美洲主要客源国和目的地国的旅游市场发展与旅游资源特点).

3. Design some classic tourist routes(设计一些经典旅游线路).

◇ **LEARNING CONTENTS**(学习内容)

1. Brazil(巴西)

2. Argentina(阿根廷)

◇ **PROBLEM ORIENTATION**(问题导向)

Why didn't South America become the main tourist source and destination of China?(为什么南美洲没有成为中国主要的旅游客源地和目的地?)

Section 1 General Situation of South America （南美洲概况）

区域概况(Regional Overview)

1. 地理位置及范围(Geographical Location and Scope)

南美旅游区位于西半球美洲大陆南部,东临大西洋,西濒太平洋,北临加勒比海,南隔德雷克海峡与南极洲相望,北部与北美洲旅游区以巴拿马运河为界。总面积1 784万平方千米。

The South America Tourism Region is located in the southern part of the American continent in the western hemisphere, bordering the Atlantic Ocean to the east, the Pacific Ocean to the west, the Caribbean Sea to the north, and Antarctica to the south across the Drake Channel. The dividing line on land between the South American Tourism Region and the North American Tourism Region is the Panama Canal. The total area is 17.84 million km^2.

CHAPTER 5　The South America Tourism Region(南美洲旅游区)

南美洲地图　SOUTH AMERICA

资料来源：标准地图服务网站，审图号：GS(2020)4394号。

2. 自然风貌(Natural Features)

南美洲旅游区地形可分为三个南北向纵列带:西部为狭长的安第斯山,中部为广阔平坦的平原低地,东部为波状起伏的高原。其中平原约占全洲面积的60%,海拔3 000米以下的高原、丘陵和山地约占全洲面积的33%,海拔3 000米以上的高原和山地约占全洲面积的7%。全洲平均海拔600米。安第斯山脉是世界上最长的山脉,也是世界最高大的山系之一,大部分海拔3 000米以上。南美洲东部有宽广的巴西高原、圭亚那高原,南部有巴塔哥尼亚高原。其中巴西高原面积500多万平方千米,为世界上面积最大的高原。平原自北向南有奥里诺科平原、亚马孙平原和拉普拉塔平原。其中亚马孙平原面积约560万平方千米,是世界上面积最大的冲积平原。

海岸线长约28 700千米,比较平直,多为侵蚀海岸。缺少大半岛、海湾,岛屿不多。南美洲是世界上火山较多、地震频繁且多强烈地震的一个洲,以太平洋沿岸地区最为频繁。

南美洲水系以科迪勒拉山系的安第斯山为分水岭,东西分属于大西洋水系和太平洋水系。太平洋水系源短流急,且多独流入海。大西洋水系的河流大多源远流长、支流众多、水量丰富、流域面积广。其中,亚马孙河是世界上流域面积最广、流量最大的河流。南美洲水系内流区域很小,内流河主要分布在南美西中部的荒漠高原和阿根廷的西北部。南美洲除最南部外,河流终年不冻。

南美旅游区大部分地区属热带雨林气候和热带草原气候。

The landscape of South America tourism region can be divided into three north-south longitudinal belts: the long and narrow Andes to the west, the middle of the vast flat plain lowlands in the middle, and the undulating plateaus to the east. The Andes in the Cordillera Mountains divide the water system into the Atlantic Ocean in the east and the Pacific Ocean in the west. The Amazon River is the world's largest rivers in terms of drainage area and discharge volume. Most of the region is tropical rainforest and savanna climate.

3. 民族与宗教(Nationality and Religion)

南美旅游区总人口约4.34亿(2019年)。地域分布不均衡,西北部和东南沿海一带人口稠密;亚马孙平原是世界人口密度最小的地区之一,每平方千米不到一人。人口分布的另一特点是人口高度集中在少数大城市。民族成分复杂,有印第安人、白人、黑人及各种不同的混血种人,其中以印欧混血种人最多。语言比较复杂,印第安人用印第安语,巴西的官方语言为葡萄牙语,其他国家均以西班牙语为官方语言。居民绝大多数信天主教,少数信基督教。

South America tourism region has a total population of about 434 million (2019). The ethnic composition is complex, mainly the Indo-European mixed. South America is predominantly a continent of Catholics.

二 旅游业（Tourism）

南美旅游区西部南北纵贯的安第斯山，是世界上最长的山脉，为环太平洋火山地震带的一部分，群山错列、峡谷幽深的崇山峻岭和烟雾缭绕的火山奇观极具特色。中部有世界面积最大的亚马孙平原和世界第一大河亚马孙河，生物种类极其丰富，素有"天然动物植物园"之称，是世界上面积最大的热带雨林景观区，是开展科学考察和热带丛林探险等专题旅游活动的基地。由于降水量丰富、地势起伏大，这里形成了许多著名的瀑布。

The Andes, which runs from north to south in the western part of the South America tourism region, is the longest mountain range in the world. It is part of the Pacific Rim Volcanic Seismic Belt. The mountains are staggered, the canyons are deep, and the volcanic spectacles are unique. In the middle of the region, there are the world's largest Amazon Plain and the world's largest river, the Amazon River, with extremely rich biological species, most of which are endemic. Known as the "Natural Animal and Botanical Garden", it is the world's largest tropical rainforest landscape area, and the base for scientific expeditions and tropical jungle explorations. Many of the world's most famous waterfalls have been formed due to the abundant rainfall and rugged terrain.

南美旅游区是世界古代文明的发祥地之一，这里孕育了灿烂的古印第安文明，曾经创造了玛雅文化、托尔特克文明和阿兹特克文明等光辉灿烂的古文明，留下了许多规模宏大的石结构古建筑及其废墟，如神庙、金字塔、祭坛、宫殿、卫城、广场等，具有较高的历史价值。这里的文化和生活方式以及艺术、宗教、建筑等受西班牙、葡萄牙、法国、意大利等拉丁语国家移民的影响较大，经过长期发展，形成了自身的特色。

独特而多姿多彩的旅游资源为南美旅游业的发展奠定了坚实的基础，南美旅游区最主要的旅游类型是海滨度假旅游，其中以巴西最为突出。

南美旅游区一直是全球游客青睐的旅游目的地之一。近年来，南美国家的旅游业一直保持强劲增长势头。巴西和阿根廷是南美地区旅游业的领头羊。具有印第安色彩的秘鲁旅游业也是拉美增长较快的旅游市场之一。智利的旅游业发展很快，是其经济发展的支柱产业之一，在相关行业的各类评选中屡获殊荣。南美旅游区各国公民多以短程旅游为主，到中国旅游的人数很少。

总体来看，南美旅游业起步较晚，国际旅游收入和接待国际游客量总体水平较低，在世界旅游市场中所占的比重较小。南美旅游业发展水平低于北美洲和欧洲，除疫情因素外，政治不稳定性、腐败和犯罪等因素都给旅游业发展带来负面影响。

由于世界杯、奥运会等全球性赛事给南美洲带来高关注度，再加上智利、厄瓜多尔、阿根廷等南美国家先后对中国出台签证利好政策，中国游客赴南美旅游增长强劲。中国游客最偏爱的热门目的地包括巴西、阿根廷、智利和玻利维亚。一些游客也开始尝试新的目的地，前往乌拉圭、厄瓜多尔、哥伦比亚等国，但游客数量相对较少。

The tourism of South America tourism region started late, in spite of its magnificent natural landscape. The overall international tourism income and the number of international tourists received are relatively low, with a low proportion in the world tourism market. Most of the citizens of South America tourism region travel mainly for short distance, and the number of tourists to China is very few. Most of the countries in the region are still not China's tourist destination, and the number of Chinese travelers to South America tourism region is still low.

Section 2　Brazil(巴西)

PART 1(第一部分)

1. 国土疆域(Territory)

巴西位于南美旅游区东部,北邻法属圭亚那、苏里南、圭亚那、委内瑞拉和哥伦比亚,西接秘鲁、玻利维亚,南接巴拉圭、阿根廷和乌拉圭,东濒大西洋。国土面积约851.49万平方千米,为南美旅游区第一大国家。海岸线长约7 400千米。

Brazil is located in the southeast of the South America Tourism Region. It is bordered by French Guyana, Suriname, Guyana, Venezuela and Colombia in the north, Peru and Bolivia in the west, Paraguay, Argentina and Uruguay in the south, and the Atlantic Ocean in the east. It covers an area of 8 514 900 km², and the largest country in the South America Tourism Region. The coastline is about 7 400 kilometers long.

2. 自然风貌(Natural Features)

巴西地形以平原和低缓高原为主,自北而南可分为五个地形区:圭亚那高原、巴西高原、亚马孙平原、沿海平原、巴拉圭低地。巴西高原和亚马孙平原绝大部分位于巴西境内。横贯北部的亚马孙河是世界上流域面积最广、流量最大的河流。素有"地球之肺"之称的亚马孙热带雨林总面积达550万平方千米,其中大部分位于巴西境内。

巴西绝大部分领土位于南回归线与赤道之间,国土的80%位于热带,除最南端属亚热带气候外,其余地区属热带气候,北部亚马孙平原为热带雨林气候,年平均气温27~29 ℃。中部高原为热带草原气候,分旱、雨两季,年平均气温18~28 ℃。

Brazil is dominantly plains and low slopped plateaus. From north to south, it can be divided into five topographical areas: Guyana Plateau, Brazil Plateau, Amazon Plain, Coastal Plain, and Paraguay Lowland. The vast majority of Brazil's land lies between the

Tropic of Capricorn and the Equator, with 92% of the land being in the tropics. The rest part has a tropical climate except for the south, which has a subtropical humid climate.

3. 人口民族(Population and Ethnicity)

巴西人口约2.1亿(2020年),人口密度为每平方千米24.66人。大西洋沿岸人口稠密,内陆地区人口稀少,东南地区是巴西人口最多的地区。白种人和黑白混血种人占人口的92%以上,其余为黑种人、黄种人和印第安人。官方语言为葡萄牙语。居民主要信奉天主教和基督教福音教派。

Brazil has a population of about 210 million (2020) with a population density of 24.66 people per square kilometer. They are mainly white and mixed race. The population is predominantly Catholic.

4. 发展简史(Brief History of Development)

1500年4月22日,葡萄牙航海家佩德罗·卡布拉尔抵达巴西。他将这片土地命名为"圣十字架",并宣布归葡萄牙所有。由于殖民者的掠夺是从砍伐巴西红木开始的,"红木"(Brasil)一词逐渐代替了"圣十字架",成为巴西国名,并沿用至今。1822年9月7日宣布巴西完全脱离葡萄牙独立,建立巴西帝国。1889年11月15日推翻帝制,成立巴西合众国。1968年改国名为巴西联邦共和国。巴西历史上有过几次大的移民浪潮,仅1884至1962年间,迁居巴西的移民即达497万多人,主要来自葡萄牙、西班牙、意大利、德国、法国、波兰和阿拉伯国家。

On September 7, 1822, a complete independence from Portugal was proclaimed and the Brazilian Empire was founded. The United States of Brazil was established in 1889. In 1968 it was renamed the Federal Republic of Brazil.

5. 政治经济(Politics and Economy)

巴西的首都为巴西利亚,国花为毛蟹爪兰,货币为雷亚尔。

巴西实行总统制共和制。国会是国家最高权力机构,国会由参、众两院组成。两院议长、副议长每两年改选一次,同一届议员任期内不可连选连任。根据1988年10月5日颁布的宪法,联邦最高法院、联邦法院、高等司法法院、高等劳工法院、高等选举法院、高等军事法院和各州法院行使司法权。目前登记的政党有33个,主要有劳工党、巴西民主运动党、民主社会党、民主工党等。

巴西经济发达,经济实力居南美旅游区各国之首。服务业、工业、农牧业为国民经济的支柱。主要工业部门是钢铁、汽车、造船、石油、水泥、化工、冶金、航空、纺织等。咖啡、蔗糖、柑橘等农产品产量居世界首位。交通发达,旅游基础设施较完善,旅游业发展很快。

Brazil is a presidential republic. Brazil has developed economy, and its economic power ranks first among the countries in South America tourism region. The services, industry, agriculture and animal husbandry are the pillars of national economy. The tourism develops rapidly, with well developed transportation and complete tourism infrastructure.

6. 旅游市场(Tourism Market)

旅游行业在推动巴西经济发展方面发挥了重要作用。巴西旅游部的数据显示,2019年上半年,巴西接待外国游客约277万人,巴西国家旅游计划的目标是在2022年达到1 200万人次,实现1 900亿美元的收入。

近几年,巴西的生态旅游生气勃勃,游客人数每年以20%的速度增加。巴西生态旅游发展迅速得益于巴西丰富的生态旅游资源:南有气势雄伟的伊瓜苏瀑布,北有奔流滚滚的亚马孙河,东有秀丽的大西洋海滩,西有一望无际的潘塔纳尔大沼泽。巴西环境部公布的一项调查数据显示,2019年巴西137个国家保护区(UC)共接待游客1 533万人次,同比增长20%。访问量最大的两个保护区分别是里约热内卢的蒂茹卡国家公园和巴拉那州的伊瓜苏国家公园,分别接待游客295.39万人次和202.04万人次。大西洋沿岸森林保护区是游客访问量最大的生物群落,游客接待量占总量的67%,且最受游客欢迎的十大保护区中有四个属于该类生物群落。

巴西是南美旅游区的旅游大国,巴西是南美洲最大的旅游市场,主要客源国是邻国及美国、加拿大等。巴西公民出游的主要目的地也是邻国,远程旅游的人数很少。

近年来,巴西开始重视中国市场,巴西旅游部旨在通过路演、强强联合、增加航班、数字化营销等方式加深中国旅游市场对巴西自然景观和独具当地特色的历史文化遗产的了解,特别是2019年巴西宣布对中国游客免签,并提出2022年实现到访巴西的中国游客数量突破50%增长的目标。与此同时,巴西作为我国公民出境旅游行程最长的国家之一,是中国极具潜力的旅游目的地市场,中国公民赴巴西旅游人数将保持10%以上的年增长速度。

Brazil is South America's largest tourism market, and the main sources are some neighboring countries, the United States, Canada, etc. Neighboring countries are also the main destinations for Brazilian citizens, and the number of long-distance travelers is few. As one of the longest outbound travel itineraries for Chinese citizens, Brazil is a potential destination market for China. In recent years, Chinese citizens have been increasingly enthusiastic about traveling to Brazil.

PART 2(第二部分)

Tourism Resources(旅游资源)

Brazil is the biggest country in South America. It is a wealthy country full of incredible and various landscapes ranging from striking beaches to diverse rainforest,

Brazil counts with the major biodiversity of the world, colorful traditions and festivals and a rich history.

Brazil is one of the most diverse countries with very varied geographical areas such as semi-arid areas, mountains, plains, tropical, subtropical and climates that range from dry to rainy tropical and equatorial climate which enhance the development of different ecosystems, such as the Amazon Rainforest, which has the greatest biological diversity of world, the Atlantic Forest and the Cerrado.

Tourism in Brazil is a growing sector and key to the economy of several regions of the country. Natural areas are its most popular tourism product, a combination of ecotourism with leisure and recreation, mainly sun and beach, and adventure travel, as well as cultural tourism. Among the most popular destinations are the Amazon Rainforest, beaches and dunes in the northeast region, the Pantanal in the center-west region, beaches at Rio de Janeiro and Santa Catarina, cultural tourism in Minas Gerais and business trips to São Paulo city.

巴西是南美洲最大的国家。巴西是一个富饶的国家,到处都是不可思议的景观,从海滩到雨林,巴西拥有世界上最丰富的生物多样性、丰富多彩的传统节日以及深厚的历史。

巴西地理区域迥异,气候多样。如半干旱地区、山区、平原、热带、亚热带,从干旱到多雨的热带和赤道气候,促进了不同生态系统的发展,如亚马孙热带雨林,是全世界物种最多的热带雨林。

巴西的旅游业发展较快。自然区域是最受欢迎的旅游产品,是生态旅游与休闲娱乐的结合,主要包括阳光和海滩、探险旅游和文化旅游。最受欢迎的旅游目的地包括亚马孙热带雨林、东北部地区的海滩和沙丘、中西部地区的潘塔纳尔、里约热内卢和圣卡塔琳娜的海滩、米纳斯吉拉斯的文化旅游和圣保罗市的商务旅行等。

1. Rio de Janeiro(里约热内卢)

Rio de Janeiro, in English "River of January", is the name of both a state and a city in southeastern Brazil. Commonly known as Rio, the city is also nicknamed A Cidade Maravilhosa—"The Marvelous City".

It is famous for its spectacular natural setting, its carnival celebrations, samba and other music, hotel-lined tourist beaches, such as Copacabana, Ipanema, and Leblon and pavements decorated with black and cream swirl pattern mosaics. Some of the most famous local landmarks in addition to the beaches include the giant statue of Jesus, known as Christ the Redeemer "Cristo Redentor" on the top of Corcovado mountain; Sugarloaf Mountain with its cable car; the Sambódromo, a giant permanent parade stand used during Carnival; and Maracanã stadium, the world's largest. Rio also boasts the world's largest forest inside an urban area, called Floresta da Tijuca, or "Tijuca Forest".

Central to the Carioca lifestyle is the beach. From dawn until dusk and even after dark, the residents of Rio can be found enjoying the long stretches of sandy coastline with which the city is blessed. The beach is not merely a place to absorb the sun's rays but also an important venue for sports, socializing and even business. It is a people-watcher's paradise—clothing is minimal and bodies are bronzed and beautiful. The famous Copacabana and Ipanema beaches are magnets for Brazilians and tourists alike.

里约热内卢是巴西东南部一个州和一个城市的名字,也被称为"神奇的城市"。

它以其壮观的自然环境、嘉年华庆典、桑巴舞和音乐、酒店林立的海滩以及用黑色和奶油色漩涡图案马赛克装饰的人行道而闻名。除海滩之外,当地最著名的地标还包括科科瓦多山上被称为"救世主基督"的巨型耶稣雕像和面包山等。里约热内卢还拥有世界上最大的城市森林——蒂茹卡森林。

这里生活的中心是海滩,从黎明到黄昏,甚至天黑之后,里约的居民们都可以欣赏到绵延多沙的海岸线,海滩不仅是一个充满阳光的地方,也是体育、社交甚至商务的重要场所。

2. Salvador(萨尔瓦多)

Salvador is undoubtedly one of the most beautiful cities in the world. Due to its very beauty and to a series of unique features, it has become a primary destination for international tourism. Famous for its history, for the legacy left by people from other continents, for the religious syncretism and for its hospitable people, the capital of the state of Bahia has staged and has been the object of several studies, conducted by professionals from different fields.

Salvador is divided into an upper and lower section (cidade alta and cidade baixa). The enormous Lacerda elevator goes from one level to the other and gives you great views over the city. Pelourinho, the old colonial part of the city, is part of the cidade alta. It is also the tourist epicenter of Salvador, and for good reason: most of the neighborhood is a pedestrian district, with cobblestone streets, many churches, and brightly-painted buildings.

萨尔瓦多无疑是世界上最美丽的城市之一,它的美丽和独有的特点使它成为国际旅游的主要目的地,并以其历史、其他大陆留下的遗产、宗教融合和热情好客的人民而闻名。

3. São Paulo(圣保罗)

São Paulo overwhelms the senses with its sheer size. With over 10 million inhabitants, it is Brazil's third largest city and the largest city in South America. São Paulo and its rival Brazilian city, Rio de Janeiro, have often been compared to New York and Los Angeles respectively. If Rio has gained fame for its striking natural setting, São Paulo's attraction lies in its people and its vibrant cultures. The Avenida Paulista's canyon of upthrusting skyscrapers only hints at the city's sources of energy. A more cosmopolitan city than its counterpart, São Paulo possesses significant ethnic minority communities, including substantial Japanese, Italian, and Arab and Lebanese Christian neighbourhoods.

The array of nationalities living in São Paulo has made it a legendary city among gourmands: Japanese, Italian nuova cucina, Brazilian, Chinese, Jewish, and Arab restaurants are all familiar parts of the city's landscape. Brazil's famously good beef is put to good use at the numerous rodizios and churrascarias. Succulent, roasted cuts of meat are circulated around the tables and cut to patrons' order. In fact, people often visit São Paulo just to dine out. The Jardins district is the center of the dining scene, and thus the center of the São Paulo social scene. Paulistanos eat late—restaurants often don't begin serving until 9:00 p. m. or 10:00 p. m., and it is common for them to stay open until 3:00 a. m..

圣保罗是世界第三大城市和南美洲最大的城市。圣保罗和里约热内卢经常被比作纽约和洛杉矶。圣保罗的吸引力在于它的人民和充满活力的文化。圣保罗拥有大量的少数民族社区，包括大量的日本、意大利、阿拉伯和黎巴嫩基督教社区。

不同国家和民族的人生活在圣保罗，使它成为一座美食爱好者眼中的传奇城市：日本、意大利、巴西、中国、犹太和阿拉伯餐馆都是这座城市景观中熟悉的部分。

Section 3　Argentina（阿根廷）

PART 1（第一部分）

1. 国土疆域（Territory）

阿根廷位于南美旅游区东南部，面积约 278.04 万平方千米，仅次于巴西，是南美旅游区第二大国。东濒大西洋，南与南极洲隔海相望，西部与智利为邻，北部、东部与玻利维亚、巴拉圭、巴西、乌拉圭接壤。南北长约 3 694 千米，东西宽约 1 423 千米，海岸线长约 4 725 千米。

Argentina is located in the southeast of the South America. Tourism Region, with an area of 2.78 million km², second only to Brazil, and is the second largest country in the South America tourism region. It borders the Atlantic Ocean in the east, facing Antarctica across the sea in the south, Chile in the west, and Bolivia, Paraguay, Brazil and Uruguay in the north and east. The maximum distance from north to south is about

3 694 km. The maximum distance between east and west is about 1 423 km. The coastline is about 4 725 km long.

2. 自然风貌(Natural Features)

阿根廷地势西高东低。西部是绵延起伏、巍峨壮丽的安第斯山,约占全国面积的30%;东部和中部的潘帕斯草原是著名的农牧区;北部主要是格兰查科平原,多沼泽、森林;南部是有名的巴塔哥尼亚高原。

拉普拉塔河全长4 100千米,为南美第二大水系。南部安第斯山区多冰蚀湖。

南北气温相差大,自然景观种类多样。北部属热带气候,中部属亚热带气候,南部为温带气候。年平均气温北部24 ℃,南部5.5 ℃。

The landscape of Argentina is high in the west and low in the east. There are the Andes to the west, the Pampas to the east and middle, the Gran Chaco Plain to the north, and the famous Patagonia Plateau to the south.

La Plata-Parana River is the second largest river system in South America with a total length of 4 100 kilometers.

The north belongs to tropical climate, the middle belongs to subtropical climate, and the south is temperate climate.

3. 人口民族(Population and Ethnicity)

阿根廷人口总数约4 537.7万(2020年),人口密度约为每平方千米16.32人。白人和印欧混血种人占95%,白人多属意大利和西班牙后裔。阿根廷官方语言为西班牙语。居民主要信奉天主教。

Argentina has a total population of about 45 377 000 (2020), with a population density of about 16.32 persons per square kilometer. The majority of the population is Catholic.

4. 发展简史(Brief History of Development)

16世纪前阿根廷居住着印第安人。16世纪中叶沦为西班牙殖民地。1810年5月25日爆发反对西班牙统治的"五月革命"。1816年7月9日宣布独立。1853年制定宪法,建立阿根廷联邦共和国。

The Indians lived before the 16th century. It became a Spanish colony in the middle of the 16th century. The Federal Republic of Argentina was founded in 1853.

5. 政治经济(Politics and Economy)

阿根廷的首都为布宜诺斯艾利斯,国花为赛波花,货币为比索。

阿根廷为联邦制的共和国,实行代议制民主。国家最高权力机构是议会,由参、众两院组成,拥有联邦立法权。参、众议员均由直选产生,可连选连任。司法机构由最高法院和各联邦法院组成。最高法院由正副院长和5名大法官组成,院长和法官由总统提名后经参议院批准任命,任期三年,可连选连任。另设法官理事会,负责挑选联邦法院法官并管理全国司法事务。实行多党制,有全国性政党57个,主要有正义党、"变革联盟"等。

阿根廷是南美旅游区中经济较发达的国家之一,与巴西、墨西哥并称为南美三大工业国。阿根廷的工业门类较齐全,主要有钢铁、电力、汽车、石油、化工、纺织、机械、食品等,其中核工业发展水平居拉美前列。农牧业发达,是世界粮食和肉类的重要生产国和出口国,素有"世界粮仓肉库"之称。

交通运输业发达,陆、海、空运能力均居拉美国家前列,国内交通运输以陆运为主。

Argentina is a federal republic and one of the more economically developed countries in South America tourism region, with a complete range of industries, together with Brazil and Mexico, known as the three major industrial nations in South America. Agriculture and animal husbandry is very developed in Argentina. It is an important producer and exporter of grain and meat in the world. Its transportation industry is well developed, with its land, sea and air transport capacity ranking front in Latin American countries.

6. 旅游市场(Tourism Market)

旅游业是阿根廷的支柱产业之一。阿根廷是南美洲第二大国际旅游目的地,到阿根廷旅游人数最多的六个国家和地区是:智利、乌拉圭、巴拉圭、巴西、欧洲和美国。根据阿根廷旅游部的统计,在2019年上半年,智利游客的入境人数增长了28%,而来自欧洲国家的游客则增长了13%。

布宜诺斯艾利斯市是阿根廷最具吸引力的城市。阿根廷旅游部的统计数据显示,2019年上半年布宜诺斯艾利斯就接待了1 465 025名外国游客,游客消费额为348.9亿比索,比2018年增长了25%。外国游客平均在住宿上花费900美元。

在南美洲地区,中国游客最偏爱的国家是巴西,其次是阿根廷,阿根廷是中国极具潜力的远程旅游市场之一,也是我国出境游客满意度最高的国家之一。但是签证难、距离远,加上航班少是阻碍中国公民前往阿根廷旅游的主要因素。

Tourism is one of Argentina's pillar industries. It is the second largest international tourist destination in South America, and Europe and Brazil are the main source of tourists to Argentina. Brazil, Chile and Uruguay are the main destinations for Argentines. In recent years, the number of Chinese tourists traveling to Argentina has been increasing, making Argentina one of the countries with the highest degree of satisfaction among Chinese outbound tourists.

PART 2(第二部分)

Tourism Resources(旅游资源)

The Argentina is provided with a vast territory and a huge variety of climates and microclimates ranging from snowy climate, polar and subpolar in the south to the tropical climate in the north, through a vast expanse of temperate climate and natural wonders like the Aconcagua, the highest mountain in the world outside the Himalayas, the widest river and estuary of the planet (La Plata River), the huge and very mighty Iguazú Falls, some of the flattest and wide meadows-plains of the planet (as the Humid Pampas, a large ocean-sea coast in the Argentine Sea), culture, customs and gastronomy famous internationally, a higher degree of development (very high compared to other Latin American countries), good quality of life and people, and relatively well prepared infrastructure make this country one of the most visited of South America.

Mainly for its beautiful landscapes and then for its cultural heritage, Argentina is receiver of massive amounts of travelers: the Argentine territory stretches from the highest peaks of the Andes in the west to the great rivers and extensive beaches and cliffs of Argentine Sea in the east; from the tropical rainforest of the Yungas north to the valleys, glaciers, lakes and cold forests of Andean Patagonia in the south, and to Argentine Antarctica. Through the warm landscapes of tropical climates contrasting, in a huge gradient microclimates, the polar climates or extensive and very fertile grasslandss with the World's most flatter plains contrasting with the highest mountains outside Asia, contrasted with also vast desert areas plethoric of geoforms for the annual running extensive and extreme Dakar rally race, the high mountain ranges, the pleasant Pampeanas mountains and the temperate Atlantic beaches and its extensive coastlines. The huge distances require in most cases air travel.

The Misiones rainforest, Argentine Yungas and areas of the Argentine Andean Patagonia are scientifically considered as biodiversity hotspots large areas worldwide. The great biodiversity and the large number of different landscapes and climates make Argentina a diverse country where appear to meet multiple countries together harmoniously (fertile temperate, deserts, cold forest, warm tropical and subtropical jungles, glacier areas, cold forests, maritime with cliffs, rias and fjords, etc.).

阿根廷幅员辽阔，气候和小气候种类繁多。这里有独特的自然奇观，如南美洲最高峰阿空加瓜山、地球上最宽的河流和河口（拉普拉塔河）、壮观的伊瓜苏瀑布、最平坦、最宽阔的草原平原（如潘帕斯草原），文化风俗和美食也享誉世界。阿根廷经济发展程度较高，人民生活质量高，相对完善的基础设施使这个国家成为南美洲游客最多的国家之一。

米西奥内斯的热带和阿根廷安第斯-巴塔哥尼亚地区是世界生物多样性热点地区。生物多样性以及不同的景观和气候使阿根廷成为一个多元化的国家。

1. Tango—The Quintessence of Argentine Culture(探戈——阿根廷文化的精髓)

Tango is a partner dance that originated in the 1890s along La Plata River, the natural border between Argentina and Uruguay, and soon spread to the rest of the world.

Tango is a dance that has influences from European and African culture. Dances from the candombe ceremonies of former slave peoples helped shape the modern day Tango. The dance originated in lower-class districts of Buenos Aires and Montevideo. The music derived from the fusion of various forms of music from Europe.

In Argentina, the onset in 1929 of the Great Depression, and restrictions introduced after the overthrow of the Hipólito Yrigoyen government in 1930 caused tango to decline. Its fortunes were reversed as tango became widely fashionable and a matter of national pride under the government of Juan Perón. Tango declined again in the 1950 s as a result of economic depression and the banning of public gatherings by the military dictatorship; male-only Tango practice—the custom at the time—was considered "public gathering". That, indirectly, boosted the popularity of rock and roll because, unlike Tango, it did not require such gatherings.

Argentine tango is the main subject in many films. On August 31, 2009, UNESCO approved a joint proposal by Argentina and Uruguay to include the tango in the UNESCO Intangible Cultural Heritage Lists. Argentina regards tango as the quintessence of its culture.

探戈是一种舞伴舞蹈,起源于19世纪90年代阿根廷和乌拉圭的天然边界——拉普拉塔河,并很快传播到世界其他地区。

探戈是一种受到欧洲和非洲文化影响的舞蹈。从前奴隶的坎东贝仪式上的舞蹈塑造了现代探戈。这种舞蹈起源于布宜诺斯艾利斯和蒙得维的亚的下层社会。

探戈在胡安·贝隆政府统治时期变得越来越流行,它激起了阿根廷人的民族自豪感,并被视为阿根廷文化的精髓。

阿根廷探戈是许多电影的主题。2009年8月31日,联合国教科文组织批准了阿根廷和乌拉圭将探戈列入联合国教科文组织非物质文化遗产名录的联合提案。

2. Buenos Aires(布宜诺斯艾利斯)

Buenos Aires is the capital and largest city of Argentina, and the second largest metropolitan area in South America. It is located on the southern shore of the estuary of the Río de la Plata, on the continent's southeastern coast. The Greater Buenos Aires conurbation, which also includes several Buenos Aires Province districts, constitutes the third largest conurbation in Latin America, with a population of around fifteen and a half million.

Buenos Aires is a top tourist destination, and is known for its European-style architecture and rich cultural life, with the highest concentration of theaters in the world. It is regarded as the "Paris of South America".

布宜诺斯艾利斯位于南美洲东南岸、拉普拉塔河南岸，是阿根廷首都和最大城市，也是南美洲第二大都市区。

布宜诺斯艾利斯是一个顶级旅游目的地，以欧式建筑和丰富的文化生活著称，拥有世界上最集中的剧院，被称为"南美洲的巴黎"。

3. Rosario(罗萨里奥)

Rosario is the largest city in the province of Santa Fe, in central Argentina. It is located 300 km northwest of Buenos Aires, on the western shore of the Paraná River. Rosario is the third most populous city in the country, and is also the most populous city in Argentina that is not a state capital, with a growing and important metropolitan area. It has developed into an industrial and commercial center and destination for a significant number of people on business. On its riverside promenade stands the Monumento Nacional a la Bandera (National Monument to the Flag), where the Argentine National Flag was raised for the first time. One of its main attractions includes the neoclassical architecture that has been retained over the centuries in hundreds of residences, houses, and public buildings.

罗萨里奥是阿根廷中部圣菲省最大的城市，位于布宜诺斯艾利斯西北 300 千米的巴拉那河西岸，是根廷第三大人口城市。目前，它已发展成为一个工业和商业中心和旅游目的地。

4. Cordoba(科尔多瓦)

Cordoba is the capital of Córdoba Province and the second largest city in Argentina after the autonomous city of Buenos Aires. It was one of the first Spanish colonial capitals of the region. The National University of Córdoba is the oldest university of the country and the second to be inaugurated in Latin America. It was founded in 1613 by the Jesuit Order. Cordoba has many historical monuments preserved from Spanish colonial rule, especially buildings of the Roman Catholic Church. The most recognizable is perhaps the Jesuit Block, declared in 2000 as a World Heritage Site by UNESCO which consists of a group of buildings dating from the 17th century, including the Colegio Nacional de Monserrat and the colonial university campus. Córdoba is one of the most picturesque of Argentina because it has a historical center with beautiful Baroque Colonial architecture mixed with tall modern buildings that give the city a great tourist attraction. With many contrasting features—it is both a cultural and tourist-like destination, a traditional and modern city, with an industrialized as well as a home-made production.

科尔多瓦是阿根廷第二大城市,仅次于布宜诺斯艾利斯。它是阿根廷最早的西班牙殖民首都之一。国立科尔多瓦大学是阿根廷历史最悠久的大学,也是拉丁美洲第二所落成的大学,由耶稣会于1613年建立。科尔多瓦有许多西班牙殖民统治时期保存下来的历史遗迹,如罗马天主教堂和耶稣会街区。科尔多瓦是一座风景如画的城市,其独特的历史、美丽的巴洛克殖民地建筑与高大的现代建筑,使这座城市成为一个著名的旅游胜地。

5. Ushuaia(乌斯怀亚)

Ushuaia, the southernmost city in the world, in Tierra del Fuego, typical destination of the south of the country, attracts visitors with a very important tourist with excursions, gastronomy and the feeling of being literally at the end of the world. North of the island, the city of Rio Grande is attractive by his old neighborhood of wooden houses painted varied or subtly and by excellent trout fishing. Further south, it is famous railway from Ushuaia and reaches the Tierra del Fuego National Park, bayside of Lapataia. Cruises are also offered by the Beagle Channel, observing colonies of South American sea lions, and a visit to Lighthouse Les Eclareurs, the beautiful Lake Fagnano (or Kami) or almost inaccessible Staten Island where is the Lighthouse of the End of the World, the landscape of Fueguan forests takes an almost magical appearance during the austral autumn to be covered with reddish the foliage of the dense forests.

乌斯怀亚位于火地岛,是世界上最南端的城市,是阿根廷南部的旅游目的地。这里五颜六色的木屋和鳟鱼捕捞,使这座城市非常吸引人。

6. Iguazú Falls(伊瓜苏瀑布)

Iguazú Falls, located in the northeast, area of subtropical forest, on the border with Brazil are one of the world's natural wonders, has good infrastructure development and touristic with very different walks. Lined with dense forests, the Iguazú river flows into 275 waterfalls, plunging more than 70 meters with a deafening noise over 2.7 km. As this huge volume of water reaches the bottom, spray rises, and rainbows are formed in the sky. A variety of the original fauna and flora completes the setting for the waterfalls within the protection of the Iguazú National Park. This park, located at eighteen kilometres from Puerto Iguazú, was declared Natural Heritage of Humanity by UNESCO. The famous falls are inside this park. The frontier with Brazil goes through the Garganta del Diablo (Devil's Throat). The National Park is full of the exotic subtropical vegetation which surrounds the falls and has 2 000 plant species and 400 bird species. Its most impressive fall is called Garganta del Diablo.

伊瓜苏瀑布位于亚热带森林区的东北部,与巴西接壤,是世界自然奇观之一,基础设施发达。在茂密的森林中,伊瓜苏河流入275个瀑布,瀑布落差超过70米,震耳欲聋的声音可达2.7千米以外。当大量的水落到底部时,水花溅起,在天空中形成美丽的彩虹。

这里已开辟为国家公园,并被联合国教科文组织列入人类自然遗产。国家公园内充满了奇异的亚热带植被,瀑布环绕,有2 000种植物和400种鸟类。

7. Lago Argentino(阿根廷湖)

Lago Argentino is a lake in the Patagonian province of Santa Cruz, Argentina. It is the biggest freshwater lake in Argentina, with a surface area of 1 415 km². It has an average depth of 150 m. The lake lies within the Los Glaciares National Park in a landscape with numerous glaciers and is fed by the glacial meltwater of several rivers, the water from Lake Viedma brought by the La Leona River, and many mountain streams.

The glaciers, the nearby town of El Calafate and the lake itself are important tourist destinations. The lake in particular is appreciated for fishing.

阿根廷拉戈湖是阿根廷巴塔哥尼亚省圣克鲁斯的一个湖泊,是阿根廷最大的淡水湖,面积1 415平方千米,平均深度为150米。该湖位于罗斯·格拉希亚雷斯冰川国家公园内,拥有众多的冰川,由冰川融水、湖水和许多山涧提供水源。

8. Bariloche(巴里洛切)

Bariloche, is a city in the province of Río Negro, Argentina, situated in the foothills of the Andeson the southern shores of Nahuel Huapi Lake. It is located within the Nahuel Huapi National Park. After development of extensive public works and Alpine-styled architecture, the city emerged in the 1930s and 1940s as a major tourism center with ski, trekking and mountaineering facilities.

Tourism, both domestic and international, is the main economic activity of Bariloche, all year around. While popular among Europeans, the city is also very popular among Brazilians. One of the most popular activities is skiing. Most tourists visit Bariloche in its winter (summer for North Americans and Europeans). The main ski station is the one at Cerro Catedral. During the summer, beautiful beaches such as Playa Bonita and Villa Tacul welcome sun-bathers; brave lake swimmers venture into its cold waters (chilled by melting snow).

The fishing season is another great attraction. Bariloche is the biggest city of a huge Lakes District, and serves as a base for many excursions in the region. Trekking in the mountains, almost completely wild and uninhabited with the exception of a few high-mountain huts operated by Club Andino Bariloche, is also a popular activity. The city is noted for its chocolates and Swiss-style architecture.

巴里洛切坐落在阿根廷西部安第斯山麓、纳韦尔瓦皮湖的南岸,以巧克力和瑞士风格的建筑而闻名。这座城市在 20 世纪 30—40 年代成为一个主要的旅游中心。

旅游业是巴里洛切的主要产业,滑雪、徒步和登山设施齐全,它不仅受到巴西人的欢迎,也很受欧洲人的欢迎。

Sum up(本章小结)

1. 南美旅游区既不是世界上国际旅游业发达地区,也不是中国的主要旅游目的地,但是其旅游资源丰富,文化独具特色,是极具潜力的旅游区。

2. 本章从地理位置及范围、自然风貌、民族与宗教、旅游市场等方面介绍了南美旅游区的基本概况。

3. 本章选取了巴西、阿根廷两个国家,它们是南美旅游区比较重要的目的地国和客源国。

4. 每个国家的介绍分为两部分,第一部分介绍了各国的国土疆域、自然风貌、人口民族、发展简史、政治经济和旅游市场的基本概况;第二部分介绍了各国的旅游资源。

Reviewing and Thinking(复习与思考)

1. 南美旅游区的自然风貌有何特色?对旅游有何影响?
2. 南美旅游区为什么目前无法成为世界重要的客源地和旅游目的地?
3. 巴西旅游资源的主要特征是什么?在发展旅游业方面有何优势?
4. 为什么说巴西发展生态旅游得天独厚?
5. 简述阿根廷旅游资源与主要旅游景点。
6. 试设计中国—巴西、阿根廷十六日游的经典路线。

CHAPTER

6

The Africa Tourism Region
（非洲旅游区）

◇ **LEARNING OBJECTIVES（学习目标）**

1. Understand the basic situation of the major tourist source and destination countries in Africa（了解非洲主要客源国和目的地国的基本情况）.

2. Master the tourism market development and tourism resources characteristics of the main source and destination countries in Africa（掌握非洲主要客源国和目的地国的旅游市场发展与旅游资源特点）.

3. Design some classic tourist routes（设计一些经典旅游线路）.

◇ **LEARNING CONTENS（学习内容）**

1. Egypt（埃及）
2. Morocco（摩洛哥）

◇ **PROBLEM ORIENTATION（问题导向）**

What are the reasons for the underdevelopment of African tourism market?（非洲旅游市场不发达的原因是什么？）

Section 1　General Situation of Africa（非洲概况）

一　区域概况（Regional Overview）

1. 地理位置及范围（Geographical Location and Scope）

非洲是"阿非利加洲"的简称，位于东半球的西部，地跨赤道南北，东濒印度洋，西临大西洋，北隔地中海和直布罗陀海峡与欧洲相望，东北隅以狭长的红海与苏伊士运河紧邻亚洲。面积约 3 020 万平方千米（包括附近岛屿）。约占世界陆地总面积的 20.4%，仅次于亚洲，为世界第二大洲。

非洲目前有 60 个国家和地区。在地理上，习惯将非洲分为北非、东非、西非、中非和南非五个地区。

北非包括埃及、苏丹、利比亚、突尼斯、阿尔及利亚、摩洛哥、亚速尔群岛、马德拉群岛。

东非包括埃塞俄比亚、厄立特里亚、索马里、吉布提、肯尼亚、坦桑尼亚、乌干达、卢旺达、布隆迪和塞舌尔。

西非包括毛里塔尼亚、西撒哈拉、塞内加尔、冈比亚、马里、布基纳法索、几内亚、几内亚比绍、佛得角、塞拉利昂、利比里亚、科特迪瓦、加纳、多哥、贝宁、尼日尔、尼日利亚和加

非洲地图 AFRICA

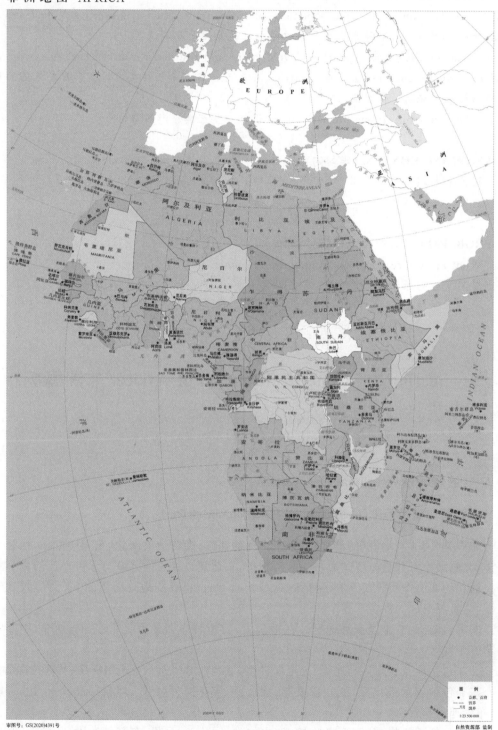

资料来源：标准地图服务网站，审图号：GS(2020)4391号。

那利群岛。

中非包括乍得、中非、喀麦隆、赤道几内亚、加蓬、刚果(布)、刚果(金)、圣多美和普林西比。

南非包括赞比亚、安哥拉、津巴布韦、马拉维、莫桑比克、博茨瓦纳、纳米比亚、南非、斯威士兰、莱索托、马达加斯加、科摩罗、毛里求斯、留尼汪、圣赫勒拿等。

Africa is the abbreviation of "Afrika Island", located in the west of the Eastern Hemisphere, across the north and south of the equator. It borders the Indian Ocean in the east, the Atlantic Ocean in the west, and Europe across the Mediterranean Sea and the Strait of Gibraltar to the north. The northeast corner is adjacent to Asia by the long and narrow Red Sea and the Suez Canal. The area is about 30.2 million km² (including nearby islands). It is the second largest continent in the world with about 20.4% of the world's total land area, second only to Asia.

There are currently 60 countries and regions in Africa. Geographically, it is customary to divide Africa into five regions: North Africa, East Africa, West Africa, Central Africa and South Africa.

2. 自然风貌(Natural Features)

非洲大陆海岸线全长 30 500 千米,海岸比较平直,缺少海湾与半岛。非洲是世界各洲中岛屿数量最少的一个洲。除马达加斯加岛外,其余多为小岛。非洲为一高原大陆,平均海拔 650 米。地势东南高、西北低。乞力马扎罗山是一座活火山,海拔 5 895 米,为非洲最高峰,山岳景观秀丽。非洲东部的大裂谷是世界上最长的裂谷带,是非洲地震最频繁、最强烈的地区,也是非洲自然旅游资源最丰富的地区。

非洲的大河流受到地质构造和其他自然因素的影响,水系较复杂,多急流、瀑布。湖泊多分布在东非裂谷带。

在希腊文中,"阿非利加"是阳光灼热的意思。赤道横贯非洲的中部,非洲 75%的土地受到太阳的垂直照射,年平均气温在 20 ℃ 以上的热带占全洲的 95%,其中有一半以上地区终年炎热,故有"热带大陆"之称。境内降水较少,仅刚果盆地和几内亚湾沿岸一带年平均降水量在 1 500 毫米以上,年平均降水量在 500 毫米以下的地区占全洲面积的 50%。刚果盆地和几内亚湾沿岸一带属热带雨林气候。地中海沿岸一带夏热干燥,冬暖多雨,属地中海气候。北非撒哈拉沙漠、南非高原西部雨量极少,属热带沙漠气候。其他广大地区夏季多雨,冬季干旱,属热带草原气候。马达加斯加岛东部属热带雨林气候,西部属热带草原气候。

The coastline of African continent is relatively straight, lacking bays and peninsulas. Africa is a plateau continent with an average elevation of 650 m. Kilimanjaro, an active volcano, 5 895 m above sea level, is the highest mountain in Africa; The Great Rift Valley in East Africa is the longest rift belt in the world. The main rivers are the Nile, the Congo River, the Niger River and so on. The equator has traversed the middle of Africa, which is known as the "tropical continent".

3. 民族与宗教(Nationality and Religion)

非洲人口总数约12.86亿人(2019年),仅次于亚洲,居世界第二位。但非洲人口分布极不均衡,尼罗河沿岸及三角洲地区,每平方千米约1 000人;撒哈拉、纳米布、卡拉哈迪等沙漠和一些干旱草原、半沙漠地带每平方千米不到1人,还有大片的无人区。非洲是世界上民族成分最复杂的地区。非洲大多数民族属于黑种人,其余属白种人和黄种人。

非洲信仰的宗教主要有三种:传统宗教、伊斯兰教和基督教。

African has a total population of 1.286 billion (2019), but it is distributed extremely uneven. The majority of African ethnic groups are black people, and the rest belong to white and yellow people. The residents mainly profess the primitive religion, Islam and Christianity.

4. 经济(Economy)

历史上非洲各国的经济曾长期遭受西方发达国家的控制,使非洲成为世界上经济发展水平最低的洲,大多数国家经济落后。农业人口约占全洲总人口的2/3,许多经济作物的产量在世界上占有重要地位,如咖啡、花生、可可、丁香、棕榈油等。采矿业和轻工业是非洲工业的主要部门。非洲是世界交通运输业比较落后的一个洲,还没有形成完整的交通运输体系。交通运输以公路为主,海运业占一定地位。航空业发展较快。

Historically, the economy of African countries has been under the control of Western developed countries for a long time, which makes Africa the continent with the lowest economic growth in the world, and most countries are economically underdeveloped.

二 旅游业(Tourism)

非洲大陆幅员辽阔、历史悠久、文化独特。拥有丰富的历史文化遗迹、秀丽的自然风光和奇异的野生动植物,具有发展旅游业的巨大潜力。15世纪以来,由于长期遭受西方殖民主义的侵略与掠夺,非洲大多数国家都属于发展中国家,经济相对比较落后,旅游基础设施不完善。一些国家和地区甚至长期社会动荡、战乱频繁、自然灾害严重,影响着旅游业的发展。

The African continent has a vast territory, a long history and a unique culture. With rich historical and cultural relics, beautiful natural scenery and exotic wildlife forms, it has great potential for tourism development. Since the 15th century, most of the African countries that are now independent are all developing countries with relatively backward economy and imperfect tourism infrastructure due to the long-term invasion and plunder of Western colonialism. Long-term social unrest, frequent wars and serious natural disasters in some countries and regions have affected the development of tourism.

最近 20 年来,非洲许多国家开始重视旅游开发,充分利用本地独有的自然风光和民俗风情,针对游客的猎奇心理,大力开展各种专项旅游活动,如特色风光游、沙漠探险游、历史考古游等,吸引着来自世界各地的游客。近年来旅游业发展较快的国家有埃及、摩洛哥、突尼斯、南非、肯尼亚、乌干达、毛里求斯和塞舌尔等。

尽管非洲旅游业发展潜力巨大,但其接待游客数和旅游业收入在全球旅游行业中所占比重仍然很低。UNWTO 发布报告称,2018 年,非洲共接待游客 7 834 万人,同比增长 10.5%,占全球比重仅 5.6%;创收约 500 亿美元,同比增长 13.1%,占全球比重仅 3.4%。2018 年,非洲接待游客数量最多的国家前五位分别是摩洛哥、埃及、南非、突尼斯和津巴布韦。非洲旅游业收入最多的国家前五位分别是埃及、南非、摩洛哥、坦桑尼亚和突尼斯。

随着中非关系进一步加强,2018 年共有 20 个非洲国家和地区对中国游客实施免签或落地签政策。埃及、突尼斯、摩洛哥、阿尔及利亚、毛里求斯、肯尼亚、南非等国家都是中国游客青睐的目的地。中青旅遨游网发布的《2018 中国公民非洲旅游报告》显示,中国赴非游客人数再创新高,增长速度持续保持高位,年均增幅超过 40%;中国游客出境游十大首选目的地中非洲国家占比达 30%。当然,中国人在非洲旅游目的地选择上,具有鲜明的"南北开花、中间突破、海岛添彩"的特点,即北部非洲以埃及为重点,逐渐向摩洛哥、突尼斯等国扩展;南部以南非为重点,逐渐向纳米比亚、博茨瓦纳、津巴布韦等国扩展;中部以肯尼亚、坦桑尼亚、埃塞俄比亚等国为重点。同时,非洲的毛里求斯、塞舌尔等高端精品海岛在中国市场也颇受欢迎,已成为具有鲜明特点和独特优势的海岛旅游目的地。

In recent years, tourism has developed rapidly in Egypt, Morocco, Tunisia, South Africa, Kenya, Uganda, Mauritius and Seychelles. The top 5 tourist destinations in Africa are Morocco, Egypt, South Africa, Tunisia and Zimbabwe.

Africa has become a major outbound destination for Chinese tourists, with the continuous communication between China and Africa.

Section 2　Egypt(埃及)

PART 1(第一部分)

1. 国土疆域(Territory)

埃及地跨亚、非两洲,大部分位于非洲东北部,只有苏伊士运河以东的西奈半岛位于亚洲西南角。北濒地中海,西连利比亚,南接苏丹,东临红海并与巴勒斯坦、以色列接壤,地处亚、非、欧三洲交通要道,面积约100.1万平方千米。

Egypt is across Asia and Africa, most of which is located in the northeast of Africa. Only the Sinai Peninsula east of the Suez Canal is located in the southwest corner of Asia. It is bordered by the Mediterranean Sea in the north, Libya in the west, Sudan in the south, the Red Sea in the east and adjacent to Palestine and Israel. It is located at the crossroads of Asia, Africa and Europe, with an area of about 1.001 million km².

2. 自然风貌(Natural Features)

埃及海岸线长约2 900千米,全境95%为沙漠。世界最长河流尼罗河从南到北流贯全境,境内长1 350千米,两岸形成狭长的河谷,在首都开罗以北形成2.4万平方千米的三角洲。苏伊士运河是连接亚、非、欧三大洲的交通要道。

埃及大部分地区属热带沙漠气候,终年炎热干燥,尼罗河三角洲和北部沿海地区属地中海气候。1月平均气温12 ℃,7月平均气温26 ℃,年平均降水量50～200毫米。沙漠地区气温可达40 ℃,年平均降水量不足30毫米。

95% of Egypt is covered by desert. The Nile, the world's longest river, runs through the country from south to north, and the Suez Canal is the main artery connecting Asia, Africa and Europe. Most areas of Egypt is a tropical arid climate, hot and dry all year round. Only the Nile delta and the north coast area is Mediterranean climate.

3. 人口民族(Population and Ethnicity)

埃及人口总数约1亿(2021年),人口密度约为每平方千米99.13人。由于埃及95%的国土面积为无法居住的荒漠,能够居住的国土面积只有5万多平方千米,因此人口聚居高度集中,主要集中在尼罗河三角洲地区。埃及的官方语言是阿拉伯语。伊斯兰教为国教,信徒主要是逊尼派,约占总人口的84%。

Egypt has a total population of about 100 million (2021), with a population density of about 99.13 people per square kilometer. Most of the population live in the Nile Delta. Islam is the state religion and its adherents are mainly Sunnis.

4. 发展简史(Brief History of Development)

埃及是世界四大文明古国之一,具有悠久的历史和文化。公元前3200年,美尼斯统一埃及建立了第一个奴隶制国家,经历了早王国、古王国、中王国、新王国和后王朝时期,共30个王朝。当时的埃及国王被称为"法老",古王国时期法老开始大规模兴建金字塔。中王国时期经济发展迅速、文艺复兴。新王国时期生产力显著提高,开始对外扩张,一度成为当时地中海流域的军事强国。后王朝时期,内乱频繁,外患不断,国力日衰。公元前525年埃及被波斯人征服。公元前30年罗马执政屋大维出兵侵入埃及,从此埃及被罗马帝国统治长达 600 余年,使埃及成为当时主要的基督教国家之一。公元 641 年,阿拉伯人入侵,埃及逐渐阿拉伯化。1517 年沦为奥斯曼土耳其帝国的一个行省。1798 年被法军占领。1882 年成为英国殖民地。1914 年成为英国的"保护国"。1922 年 2 月 28 日,英国宣布埃及为独立国家,但保留对国防、外交、少数民族等问题的处置权。1952 年 7 月 23 日,以纳赛尔为首的自由军官组织推翻法鲁克王朝,成立革命指导委员会,掌握国家政权。1953 年 6 月 18 日宣布成立埃及共和国。1958 年 2 月同叙利亚合并成立阿拉伯联合共和国(简称"阿联")。1961 年叙利亚发生政变,退出"阿联"。1971 年 9 月 1 日改名为阿拉伯埃及共和国。

Egypt is one of the four ancient civilizations in the world. In 3200 BC, Menes united Egypt and established the first slavery state. Around 641 AD, the Arabs invaded and established the Arab State. It became a province of the Ottoman Empire in 1517 and became a British colony in 1882. The Republic of Egypt was proclaimed on June 18, 1953. It was renamed the Arab Republic of Egypt on September 1, 1971.

5. 政治经济(Politics and Economy)

首都为开罗,国花为莲花,货币为埃及镑。

埃及的政体是总统制共和制。总统是国家元首兼武装部队最高统帅,由人民议会提名,公民投票选出,任期 6 年。由总统任命副总统、总理及内阁部长。议会是最高立法机关。议员由普选产生,任期 5 年。法院包括最高法院、上诉法院、中央法院和初级法院以及行政法院,开罗还设有最高宪法法院。检察机构包括总检察院和地方检察分院。

埃及经济属开放型市场经济,拥有相对完整的工业、农业和服务业体系。服务业约占国内生产总值50%。工业以纺织、食品加工等轻工业为主。农村人口占总人口的55%,农业占国内生产总值的14%。石油天然气、旅游、侨汇和苏伊士运河是四大外汇收入来源。

Egypt has an open market economy with a relatively complete system of industry, agriculture and services. Petrol and natural gas, tourism, remittances and the Suez Canal are the top four sources of foreign exchange in Egypt.

6. 旅游市场(Tourism Market)

埃及历史悠久,名胜古迹很多,具有发展旅游业的良好条件。埃及政府历来十分重视旅游业。旅游业是埃及的支柱产业之一,是埃及最主要的外汇来源。

埃及接待的海外游客70%来自欧洲,其中输出游客最多的 10 个国家依次为俄罗斯、德国、英国、意大利、法国、波兰、乌克兰、利比亚、沙特阿拉伯和美国。

自 2011 年政局陷入动荡后,埃及旅游业严重萎缩。近年来,埃及实施旅游业改革计划,旅游业发展显著。2019 年埃及的游客总数为 1 310 万,2018 年和 2017 年分别为 1 130 万和 830 万。2019 年访埃游客人数仍然低于 2010 年的峰值。

埃及出境旅游的主要旅游目的地是欧洲和地中海沿岸各国。随着中埃两国经贸往来和文化交流的进一步加深,前往中国的埃及旅游者人数在逐年增加。

自 2008 年起,埃及已成为中国在非洲及中东地区的第一大旅游目的地国。

The Egyptian government has always attached great importance to tourism, which is one of Egypt's pillar industries and its main source of foreign exchange. 70% of the overseas tourists to Egypt are from Europe, and the main outbound tourist destination are Europe and the Mediterranean coastal countries. In recent years, the number of Chinese tourists to Egypt has always been on the rise, and China has become the fourth largest source of tourists to Egypt.

PART 2(第二部分)

Tourism Resources(旅游资源)

1. Cairo(开罗)

Cairo is the capital of Egypt and, with a total population in excess of 22.8 million people, one of the largest cities in both Africa and the Middle East (the regions which it conveniently straddles). It is also the 19th largest city in the world, and among the world's most densely populated cities.

Situated on the River Nile, Cairo is famous for its own history, preserved in the fabulous medieval Islamic city and Coptic sites in Old Cairo. The Egyptian Museum in the center of town is a must see, with its countless Ancient Egyptian artifacts, as is shopping at the Khan al-Khalili bazaar. No trip to Cairo would be complete, for example, without a visit to the Giza Pyramids, and to the nearby Saqqara Pyramid Complex, where visitors will see Egypt's first step pyramid built by the architect Imhotep for the third dynasty pharaoh Djoser.

Though firmly attached to the past, Cairo is also home to a vibrant modern society. The Midan Tahrir area situated in downtown Cairo area, built in the 19th century under the rule of Khedive Ismail, has strived to be a "Paris on the Nile". There also are a number of more modern suburbs including Ma'adi and Heliopolis, while Zamalek is a quiet area on Gezira Island, with upscale shopping. Cairo is best in the fall or spring, when the weather isn't so hot. A felucca ride on the Nile is a good way to escape from the busy city, as is a visit to Al-Azhar Park.

Cairo is the ancient capital of the world famous culture. This cultural atmosphere looks attractive. The city has 250 mosques. The most famous mosque is Al-Azhar Mosque. It is the oldest university in Arabia world Al-Azhar University is located. The University was founded in 972 years. People study the laws of Islam, the history of Arabia literature and philosophy. The Egyptian Museum is a museum of pearl in the world. It is located in the Liberation Square, built in 1863. More than 63 000 pieces of cultural relics are on display here. Cairo tower is the most obvious sign of modern Cairo, about 190 meters high.

The best time to visit Cairo is during the winter from November to March, when daytime temperature generally stays below 25 ℃, with nighttime temperature around 10 ℃ with occasional rain showers clearing the air.

开罗是埃及的首都,是非洲和中东最大的城市之一,是世界上第 19 大城市,也是世界上人口最密集的城市之一。

开罗位于尼罗河之滨,以其历史而闻名。位于市中心的埃及博物馆有无数的古埃及文物,吉萨金字塔和附近的萨卡拉金字塔群,都是不可错过的景观。

开罗是世界著名的文化古都。这个城市有 250 座清真寺,最著名的清真寺是爱资哈尔清真寺。建于 1863 年的埃及博物馆位于解放广场,这里陈列着 63 000 多件文物。爱资哈尔大学建于公元 972 年,是阿拉伯世界最古老的大学,人们在这里学习伊斯兰教的法律、阿拉伯文学和哲学。

2. Pyramid(金字塔)

The most famous pyramids are the Egyptian pyramids. The pyramid is the ancient Egyptian king's mausoleum built for himself. Egyptian pyramids are huge structures built of brick or stone, some of which are among the world's largest constructions. They are shaped as a reference to the rays of the sun. Most pyramids had a polished, highly reflective white limestone surface, to give them a shining appearance when viewed from a distance. The capstone was usually made of hard stone—granite or basalt—and could be plated with gold, silver, or electrum and would also be highly reflective. Ancient Egyptian pyramids were in most cases placed west of the river Nile, near Cairo. The Great Pyramid of Giza is the largest in Egypt and one of the largest in the world. It is praised for one of ancient seven greatest miracles in the world. It is the only one to survive into modern times.

The Great Pyramid of Giza, which was probably completed around 2465 BC, is the oldest of the Giza pyramids and the largest pyramid in the world, and is the only surviving monument of the Seven Wonders of the Ancient World. The Pyramid of Khafre is believed to have been completed around 2532 BC, at the end of Khafre's reign. Khafre ambitiously placed his pyramid next to his fathers. It is not as tall as his father's pyramid but he was able to give it the impression of appearing taller by building it on a site with a foundation 10 m higher than his father's. Along with building his pyramid, Khafre commissioned the building of the giant Sphinx as guardian over his tomb. The face of a human, possibly a depiction of the pharaoh, on a lion's body was seen as a symbol of divinity among the Greeks fifteen hundred years later. The Great Sphinx is carved out the limestone bedrock and stands about 20 m tall. Menkaure's pyramid dates to circa 2490 BC and stands 65 m high making it the smallest of the Great Pyramids.

最著名的金字塔是埃及金字塔。金字塔是古埃及国王为自己建造的陵墓。埃及金字塔是用砖或石头建造的巨大建筑，其中一些是世界最大的建筑。它们的形状参照太阳光线。大多数金字塔都有一个抛光的、高反射的白色石灰石表面，从远处看，它们闪闪发光。古埃及金字塔大多位于尼罗河以西，开罗附近。

吉萨大金字塔是埃及最大的金字塔，也是世界上最大的金字塔之一，是古代世界七大奇迹中仅存的遗迹，完成于公元前 2465 年。哈夫拉金字塔大约建于公元前 2532 年。孟卡拉金字塔大约建于公元前 2490 年，高 65 米，是世界上最小的金字塔。

在巨大的金字塔的前面，在石灰岩基岩上还建造了巨型狮身人面像，高约 20 米，它作为法老坟墓的守护者，也被视为神的象征。

3. The Nile(尼罗河)

The Nile is one of the world's great waterways, at 6 670 kilometers generally regarded as the longest river in the world and among the most culturally significant natural formations in human history. The Nile Valley and Delta is the cradle of Egyptian culture and the birthplace of one of world culture. Along most of its length through Egypt, the Nile has scoured a deep, wide gorge in the desert plateau.

The Nile Valley is a canyon running 660 miles long with a floodplain occupying 4 250 square miles. The Delta spans some 8 500 square miles and is fringed in its coastal regions by lagoons, wetlands, lakes and sand dunes. The Delta represented 63% of the inhabited area of Egypt, extending about 200 kilometers from south to north and roughly 400 kilometers from east to west.

In ancient Egypt, the flooding of the Nile was predictable enough for the Egyptians to plan their yearly crops around it. It flooded annually some time from June to September. The ancient Egyptians learned partial control of the flood waters of the Nile by means of irrigation. In addition to being a source of water for their crops, the Nile River was a source of fish and a major artery linking parts of Egypt as well as linking Egypt to its neighbors.

The Nile represents life itself to the people of Egypt, ancient and modern. In fact, for thousands of years, the river has made life possible for hundreds of thousands of people and animals, and has shaped the culture we today are only beginning to truly understand.

There are many boats on the Nile, such as the Pharaoh boats. It is enjoyable to boat and watch lovely scenes on both sides of the Nile on night Pharaoh boats.

尼罗河是世界上最长的河流，全长 6 670 千米，也是人类历史上最具文化意义的自然形态之一。尼罗河流域和三角洲是埃及文化的摇篮和世界文化的发源地之一。尼罗河流经埃及的大部分地区,在沙漠高原上冲刷出一条又深又宽的峡谷。尼罗河沿岸有潟湖、湿地、湖泊和沙丘。

在古代,埃及人就能预测尼罗河每年6月到9月的某个时候会发生洪水,以此在尼罗河周围规划农作物的种植,并能通过灌溉部分控制尼罗河的洪水。

无论是古代还是现代,尼罗河代表着埃及人民的生命。几千年来,这条河使成千上万的人和动物得以生存,并塑造了我们今天才开始真正了解的文化。乘船在尼罗河上游览,可以欣赏尼罗河两岸的美丽景色。

4. Pharaoh Village(法老村)

Pharaoh Village is an island located in the city of Cairo on the Nile River, covering an area of about 200 acres. It is built by the fund in 1984 after the Egypt's first ambassador Dr. Hassan Rajab's discovery of papyrus papermaking process lost one thousand years. Entering the village, there are many statues among the papyrus and flowers. In addition to the statues, there built the Pharaohs temples of the ancient style. The last part of the Pharaoh village is the farmhouses with white walls and the roof of palm leaves, simple and quiet. The village shows the economic and social life of the ancient Egyptians thousands of years ago.

法老村位于开罗市尼罗河畔的一座小岛上,占地约200英亩。是埃及首任驻华大使哈桑·拉贾布博士在发现失传一千年的纸草造纸工艺后于1984年集资修建的。进入村庄,在纸莎草和鲜花中有许多雕像,有古代风格的法老神庙,还有法老村的农舍,农舍有白色的墙壁和棕榈叶的屋顶,简单而安静。这个村庄展示了几千年前古埃及人的经济和社会生活。

Section 3　Morocco(摩洛哥)

PART 1(第一部分)

1. 国土疆域(Territory)

摩洛哥王国位于非洲西北端。东部、东南部接壤阿尔及利亚,南邻西撒哈拉,西濒大西洋,北隔直布罗陀海峡与西班牙相望,扼守大西洋进入地中海的门户。国土面积约45.9万平方千米。

The Kingdom of Morocco is located at the northwestern tip of Africa. It borders

Algeria in the east and southeast, Western Sahara in the south, the Atlantic Ocean in the west, Spain across the Strait of Gibraltar in the north, guarding the gateway of the Atlantic Ocean into the Mediterranean Sea. It covers an area of 459 000 km^2.

2. 自然风貌(Natural Features)

摩洛哥地形复杂,以山地和高原为主,中部和北部为峻峭的阿特拉斯山脉,东部和南部是高原和前撒哈拉高原,仅西北沿海一带为狭长低缓的平原。

乌姆赖比阿河是第一大河,长 556 千米,德拉河是最大的间歇河,长 1 150 千米。主要河流还有木卢亚河、塞布河等。

摩洛哥西北部为地中海气候,夏季炎热干燥,冬季温和湿润,1 月平均气温 12 ℃,7 月份 22~24 ℃。降水量为 300~800 毫米。中部属亚热带山地气候,温和湿润,气温随海拔高度而变化。东部、南部为热带沙漠气候,年平均气温约 20 ℃。年降水量在 250 毫米以下,南部不足 100 毫米。由于斜贯全境的阿特拉斯山挡住了南部撒哈拉沙漠的热浪的侵袭,加之濒临大西洋和地中海的地理位置,使摩洛哥气候温和宜人,四季花木繁茂,赢得"烈日下的清凉国土"的美誉。摩洛哥是个风景如画的国家,还享有"北非花园"的美称。

Morocco has a complex landform, mainly mountains and plateaus. Morocco has a Mediterranean climate in the northwest, a subtropical mountain climate in the middle, and a tropical dessert climate in the south. Morocco has a mild and pleasant climate with flourishing flowers all year round, earning the reputation of "cool land under the scorching sun".

3. 人口民族(Population and Ethnicity)

摩洛哥人口约 3 621 万(2021 年),人口密度为每平方千米 78.89 人,主要是阿拉伯人。官方语言为阿拉伯语,通用法语。居民主要信奉伊斯兰教。

Morocco has a population of about 36 210 000 (2021) with a population density of 78.89 people per square kilometer. The residents mainly profess Islam.

4. 发展简史(Brief History of Development)

摩洛哥是非洲最古老的国家之一。公元 7 世纪阿拉伯人进入,并于 8 世纪建立第一个阿拉伯王国。从 15 世纪起,西方列强先后入侵。1956 年摩洛哥独立。1957 年 8 月 14 日正式定国名为摩洛哥王国,苏丹改称国王。

The Arabs entered Morocco in the 7th century. The first Arab empire in Morocco's history was founded in the 8th century. From the beginning of the 15th century, Western powers invaded one after another. On August 14, 1957, it was officially named the Kingdom of Morocco.

5. 政治经济(Politics and Economy)

首都为拉巴特,国花为康乃馨,货币为迪拉姆。

摩洛哥是君主立宪制的伊斯兰国家,国王拥有最高权力。国王是国家元首、宗教领袖、武装部队最高统帅;首相拥有提名和罢免大臣、解散议会等权力。议会由众议院和参议院两院组成。司法机构分四级:最高法院、上诉法院(21个)、初级法院(68个)和初级法院派驻的法官处。实行多党制。现有35个政党,各党均宣布拥护国王和伊斯兰教,在大政方针上与国王保持一致。主要政党有公正与发展党、独立党、人民运动、进步与社会主义党等。

摩洛哥经济总量在非洲排名第五,在北非排名第三。磷酸盐出口、旅游业、侨汇是摩洛哥经济的主要支柱。工业企业主要部门有农业食品加工、化工医药、纺织服装、采矿和机电冶金工业。摩洛哥是世界磷酸盐出口第一大国。手工业在国民经济中占重要地位,主要产品有毛毯、皮革制品、金属加工品、陶瓷和木制家具。农业是国民经济主要部门,出口农产品主要有柑橘、橄榄油等。渔业资源丰富,是非洲最大的渔业产品生产国。陆路交通较发达,在国内运输业中占主导地位。

Morocco is an Islamic constitutional monarchy and mainly based on agriculture and mining, among which mining is the pillar industry; Agriculture is the main sector of national economy. Tourism is well developed.

6. 旅游市场(Tourism Market)

摩洛哥是一个文明古国,也是世界上自然风光最美丽的国家之一,拥有绵长的大西洋和地中海海岸线,还有撒哈拉沙漠、雪山和古城,阿拉伯风情浓郁,旅游资源十分丰富,旅游业发达,休闲旅游是摩洛哥旅游的基本特色。

摩洛哥是非洲第一大旅游目的地国,是其国民经济的支柱产业,是本国第二大平衡国际收支来源。

2019年1—8月,摩洛哥接待游客共计926.6万人次,同比增长6.4%。主要客源国依次为法国、西班牙、英国、德国等国。俄罗斯和捷克作为摩洛哥新兴的旅游客源市场,来摩旅游的人数增长很快。美国和加拿大等北美国家游客数量也有不同程度的增长。

随着中摩双方的交流加深,特别是自2016年6月1日起,摩洛哥正式实施中国公民赴摩洛哥免签的政策以来,中国赴摩洛哥旅游的游客数量增长很快。为进一步提升对中国游客的吸引力,摩洛哥正着手改善酒店和交通设施,摩洛哥和中国的直航线路也指日可待。

Morocco is the first tourist destination country in Africa. Tourism is the pillar industry of its national economic development. The main tourist sources are France, Spain, the United Kingdom, Germany and so on. Russia and the Czech Republic as Morocco's emerging tourist source markets, and the number of tourists to Morocco is growing rapidly.

PART 2(第二部分)

Tourism Resources(旅游资源)

Tourism is one of the most important sectors in Morocco's economy, it is well developed with a strong tourist industry focused on the country's coast, culture, and history. Tourism is the second largest foreign exchange earner in Morocco after the phosphate industry. Morocco's relatively high amount of tourists has been aided by its location. Morocco is close to Europe and attracts visitors to its beaches.

Tourism is increasingly focused on Morocco's culture, such as its ancient cities. The modern tourist industry capitalizes on Morocco's ancient Roman and Islamic sites, and on its landscape and cultural history. 60% of Morocco's tourists visit for its culture and heritage. Agadir is a major coastal resort and has a third of all Moroccan bed nights. It is a base for tours to the Atlas Mountains. Other resorts in north Morocco are also very popular. Casablanca is the major cruise port in Morocco, and has the best developed market for tourists in Morocco, Marrakech in central Morocco is a popular tourist destination, but is more popular among tourists for one- and two-day excursions that provide a taste of Morocco's history and culture. The Majorelle botanical garden in Marrakech is a popular tourist attraction.

Activity and adventure tourism in the Atlas and Rif Mountains are the fastest growth area in Moroccan tourism. These locations have excellent walking and trekking opportunities from late March to mid-November. The government is investing in trekking circuits. They are also developing desert tourism in competition with Tunisia.

旅游业是摩洛哥经济中最重要的部门之一,是摩洛哥仅次于磷酸盐工业的第二大外汇收入来源。

摩洛哥充分利用古罗马和伊斯兰遗址、自然景观及文化历史发展旅游业。阿加迪尔是主要的海滨度假胜地。卡萨布兰卡是摩洛哥的主要邮轮港口,拥有摩洛哥最发达的旅游市场,摩洛哥中部的马拉喀什是一个受欢迎的旅游目的地。马拉喀什的马约尔植物园也是一个受欢迎的旅游景点。

阿特拉斯山和里夫山是摩洛哥旅游业增长最快的地区,这里是徒步旅行的好去处,政府正在投资建设更多的徒步线路。同时,为了与突尼斯竞争,他们正在开发沙漠旅游。

1. Casablanca(卡萨布兰卡)

Casablanca is the largest city of Morocco, located in the northwestern part of the country on the Atlantic Ocean. It is also the largest city in the Maghreb, as well as one of the largest and most important cities in Africa, both economically and demographically. Casablanca has been called the "Miami of Morocco" due to its incredible art deco architecture. While the city embraces its French history with detailed city planning in the early 20th century, Casablanca's modern ambiance is very different from other Moroccan cities. It is Morocco's financial and cultural center, filled with industry, media, fashion and commerce.

Casablanca is home to the Hassan Ⅱ Mosque, designed by the French architect Michel Pinseau. It is situated on a promontory on the Atlantic. The mosque has room for 25 000 worshippers inside, and a further 80 000 can be accommodated in the mosque's courtyard. Its minaret is the world's tallest at 210 metres. The mosque is also the largest in North Africa, and the third largest in the world.

A popular site among locals is the small island Marabout de Sidi Abderrahmane. It is possible to walk across to the rocky island at low tide.

卡萨布兰卡位于该国西北部，濒临大西洋，是摩洛哥最大的城市，是马格里布最大的城市，也是非洲最大和最重要的城市之一。卡萨布兰卡因其装饰艺术建筑而被称为"摩洛哥的迈阿密"。卡萨布兰卡在20世纪初的城市规划中融入了法国历史，它的现代氛围与其他摩洛哥城市截然不同。它是摩洛哥的金融和文化中心，也是工业、媒体、时尚和商业中心。

卡萨布兰卡是哈桑二世清真寺的所在地，该清真寺由法国建筑师米歇尔·潘索设计。清真寺位于大西洋的一个海角上。它的宣礼塔塔高达210米，是世界最高的。它是北非最大的清真寺，也是世界第三大清真寺。

2. Rabat(拉巴特)

Rabat is the capital of Morocco and its seventh largest city center. The city is located on the Atlantic Ocean at the mouth of the river Bou Regreg. On the facing shore of the river lies Salé, the city's main commuter town. Rabat, Temara, and Salé form a conurbation of over 1.8 million people. Silt-related problems have diminished Rabat's role as a port; however, Rabat and Salé still maintain important textile, food processing and construction industries. In addition, tourism and the presence of all foreign embassies in Morocco serve to make Rabat one of the most important cities in the country.

The Moroccan capital was awarded second place in "Top Travel Destinations of 2013" by CNN. It is one of four Imperial cities of Morocco, and the Medina of Rabat is listed as a World Heritage site.

The Mausoleum of Mohammed Ⅴ is a historical building located on the opposite side of the Hassan Tower on the Yacoub al-Mansour esplanade in Rabat, Morocco. It contains the tombs of the Moroccan king and his two sons, late King Hassan Ⅱ and Prince Abdallah. The building is considered a masterpiece of modern Alaouite Dynasty architecture, with its white silhouette, topped by a typical green tiled roof, green being the color of Islam. Hassan Tower or Tour Hassan is the minaret of an incomplete mosque in Rabat, Morocco. The tower, made of red sandstone, along with the remains of the mosque and the modern Mausoleum of Mohammed Ⅴ, forms an important historical and tourist complex in Rabat.

拉巴特位于大西洋的布雷格雷格河口,是摩洛哥首都和第七大城市中心。拉巴特是摩洛哥重要的纺织、食品加工和建筑业中心,而旅游业和所有外国驻摩洛哥大使馆的存在使拉巴特成为摩洛哥最重要的城市之一。拉巴特阿拉伯人区已被列为世界遗产,拉巴特被CNN评为"2013年最佳旅游目的地"第二名。

穆罕默德五世的陵墓是一座历史建筑,它被认为是现代阿拉维王朝建筑的杰作,白色轮廓,顶部是典型的绿色瓷砖屋顶,绿色是伊斯兰教的颜色。由红砂岩建成的哈桑塔、连同清真寺和穆罕默德五世的陵墓,构成了拉巴特重要的历史和旅游综合体。

3. Tangier(丹吉尔)

Tangier is a major city in northern Morocco, with a population of approximately 974 000. It is located on the North Africa coast at the western entrance to the Strait of Gibraltar where the Mediterranean Sea meets the Atlantic Ocean off Cape Spartel. The history of Tangier is very rich, due to the historical presence of many civilizations and cultures starting from before the 5th century BC.

The Dar-el-Makhzen (or Sultanate Palace) is a historical building in Tangier, Morocco, which was the seat of residence for the Sultans of Morocco when staying in the city. It was built in the Kasbah on one of the highest points of the city overlooking the Medina and the Strait of Gibraltar. Currently it is used by two museums, the Museum of Moroccan Arts and the Museum of Antiquities. Tangier Grand Mosque is a large mosque in the Grand Socco area of central Tangier, Morocco. It was built on the site of a former Portuguese cathedral which in turn stood on a Roman temple dedicated to Hercules. The Caves of Hercules are situated 14 km of Tangier in the Cap Spartel area. It is a place of great beauty and archeological significance.

丹吉尔是摩洛哥北部的一个主要城市,位于北非海岸、直布罗陀海峡的西部入口处。丹吉尔历史悠久,在公元前5世纪之前就有许多文明和文化。

苏丹王宫是丹吉尔的一座历史建筑,曾是摩洛哥苏丹在该市的住所。摩洛哥艺术博物馆、古物博物馆、丹吉尔大清真寺、"非洲洞"等都是不容错过的地方。

4. Fez(非斯)

Fez is the third largest city of Morocco. The city has two old medinas, the larger of which is Fes el Bali. It is listed as a UNESCO World Heritage Site and is believed to be one of the world's largest car-free urban areas. Al-Qarawiyyin, founded in 859 AD, is the oldest continuously functioning madrasa in the world. The city has been called the "Mecca of the West" and the "Athens of Africa".

The Madrasa Bou Inania is a madrasa in Fes, Morocco, founded in 1351-1356 AD. It is widely acknowledged as an excellent example of Marinid architecture. The madrasa functioned both as an educational institute and as a congregational mosque. The madrasa is one of the few religious places in Morocco that is accessible for non-Islamic visitors. The Zaouia Moulay Idriss Ⅱ is a zaouia (shrine) in Fes, Morocco, dedicated to and tomb of Moulay Idriss Ⅱ. Moulay Idriss Ⅱ is the patron saint of the city of Fez, and it is believed that visiting his zaouia is beneficial for strangers visiting the city, boys before being circumcised and women wanting to facilitate childbirth. The University of al-Qarawiyyin or al-Karaouine is a university located in Fez, Morocco. It is the oldest existing, continually operating and the first degree awarding educational institution in the world according to UNESCO and Guinness World Records and is sometimes referred to as the oldest university. The al-Qarawiyyin mosque-religious school/college was founded by Fatima al-Fihri in 859 with an associated school, or madrasa, which subsequently became one of the leading spiritual and educational centers of the historic Muslim world.

非斯是摩洛哥第三大城市。这座城市有两个古老的麦地那,其中较大的是 Fes el Bali。非斯被联合国教科文组织列为世界遗产。Al-Qarawiyyin 建立于公元 859 年,是世界上最古老的伊斯兰学校。这座城市被称为"西方的麦加"和"非洲的雅典"。

布伊纳尼亚学校也是非斯的一所伊斯兰学校,建于 1351—1356 年。它被认为是马里尼建筑的一个优秀范例,它既是一个教育机构,也是一个教会清真寺。伊斯兰学校是摩洛哥为数不多的非伊斯兰游客可以进入的宗教场所之一。

Sum up(本章小结)

1.非洲是世界上经济发展水平最低的地区,非洲旅游区也是国际旅游业欠发达地区,且内部发展极不平衡,其中北部的埃及、摩洛哥,南部的南非,东部的肯尼亚、坦桑尼亚等国家旅游业相对发达。非洲拥有丰富的历史文化遗迹、秀丽的自然风光和奇异的野生动植物,具有发展旅游业的巨大潜力。

2.本章从地理位置及范围、自然风貌、民族与宗教、旅游市场等方面介绍了非洲旅游区的基本概况。

3.本章选取了埃及、摩洛哥两个国家,它们是非洲旅游区最重要的目的地国和客源国。

4.每个国家的介绍分为两部分,第一部分介绍了各国的国土疆域、自然风貌、人口民族、发展简史、政治经济和旅游市场的基本概况,第二部分介绍了各国的旅游资源。

Reviewing and Thinking(复习与思考)

1. 非洲的旅游资源有什么特色？
2. 为什么非洲没有成为国际旅游的重要市场？有哪些制约因素？
3. 埃及和摩洛哥各有哪些主要景点？

CHAPTER 7

The Oceania Tourism Region
（大洋洲旅游区）

◇ **LEARNING OBJECTIVES**(学习目标)

1. Understand the basic situation of the major tourist source and destination countries in Oceania(了解大洋洲主要客源国和目的地国的基本情况).

2. Master the tourism market development and tourism resources characteristics of the main tourist source and destination countries in Oceania(掌握大洋洲主要客源国和目的地国的旅游市场发展与旅游资源特点).

3. Design some classic tourist routes(设计一些经典旅游线路).

◇ **LEARNING CONTENTS**

1. Australia(澳大利亚)
2. New Zealand(新西兰)

◇ **PROBLEM ORIENTATION**(问题导向)

Why can Oceania become a new tourist destination in China? (大洋洲为什么能成为中国新的旅游目的地?)

Section 1　General Situation of Oceania(大洋洲概况)

一　区域概况(Regional Overview)

大洋洲旅游区位于太平洋西南部和南部,介于亚洲旅游区和南极洲之间,西临印度洋,东濒太平洋。大洋洲旅游区包括澳大利亚大陆、塔斯马尼亚岛、新西兰南北二岛、新几内亚岛以及太平洋上的三大岛群(即波利尼西亚、密克罗尼西亚和美拉尼西亚三大岛群)等1万多个岛屿。陆地总面积约897万平方千米,约占世界陆地总面积的6%。大洋洲旅游区现有14个独立国家,其余10个地区尚在美、英、法等国的管辖之下。

The Oceania Tourism Region is located in the southwest and south of the Pacific Ocean, between the Asian tourism region and Antarctica, adjacent to the Indian Ocean in the west and the Pacific Ocean in the east. The Oceania tourism region includes the Australian mainland, Tasmania, New Zealand, New Guinea and three major island groups in the Pacific Ocean (namely Polynesia, Micronesia and Melanesia). There are more than 10 000 islands in total. The total land area is about 8.97 million km², accounting for about 6% of the world's total land area. There are currently 14 independent countries

资料来源:标准地图服务网站,审图号:GS(2020)4396 号。

in Oceania tourism region, and the remaining 10 regions are still under the jurisdiction of the United States, Britain, France and other countries.

大洋洲旅游区地形分为大陆和岛屿两部分,大陆海岸线长约 19 000 千米,澳大利亚独占整个大陆。岛屿面积约为 133 万平方千米,其中新几内亚岛最大,是世界第二大岛。全洲高原、山地和丘陵众多,平原较小。大洋洲有活火山 60 多座(不包括海底火山),火山旅游资源丰富。

大洋洲旅游区大部分处在南、北回归线之间,绝大部分地区属热带和亚热带,除澳大利亚的内陆地区属大陆性气候外,其余地区属海洋性气候。除澳大利亚外,全区其他各地气候温差不大。生物旅游资源多种多样,全年适宜旅游。

大洋洲旅游区总人口约 4 126 万人(2019 年),约占世界总人口的 0.5%。其中欧洲人后裔约占 70%以上,集中在澳大利亚和新西兰两国。各岛国人口密度差异显著,巴布亚人、澳大利亚土著人、塔斯马尼亚人、毛利人、美拉尼西亚人、密克罗尼西亚人和波利尼西亚人等当地居民约占总人口的 20%,此外还有混血种人、印度人、华人和日本人等。绝大部分居民信奉基督教,少数人信奉天主教,印度人多信奉印度教。大部分居民通用英语,太平洋三大岛群上的当地居民,分别使用波利尼西亚语、密克罗尼西亚语和美拉尼西亚语。

The landscape of Oceania tourism region is divided into mainland and island: the mainland coastline is about 19 000 km long, Australia has the whole continent to itself. Oceania has more than 60 active volcanoes (not including submarine volcanoes) and is rich in volcanic tourism resources. Most of Oceania tourism region is tropical and subtropical, except for a continental climate in the inland of Australia, and the rest of the region belongs to a maritime climate. The vast majority of the population is Christian.

旅游业(Tourism)

　　大洋洲旅游区地处赤道南北,岛屿众多。岛屿多属珊瑚礁型,有世界上最大的珊瑚礁群——大堡礁(它位于澳大利亚东北海岸的珊瑚海上,断续绵延2 000 km,有3 000余个岛礁,面积21万 km²)。此地处处是浪漫的热带海岛风光,是休闲、度假的天堂。同时,由于全区地广人稀、远离其他大陆且发现较晚,因而保持了比较原始的风貌,动植物都非常独特,如袋鼠、笑鸟等都是这里独有的动物。对于厌倦了城市生活的人们来说,大洋洲是一块新奇而神秘的大陆。蔚蓝的大海、白色的沙滩、五光十色的珊瑚、广阔的沙漠和迷人的热带森林景观,构成了一幅绚丽的图画,令人向往。

　　20世纪50年代以来,大洋洲以其丰富的自然旅游资源和独特的毛利文化成为全世界发展较快的旅游区。在这个旅游区内有两种类型的国家:一类是发达国家澳大利亚和新西兰,旅游基础接待设施良好,旅游入境人数成倍增长,旅游创汇居世界前列,游客多以欧美国家和亚洲的日本等经济实力较强的国家为主。出境旅游势头强劲,目前这两个国家到中国来旅游的游客已占中国海外游客总数的4%左右,已成为中国主要的客源国。另一类是发展中国家,由于经济实力的差距,旅游业发展速度相对较慢,多以海岛旅游为主,游客多是周边国家的居民。

Oceania tourism region is located in the north and south of the equator. There are many islands, which are coral reefs, and unique fauna and flora. Since the 1950s, Oceania has become a fast developing tourism region in the world with its rich natural tourism resources and unique Maori culture.

Section 2　Australia(澳大利亚)

PART 1(第二部分)

1. 国土疆域(Territory)

　　澳大利亚联邦位于南太平洋和印度洋之间,由澳大利亚大陆、塔斯马尼亚等岛屿和海外领土组成。东濒太平洋的珊瑚海和塔斯曼海，北、西、南三面临印度洋及其边缘海。海岸线长 36 735 千米。澳大利亚是世界上唯一一个独占一个大陆的国家。整个澳大利亚位于南纬 10°41′和 43°39′之间，国土面积约 769.2 万平方千米，居世界第六位，仅次于俄罗斯、加拿大、中国、美国和巴西，占大洋洲面积的 85%。

The Commonwealth of Australia, located between the South Pacific and the Indian Ocean, is composed of the Australian mainland, Tasmania island and overseas territories. Australia is surrounded by the sea on all sides, bordering the Coral Sea of the Pacific Ocean and the Tasman Sea in the east, the Indian Ocean in the north, west and south. Australia is the only country in the world whose territory spans the whole continent. Australia is located between 10°41′ and 43°39′ south latitude, covering the area of 7.692 million km^2, ranking sixth in the world, second only to Russia, Canada, the United States, China and Brazil, accounting for 85% of the area of Oceania.

2. 自然风貌(Natural Features)

澳大利亚海岸线长 36 735 千米。虽四面环水，沙漠和半沙漠却占全国面积的 35%。全国分为东部山地、中部平原和西部高原 3 个地区。森林面积为 106 万平方千米，覆盖率为 20%。最长河流墨尔本河长 3 490 千米。在东部沿海有全世界最大的珊瑚礁——大堡礁。明媚秀丽的海滩、险峻奇绝的壮丽峡谷、辽阔荒凉的内陆风光、举世闻名的大堡礁具有无与伦比的迷人魅力，每年都吸引着数百万的旅游者前来度假。

澳大利亚是世界上最干燥的大陆。按照气候带的划分，澳大利亚的北部为热带，中部为辽阔的干旱地带，大部分属温带。澳大利亚的气候比较温和，全年温差不大。最湿润的地方是东北热带地区和塔斯马尼亚州西南地带。最冷的地区位于塔斯马尼亚的高原地区和东南大陆的边缘地带。内陆地区干旱少雨，年降水量不足 200 毫米，东部山区的降水量 500~1 200 毫米。澳大利亚的四季正好与中国相反。夏季由 12 月份开始，3 至 5 月份是秋季，6 月进入冬季，9 月则是春季的开始。南回归线以北地区年平均气温为 23~26 ℃，回归线以南地区温差稍微明显一些，冬季平均气温为 14 ℃，夏季为 26 ℃。生物旅游资源独特，全年大部分时间适宜旅游。

Although Australia is surrounded by water on all sides, about 35% of the land is dominated by deserts and semi-arid land. The country is topographically divided into 3 regions: the eastern mountains, the central plains and the western plateaus. Australia is the driest continent in the world. According to the division of climate zone, the northern part of Australia is tropical, the central part is vast arid zone, and the southern part is temperate zone. Biological tourism resources are unique, and most of the year is suitable for tourism.

3. 人口民族(Population and Ethnicity)

澳大利亚人口约 2 569 万(2020 年),人口密度为每平方千米 3.34 人。其中英国及爱尔兰后裔占 74%,亚裔占 5%,土著居民占 2.7%,其他民族占 18.3%。英语为官方语言。约 63.9% 的居民信仰基督教,5.9% 的居民信仰佛教、伊斯兰教、印度教等其他宗教。无宗教信仰或宗教信仰不明人口占 30.2%。

Australia has a population of about 25.69 million (2020) with a population density of 3.34 people per square kilometer, of which 74% are of British and Irish descendants. Residents mainly believe in Christianity.

4. 发展简史(Brief History of Development)

澳大利亚原为土著人居住。1770 年,英国航海家詹姆斯·库克在澳大利亚东海岸登陆,并宣布英国占有这片土地。1788 年 1 月 26 日,英国首批移民抵达澳大利亚,这一天后来被定为澳大利亚的国庆日。此后,英国陆续在澳大利亚各地建立了一些分散的殖民区。1900 年 7 月英议会通过《澳大利亚联邦宪法》,1901 年 1 月 1 日,澳大利亚各殖民区改为州,成立澳大利亚联邦。1931 年澳大利亚成为英联邦内的独立国。

In 1770 Australia became a British colony. On January 1, 1901, the colonial districts of Australia formed the Commonwealth of Australia and became the British Dominion. In 1931 Australia became an independent country within the Commonwealth Nations.

5. 政治经济(Politics and Economy)

澳大利亚的首都为堪培拉,国花为金合欢,货币为澳大利亚元。

国家政体为联邦议会制。英国女王是澳大利亚的国家元首,由女王任命的总督为法定的最高行政长官。总理由总督提名,由女王任命。联邦议会是澳大利亚的最高立法机构,由女王(澳总督为其代表)和参、众两院组成。

联邦众议院议员 151 名,按各州人口比例选出,任期 3 年。参议院议员 76 名,6 个州每州 12 名,2 个地区各 2 名,各州参议员任期 6 年,每 3 年改选一半,各地区参议员任期 3 年。

联邦政府由众议院多数党或党派联盟组成,政府一般任期 3 年。

澳大利亚是一个后起的工业化国家,农牧业发达,自然资源丰富,盛产羊、牛、小麦和蔗糖,同时也是世界重要的矿产品生产和出口国。农牧业、采矿业为传统产业;近年来,制造业和高科技产业有较快发展;服务业是澳大利亚经济最重要和发展最快的部门,经过 30 多年的经济结构调整,已成为国民经济支柱产业,占国内生产总值 80% 以上。

20 世纪 70 年代以来,澳大利亚进行了一系列的经济改革,大力发展对外贸易,经济持续较快增长。自 2009 年以来,由于全球经济放缓,石油和铁矿石等大宗商品的价格下降,澳大利亚经济下滑。2019—2020 财年经济出现负增长,国内生产总值 1.95 万亿澳元,人均 GDP 约 7.6 万澳元。

Australia has a federal parliamentary system of government. It is a rising industrialized country. In recent years, manufacturing and high-tech industries have developed rapidly, and services is the most important and fastest developing sector of Australian economy.

6. 旅游市场(Tourism Market)

澳大利亚以其湛蓝的海水、金色的沙滩、色彩斑斓的海底花园(大堡礁)、茫茫无际的沙漠、郁郁葱葱的热带雨林景观、风景秀丽的山涧洞府、奇特古老的民俗风情、绚丽多姿的文化艺术、举世无双的动物奇观，成为全世界最令游客心驰神往的目的地之一。

近年来，海外游客来澳人数总体呈上升趋势，但国内游客仍是主导。由于澳元汇率走低、全球经济回暖、廉价航空公司瞄准亚洲市场等因素，澳大利亚成为入境旅游热门目的地。目前，澳大利亚排名前五位的客源国分别是中国、新西兰、美国、英国和日本；与此同时，旅游总消费排名前五位的国家分别是中国、美国、英国、新西兰和日本。毋庸置疑，中国已经成为澳大利亚头号旅游客源国。澳大利亚旅游资源丰富，著名的旅游城市和景点有悉尼、墨尔本、布里斯班、阿德莱德、珀斯、大堡礁、黄金海岸和达尔文等。

2018年共有850万海外游客选择澳大利亚作为其休闲度假目的地，创下历史最高纪录，为澳大利亚创造高达440亿澳元的经济收入。澳大利亚国际旅游的增长在很大程度上主要受亚洲市场的推动，中国继续稳居其作为澳大利亚头号旅游市场的地位，2018年中国市场共计输送130万游客，旅游支出达到117亿澳元，游客量和消费支出分别增长5%和13%。

近年来，澳大利亚也成为中国游客优先选择的目的地之一，中国游客的数量持续增长，中国游客赴澳旅游支出也超过其他任何国家的游客。据澳洲统计局和旅游局预测，中国赴澳游客的数量将以每年5.1%的增长率增长，到2023年，总数将达到9 700万人，有望在4年内超过新西兰，中国将成为澳大利亚海外游市场的主力军。

澳大利亚每年出境游人口比例相当高。在最受澳大利亚游客欢迎的海外旅游目的地国排名当中，中国居第七位，排名依次为新西兰、英国、美国、印尼、斐济、泰国和中国。近年来澳大利亚来华旅游人数呈增长趋势，2018年来华游客人数为75.19万人次，十年增长34%。

目前澳大利亚旅华市场面临几个有利的因素。首先，中澳两国经贸关系的加强推动了商务旅游的发展。商务旅游占澳大利亚旅华总人数的20%以上，商务旅游的增加对总体入境人数的增长有很大的贡献。其次，中国旅游的快速增长，以及有吸引力的目的地形象在全球深入人心。在全球备受恐怖活动威胁的形势下，中国局势稳定、游客安全有保障。同时，中国丰富的旅游产品、快速发展的经济和不断改善的基础设施，对澳大利亚游客有很大的吸引力；最后，中澳两国间的航空运力不断增加为旅游市场的进一步拓展提供了交通运力保障。目前在中澳航线上，中国国航和东方航空每周均有7个航班、南方航空有4个航班直抵澳大利亚。航空公司和旅游公司的密切合作也促进了澳大利亚来华旅游的发展。

At present, Australia's top five tourist sources are China, New Zealand, the United States, the United Kingdom and Japan. The top five countries in total tourism consumption are China, the United States, the UK, New Zealand and Japan. In recent years, Australia has also become one of the top destinations for Chinese tourists, whose number has continued to grow and who spend more on Australian tourism than tourists from any other country.

PART 2(第二部分)

Tourism Resources(旅游资源)

Popular Australian destinations include the coastal cities of Sydney and Melbourne, as well as other high profile destinations including regional Queensland, the Gold Coast and the Great Barrier Reef, the world's largest reef. Uluru and the Australian outback are other popular locations, as is the Tasmanian wilderness. The unique Australian wildlife is also another significant point of interest in the country's tourism.

澳大利亚受欢迎的目的地包括悉尼和墨尔本等沿海城市,以及昆士兰地区、黄金海岸和世界上最大的珊瑚礁大堡礁等地。乌鲁鲁(即艾尔斯岩)和澳大利亚内陆也是澳大利亚受欢迎的地方。澳大利亚独特的野生动物是该国旅游业的另一大特色兴趣点。

1. Natural Tourism Resources(自然旅游资源)

1)The Great Barrier Reef(大堡礁)

The Great Barrier Reef is the world's largest coral reef system composed of over 2 900 individual reefs and 900 islands stretching for over 2 300 kilometres over an area of approximately 344 400 km^2. The reef is located in the Coral Sea, off the coast of Queensland, Australia.

The Great Barrier Reef can be seen from outer space and is the world's biggest single structure made by living organisms. This reef structure is composed of and built by billions of tiny organisms, known as coral polyps. It supports a wide diversity of life and was selected as a World Heritage Site in 1981. CNN labeled it one of the seven natural wonders of the world.

A large part of the reef is protected by the Great Barrier Reef Marine Park, which helps to limit the impact of human use, such as fishing and tourism. Other environmental pressures on the reef and its ecosystem include runoff, climate change accompanied by mass coral bleaching, and cyclic population outbreaks of the crown-of-thorns starfish. According to a study published in October 2012 by the Proceedings of the National Academy of Sciences, the reef has lost more than half its coral cover since 1985.

The Great Barrier Reef has long been known to and used by the Aboriginal Australian and Torres Strait Islander people, and is an important part of local groups' cultures and spirituality. The reef is a very popular destination for tourists, especially in the Whitsunday Islands and Cairns regions. Tourism is an important economic activity for the region, generating over $3 billion per year.

大堡礁位于澳大利亚昆士兰海岸附近的珊瑚海中,是世界上最大的珊瑚礁系统,由2 900多个珊瑚礁和900多个岛屿组成,绵延2 300多千米,面积约344 400平方千米。

大堡礁是世界上最大的由数十亿的微小生物组成的单一结构的珊瑚礁,也被称为珊瑚虫。1981年它被列为世界遗产。美国有线电视新闻网将其列为世界七大自然奇观之一。

大堡礁海洋公园保护着大堡礁的很大一部分,这有助于限制人类的影响,如捕鱼和旅游业。

大堡礁很早就被澳大利亚的土著居民和托雷斯海峡岛民所熟知和利用,是当地群体文化和精神的重要组成部分。珊瑚礁是一个非常受欢迎的旅游目的地,旅游业是当地的一项重要经济活动,每年带来30多亿美元的收入。

2)The Blue Mountains(蓝山山脉)

The Blue Mountains is a mountainous region and a mountain range located in New South Wales, Australia. It is a magical place any time of the year—glowing in autumn, cool in winter, colourful in spring and refreshing in summer. The Blue Mountains is densely populated by oil bearing Eucalyptus trees. The atmosphere is filled with finely dispersed droplets of oil, which, in combination with dust particles and water vapor, scatter short-wave length rays of light which are predominantly blue in color. The Greater Blue Mountains was inscribed on the World Heritage List in 2000 and was one of 15 World Heritage places included in the National Heritage List on 21 May 2007.

蓝山山脉是位于澳大利亚新南威尔士州的山脉。这里在任何季节都是一个神奇的地方,秋高气爽、冬凉、春艳、夏爽。蓝山上密布着众多油性桉树,大气中弥漫着很细的油滴,这些油滴与尘埃颗粒和水蒸气结合在一起,散射出以蓝色为主的短波光线。蓝山山脉于2000年被列入《世界遗产名录》,是2007年5月21日被列入《国家遗产名录》的15个世界遗产地之一。

3)Bondi Beach(邦迪海滩)

Bondi Beach is a popular beach and the name of the surrounding suburb in Sydney, New South Wales, Australia. Bondi Beach is located 7 km east of the Sydney central business district, in the local government area of Waverley Council, in the Eastern Suburbs. Bondi, North Bondi and Bondi Junction are neighboring suburbs. Bondi is one of the most visited tourist sites in Australia.

邦迪海滩是一个受欢迎的海滩。邦迪海滩位于悉尼中央商务区以东7千米处,是澳大利亚游客最多的景点之一。

4) Phillip Island(菲利普岛)

Phillip Island is an Australian island about 140 km south-southeast of Melbourne, Victoria. Named after Arthur Phillip, the first Governor of New South Wales, Phillip Island forms a natural breakwater for the shallow waters of the Western Port. It is 26 km long and 9 km wide, with an area of about 100 km². It has 97 km of coastline and is part of the Bass Coast Shire.

A 640 m concrete bridge (originally a wooden bridge) connects the mainland town San Remo with the island town Newhaven. In the 2011 census the island's permanent population was 9 406, compared to 7 071 in 2001. During the summer, the population swells to 40 000. 60% of the island is farmland devoted to grazing of sheep and cattle.

菲利普岛是澳大利亚的一个岛屿，位于维多利亚州墨尔本东南偏南约 140 千米处。菲利普岛以新南威尔士州首任总督阿瑟·菲利普的名字命名，形成了西港浅水区的天然防波堤。它长 26 千米，宽 9 千米，面积约 100 平方千米，有 97 千米的海岸线，是巴斯海岸郡的一部分。岛上 60% 的土地用于放牧。

5) Ayers Rock(艾尔斯岩)

Ayers Rock is also known by its Aboriginal name "Uluru". It is a sacred part of Aboriginal creation mythology. Uluru is considered one of the great wonders of the world and one of Australia's most recognizable natural icons. Uluru is a large magnetic mound large not unlike Silbury Hill in England. It is located on a major planetary grid point much like the Great Pyramid in Egypt.

Ayers Rock is a large sandstone rock formation in central Australia, in the Northern Territory. It is located in Uluru-Kata Tjuta National Park. It is the second largest monolith in the world (after Mount Augustus, also in Australia), more than 318 m high and 8 km around. It also extends 2.5 km into the ground. It was described by explorer Ernest Giles in 1872 as "the remarkable pebble".

Uluru is an inselberg, literally "island mountain", an isolated remnant left after the slow erosion of an original mountain range. Uluru is also often referred to as a monolith, although this is a somewhat ambiguous term because of its multiple meanings, and thus a word generally avoided by geologists. The remarkable feature of Uluru is its homogeneity and lack of jointing and parting at bedding surfaces, leading to the lack of development of scree slopes and soil. These characteristics led to its survival, while the surrounding rocks were eroded. For the purpose of mapping and describing the geological history of the area, geologists refer to the rock strata making up Uluru as the Mutitjulu Arkose, and it is one of many sedimentary formations filling the Amadeus Basin.

艾尔斯岩以其土著名字"乌鲁鲁"而闻名。它是土著神话中的神圣之地，乌鲁鲁被认为是世界上伟大的奇迹之一,也是澳大利亚最著名的自然标志之一。乌鲁鲁是一个巨大的磁丘,与英国的锡尔伯里山类似,像埃及金字塔一样位于一个行星网格点上。

艾尔斯岩位于北领地的乌鲁鲁-卡塔丘塔国家公园,是澳大利亚中部的一种大型砂岩构造,是世界上第二大的巨石,高 318 米,周长 8 千米,还延伸到地下 2.5 千米。

艾尔斯岩是原始山脉缓慢侵蚀后留下的孤立遗迹,其显著特征是其均匀性和层理面缺乏接合和分离,导致碎石边坡和土壤缺乏发育。

2. Cultural Tourism Resources(人文旅游资源)

1)Lake Burley Griffin(伯利·格里芬湖)

Lake Burley Griffin is an artificial lake in the center of Canberra, the capital of Australia. It was completed in 1963 after the Molonglo River—which ran between the city center and Parliamentary Triangle—was dammed. It is named after Walter Burley Griffin, the American architect who won the competition to design the city of Canberra.

The lake is an ornamental body with a length of 11 kilometers; at its widest, it measures 1.2 kilometers. It has an average depth of 4 meters and a maximum depth of about 18 meters near the Scrivener Dam. Its flow is regulated by the 33-metre (108 ft) tall Scrivener Dam, designed to handle floods that occur once in 5 000 years. In times of drought, water levels can be maintained through the release of water from Googong Dam, located on an upstream tributary of the Molonglo River.

伯利·格里芬湖是澳大利亚首都堪培拉市中心的一个人工湖。它以堪培拉城市设计总监美国建筑师沃尔特·伯利·格里芬的名字命名。伯利·格里芬湖极具观赏性,长 11 千米,最大宽度为 1.2 千米,平均深度为 4 米,最大深度约为 18 米。

2)The Sydney Opera House(悉尼歌剧院)

The Sydney Opera House is a multi-venue performing arts centre in Sydney, New South Wales, Australia. Situated on Bennelong Point in Sydney Harbour, close to the Sydney Harbour Bridge, the facility is adjacent to the Sydney central business district and the Royal Botanic Gardens, between Sydney and Farm Coves.

Though its name suggests a single venue, the project comprises multiple performance venues which together are among the busiest performing arts center's in the world—hosting over 1 500 performances each year attended by some 1.2 million people. The venues produce and present a wide range of in-house productions and accommodate numerous performing arts companies, including four key resident companies: Opera Australia, The Australian Ballet, the Sydney Theatre Company and the Sydney Symphony Orchestra. As one of the most popular visitor attractions in Australia, more than seven million people visit the site each year, with 300 000 people participating annually in a guided tour of the facility.

Identified as one of the 20th century's most distinctive buildings and one of the most famous performing arts centers in the world, the facility is managed by the Sydney Opera House Trust, under the auspices of the New South Wales Ministry of the Arts. The Sydney Opera House became a UNESCO World Heritage Site on 28 June 2007.

悉尼歌剧院是位于澳大利亚新南威尔士州悉尼市的一个多场馆的表演艺术中心，也是世界上最繁忙的表演艺术中心之一，每年举办超过1 500场演出，约120万人参加，是澳大利亚最受欢迎的旅游景点之一。

悉尼歌剧院是20世纪最具特色的建筑之一，也是世界最著名的表演艺术中心之一，由悉尼歌剧院信托基金会管理，由新南威尔士州艺术部赞助。悉尼歌剧院于2007年6月28日成为联合国教科文组织世界遗产。

 知识拓展 7.1　树袋熊（见二维码）

Section 3　New Zealand（新西兰）

PART 1（第一部分）

1. 国土疆域(Territory)

新西兰位于太平洋西南部，西隔塔斯曼海与澳大利亚相望，相距1 600千米，由北岛、南岛及一些小岛组成，面积约27万平方千米。

全国共分为11个大区，设有67个地区行政机构（其中包括13个市政厅、53个区议会和查塔姆群岛议会)。主要城市有惠灵顿、奥克兰、克赖斯特彻奇(基督城)、哈密尔顿、达尼丁等。

New Zealand is located in the southwest of the Pacific Ocean. It faces Australia across the Tasman Sea in the west, 1 600 km away. New Zealand is composed of North Island, South Island, and some small islands nearby, with an area of about 270 000 km^2.

The country is divided into 11 regions, with 67 regional administrations (including 13 city halls, 53 district boards and the Chatham Islands Council). The main cities are Wellington, Auckland, Christchurch, Hamilton, Dunedin, etc.

2. 自然风貌(Natural Features)

新西兰海岸线长约1.5万千米。境内多山,平原狭小,山地和丘陵约占总面积的75%以上。北岛多火山和温泉,南岛多冰河与湖泊,其中库克峰海拔3 754米,为全国最高峰。新西兰是一个冰与火共存的国家,南岛、北岛风格迥异的冰火奇景的完美结合,呈现出令人惊讶的独特魅力,令人心醉神迷,流连忘返。

新西兰一年四季气候温和,温差不大。绝大部分属温带海洋性气候,阳光充足,雨量丰富,植物茂盛。平均气温夏季20 ℃左右,冬季10 ℃左右。年平均降水量600～1 500毫米。全年适宜旅游,冬季、秋季为最佳旅游季节。

New Zealand is a country of mountains and narrow plains, with mountains and hills accounting for more than 75% of its total land. The North Island has many volcanoes and springs, the South Island has many glacier and lakes. Most of the country has a temperate marine climate. It is suitable for tourism throughout the year, but winter and autumn are the best seasons.

3. 人口民族(Population and Ethnicity)

新西兰人口约511.2万(2020年),人口密度为每平方千米18.93人。其中欧洲移民后裔占70%,毛利人占17%,太平洋岛国裔占8%(部分为多元族裔认同)。官方语言为英语、毛利语。近一半居民信奉基督教。

New Zealand has a population of about 5.112 million (2020) with a population density of 18.93 people per square kilometer, of which 74% are descendants of European immigrants. Residents mainly believe in Christianity.

4. 发展简史(Brief History of Development)

1350年起,毛利人就在此定居,成为新西兰最早的居民。1642年,荷兰航海家阿贝尔·塔斯曼在此登陆。1769年至1777年,英国库克船长先后5次来到新西兰。此后英国向新西兰大批移民并宣布占领新西兰。1840年英国迫使毛利人族长签订《威坦哲条约》,新西兰成为英国殖民地。1907年新西兰独立,成为英国的自治领,政治、经济、外交仍受英国控制。1947年成为主权国家,同时是英联邦成员。

The Maoris settled in 1350 AD and became New Zealand's first inhabitants. In the 18th century, the British emigrated to New Zealand in large numbers and declared their occupation. New Zealand became independent in 1907 and a sovereign nation in 1947, a member of the Commonwealth of Nations.

5. 政治经济(Politics and Economy)

新西兰的首都为惠灵顿,国花为银厥,货币为新西兰元。

新西兰实行英国式的议会民主制。英国女王是新西兰的国家元首,女王任命的总督作为其代表行使管理权。总督与部长组成的行政会议是法定的最高行政机构。内阁掌握实权,由议会多数党组成。议会只设众议院,由普选产生,任期3年。无成文宪法,其宪法是由英国议会和新西兰议会先后通过的一系列法律和修正案以及英国枢密院的某些决定构成的。

新西兰是经济发达国家,早期主要经济产业为农业,农牧产品出口占出口总量的50%。羊肉和奶制品出口量居世界第一位,羊毛出口量居世界第三位。后来,新西兰转型为具有国际竞争力的工业化市场经济,对外贸易、服务业和旅游业等相对发达。2020年国内生产总值为3 220亿新元,人均GDP约6.3万新元。

New Zealand has a parliamentary democracy of the British style. New Zealand is an economically developed country. In the early stage, its main economic industry was agriculture, and the export of agricultural and animal husbandry products accounted for 50% of the total export. Later, New Zealand transformed into an industrialized market economy with international competitiveness, coupled with relatively developed foreign trade, services and tourism.

6. 旅游市场(Tourism Market)

新西兰是全球最美丽的国家之一。约有30%的国土为保护区。拥有3项世界遗产、14个国家公园、3座海洋公园、数百座自然保护区和生态区。优美的沙滩、幽静的峡湾、葱茏的山峰、秀丽的湖泊、多样的人文风情、传统的乡村农庄、珍稀的动物,无不散发着诱人的魅力,吸引着世界各地的旅游者慕名而来,每年入境旅游人数有200万人次左右,纯新西兰旅游观光约占60%,随着《指环王》《钢琴课》和《垂直极限》等一系列国际知名影片在新西兰的成功拍摄,新西兰已成为广大游客心目中神圣的"中土"世界。

在全球整体入境旅游不景气的背景下,新西兰的入境旅游维持在稳定的水平,主要客源市场为澳大利亚、中国、美国、韩国等。新西兰统计局数据显示,2018年总体游客到访量为451 344人次,相比去年增长9.7%,人均消费达3 943美元。其中度假游客到访量为343 648人次,相比去年增长11.7%,人均消费达3 898美元。

新西兰出境旅游市场,依次为大洋洲(83%)、亚洲(13%)、欧洲(8%)和美洲(7%),其中澳大利亚、美国、斐济和英国是最受欢迎的目的地。

新西兰出境游中,主要目的是度假旅游(42%),其次是探亲访友(29%)和商务旅游(18%)。在过去的几年中,度假游减少了,而探亲访友增加了。

自 2017 年 5 月 8 日起,中国游客个人多次往返新西兰的旅游签证有效期由三年延长至五年,且持中国护照的游客能使用自助通关系统(目前称为 eGates)来实现快速通关。2019 年为"中国—新西兰旅游年",这些举措进一步促进了中国公民前往新西兰旅游。

近年来,新西兰来华旅游逐年增长,2018 年,新西兰来华旅游人数为 14.64 万人次,十年增长 45%。新西兰旅游局表示,目前中国市场上提供的旅游产品质量参差不齐,有些旅游团的行程为了降低成本,没有真正地带旅客游览景点,有些旅游团只是注重购物,游客没有真正欣赏到中国的大好河山。鉴于此,中国对新西兰游客市场推广的重点必须放在加强旅游产品的包装、提高旅游产品质量方面,让游客尽情欣赏中国的美景,感受中国的传统文化。

Inbound tourism remains stable in New Zealand, and the main source markets are Australia, China, the United States, South Korea, etc.

Oceania (83%), Asia (13%), Europe (8%) and the Americas (7%) are the most popular destinations for New Zealand outbound tourism.

In recent years, the number of Chinese tourists to New Zealand has grown rapidly. In recent years, New Zealand tourism to China has increased year by year.

PART 2(第二部分)

Tourism Resources(旅游资源)

Tourism is an important industry in New Zealand. Many international tourists spend time in Auckland, Christchurch, Queenstown, Rotorua, and Wellington. Other high-profile destinations include the Bay of Islands, Waitomo Caves, Aoraki / Mount Cook, Milford Sound, Lake Taupo, Dunedin.

旅游业是新西兰的重要产业。许多国际游客在奥克兰、克赖斯特彻奇、皇后镇、罗托鲁阿和惠灵顿度过。其他引人注目的目的地包括岛屿湾、怀托摩萤火虫洞、奥拉基/库克山、米尔福德峡湾、陶波湖、达尼丁等。

1. Auckland(奥克兰)

Auckland is New Zealand's largest city and main transport hub. Also Auckland Domain is one of the largest parks in the city, close to the Auckland CBD and having a good view of the Hauraki Gulf and Rangitoto Island. Smaller parks close to the city centre are Albert Park, Myers Park, Western Park and Victoria Park.

While most volcanic cones in the Auckland volcanic field have been affected by quarrying, many of the remaining cones are now within parks, and retain a more natural character than the surrounding city. Prehistoric earthworks and historic fortifications are in several of these parks, including Mount Eden, North Head and Maungakiekie / One Tree Hill.

Other parks around the city are in Western Springs, which has a large park bordering the MOTAT museum and the Auckland Zoo. The Auckland Botanic Gardens are further south, in Manurewa.

Ferries provide transport to parks and nature reserves at Devonport, Waiheke Island, Rangitoto Island and Tiritiri Matangi. The Waitakere Ranges Regional Park to the west of Auckland offers beautiful and relatively unspoiled bush territory, as do the Hunua Ranges to the south.

奥克兰是新西兰最大的城市和主要的交通枢纽。奥克兰中央公园也是该市最大的公园之一。

虽然奥克兰火山区的大多数火山锥都受到采石活动的影响,但许多火山锥仍保留在公园内,并保留了比周围城市更自然的特征。公园内还有史前工程和历史防御工事,例如伊甸山。

2. Wellington(惠灵顿)

Wellington is the capital city and second most populous urban area of New Zealand. It is located at the south-western tip of the North Island. Wellington is marketed as the "coolest little capital in the world" by Positively Wellington Tourism, an award-winning regional tourism organization set up as a council controlled organization by Wellington City Council in 1997. Popular tourist attractions include Museum of Wellington City & Sea, Wellington Zoo, Zealandia and Wellington Cable Car. Wellington is a popular conference tourism destination due to its compact nature, cultural attractions, award-winning restaurants and access to government agencies.

惠灵顿位于北岛的西南端,是新西兰的首都和第二大城市,被誉为"世界上最酷的小首都"。受欢迎的旅游景点包括惠灵顿城市和海洋博物馆、惠灵顿动物园和惠灵顿缆车。惠灵顿还是一个受欢迎的会议旅游目的地。

3. Lake Taupo(陶波湖)

Lake Taupo is a lake situated in the North Island of New Zealand. It lies in the caldera of the Taupo Volcano. With a surface area of 616 square kilometres, it is the largest lake by surface area in New Zealand, and the second largest freshwater lake by surface area in geopolitical Oceania after Lake Murray (Papua New Guinea).

Lake Taupo has a perimeter of approximately 193 kilometres and a deepest point of

186 metres. It is drained by the Waikato River (New Zealand's longest river), while its main tributaries are the Waitahanui River, the Tongariro River, and the Tauranga Taupo River. It is a noted trout fishery with stocks of introduced brown trout and rainbow trout.

陶波湖是一个位于新西兰北岛的湖泊，由陶波火山的火山口积水而成。陶波湖周长约 193 千米，最深 186 米，面积 616 平方千米，是新西兰面积最大的湖泊，这里盛产鳟鱼。

4. Rotorua(罗托鲁阿)

Rotorua is a major destination for both domestic and international tourists; the tourism industry is by far the largest industry in the district. It is known for its geothermal activity, and features geysers—notably the Pohutu Geyser at Whakarewarewa—and hot mud pools. This thermal activity is sourced to the Rotorua caldera, on which the town lies. Rotorua is home to the Waiariki Institute of Technology.

The Lakes of Rotorua are a collection of many lakes surrounding Rotorua.

The Rotorua region has 17 lakes, known collectively as the Lakes of Rotorua. Fishing, waterskiing, swimming and other water activities are popular in summer. The lakes are also used for event venues; Rotorua hosted the 2007 World Waterski Championships and Lake Rotorua was the venue for the World Blind Sailing Championships in March 2009. Lake Rotorua is also used as a departure and landing point for float planes.

罗托鲁阿是新西兰的主要旅游目的地，旅游业是这里最大的产业。它以地热资源而闻名，以间歇泉和热泥浆池为特色。

罗托鲁阿湖是罗托鲁阿周围许多湖泊的集合体，这里有 17 个湖泊，适合钓鱼、滑水、游泳。罗托鲁阿曾举办 2007 年世界水上运动锦标赛。

5. Dunedin(达尼丁)

Known as the "Edinburgh of New Zealand", Dunedin is the country's city of the south, wearing its Scottish heritage with pride. Surrounded by dramatic hills and at the foot of a long, picturesque harbour, Dunedin is one of the best-preserved Victorian and Edwardian cities in the Southern Hemisphere. The accommodation is good and plentiful; the nightlife buzzes with funky bars and delicious restaurants and the natural attractions are unique and fascinating.

Don't miss a drive up the Otago Peninsula, the views are endless and the beaches are beautifully rugged. Nestled at the foot of Taiaroa Head is the Royal Albatross Centre, the only place in the world on the mainland where you can view Northern Royal

Albatross in their natural habitat. On Dunedin's doorstep you will also find incredible wildlife including the world's rarest penguin colonies.

达尼丁是新西兰南部的城市，被誉为"英国的爱丁堡"，这里的人们自豪地穿着苏格兰传统服饰。达尼丁是南半球保存最完好的维多利亚和爱德华时代建筑的城市之一，周围群山环绕，自然景色独特而迷人，山脚下有风景如画的海港。

皇家信天翁中心奥塔哥半岛的泰瓦罗瓦角，是世界上唯一一个可以看到北方皇家信天翁自然栖息地的地方。在达尼丁，你还会发现不可思议的野生动物，如世界上最稀有的企鹅群。

6. Christchurch(克赖斯特彻奇)

The large number of public parks and well-developed residential gardens with many trees has given Christchurch the name of The Garden City.

Christchurch, New Zealand is interwoven by two rivers linking parks, gardens and avenues. Bordered by the Port Hills and the Pacific Ocean, it is situated on the Canterbury Plains with the Southern Alps as a majestic backdrop. The award-winning Christchurch Botanic Gardens feature one of the finest collections of exotic and native plants found in New Zealand.

In February 2011, Christchurch was hit by a huge earthquake. Much of the central city with its classic neo-gothic architecture was destroyed. But it remains a beautiful city, a city where you can cycle alongside the river, stay in good hotels and indulge in fine sophisticated dining, and a city where, just 15 minutes from the center you can scramble up mountain bike tracks or ride a wave at a surf beach.

The buildings may have been damaged but the soul of the city and the welcoming spirits of the people remain very much intact. Innovative shops and businesses are springing up as the city rebuilds.

You can explore the city by foot, on an open top bus, tram or even relax in a punt as you float down the Avon River on a punt. Experience polar life at the International Antarctic Centre, see the rare kiwi at Willowbank Wildlife Reserve, dive into aviation history at the Air Force Museum or visit Orana Wildlife Park, New Zealand's only open range zoo.

克赖斯特彻奇拥有众多的公园和树木繁茂的住宅花园，因此得名"花园之城"。

克赖斯特彻奇以南阿尔卑斯山为雄伟的背景，位于坎特伯雷平原上，毗邻港口山和太平洋，由两条河流交织而成，连接着公园、花园和大街。

你可以步行、乘坐敞篷巴士、电车，甚至可以坐着平底船在雅芳河上漂流。你可以在国际南极中心体验极地生活，在柳岸野生动物保护区观赏稀有的几维鸟，在空军博物馆了解航空史，或参观新西兰唯一的开放动物园奥拉纳野生动物园。

7. Queenstown(皇后镇)

Queenstown is a resort town in Otago in the southwest of New Zealand's South Island.

It is built around an inlet called Queenstown Bay on Lake Wakatipu, a long thin Z-shaped lake formed by glacial processes, and has spectacular views of nearby mountains such as The Remarkables, Cecil Peak, Walter Peak and just above the town; Ben Lomond and Queenstown Hill.

Queenstown is now known for its commerce-oriented tourism, especially adventure and ski tourism. A resort town, Queenstown boasted 220 adventure tourism activities in 2012. Skiing and snowboarding, jet boating, whitewater rafting, bungy jumping, mountain biking, skateboarding, tramping, paragliding, sky diving and fly fishing are all popular.

Queenstown is a major center for snow sports in New Zealand, with people from all over the country and many parts of the world travelling to ski at the four main mountain ski fields (Cardrona Alpine Resort, Coronet Peak, The Remarkables and Treble Cone). Cross country skiing is also available at the Waiorau Snowfarm, near Cardrona village. The 100-year-old twin screw coal fired steamer TSS Earnslaw traverses Lake Wakatipu.

Queenstown lies close to the center of a small wine producing region, reputed to be the world's southernmost. The Two Paddocks vineyard is owned by local actor Sam Neill.

皇后镇是新西兰南岛西南部奥塔哥的一个度假小镇。

皇后镇以商业旅游闻名，特别是冒险和滑雪旅游，这里的滑雪和滑雪板、喷气艇、白水漂流、蹦极、山地自行车、滑板、蹦床、滑翔伞、跳伞和飞钓都很受游客欢迎。

皇后镇是新西兰主要的冰雪运动中心，来自全国各地和世界各地的人们前往四个主要的高山滑雪场滑雪——卡德罗纳高山度假村、皇冠峰滑雪场、The Remarkables 滑雪场和三锥山滑雪场。

8. Aoraki / Mount Cook(奥拉基/库克山)

Aoraki / Mount Cook is the highest mountain in New Zealand. Its height since 2014 is listed as 3 724 m, having earlier been measured at 3 754 m. It lies in the Southern Alps, the mountain range which runs the length of the South Island. A popular tourist destination, it is also a favorite challenge for mountain climbers. Aoraki / Mount Cook consists of three summits lying slightly south and east of the main divide, the Low Peak, Middle Peak and High Peak, with the Tasman Glacier to the east and the Hooker Glacier to the west.

The mountain is in the Aoraki / Mount Cook National Park, in the Canterbury region. The park was established in 1953 and along with Westland Tai Poutini National Park, Mount Aspiring National Park and Fiordland National Park forms one of the UNESCO World Heritage Sites. The park contains more than 140 peaks standing over 2 000 meters and 72 named glaciers, which cover 40% of its 700 square kilometers.

The settlement of Mount Cook Village is a tourist center and base camp for the mountain. It is 7 km from the end of the Tasman Glacier and 12 km south of Aoraki / Mount Cook's summit.

奥拉基/库克山是新西兰最高的山,高 3 724 米。它位于南阿尔卑斯山脉,山脉贯穿南岛。作为一个受欢迎的旅游目的地,它是登山者的最爱。它由位于主分水岭偏南和偏东的三座山峰组成,分别为低峰、中峰和高峰,东有塔斯曼冰川,西有胡克冰川。

这座山属于奥拉基/库克山国家公园,该公园成立于 1953 年,与西部泰普提尼国家公园、阿斯帕林山国家公园和峡湾国家公园一起构成联合国教科文组织世界遗产之一。公园内有 140 多座山峰,海拔超过 2 000 米,有 72 座命名的冰川。库克山村的居民点是一个旅游中心和山区的大本营。

知识拓展 7.2　毛利人迎宾仪式(见二维码)

Sum up(本章小结)

1. 大洋洲旅游区以其丰富的自然旅游资源和独特的毛利文化成为全世界发展较快的旅游区,它也是中国新兴的主要旅游目的地和客源地区。

2. 本章从地理位置及范围、自然风貌、民族与宗教、旅游市场等方面介绍了大洋洲旅游区的基本概况。

3. 本章主要选取了澳大利亚、新西兰两个国家进行介绍,它们是大洋洲旅游区最发达的目的地国和客源国。

4.每个国家的介绍分为两部分,第一部分介绍了各国的国土疆域、自然风貌、人口民族、发展简史、政治经济和旅游市场的基本概况;第二部分介绍了各国的旅游资源。

 Reviewing and Thinking(复习与思考)

1.澳大利亚的旅游资源有何特色?
2.试结合澳大利亚的旅游资源特色,设计一条最适合中国游客的自助游旅游线路。
3.新西兰的旅游资源有何特色?
4.试结合新西兰旅游资源特色,设计一条最适合中国游客的自助游旅游线路。

Reference(参考文献)

[1] 毕世鸿等.新加坡[M].北京:社会科学文献出版社,2016.

[2] 曹景洲.海外旅游目的地概况[M].北京:中国旅游出版社,2011.

[3] 崔筱力.中国主要客源国(地区)概况[M].(2版).厦门:厦门大学出版社,2019.

[4] 丁勇义,李玥瑾,张景,等.中国旅游客源国概况[M].北京:清华大学出版社,2019.

[5] 乔凡尼·朱塞佩·贝拉尼.美丽的地球:非洲[M].董庆,译.北京:中信出版集团股份有限公司,2016.

[6] 《国家地理》编委会,《国家地理系列》编委.国家地理·世界卷[M].北京:蓝天出版社,2009.

[7] 胡华.中国旅游客源国与目的地国概况[M].北京:中国旅游出版社,2012.

[8] 日本大宝石出版社.走遍全国:德国[M].金松,赵征环,译.北京:中国旅游出版社,2015.

[9] 金版童书.世界地理百科[M].南昌:江西美术出版社,2019.

[10] 吕夏乔.欧洲常识[M].北京:新世界出版社,2015.

[11] 吕夏乔.非洲常识[M].南京:江苏人民出版社,2015.

[12] 彭淑清.中国旅游海外客源市场概况[M].武汉:华中科技大学出版社,2009.

[13] 《亲历者》编辑部.南美洲旅行 Let's Go[M].(2版).北京:中国铁道出版社,2017.

[14] 任佳,李丽.印度[M].北京:社会科学文献出版社,2016.

[15] 孙克勤.中国客源国概况[M].(2版).北京:旅游教育出版社,2014.

[16] 史蒂芬.霍拉克,等.加拿大[M].北京:中国旅游出版社,2015.

[17] 宋瑞.2018~2019年中国旅游发展分析与预测[M].北京:社会科学文献出版社,2019.

[18] 滕藤.简明西欧百科全书[M].北京:中国社会科学出版社,2019.

[19] 《图行世界》编辑部.全球最美的地方特辑:欧洲[M].北京:中国旅游出版社,2011.

[20] 王佩良.主要旅游客源国概况[M].北京:高等教育出版社,2014.

[21] 王兴斌.中国旅游客源国概况[M].(8版).北京:旅游教育出版社,2019.

[22] 伍百军.中国主要旅游客源国和目的地国概况[M].北京:电子工业出版社,2013.

[23] 陈福义,张金霞.中国主要旅游客源国和目的地国概况[M].北京:清华大学出版社,2007.

[24] 周昌军,周红雨.中国旅游客源市场概况(中英双语)[M].天津:南开大学出版社,2009.

[25] 日本《走遍全球》编辑室.走遍全球:澳大利亚[M].马谦,王启文,译.北京:中国旅游出版社,2019.

[26] 天域北斗数码科技有限公司.世界地理地图集[M].北京:中国地图出版社,2015.

教学支持说明

普通高等学校"十四五"规划旅游管理类精品教材系华中科技大学出版社"十四五"规划重点教材。

为了改善教学效果,提高教材的使用效率,满足高校授课教师的教学需求,本套教材备有与纸质教材配套的教学课件(PPT电子教案)和拓展资源(案例库、习题库视频等)。

为保证本教学课件及相关教学资料仅为教材使用者所得,我们将向使用本套教材的高校授课教师免费赠送教学课件或者相关教学资料,烦请授课教师通过电话、邮件或加入旅游专家俱乐部QQ群等方式与我们联系,获取"教学课件资源申请表",准确填写后发给我们,我们的联系方式如下:

地址:湖北省武汉市东湖新技术开发区华工科技园华工园六路

邮编:430223

电话:027-81321911

传真:027-81321917

E-mail:lyzjjlb@163.com

旅游专家俱乐部QQ群号:306110199

旅游专家俱乐部QQ群二维码:

群名称:旅游专家俱乐部
群　号:306110199

教学课件资源申请表

填表时间：_____年___月___日

1. 以下内容请教师按实际情况写,★为必填项。
2. 学生根据个人情况如实填写,相关内容可以酌情调整提交。

★姓名		★性别	□男 □女	出生年月		★职务	
						★职称	□教授 □副教授 □讲师 □助教

★学校		★院/系	
★教研室		★专业	
★办公电话		家庭电话		★移动电话	
★E-mail（请填写清晰）			★QQ号/微信号	
★联系地址		★邮编	

★现在主授课程情况	学生人数	教材所属出版社	教材满意度
课程一			□满意 □一般 □不满意
课程二			□满意 □一般 □不满意
课程三			□满意 □一般 □不满意
其 他			□满意 □一般 □不满意

教材出版信息			
方向一		□准备写 □写作中 □已成稿 □已出版待修订 □有讲义		
方向二		□准备写 □写作中 □已成稿 □已出版待修订 □有讲义		
方向三		□准备写 □写作中 □已成稿 □已出版待修订 □有讲义		

请教师认真填写表格下列内容,提供索取课件配套教材的相关信息,我社将根据每位教师/学生填表信息的完整性、授课情况与索取课件的相关性,以及教材使用的情况赠送教材的配套课件及相关教学资源。

ISBN(书号)	书名	作者	索取课件简要说明	学生人数（如选作教材）
			□教学 □参考	
			□教学 □参考	

★您对与课件配套的纸质教材的意见和建议,希望提供哪些配套教学资源：